ARM CANDY

First published in the United Kingdom in 2015 by
Pavilion
1 Gower Street
London
WC1E 6HD

ISBN 9781910496152

A CIP catalogue record for this book is available from the
British Library.

10 9 8 7 6 5 4 3 2 1

Repro by Mission Productions Ltd, Hong Kong
Printed and bound by Toppan Leefung Printing Ltd, China

This book can be ordered direct from the publisher at
www.pavilionbooks.com

LAURA STRUTT

ARM CANDY

FRIENDSHIP BRACELETS
TO MAKE AND SHARE

PAVILION

CONTENTS

INTRODUCTION

It's so simple to arm yourself with some pretty beads and a few other craft supplies and start making beautiful bracelets for yourself, or as gifts for your friends. You could even hold an arm candy party for your chums, making your bracelets together. The materials you'll be using aren't particularly valuable, but the time spent and the gift of friendship they signify will be truly treasured.

You'll find that the projects are easy and quick-to-make, even if you are trying out a new technique like the loom-band design. Suggestions for colour combinations are shown in the photographs, but you can get creative with your own colour choices if you prefer.

As well as designs that feature the usual jewellery materials and findings, there are projects made from common crafting items like embroidery thread, washi tape and spray paint. So if you have any of these materials in your cupboard left over from other projects you will be able to use them up. There are even no-cost projects that make use of recycled materials, like the T-shirt Yarn Bracelet.

So gather what you need and get crafting!

CHEVRON FRIENDSHIP BAND

Woven friendship bands are so much fun to make. Before you know it you'll have mastered this technique for making neat little woven knots and you'll be whipping up a stack in all your favourite colour combinations!

YOU WILL NEED

> EMBROIDERY THREAD, IN TWO COLOURS

> SCISSORS

> SAFETY PIN OR WASHI TAPE

CUSTOMISATION TIP

Create wider bands or add in more colours by simply increasing the number of strands of embroidery thread you use, keeping to an even number.

USE A SERIES OF SIMPLE LITTLE KNOTS TO CRAFT A COLOURFUL COLLECTION OF WOVEN BANGLES

1 You will need four embroidery thread lengths in colour A and four lengths in colour B. Trim the lengths to around 80 cm long. Knot the lengths together 10 cm from the end.

2 Divide the short lengths above the knot into three sections: two with three strands and one with two strands, and braid from the knot to 2 cm from the end. Knot the threads together at the far end of the braid to secure. Insert a safety pin into the knot – or use a section of washi tape – and secure to a firm surface (you can use a cushion, ironing board or even the leg of your jeans).

3 Spread the threads out and arrange them so that they are laying, from left to right, two colour A, four colour B and two colour A threads. Separate these threads to create two halves, each with two strands of thread A outermost and two of thread B innermost.

4 To create the friendship band you'll work lots of little knots. To make a knot, bring the first thread over the second, passing it under and bringing the end through the loop.

5 Draw up closely to tighten the knot into position.

6 Repeat step 4 to make a second knot with the same threads in the same way. These two knots count as one woven stitch on the bracelet. Begin the chevron. Take the threads on the far left and create one woven stitch (see steps 4, 5 and 6) on the thread to the right-hand side of it. Continuing with this thread, repeat to create another woven stitch on the next thread and then the thread following it. The initial thread will now lie at the centre of the strands.

QUICK TIP

Be sure to draw up each of the little knots you make (see steps 4 and 5) to create the chevron pattern neatly and tightly. This will help to create an even finish to the friendship band without any holes or gaps in the woven stitches.

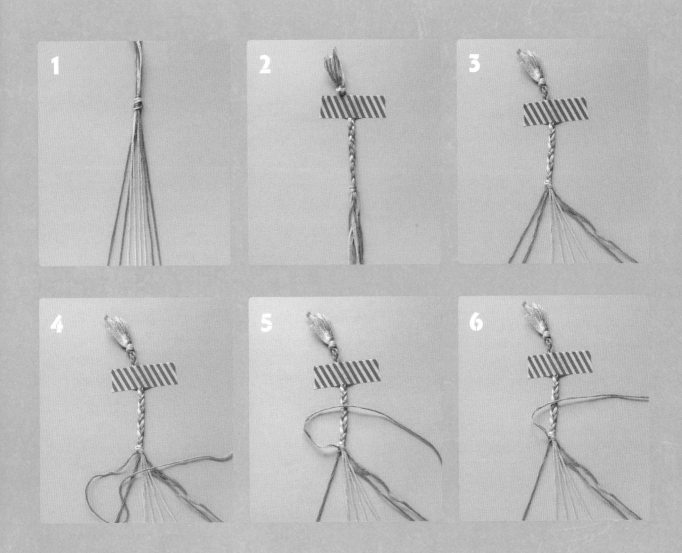

7 Complete the point of the chevron. Make a single woven stitch over the next three threads to end in the centre. Join the point of the chevron by working the two inner threads together with one woven stitch.

8 Begin making the second half of the chevron. Return to the outermost thread on the left-hand side and repeat to create three woven stitches to reach the centre of the section. Then work three woven stitches from the right-hand side to meet at the centre and join the two centre threads with a single woven stitch. This will create the first V in the chevron pattern in thread colour A, with each one being made up of two lines of woven stitches meeting in the centre.

9 Begin the second chevron. Take the threads on the far left and create one woven stitch (see steps 4 and 5) on the thread to the right-hand side of it. Continuing with this thread, repeat to create another woven stitch on the next thread and then the thread following it. The thread will now lie at the centre of the strands.

10 Moving to the other side, begin making the second half of the chevron. Make a single woven stitch over the next three threads to end in the centre. Join the point of the chevron by working the two inner threads together with one woven stitch.

11 Return to the outermost thread on the left-hand side and repeat to create three woven stitches to reach the centre of the section. Then work three woven stitches from the right-hand side to meet at the centre and join the two centre threads. This will create the next V in the chevron pattern with two lines of woven stitches in thread colour B.

12 Continue working steps 6–11 to repeat the chevron pattern for the desired length. Tie a knot at the bottom of the bracelet to secure the woven design. Divide the thread into three sections – two with three strands and one with two strands and braid to 2 cm before the end. Tie in a knot at the bottom to secure and trim the ends neatly before tying to your wrist or gifting to a friend.

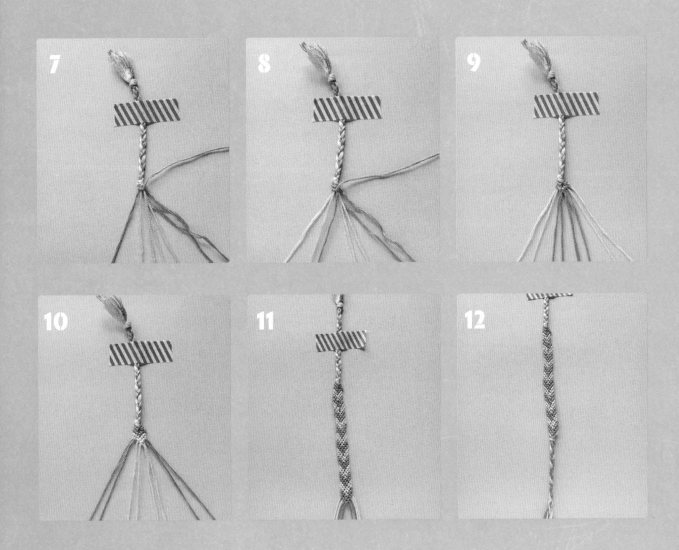

CHARM MOTIF BRACELET

A large charm in a graphic flower shape makes a great focal point for this simple statement bracelet. Team it with colourful cord, and you'll create a finished result in no time.

YOU WILL NEED

> MEDIUM BOOTLACE CORD, IN TWO COLOURS, 40 CM OF EACH

> SCISSORS

> CHARM OF YOUR CHOICE

> FOLDOVER CORD ENDS X 2

> SLIM FLAT-NOSE JEWELLERY PLIERS X 2 PAIRS

> JUMP RINGS X 2

> BRACELET TOGGLE CLASP

CUSTOMISATION TIP

Pick any statement charm with large open sections – these will work best as they give you a section through which to thread the cord. Try using a purchased heart or star, or even make your own openwork shape from jewellery wire.

CREATE A STATEMENT BRACELET
WITH A LARGE CHARM

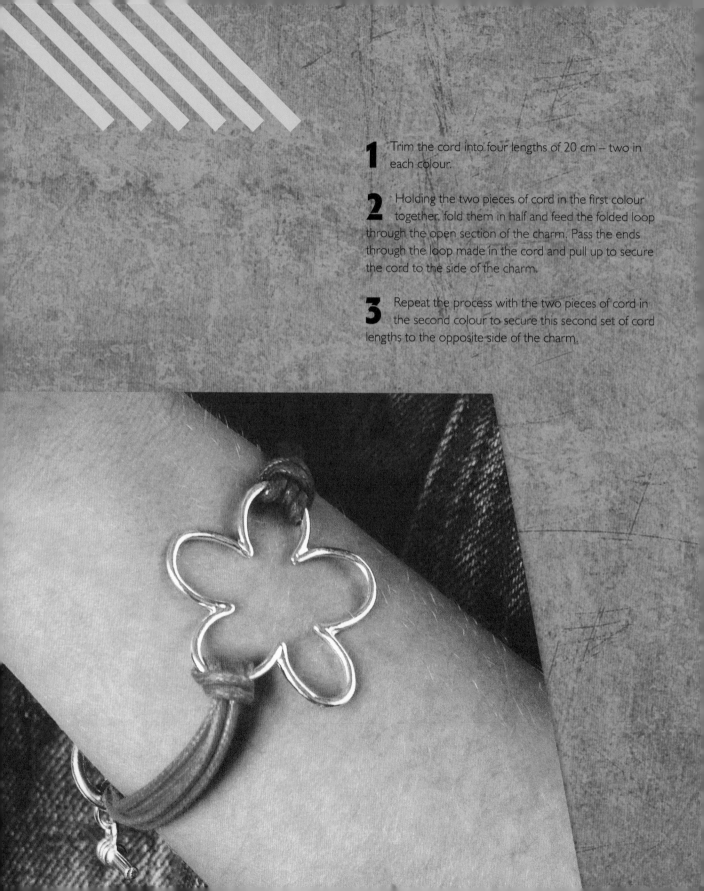

1 Trim the cord into four lengths of 20 cm – two in each colour.

2 Holding the two pieces of cord in the first colour together, fold them in half and feed the folded loop through the open section of the charm. Pass the ends through the loop made in the cord and pull up to secure the cord to the side of the charm.

3 Repeat the process with the two pieces of cord in the second colour to secure this second set of cord lengths to the opposite side of the charm.

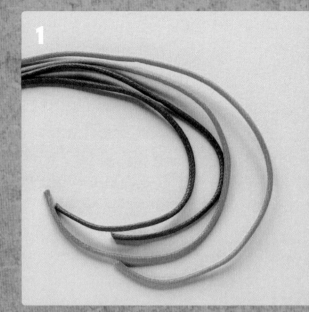

4 Working on each side in turn, secure the four ends of the cord into the cord ends, folding over and pressing them closed with one set of the flat-nose jewellery pliers.

5 Use both pairs of jewellery pliers to twist a jump ring open (see tip). Slide the ring through the loop on the first cord end and then through one end of one half of the bracelet clasp. Twist back to secure.

6 Repeat step 5 with the second jump ring to secure the second part of the bracelet clasp on the opposite side of the bracelet.

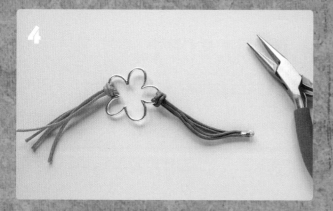

QUICK TIP

When opening jump rings to secure the clasp, work carefully. Twist the two sections apart by holding the ends of each section in a set of pliers held in each hand, then rotating the pliers away from each other. By twisting the rings apart, rather than pulling them open, you will be able to close them back neatly – just reverse the twist process to restore the original perfect circle shape.

T-SHIRT YARN BRACELET

Cotton jersey ribbon yarns are great for making colourful, soft accessories. Why not use old T-shirts to make the yarn yourself and create new arm candy at zero cost?

YOU WILL NEED

❯ T-SHIRT YARN (OR T-SHIRTS CUT INTO STRIPS)

❯ SCISSORS

❯ SEWING NEEDLE AND THREAD

CUSTOMISATION TIP

Make a chunkier bracelet by using six strands of T-shirt yarn. Hold the yarns in three sets of two, and work the braid in the same way as the three-strand version.

UPCYCLE OLD T-SHIRTS TO CREATE STUNNING BOLD BRACELETS

1 Cut T-shirt yarn – or strips from old unwanted T-shirts – into 30 cm lengths in multiples of three different colours, shades or designs.

2 Knot one end of a set of three strands of yarns or T-shirt strips together and spread out the free lengths neatly, ready to braid.

3 Create the braid by taking the strand on the left-hand side and bringing it over to the centre of the set of three strands. Move to the right-hand side and bring the strand in towards the centre. This creates the braid.

4 Continue braiding the strands by bringing the outermost strands in towards the centre in turn.

QUICK TIP

Create your own T-shirt yarn by cutting old unwanted T-shirts into 3-cm wide, 30-cm long strips ready to be braided.

QUICK TIP

Strips cut from T-shirts, or T-shirt yarn, can be very stretchy. Pull and stretch the lengths of yarn slightly before braiding so that the bracelets won't stretch as you wear them and become too large.

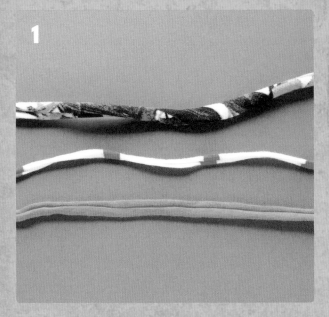

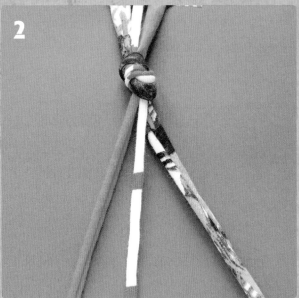

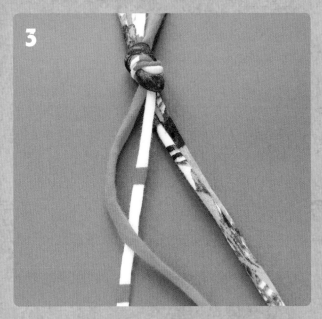

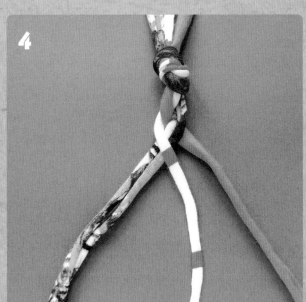

5 Continue working the strands together until the braided strip is 4 cm longer than the circumference of your wrist.

6 Using the needle and thread, work a few stitches through the base of the braid to secure the ends in place, knot securely and fasten off. Remove the knot from the other end of the braid and work a few stitches through the strands to secure the braid on the opposite end. Knot securely and fasten off.

7 Trim five of the six ends of the strands to 2 cm from the end of the braid, leaving one strand untrimmed. Without twisting the braided strip, overlap the two sets of shorter ends and, with the needle and thread, work a few stitches through the join to secure the braid in a circle. Knot securely and fasten off.

8 Wrap the remaining (untrimmed) strand neatly around the join to conceal the ends. With a needle and thread, work a few stitches to secure the wrapped section on the inside of the bangle to finish. Knot the thread securely and fasten off.

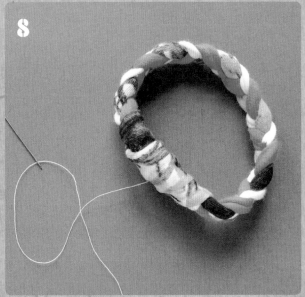

WASHI TAPE BANGLE

A paper crafter's favourite, washi tape comes in a huge range of different prints and colours. Pick your favourite combinations to create your own statement bangle.

YOU WILL NEED

> OLD WOOD OR PLASTIC SMOOTH-FINISHED BANGLE

> SELECTION OF WASHI TAPES

> SCISSORS

> MOD PODGE DECOUPAGE GLUE (OPTIONAL)

CUSTOMISATION TIP

Create a metallic effect by using silver duct tape, adding pieces in the same manner as the washi tape. Or cut shapes and accents from duct tape to add a custom finish to your bangle.

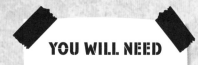
CUSTOMISE OLD BANGLES WITH WASHI TAPE FOR A FRESH NEW LOOK!

1 Clean and dry the old bangle. Plan your design using a collection of washi tapes in complementary designs.

2 Cut the washi tape into small strips slightly larger than the width of the bangle. Working around the bangle, begin securing the tapes onto its surface. Fold the cut edges neatly in towards the inside of the bangle, and make sure that each strip is fully adhered before adding the next.

3 Continue covering the outer face of the bangle with tape strips, overlapping them slightly to make sure that none of the original bangle is visible.

4 Cut two strips each measuring 3 cm longer than the inner measurement of the bangle. Carefully secure the first strip around the inside of the bracelet. Repeat to add the second strip. If the bangle is very wide, you might need to add a third strip so that all the cut edges of the folded strips are neatly covered and secured.

QUICK TIP

Washi tape is quick and easy to apply. You can reposition the strips as you work if you are not happy with the placement. However, the more you remove and reapply the strips the less sticky they become, so make sure that they are fully stuck down before moving on to the next strip.

QUICK TIP

For longevity, seal the finished bangle with a coat of decoupage glue (mod podge) or matt or shiny clear varnish to protect the tape from dirt and damage.

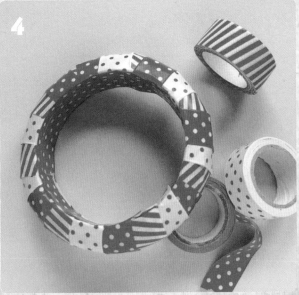

URBAN KNOT BRACELET

Impress your friends with your clever knotting technique – this chunky cord bracelet is surprisingly easy to make. Try out different colours and thicknesses, then stack for a cool armful.

YOU WILL NEED

> MEDIUM PARACORD, 3 M

> SCISSORS

> CRAFT GLUE

> PLASTIC SNAP CLIP CLASP

> WASHI TAPE OR STICKY TAPE

CUSTOMISATION TIP

Paracord is a lightweight nylon rope originally designed for parachutes, hence its name. Originally it was made only in natural and olive drab, but today there's a rainbow of hues to choose from. You can even buy the cord in neon colours and a glow-in-the-dark version that would make great bracelets for night owls on a mission!

DISCOVER HOW TO CREATE A STRIKING URBAN-STYLE BRACELET WITH THIS CLEVER PARACORD KNOT DESIGN

1 Cut a 75 cm length from the cord. Apply a small dab of craft glue to both the ends of the cut length and those of the remaining piece to prevent them from fraying. Set aside to dry. Fold the 75 cm cut length of cord in half and feed it through the opening of one half of the clasp. Push the cord loop through from front to back, then draw the ends through the loop.

2 Secure the clasp in place with a piece of washi or sticky tape. Centre the remaining length of cord and tie in a knot around the secured cord, making sure that the knot is fastened snugly to the base of the clasp. Position the lengths of knotted cord outermost. The cord secured to the clasp will sit in the centre.

3 The knots are created in two parts. You make the first part of the knot by passing the left-hand piece of cord under the centre two pieces and the right-hand piece of cord over the centre two pieces. Feed the cord from the left-hand section up and through the loop made by the cord on the right-hand side, and feed the cord from the right-hand side down and through the loop made by the cord on the left-hand side. Draw up to tighten the first part of the knot.

4 Create the second part of the knot by passing the left-hand piece of cord over the centre two pieces and the right-hand piece of cord under the centre two pieces. Feed the cord from the left-hand section down and through the loop made by the cord on the right-hand side, and feed the cord from the right-hand side up and through the loop made by the cord on the left-hand side. Draw up to tighten the final part of the knot.

QUICK TIP

Be careful when using glue: avoid contact with your skin and work in small dabs at a time to make sure that it is not visible on the finished bracelet.

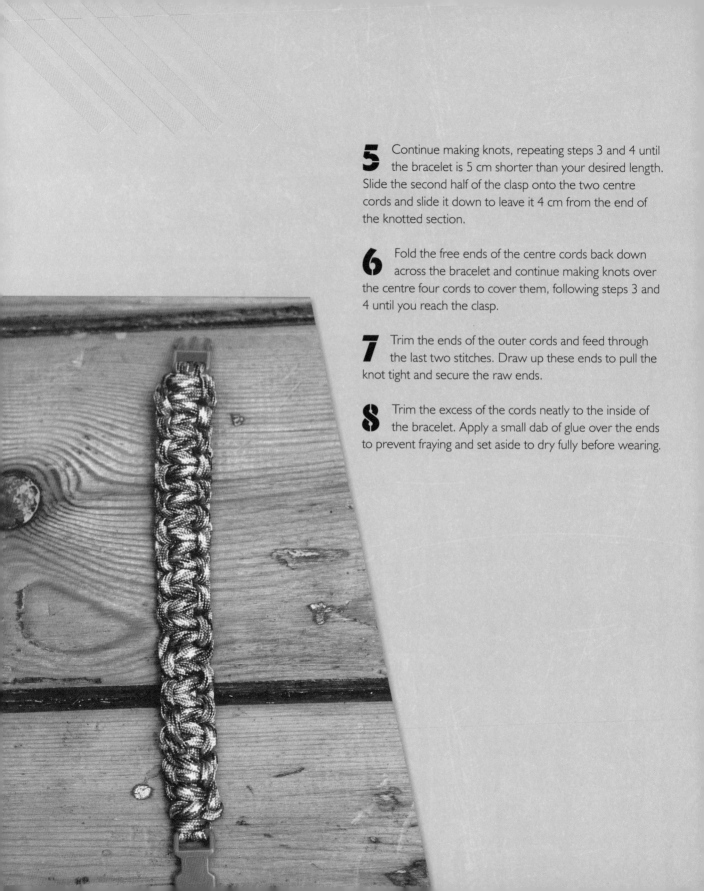

5 Continue making knots, repeating steps 3 and 4 until the bracelet is 5 cm shorter than your desired length. Slide the second half of the clasp onto the two centre cords and slide it down to leave it 4 cm from the end of the knotted section.

6 Fold the free ends of the centre cords back down across the bracelet and continue making knots over the centre four cords to cover them, following steps 3 and 4 until you reach the clasp.

7 Trim the ends of the outer cords and feed through the last two stitches. Draw up these ends to pull the knot tight and secure the raw ends.

8 Trim the excess of the cords neatly to the inside of the bracelet. Apply a small dab of glue over the ends to prevent fraying and set aside to dry fully before wearing.

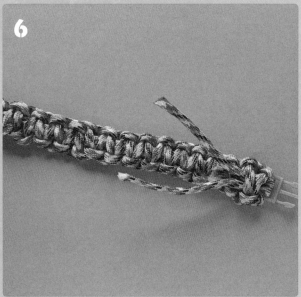

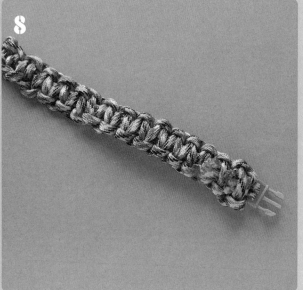

CROCHET BEADED BRACELET

Adding a scattering of bright little glass beads to a simple crochet chain worked in twine is easier than you might think – and makes a stunning festival-style bracelet.

YOU WILL NEED

› NATURAL TWINE

› SCISSORS

› GLASS BEADS, 4 MM (25–35 BEADS, DEPENDING ON WRIST MEASUREMENT)

› WASHI TAPE

› CROCHET HOOK, 5 MM SIZE

CUSTOMISATION TIP

Work with a random selection of coloured beads for a unique finish, or pick a couple of your favourite shades and create a repeated pattern for a more coordinated design.

COMBINE NATURAL TWINE AND COLOURFUL BEADS FOR TRUE BOHO STYLE!

1 Cut a 1 m length of twine and begin to thread on a selection of beads in your preferred order. Hold the other end of the twine down with washi tape to prevent the beads slipping off if needed.

2 Add a knot to one end of the twine and slide two beads to the knot before knotting again. This forms one of the ties for the bracelet.

3 Measure 10 cm in from the inner knot and knot again. At the base of this knot tie a slip knot and insert the crochet hook through the slip knot, drawing it up around the hook. Use the hook to catch the tail of the twine and draw it through the slip knot – this is a crochet chain stitch.

4 Slide the first bead to the base of the crochet chain stitch you just made, use the hook to catch the tail of the twine and draw it through the loop on the hook to make the next stitch.

QUICK TIP

If you are using larger beads, be sure to pick a larger crochet hook too. Select a hook that is 1 mm larger than the chosen beads – so, if you are using 5 mm beads, use a 6 mm crochet hook.

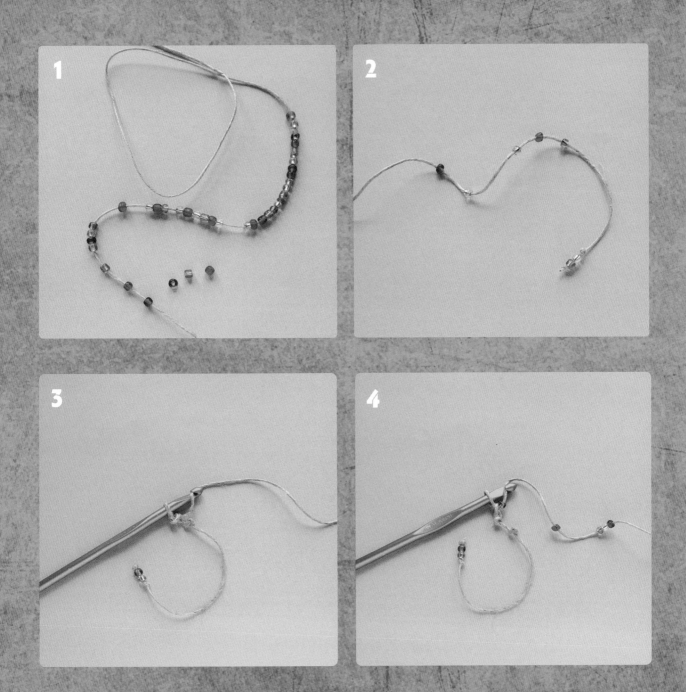

5 Continue sliding the next bead on the twine onto the base of the crochet chain stitch you have just made before catching the twine with the hook and drawing it through the loop on the hook.

6 Continue to make the crochet chain, adding beads at each stitch until the worked length is 2 cm longer than your wrist. Remove the hook and tie the twine in a knot at the base of the length of beaded crochet chain to secure. Make sure that there are two beads left on the remaining length of twine to make the end of the tie.

7 Measure 10 cm along the twine from the base of the crochet chain and make a knot. This will create the second tie.

8 Slide the two remaining beads to the outermost knot and secure in place with another knot above them. Trim away the end of the twine below the outermost knot to neaten, and knot the ties into a loop to finish the bracelet.

QUICK TIP

Threading the beads onto the twine can be a little tricky. Make sure that the ends of the twine are cut neatly as frayed ends are harder to feed beads onto.

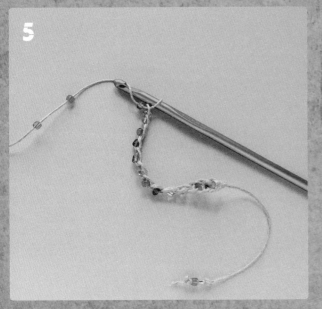

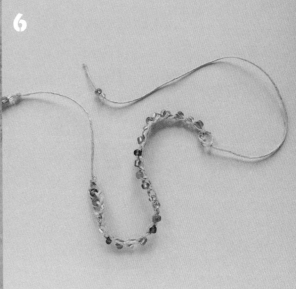

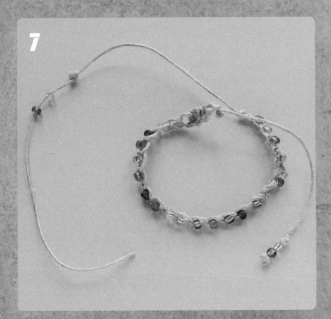

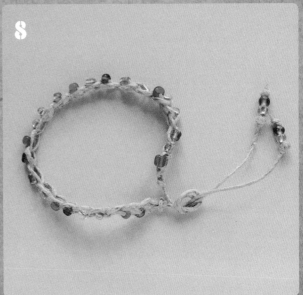

BEADED SAFETY PIN BRACELET

Make a statement accessory that your friends won't believe is made from simple safety pins embellished with tiny beads. Use one, two, three or a rainbow assortment of colours to vary the results.

YOU WILL NEED

> SAFETY PINS – MINIMUM 60

> SEED BEADS, IN THREE COLOURS

> THIN SHIRRING ELASTIC

> SCISSORS

> WASHI TAPE

CUSTOMISATION TIP

Instead of threading tiny round seed beads on the safety pins, why not try using the long type known as bugle beads for a different look.

TRANSFORM EVERYDAY SAFETY PINS

INTO A STUNNING BRACELET

WITH LASHINGS OF SEED BEADS

1 Open the safety pins and feed the seed beads onto the pin. Once the pin is full of beads, secure the safety pin closed. Repeat to fill 60 safety pins with seed beads – 30 of each colour of beads.

2 Position the safety pins in the order needed to create the design using the three colours. Make sure that the safety pins are each positioned in opposite orientation to the one next to it – one with the opening end upwards, the next with the coil end upwards. This will help them stack snugly when secured together to make the bracelet.

3 Cut a length of shirring elastic 20 cm longer than the measurement of your wrist and thread through the upper section of the row of beaded safety pins. Make sure that the elastic passes through the top section of one safety pin and the bottom part of the next, with the beaded section outermost.

4 Cut a second length of shirring elastic to 20 cm longer than the measurement of your wrist and begin threading it through the lower section of the row of safety pins. Slide the safety pins up neatly and snugly together as you work, being careful not to slide them off the other end of the elastic.

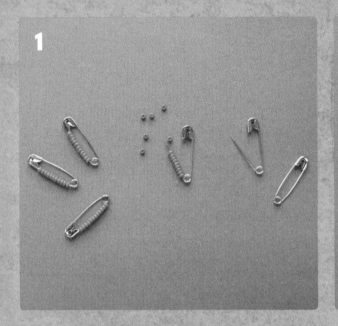

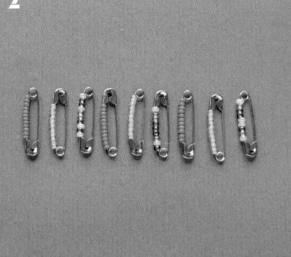

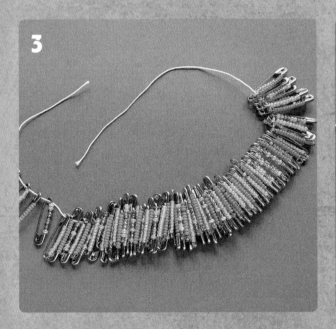

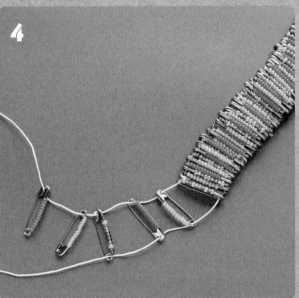

5 Holding the ends of the elastic, draw together the upper length and tighten to form the bracelet. Knot the ends together securely and trim away the excess elastic to neaten.

6 Draw up the lower length of elastic to complete the bracelet, secure tightly with a neat knot and snip away the excess elastic to neaten.

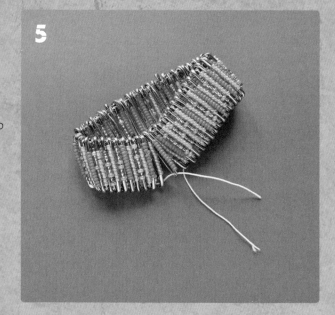

QUICK TIP

Be sure to work carefully when using safety pins, as the pin ends are very sharp and can cause injury.

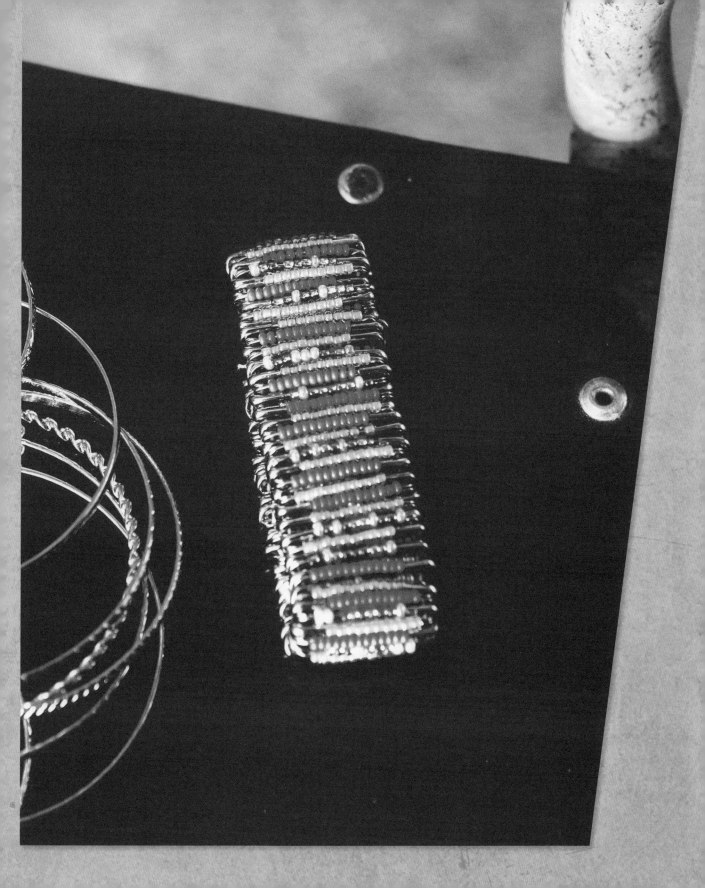

SAILOR KNOT BRACELET

The chunky sailor knot looks much more complex to make than it is, and will create a stunning statement bracelet that you can wear with pride – for an even more bold, dramatic look try working with two colours.

CUSTOMISATION TIP

Use the cord handles from fancy carrier bags for an eco-friendly bargain bracelet. Either mix cords from two bags, or use both handles from one bag to make a chic single-colour version.

TIE A STRIKING SAILOR KNOT TO MAKE A BRACELET THAT WILL REALLY WOW!

1 Cut the cord to two pieces of the required length. Fold one of the pieces of cord into half and position into a loop with the folded end lying over the tails.

2 Fold the second piece of cord in half and position under the loop of the first cord with the folded end positioned towards the fold of the first piece of cord.

3 Pass the folded end of the second cord over the folded end of the first piece of cord and then pass it under the tails of the first cord on the left-hand side.

4 Bring the folded ends of the second cord back to the right-hand side, passing it over the first part of the loop of the first cord, under the tails of the second cord and then back over the second part of the loop of the first cord. Holding the folded ends and tails of the cord on either side, carefully draw up to tighten the knot.

5 Trim the ends of the cord to the desired length for your wrist. Apply a small dab of glue to the ends and position in turn into the wide ribbon-end clasps. Use the flat-nose jewellery pliers to press the clasps closed.

6 Use the two pairs of slim flat-nose pliers to twist open the jump rings. Using the rings, secure the two parts of the lobster clasp into position on the ribbon end clasps on either side of the bracelet to finish.

QUICK TIP

When opening jump rings to secure the clasp, work carefully. Twist the two sections apart by holding the ends of each section in a set of pliers in each hand and rotating the pliers away from each other. By twisting the rings apart, rather than pulling them open, you will be able to close them back neatly by reversing the process to restore the original perfect circle shape.

QUICK TIP

Use superglue with care to avoid contact with your fingers and clothing. Work in small dabs at a time so that this is not visible on the finished piece.

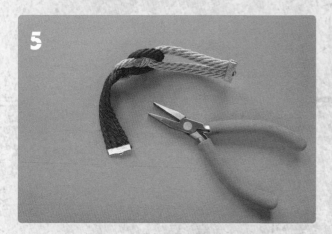

MULTI-STRANDED BRAID BRACELET

A simple braid design is enhanced by a combination of shell beads in rich colours and glossy clear glass beads, creating a dramatic designer-style accessory.

YOU WILL NEED

> TIGER TAIL WIRE, 1.5 M

> JEWELLERY WIRE CUTTERS

> SIX-STRAND SLIDE CLASP

> CRIMP BEADS X 18

> FLAT-NOSE JEWELLERY PLIERS

> TURQUOISE BEAD CHIPS X 40.6 CM STRAND (APPROX 100 BEADS)

> CORAL BEADS, 4 MM, X APPROX 70

> CLEAR GLASS BEADS, 4 MM, X APPROX 70

> NATURAL COLOUR SHELL BEADS X 40.6 CM STRAND (APPROX 90 BEADS)

CUSTOMISATION TIP

Replace the central two strands of beads with velvet or suede ribbon secured in crimp beads and mix with beads from your stash that harmonise to create your own stylish braided bracelet design. Why not try black velvet ribbon with round pearl and faceted jet beads, or light brown suede ribbon with natural shell and conker brown wood beads?

TEAM SHELL AND GLASS BEADS FOR A STYLISH BRACELET THAT WILL REALLY TURN HEADS!

1 Trim the tiger tail wire into six equal lengths, each measuring 5 cm longer than the desired length for your wrist measurement. Feed through the strand loops on one half of the clasp, slide a crimp bead onto the tiger tail wire and feed the short end of the tiger tail wire back through the crimp bead to create a loop. Use the flat-nose pliers to press the crimp bead closed to secure the wires in place. Continue to secure all six strands of tiger tail wire into the one half of the clasp with crimp beads. Use the wire cutters to trim away the short excess ends of wire neatly.

2 Working on each strand in turn, thread the selection of beads onto the tiger tail wire. Use the turquoise beads for the first two strands, the coral and the glass beads for the next two strands and the shell beads on the final two strands.

3 Make sure that all the beaded sections are the same length, then slide a crimp bead onto each length of wire and press closed with the flat-nose pliers to hold the beads neatly in place.

4 Take the outer two strands in towards the centre in turn to create a braid. Continue to loosely braid the bracelet for the entire length of the beads.

QUICK TIP

Be careful when using wire cutters: protect your eyes with safety goggles (swimming goggles work well too) and wear leather gloves as small sections of wire can be very sharp and may cause injury.

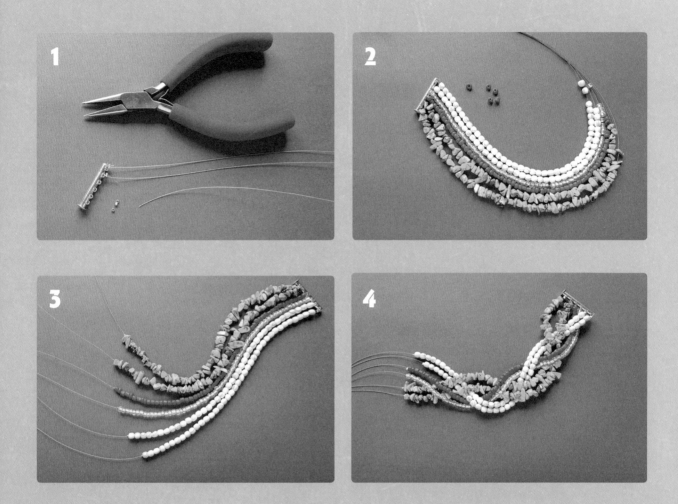

5 Slide a crimp bead onto each of the tiger tail wires before passing through the corresponding strand loops on the second half of the clasp.

6 Drawing the clasp up to the end of the braided section, feed the wire through the corresponding crimp beads in turn and press closed with the flat-nose pliers to secure. Use the wire cutters to neatly cut away the excess wire.

WIRE WORD BRACELET

Bending and manipulating jewellery wire into a message or the letters of your name is a fun way to create a personalised accessory. Why not make some for your friends too?

YOU WILL NEED

> MEDIUM-GAUGE JEWELLERY WIRE

> JEWELLERY WIRE CUTTERS

> ROUND-NOSE JEWELLERY PLIERS

> THREE STRANDS OF COLOURED CORD AND SUEDE, 10 CM EACH

> SCISSORS

> RIBBON ENDS X 2

> FLAT-NOSE JEWELLERY PLIERS

> SLIM FLAT-NOSE JEWELLERY PLIERS X 2

> LARGE JUMP RINGS X 3

> LOBSTER CLASP

CUSTOMISATION TIP

Create your own design using the wire to form your name, a fun word or a striking motif!

PERSONALISE YOUR LOOK WITH A WIRE WORD BRACELET

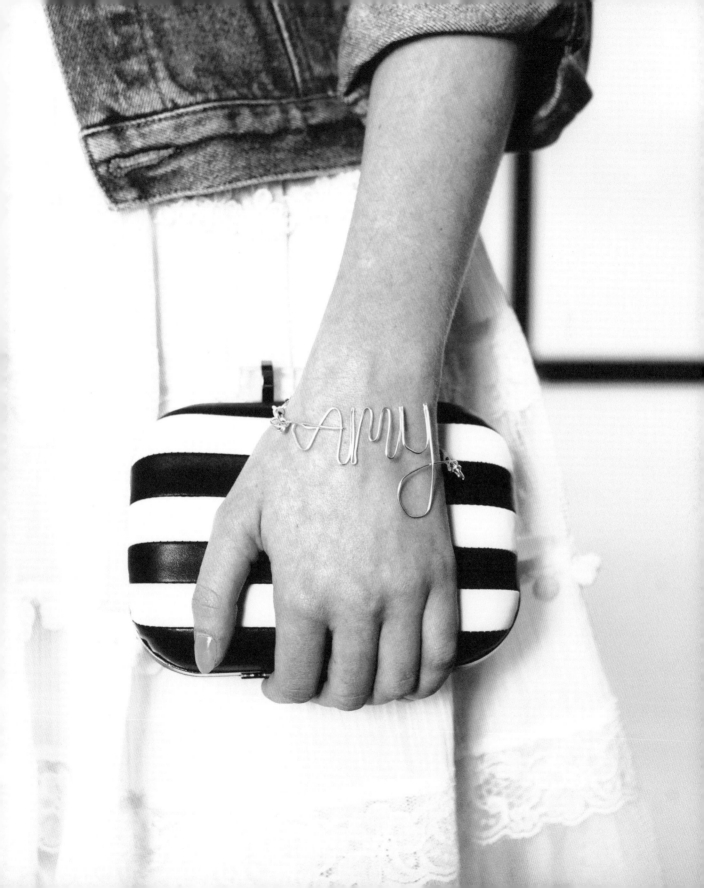

1 Cut a length of medium-gauge jewellery wire using the jewellery wire cutters. Using the round-nose pliers, create a small coil in the end of the wire. Bend and fold the wire to create your name, word or motif. Add a second small coil of wire to the other end of the wire and trim away the excess.

2 Cut the cord and suede to length. Secure the ends of the three cord and suede strands into one of the ribbon ends and use the flat-nose pliers to press closed and secure together.

3 Pass the outer cords in towards the centre in turn to create a braid. Braid the lengths together, then secure the ends in place with the second ribbon end using the flat-nose pliers.

4 Using the two pairs of slim round-nose jewellery pliers, twist open a jump ring and feed it through the small coil created at the end of the wire word and then through the ribbon end on the braid to join them together. Twist the jump ring back to close neatly.

QUICK TIP

When opening jump rings to secure the clasp, work carefully. Twist the two sections apart by holding the ends of each section in a set of pliers held in each hand, then rotating the pliers away from each other. By twisting the rings apart, rather than pulling them open, you will be able to close them back neatly — just reverse the twist process to restore the original perfect circle shape.

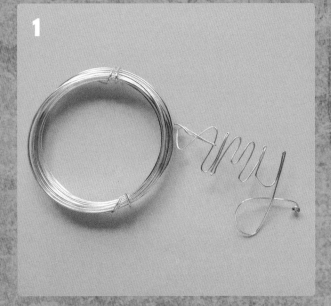

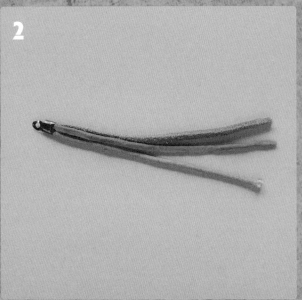

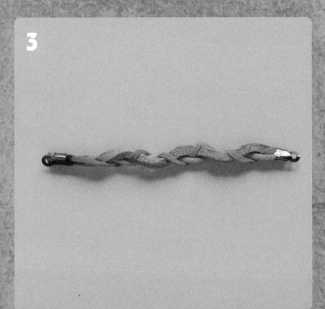

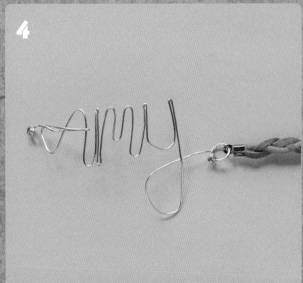

5 Repeat step 4 to add a jump ring to the other coil on the second side of the wire word (the beginning of the word).

6 In the same manner, twist open the final jump ring and use to secure the lobster clasp to the remaining ribbon end on the braided cord.

QUICK TIP

Be careful when using wire cutters: protect your eyes with safety goggles (swimming goggles work well too) and wear leather gloves as small sections of wire can be very sharp and may cause injury.

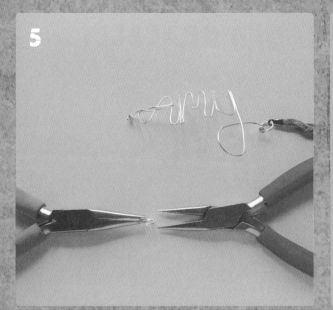

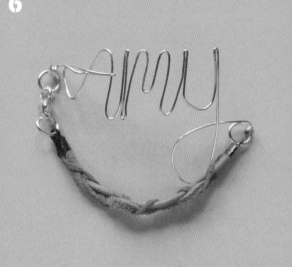

QUICK TIP

Create a guide for bending the wire into a word. Write out your word on paper so that you are happy with how it looks, then use this as a template while bending the wire.

MULTI-STRAND BEADED BRACELET

Memory wire retains its shape, making it a fantastic choice for creating this stacked strand-effect beaded bracelet. Select your favourite colour combinations for real stand-out style.

YOU WILL NEED

❯ JEWELLERY WIRE CUTTERS

❯ MEMORY WIRE

❯ ROUND-NOSE JEWELLERY PLIERS

❯ SELECTION OF BEADS (AMOUNTS ALL APPROX): GREEN SEED X 250; BLUE GLASS, 4 MM, X 110; CLEAR GLASS, 4 MM, X 60; RED GLASS, 4 MM, X 50; GOLD CUBE, 4 MM, X 7; WHITE CUBE, 4 MM, X 10; LIGHT BLUE GLASS, 4 MM, X 7; OPAQUE BLUE GLASS, 4 MM, X 7; SMALL SILVER, 3 MM, X 7

❯ JUMP RINGS X 2

❯ BRACELET TOGGLE CLASP

CUSTOMISATION TIP

Work with two contrasting colours and create a stacked stripe that runs through the individual strands.

STAND OUT FROM THE CROWD

WITH SPARKLING BEADS!

1 Use the wire cutters to carefully trim the memory wire into 6 lengths that are each 6 cm longer than your desired finished measurement around your wrist.

2 Use the round-nose jewellery pliers to create a small loop in one end of each length of memory wire.

3 Begin feeding the beads onto the lengths of memory wire. The neat end loops will prevent the beads from sliding off.

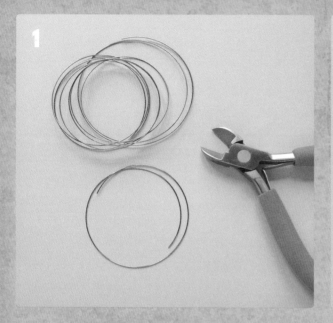

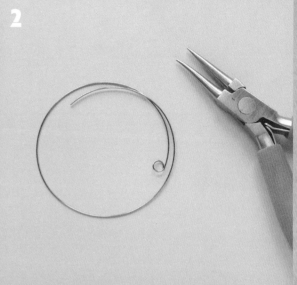

QUICK TIP

When making a wire loop, hold the wire ends level in the pliers, being careful that the ends don't extend above the pliers. Press your thumb on the end of the wire that lies on the pliers and begin rolling the pliers round to make the neat loop. Don't try to do this on one action, or your wrist will end up aching. Simply reposition the pliers and begin rolling again until the loop is finished.

4 Create a different design with the beads on each of the six lengths of memory wire. Work with different colours and shapes of beads to make each length unique.

5 Once you have finished threading beads onto each length, use the round-nose jewellery pliers to create a second small loop in the other end of the lengths of memory wire. This second loop will hold the beads securely in place on the length of wire.

6 Twist open a jump ring (see tip) and feed the loops on the ends of the memory wires into the ring. Add one half of the bracelet toggle clasp and twist closed (see tip).

7 Repeat with the second jump ring on the other side of the bracelet to join the ends of the strands together and secure the second half of the bracelet toggle clasp.

QUICK TIP

When opening jump rings to secure the clasp, work carefully. Twist the two sections apart by holding the ends of each section in a set of pliers held in each hand, then rotating the pliers away from each other. By twisting the rings apart, rather than pulling them open, you will be able to close them back neatly – just reverse the twist process to restore the original perfect circle shape.

ZIPPER BRACELET

This simple strip bracelet is created from a standard jeans zipper. The metallic teeth create a dramatic finish to this easy-to-make bracelet and the slider tab is used to hang a bead dangle.

YOU WILL NEED

〉 ZIPPER WITH METAL TEETH, 18 CM

〉 SUPERGLUE

〉 STATEMENT BEAD

〉 GLASS BEADS, 4 MM, IN TWO COLOURS, X 6

〉 SILVER HEAD PIN

〉 ROUND-NOSE JEWELLERY PLIERS

〉 JEWELLERY WIRE CUTTERS

〉 SLIM FLAT-NOSE JEWELLERY PLIERS X 2

〉 JUMP RING X 1

〉 LOBSTER CLASP

CUSTOMISATION TIP

Zipper tapes come in a range of colours and finishes, including a luxurious satin tape. Create a selection of bracelets using different zippers and hanging charms and wear them together for maximum impact.

MAKE AN IMPACT WITH A ZIPPY FASHION BRACELET!

1 With the zipper fastened and teeth placed downwards, add a line of superglue to the length of the webbing on one side of the teeth. Fold the webbing over the glue and press in place to create a thin strip. Set aside to allow the glue to dry.

2 Repeat to add a line of superglue along the webbing on the second side of the zipper and fold in to create a thin strip. Set aside to allow the glue to dry.

3 Slide three small beads, the statement bead and three more glass beads onto the head pin. Use the round-nose pliers to make a neat loop at the end of the head pin and the wire cutters to trim away the excess wire (see Quick Tip on page 66 for safety advice when working with wire cutters).

4 Use two pairs of the slim flat-nose pliers to twist open the jump ring. Push the ends of the open ring up through either side of the webbing below the closed end of the zipper. Feed on the bead charm and the lobster clasp, then twist closed neatly. Trim away the excess webbing at the zipper tab end and secure the lobster clasp to the slider tab to create the bracelet.

QUICK TIP

When opening jump rings, work carefully. Twist the two sections apart by holding the ends of each section in a set of pliers held in each hand, then rotating the pliers away from each other. By twisting the rings apart, rather than pulling them open, you will be able to close them back neatly – just reverse the twist process to restore the original perfect circle shape.

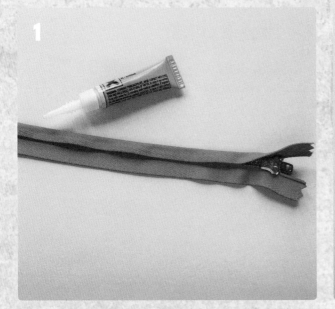

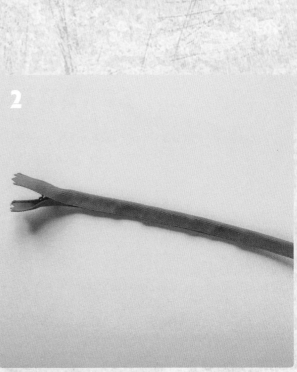

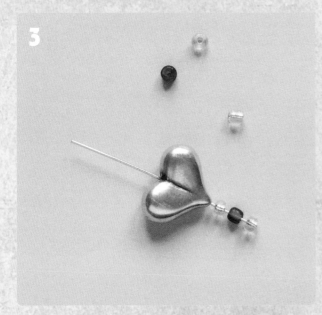

SPRAY PAINT BANGLE

Update your look in an instant with this speedy bracelet makeover. Take an old bangle, team bright acrylic-based spray paints with shining metallic markers, then unleash your creativity!

YOU WILL NEED

❯ OLD PLASTIC OR WOOD SMOOTH-SURFACED BANGLE

❯ PAPER TO COVER WORK SURFACE

❯ ACRYLIC SPRAY PAINT

❯ METALLIC MARKER

❯ PENCIL (OPTIONAL)

CUSTOMISATION TIP

Why not use the metallic markers to add your name (or your friend's name if you are making the bangle as a gift), or a favourite word or a meaningful slogan for a truly personal bracelet!

UPCYCLE OLD BANGLES WITH COLOURFUL PAINTS AND MARKERS

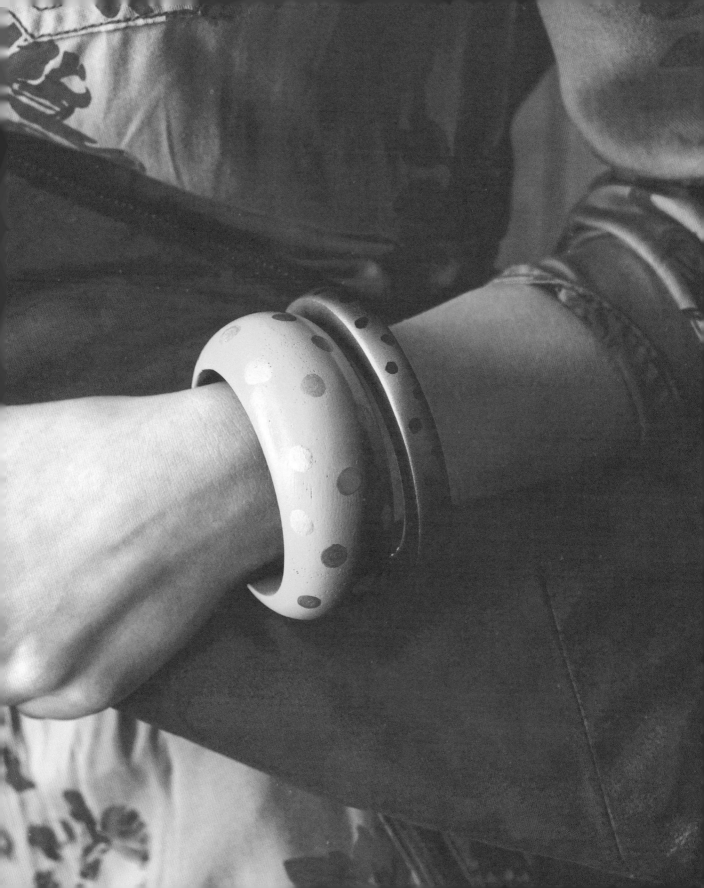

QUICK TIP

Only use spray paints in well-ventilated areas, and make sure that all surfaces are covered with protective paper. Wear old clothing that doesn't matter if some spray accidentally lands on your jeans instead of the bangle. You could also wear a decorator's protective mask if you are worried about breathing in paint fumes.

1 Clean the surface of the bangle in soapy water to remove any dust or dirt. Rinse and dry.

2 In a well-ventilated area, cover your work surface with paper to protect it from stray paint. Using an acrylic-based paint, work in small bursts of spray and repeated arching motions to cover the bangle in paint. Allow up to 60 minutes for the paint to become touch dry before turning to paint any remaining sections.

3 Once the paint is fully dry, begin to draw your design using the marker. You may want to sketch the design out in pencil lightly first to give you guide lines.

4 Complete the design, working carefully to make sure that you don't touch any of the marker elements until they are fully dry (about 20 minutes), or they may smudge.

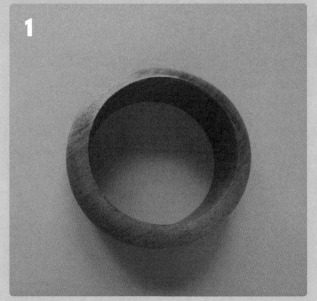

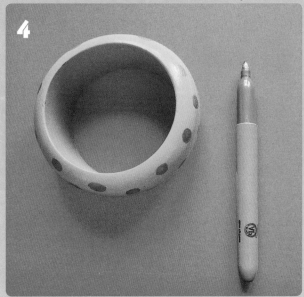

BEAD BRAID BRACELET

A handful of little golden beads and a single statement bead in a pop of contrast colour to the cord will transform a casual braided cord bracelet design into a stylish party accessory.

YOU WILL NEED

❯ THIN COTTON CORD, 2 M

❯ SCISSORS

❯ SMALL GOLD BEADS, 4 MM, X 42

❯ LARGE STATEMENT BEAD

CUSTOMISATION TIP

Mix and match cord and bead colours to create signature style bracelets for every occasion. Why not try black thread, silver beads and a silver charm instead of a statement bead for a party combination that will go with your little black dress?

METALLIC BEADS ADD A CHIC TOUCH TO A CLASSIC CORD BRACELET

1 Cut the cord to 2 lengths of 1 m each and, holding them together, fold both lengths in half. Tie a knot at the top of the fold to create a small loop through which the statement bead can pass (this will form the fastening for the bracelet).

2 Trim away one of the lengths of cord at the base of the knot and braid the remaining three lengths together for 2 cm. To create a braid, take the outer two strands in towards the centre in turn. Tie a knot to secure.

3 Thread a selection of gold beads onto each of the three strands of cord, sliding away from the cut end to prevent them from sliding off.

4 Slide the first bead up the outermost strand of cord on the left-hand side and then bring the cord to the centre. Next, slide the first bead of the outermost strand of the cord on the right-hand side and then bring the cord to the centre. The beads will be secured at each side of the braid.

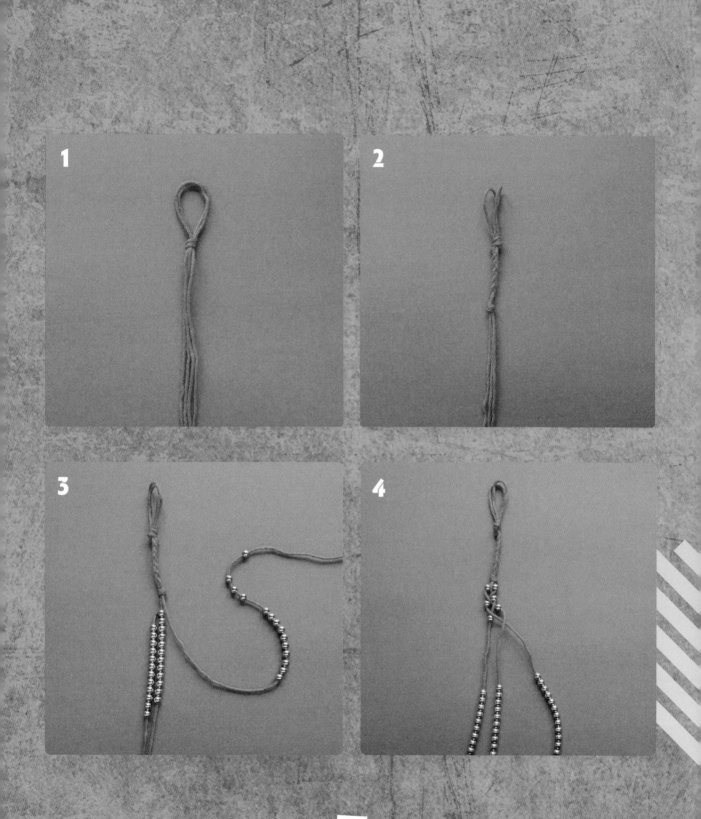

5 Continue braiding the cord, securing a bead at each side with each motion until the beaded section of the braid is the required length for your wrist, reserving one gold bead to pair with the statement bead.

6 Add a knot to the base of the braid to secure the cord and beads neatly into place.

7 Without adding more beads, braid the remaining free cord for 2 cm, then knot again. Thread the three strands of cord through the statement bead.

8 Add a single bead to the three strands of cord then knot them together securely to complete the second bracelet tie. Trim the cord below the knot to finish. To wear, wrap around your wrist and pass the statement bead through the loop to secure.

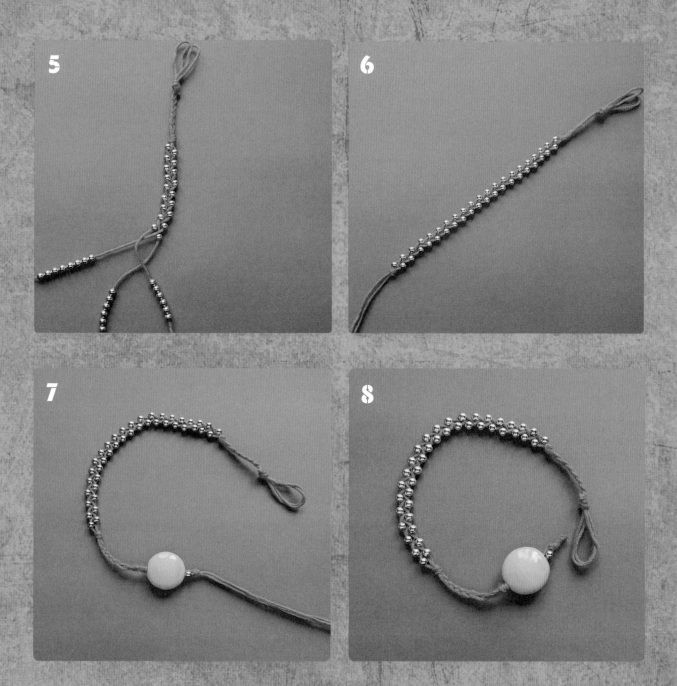

LOOM-BAND BRACELET

Fashionable loom bands are a great way to weave a bright, fun bracelet. This wide bracelet with its striking chevron design gives you plenty of space to use a rainbow of colours.

YOU WILL NEED

> LOOM BANDS IN A RANGE OF COLOURS X 6 PACKS

> LOOM-BAND LOOM, LONG

> LOOM-BAND HOOK

> LOOM-BAND FASTENING CLIP

CUSTOMISATION TIP

Try making a bracelet with even more colours to create a full rainbow, or just stick to two of your favourite shades for a dramatic striped finish.

WHY NOT WEAVE A RAINBOW COLLECTION OF LOOM BAND BRACELETS?

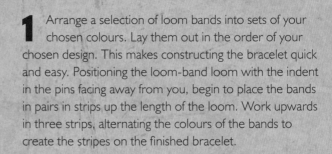

1 Arrange a selection of loom bands into sets of your chosen colours. Lay them out in the order of your chosen design. This makes constructing the bracelet quick and easy. Positioning the loom-band loom with the indent in the pins facing away from you, begin to place the bands in pairs in strips up the length of the loom. Work upwards in three strips, alternating the colours of the bands to create the stripes on the finished bracelet.

2 Turn the loom-band loom around so that the indents in the pins are facing towards you, and begin positioning the centre bands. Work across the three strips of positioned loom bands to create small triangles across the loom.

3 Twist a single loom band (black here) into a figure-eight, and position onto the lowest centre pin of the loom. This will become the closure for the bracelet.

4 Starting from the lowest band and working upwards, inset the loom-band hook into the indent in the pin behind the central triangle band, and pick up and lift the bands and pass them onto the pin above them.

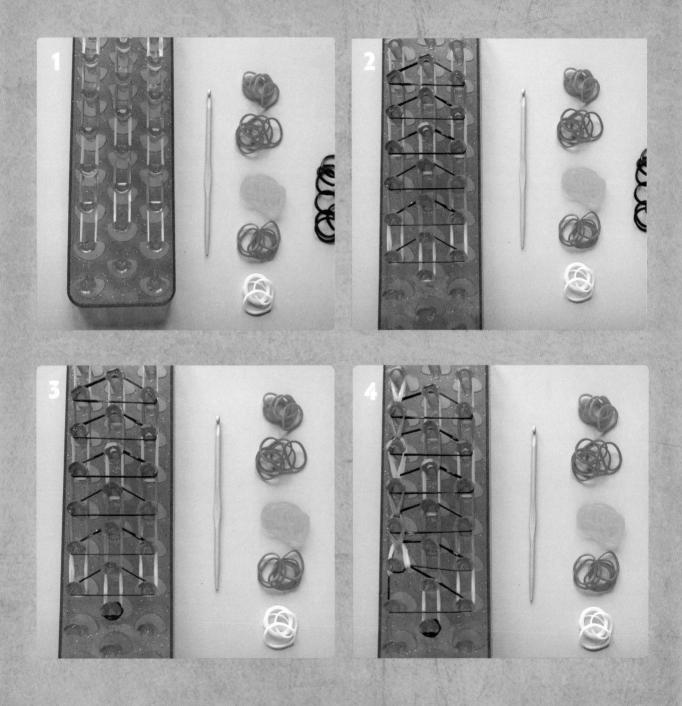

5 Repeat the process to pass the loom bands onto the pin above on the next two rows of bands.

6 Draw the outer two sections of the lowest centre triangle loom band into the centre, twisting them before placing them onto the centre pin on the loom-band loom. This twist will become the second part of the closure for the bracelet.

7 Insert the loom-band fastening into the twisted loom band to secure the fastening. Starting at the secured fastening, carefully begin to lift the bands free from the loom-band loom. Your bracelet is now ready to wear!

8 Secure the second half of the loom-band fastening clips into the small looped loom-band in the other side to create the bracelet.

QUICK TIP

The loom-band loom stretches the bands to around double their length while you are creating the design, so you need to make sure that the stripes of bands on the loom are long enough to go around your wrist when you take them off the loom. The stretched length on the loom will need to be double your wrist measurement plus 5 cm for fit.

MATERIALS

All the projects list the materials you need to make them. Some additional advice is provided here.

EMBROIDERY THREAD

Each strand of embroidery floss is usually made up of six fine strands of mercerized cotton, giving the thread a soft, silky feel. You use all the fine strands together as one thread for your bracelet. There are more than 500 colour choices on the market, so you'll be able to match your Chevron Friendship Band (see page 8) to any outfit.

CORD

You can find cord in a range of fibres, including nylon, cotton, leather and faux suede, and in a range of thicknesses. A fine cotton cord is used for the Bead Braid design (see page 78), fine waxed cotton cord for the Charm Motif Bracelet (see page 14), thicker cord for the Sailor Knot project (see page 48) and chunky paracord for the Urban Knot Bracelet (see page 30). You should always choose the same weight of cord, but you can vary the fibre and colour to customize the design.

JEWELLERY FINDINGS

Fixtures such as clasps, ribbon ends and crimp beads are known as jewellery findings. These specialist fittings are available in silver- and gold-tone metal, and also in enamelled metal in a range of colours. You can also buy sterling silver findings for a special project.

SEED BEADS

Also known as rocailles, these tiny glass beads resemble little seeds, hence the name. Japanese or Czech in origin, they are available in a huge range of colours. Japanese beads have a larger hole and are more regular in shape, but are also more costly.

WIRE

Steel memory wire is used for the Multi-strand Beaded Bracelet (see page 64) as it holds its curved shape easily. Sold in coils, it is often plated to give a silver, gold or antique brass effect. This wire is very hard, so you will need to use wire cutters designed for cutting memory wire. Jewellery wire is softer and easy to bend, so it is ideal for the Wire Word Bracelet (see page 58). It's usually made from silver plated copper, though enamelled versions are also available in a range of colours (use nylon-jawed pliers with these so you don't mark the wire as you bend it).

JEWELLERY PLIERS

You will need both flat-nose and round-nose types for the projects in this book. Round-nose pliers have jaws that taper to a point and are ideal for making loops. Position

your wire near the handle for a large loop and near the tip of the jaws for a small loop. Flat-nose types have jaws that don't taper, and are used for opening and closing jump rings and gripping wire.

LOOM BANDS
The bands are generally made of silicone rather than rubber, which is good news for those allergic to latex. There's a huge range of colours and special finishes, such as pearlised or metallic hues, available.

ACRYLIC SPRAY PAINT
Always use decorative spray paints in a well-ventilated area and cover surfaces in the immediate area. You may want to wear old clothes and disposable gloves too. Hold the can around 25 cm away from the bangle and move it back and forth in an even manner. Paint will be touch dry in around an hour (though fast-dry types will be touch dry in 10 minutes) and fully dry the next day. You can find a range of colours, including metallic effects.

WASHI TAPE
This sticky tape, as used in the Washi Tape Bangle (see page 26), is essentially a decorative masking tape that originated in Japan and has become a very popular material for a number of crafts, including card making, scrapbooking, gift wrapping and jewellery making – to name just a few!

CHARMS
The addition of charms is a quick and easy way to customise a project, such as the Zipper Bracelet (see page 70), or can be used as a focal point, such as the Charm Motif Bracelet (see page 14). These motifs in all shapes and sizes are usually found in the jewellery section of craft stores - or you can make your own accents with selections of beads and jewellery wire.

RESOURCES

If you are a keen crafter, you will probably have some of the
tools and materials for the projects in this book already – and
a few of the projects, like the T-shirt Yarn Bracelet (see page
20), simply upcycle things you will have around the home. If
you need to buy more specialist items, such as the jewellery
pliers or memory wire, you'll find pretty much everything
you need at large craft stores or haberdashery sections
in department stores such as John Lewis. If you can't find
anything on your local high street, there's a huge range of
online suppliers with an amazing choice of beads and other
bits and bobs. There are lots of wonderful online specialist
sources for jewellery supplies, though you might like to
browse for beads at a bricks and mortar store if you get the
chance as the experience of choosing from a treasure chest of
styles you can touch and feel will inspire you.

HOBBYCRAFT
www.hobbycraft.co.uk
The largest nationwide chain of craft stores stocks over 30,000 products, so you'll discover everything you need to get crafty, including jewellery making, knitting and stitching, papercraft and art materials.

FRED ALDOUS
37 Lever Street
Manchester M1 1LW
www.fredaldous.co.uk
This famous Manchester craft store has been around since 1886! Its extensive stock is now available online too.

HOMECRAFTS
www.homecrafts.co.uk
An established online craft supplier with over 16,000 products in their range.

BEADWORKS BEAD SHOP
21a Tower Street
Seven Dials, Covent Garden
London WC2H 9NS
www.beadworks.co.uk
Stocks a very large range of beads, and also findings, tools and bead kits. Products also available to purchase online.

CREATIVE BEADCRAFT
31 Smiths Court
Brewer Street
London
W1D 7DP
www.creativebeadcraft.co.uk
Established in 1920, this family-run company offers a wide range of beads, findings and tools.

BEADS DIRECT
www.beadsdirect.co.uk
The biggest online bead resource in Europe.

GEORGE WEIL
Old Portsmouth Road
Peasmarsh
GUILDFORD
Surrey GU3 1LZ
www.georgeweil.com
This mail order supplier/shop based at a warehouse near Guildford in Surrey sells a large range of traditional fine art materials and craft materials and equipment direct from the showroom and through the website.

DERAMORES
www.deramores.com
Online retailer of knitting and yarn craft supplies. Stockists of a wide range of yarns and materials, including crochet hooks and loom bands.

WEAREKNITTERS
www.weareknitters.com
Online retailer of modern knitting yarns and supplies, including a wide range of fabric or T-shirt yarns in a range of bold colours.

INDEX

ABOUT THE AUTHOR

Laura Strutt is a craft designer and maker living in Colchester with her husband and little dog, Waffle. She is the author of a number of crafting books, including on sewing, wedding and yarn crafts. Laura regularly teaches at workshops around the UK and shares lots of creative projects, how-to guides, recipes and crafty inspiration on her website www.madepeachy.com

ACKNOWLEDGEMENTS

Creating these arm candy designs for this book has been a lot of fun – there is nothing more inspiring than being surrounded by lots of brightly coloured beads, trinkets, charms and findings! There have been a number of people who have contributed to the creation of this book and thanks goes out to them all. In particular, Amy Christian, at Pavilion Books, for commissioning such a fantastic and fun book and Judith More for her fabulous attention to detail. Finally, special thanks to my husband, John Strutt, for his endless support, creative input and tolerance to being surrounded by crafty supplies 24/7!

Step-by-step photography by Laura Strutt
Main project photography by Christina Wilson

Work Out

Mathematics

GCSE

The titles in this series

MACMILLAN
WORK OUT
SERIES

Work Out

Mathematics

GCSE

G.D. Buckwell

MACMILLAN
EDUCATION

First published 1986
Reprinted 1986
Reprinted (with corrections) 1986
This edition 1987
Reprinted (with corrections) 1988

Published by
MACMILLAN EDUCATION LTD
Houndmills, Basingstoke, Hampshire RG21 2XS
and London
Companies and representatives
throughout the world

Typeset by TecSet Ltd,
Wallington, Surrey
Printed in Great Britain at The Bath Press, Avon

British Library Cataloguing in Publication Data
Buckwell, G. D.
(Macmillan work out series)
1. Mathematics—Examinations, questions,
etc.
I. Title
510'.76   QA43
ISBN 0–333–44013–7 (paper cover)
ISBN 0–333–43450–1 (export edn)

Contents

Acknowledgements

The author and publishers wish to thank the following who have kindly given permission for the use of copyright material:

The Associated Examining Board, the East Anglian Regional Examinations Board, the Joint Matriculation Board, the Northern Ireland Schools Examination Council, the Oxford and Cambridge Schools Examination Board, the Scottish Examination Board, the Southern Universities' Joint Board, the University of Cambridge Local Examinations Syndicate, the University of London School Examinations Board, the University of Oxford Delegacy of Local Examinations and the Welsh Joint Education Committee for questions from past examination papers.

Every effort has been made to trace all the copyright holders but if any have been inadvertently overlooked the publishers will be pleased to make the necessary arrangement at the first opportunity.

The University of London Entrance and Schools Examinations Council accepts no responsibility whatsoever for the accuracy or method in the answers given in this book to actual questions set by the London Board.

Acknowledgement is made to the Southern Universities' Joint Board for School Examinations for permission to use questions taken from their past papers but the Board is in no way responsible for answers that may be provided and they are solely the responsibility of the authors.

The Associated Examining Board, the University of Oxford Delegacy of Local Examinations, the University of Cambridge Local Examinations Syndicate, the Northern Ireland Schools Examination Council and the Scottish Examination Board wish to point out that worked examples included in the text are entirely the responsibility of the author and have neither been provided nor approved by the Board.

Organizations Responsible for GCSE Examinations

In the United Kingdom, examinations are administered by the following organizations. Syllabuses and examination papers can be ordered from the addresses given here:

Northern Examining Association (NEA)

Joint Matriculation Board (JMB)
Publications available from:
John Sherratt & Son Ltd
78 Park Road, Altrincham
Chesire WA14 5QQ

North Regional Examinations Board
Wheatfield Road, Westerhope
Newcastle upon Tyne NE5 5JZ

**Yorkshire and Humberside Regional
  Examinations Board (YREB)**
Scarsdale House
136 Derbyside Lane
Sheffield S8 8SE

**Associated Lancashire Schools
  Examining Board**
12 Harter Street
Manchester M1 6HL

**North West Regional Examinations
  Board (NWREB)**
Orbit House, Albert Street
Eccles, Manchester M30 0WL

Midland Examining Group (MEG)

**University of Cambridge Local
  Examinations Syndicate (UCLES)**
Syndicate Buildings, Hills Road
Cambridge CB1 2EU

**Oxford and Cambridge Schools
  Examination Board (O & C)**
10 Trumpington Street
Cambridge CB2 1QB

Southern Universities' Joint Board (SUJB)
Cotham Road
Bristol BS6 6DD

**East Midland Regional Examinations
  Board (EMREB)**
Robins Wood House, Robins Wood Road
Aspley, Nottingham NG8 3NR

West Midlands Examinations Board (WMEB)
Norfolk House, Smallbrook
Queensway, Birmingham B5 4NJ

London and East Anglian Group (LEAG)

**University of London School
  Examinations Board (L)**
University of London Publications Office
52 Gordon Square
London WC1E 6EE

**London Regional Examining Board
  (LREB)**
Lyon House
104 Wandsworth High Street
London SW18 4LF

East Anglian Examinations Board (EAEB)
The Lindens, Lexden Road
Colchester, Essex CO3 3RL

Southern Examining Group (SEG)

The Associated Examining Board (AEB)
Stag Hill House
Guildford
Surrey GU2 5XJ

**University of Oxford Delegacy of
  Local Examinations (OLE)**
Ewert Place, Banbury Road
Summertown, Oxford OX2 7BZ

**Southern Regional Examinations
  Board (SREB)**
Avondale House
33 Carlton Crescent
Southampton, Hants SO9 4YL

**South-East Regional Examinations
  Board (SEREB)**
Beloe House
2–10 Mount Ephraim Road
Royal Tunbridge Wells, Kent TN1 1EU

South-Western Examinations Board (SWExB)
23–29 Marsh Street
Bristol BS1 4BP

Scottish Examination Board (SEB)

Publications available from:
Robert Gibson and Sons (Glasgow) Ltd
17 Fitzroy Place, Glasgow G3 7SF

Welsh Joint Education Committee (WJEC)

245 Western Avenue
Cardiff CF5 2YX

Northern Ireland Schools Examinations
    Council (NISEC)

Examinations Office
Beechill House, Beechill Road
Belfast BT8 4RS

Introduction

Simply buying a book will not make you pass any examinations. However, by working from this book regularly and methodically you will improve your understanding of the key facts and have the opportunity to practise answering examination questions and so check your progress.

Each chapter is self-contained; so you should choose the topics you find particularly difficult, study the explanation and worked examples and then tackle the check test; the answers are at the back of the book. If you have problems with the check test, then go back through the earlier part of the chapter. Finally, to confirm what you have achieved, tackle the questions and exercises at the end of the chapter; again the answers are at the back.

The Examination

This book provides a framework that will enable you to tackle an examination at the age of 16 — the GCSE. In mathematics, three levels will be offered as follows:

Level	Target group	Grades available
I	Grade F	E, F, G
II	Grade D	C, D, E, F
III	Grade B	A, B, C, D

The approach used in this book is most suitable for pupils hoping to obtain grades A, B or C.

The GCSE is a new examination and for that reason, in mathematics, course work will not be compulsory until 1991. A chapter has been included on course work although at such an early stage in its development one can only speculate on the final forms it will take. It is important that if you are submitting course work, you are fully aware of the regulations in operation for your examining group.

The only guidance on examination questions that is available at the moment is in the form of specimen questions. These have not been fully tested in most cases, and therefore they give only a general idea of the nature of the papers. In some cases questions have changed very little from past questions in the hardest papers. It is for this reason that some past 'O' level questions appear in the exercises in this book, where the author feels they are relevant to the topics for that chapter.

A number of sections and questions have been marked with an asterisk. These can be omitted by most students at a first reading. You will need to check carefully whether any of these harder topics are required by your syllabus.

Remember to keep a close watch on the time during the examination. If you simply cannot answer a question, move on to the next one without wasting time. At the end, if you have time, you can have another attempt at the questions you have missed.

Revision

You will probably revise more in mathematics than in any other subject. It is essential to know and understand the basic principles and be able to apply them accurately. Therefore it is important that you plan a realistic revision programme giving yourself time to practise working out problems in all the topics included in your examination. Start by obtaining the syllabus for the mathematics paper you are taking, from the appropriate examining group (addresses are given on pages ix–xi.

Avoid panic by drawing up a revision programme which you can stick to. Just before the examination, go through the check tests included in each chapter of this book; this will improve your confidence and highlight any weak spots.

1 Set Theory

1.1 Definition

A set is a clearly defined collection of distinct objects, which are called *members* or *elements* of the set. Sets will be denoted by capital letters $A, B, C, \ldots$ and the elements or members by lower-case letters $x, y, z, \ldots$. If x belongs to a set A, we write this $x \in A$. ($\in$ stands for 'belongs to', or 'is an element of' or 'is a member of'.)

If y does not belong to a set B, we write this $y \notin B$. Sometimes it is possible to list all the elements, for example $A = \{1, 3, 4, 7\}$, $B = \{a, b, x, y\}$. For more complex sets, see the notation used in section 1.4.

1.2 Equality

Two sets A and B can only be equal if A and B contain exactly the same elements. However, the order of listing elements is not important and so $\{1, 3, 4, 6\} = \{4, 1, 6, 3\}$.

*1.3 Standard Sets

In mathematics, we are most frequently concerned with sets of numbers. In order to save repetition, certain letters are used for commonly used sets:

$\mathbb{N} = \{0, 1, 2, 3, 4, \ldots\}$
$\mathbb{Z} = \{0, \pm1, \pm2, \pm3, \ldots\}$
$\mathbb{Z}^+ = \{1, 2, 3, 4, \ldots\}$
$\mathbb{Q}$ is the set of rational numbers (see Chapter 2).
$\mathbb{R}$ is the set of all real numbers from $-\infty$ to $+\infty$.

1.4 Alternative Notation

Listing each element of a set is often not possible, or convenient. We use the following notation:

$$A = \{x : x \in \mathbb{N} \text{ and } x \text{ is even}\}.$$

We read this as A equals the set of values of x such that x belongs to $\mathbb{N}$ and is even.

Hence, $A = \{0, 2, 4, 6, \ldots\}$. Clearly this notation is very suitable to represent an *infinite set*.

$$B = \{x : x \in \mathbb{R} \text{ and } 2x - 1 \leqslant 5\}.$$

Solving $2x - 1 \leqslant 5$ (see Chapter 6 if you are unsure about inequalities) gives $2x \leqslant 6, \therefore x \leqslant 3$.

This time, x can be any number less than or equal to 3. It could be represented by part of the number line from $-\infty$ to 3, but it is impossible to list the elements. The reader will find many more examples using this notation throughout the book.

1.5 Universal Set, Complement

The set of all possible elements that we wish to consider in any problem is called the *universal set*. It is denoted by $\mathcal{E}$. The universal set is particularly useful when considering the complement of a set A, denoted by A'. A' is the set of elements of $\mathcal{E}$ that do not belong to A.

$\therefore$ If $\qquad \mathcal{E} = \{1, 2, 3, 4, 5, 6, 7, 8\} \qquad$ and $\qquad A = \{x : x \text{ is odd}\}$,

then since $\qquad\qquad\qquad\qquad\qquad A = \{1, 3, 5, 7\}$

it follows that $\qquad\qquad\qquad\qquad A' = \{2, 4, 6, 8\}$.

1.6 Intersection, Null Set

The *intersection* of two sets A and B is the set of elements that belong to both set A and set B. The symbol $\cap$ is used.

Hence $\qquad\qquad\qquad A \cap B = \{x : x \in A \text{ and } x \in B\}$

(read as 'A intersection B').
For example, if

$$A = \{1, 3, 4, 5\}, \qquad B = \{2, 3, 5, 6\} \qquad \text{and} \qquad C = \{2, 6, 7\},$$

then:
(a) $A \cap B = \{3, 5\}$.
(b) $A \cap C$ has no elements. We write this

$$A \cap C = \{ \ \} \qquad \text{or} \qquad A \cap C = \phi.$$

ϕ is known as the *null* set or the *empty* set. In this case $A \cap C = \phi$.
$A \cap C = \phi$.
   If $X \cap Y = \phi$ then the sets X and Y have no element in common. We say that X and Y are *disjoint* sets.

1.7 Union

The *union* of two sets A and B is the set of elements that belong to either set A or set B, or to both. The symbol $\cup$ is used.

Hence $\qquad\qquad A \cup B \text{ (read as '}A \text{ union } B\text{')} = \{x : x \in A \text{ or } x \in B\}$.

For example,

if $\qquad\qquad A = \{3, 4, 5, 6\} \qquad$ and $\qquad B = \{a, b, 2, 4, d\}$

then $\qquad\qquad\qquad\qquad A \cup B = \{2, 3, 4, 5, 6, a, b, d\}$.

1.8   Subsets

Sometimes we may want to indicate that all the elements of a set A belong to another set B. We say that A is a *subset* of B.
  We write this $A \subset B$.

Note: Since all the elements of A belong to A, we can say that A is a subset of A. Hence $A \subset A$.

(Some books use the symbol $\subseteq$ to indicate that a set can be a subset of itself.)

1.9   Venn Diagrams

A problem can often be made much easier if it is represented by a Venn diagram. The universal set is represented by a rectangle and the sets are represented by closed curves, usually circles or ovals. Sets required can then be indicated by shading appropriate regions. The examples in Fig. 1.1 should indicate how this is done.

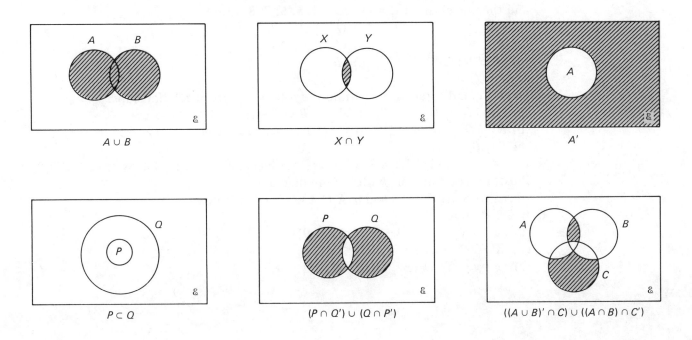

Fig. 1.1

1.10   Number of Elements

The number of elements in a set A is denoted by $n(A)$. For example,
(a) $A = \{3, 4, 7, 8, 10\}$, $n(A) = 5$,
(b) $B = \{x : 2 \leqslant x \leqslant 14 \text{ and } x \text{ is prime}\}$; since

$$B = \{2, 3, 5, 7, 11, 13\},$$

then $n(B) = 6$.

1.11 Sets of Points

Sets of points can often be conveniently represented using set notation.

$$A = \{(x, y) : y = 3x + 1\}.$$

This represents the set of points which satisfy $y = 3x + 1$, hence A is a straight line with equation $y = 3x + 1$.

Further examples of this can be found in Chapters 5 and 6. The following check exercise contains simple examples on the ideas covered so far.

Check 1

1 List the elements of the following sets:
   (a) $A = \{x : x \in \mathbb{N}, x \text{ is prime and } 8 < x < 30\}$.
   (b) $B = \{x : 4x + 3 = 9\}$.
   (c) $C = \{x : x \in \mathbb{N} \text{ and } 4x + 3 = 9\}$.
   (d) $D = \{(x \ y) : x + y = 8, x, y \in \mathbb{N}\}$.
   (e) $E = \{x : \sin x° = \frac{1}{2}, 0 \leqslant x \leqslant 360\}$.

2 If $P = \{3, 4, 5, 6\}$, $Q = \{1, 4, 5, 7\}$, $R = \{1, 2, 4, 6\}$
   and the universal set $\& = \{1, 2, 3, 4, 5, 6, 7, 8\}$, find:
   (a) $P \cap Q$ (e) $(P' \cap Q) \cup R$
   (b) R' (f) $(P \cup Q') \cap R'$
   (c) $(P \cup Q) \cap R$ (g) $(P \cup Q) \cap (Q \cup R)$
   (d) $P \cup Q'$

3 Draw Venn diagrams to illustrate the following sets or relationships:
   (a) $(A \cup B) \cap C$ (d) $A' \cap (B \cup C)$ where $A \cap B = \phi$
   (b) $P \cap (Q' \cup R')$ (e) $(X \cap Y) \cup (Y \cap Z)$ where $X \cap Z = \phi$
   (c) $P \subset (Q \cup R)$

4 If $n(A) = 5$ and $n(B) = 8$, what are the greatest and least values of $n(A \cup B)$? Illustrate your answers with a Venn diagram.

5 If $n(X) = 8$, $n(Y) = 16$ and $n(X \cap Y) = 5$, what is $n(X \cup Y)$?

6 If $\& = \mathbb{Z}$, find:
   (a) $\{x : 3 \leqslant x \leqslant 8\} \cup \{x : 5 < x < 9\}$,
   (b) $\{x : 2 < x < 7\} \cap \{x : 4 \leqslant x < 8\}$,
   (c) $\{x : x < 3\} \cup \{x : -8 \leqslant x \leqslant -5\}$.

*1.12 Logic

Set notation is an extremely powerful tool when used to represent sentences and arguments in mathematical logic.

(a) If $P = \{\text{multiples of 4}\}$ and $Q = \{\text{multiples of 2}\}$ then the relationship $P \subset Q$ could be used to represent the statement, 'All multiples of 4 are divisible by 2.'

(b) If $A = \{\text{domestic animals}\}$ and $B = \{\text{whales}\}$ then the relationship $A \cap B = \phi$ could be used to represent the statement, 'A whale is not a domestic animal.'

(c) Consider the truth of the following argument:

> All racing cars are fast.
> Some fast cars are expensive.
> Hence, there are some racing cars that are expensive.

There can be no doubt in reality, about the truth of the final statement, but look at the mathematics behind the argument.

Let $F = \{\text{fast cars}\}$, $E = \{\text{expensive cars}\}$ and $R = \{\text{racing cars}\}$.

The information given can be expressed in set notation by the two results $R \subset F$ and $F \cap E \neq \phi$.

If we now try to represent these results in a Venn diagram, we find that there are two possible diagrams satisfying these conditions. These can be seen in Fig. 1.2.

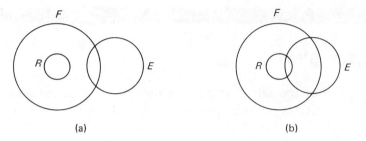

(a)   (b)

Fig. 1.2

Clearly, Fig. 1.2(a) does not satisfy the final conclusion. Hence, the final conclusion is false.

*1.13   De Morgan's Laws, Distributive Laws

There are certain results which are true for any set A. These can be used to simplify results (see Worked Example 1.1. They are:

(a) $A \cup A = A$;   (e) $A \cap A = A$;

(b) $A \cup A' = \mathcal{E}$;   (f) $A \cap A' = \phi$;

(c) $A \cup \mathcal{E} = \mathcal{E}$;   (g) $A \cap \mathcal{E} = A$;

(d) $A \cup \phi = A$;   (h) $A \cap \phi = \phi$.

De Morgan's laws:

(i) $(A \cup B)' = A' \cap B'$;

(j) $(A \cap B)' = A' \cup B'$.

The proofs of (i) and (j) given below illustrate another way of using Venn diagrams.

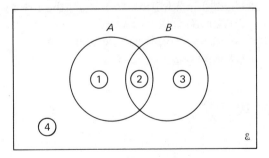

Fig. 1.3

Each region in Fig. 1.3 has been numbered 1, 2, 3 or 4.

7

$$(A \cup B)' = (① \cup ② \cup ③)' = ④$$
$$A' \cap B' = (③ \cup ④) \cap (① \cup ④) = ④$$
$$\therefore (A \cup B)' = A' \cap B'.$$

Proof of the other result is similar.

The distributive laws:
(k) $A \cup (B \cap C) = (A \cup B) \cap (A \cup C)$;
(l) $A \cap (B \cup C) = (A \cap B) \cup (A \cap C)$.

Worked Example 1.1

For the sets A and B, we define $A * B$ as the set of elements which are in A or B but not in both. The set $A * B$ is shaded in the Venn diagram, Fig. 1.4.

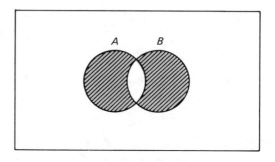

Fig. 1.4

Write down, without using $*$, sets which are equivalent to
(a) $A * A$ (c) $(A * B) \cup A$
(b) $A * A'$ (d) $(A * B) \cup B$ [L]

Solution

(a) We can write $A * B = (A \cap B') \cup (A' \cap B)$,
     hence $A * A = (A \cap A') \cup (A' \cap A) = \phi \cup \phi = \phi$.
(b) $A * A = (A \cap (A')') \cup (A' \cap A')$
           $= (A \cap A) \cup A' = A \cup A' = \mathcal{E}$.
(c) $(A * B) \cup A$ can be seen most clearly if a Venn diagram is used. If all of A is shaded in addition to $A * B$, then the whole of $A \cup B$ is shaded,
     $\therefore (A * B) \cup A = A \cup B$.
(d) As in part (c), it can be seen that
     $(A * B) \cup B = A \cup B$.

Worked Example 1.2

In a local election, 3025 constituents voted for a number of candidates, 800 voted for candidate A only, 850 voted for candidate B only, and 630 voted for candidate C only. 425 voted for A and B, 120 voted for A and C and 57 voted for B and C.

If 537 voted for none of the candidates A, B and C, how many voted for all three candidates?

Solution

This question is best solved by a Venn diagram.

If the number of people who voted for all three candidates is denoted by x, then the number in each region will be as in Fig. 1.5.

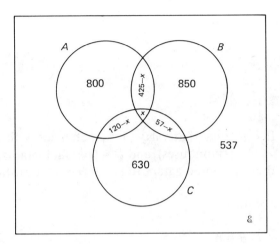

Fig. 1.5

Since the total number of people represented in the diagram is 3025, then

$$800 + (425 - x) + 850 + (120 - x) + x + (57 - x)$$
$$+ 630 + 537 = 3025.$$
$$\therefore 3419 - 2x = 3025.$$

Hence $x = 197$.
$\therefore$ 197 people voted for all three candidates.

Worked Example 1.3

Two sets P and Q are such that $P \cup Q = P$. A third set R is such that $R \cap Q = \phi$. Which of the following statements *must* be true?
(a) $P \cap R \neq \phi$;   (b) $P \cap Q \cap R = \phi$;   (c) $Q \subset P \cup R$.

Solution

The main difficulty with this type of problem is that the given information can be represented by more than one Venn diagram. All possibilities must be considered before attempting an answer.

$P \cup Q = P$ means that Q is a subset of P.
$R \cap Q = \phi$ only means that R does not overlap Q. The three possibilities are shown in Fig. 1.6.
(a) Fig. 1.6(c) shows that $P \cap R \neq \phi$ can be false.
(b) In each diagram $P \cap Q \cap R = \phi$, hence the statement is true.
(c) Since $P \cup R$ contains all of P, and Q is a subset of P, then $Q \subset P \cup R$ must be true.

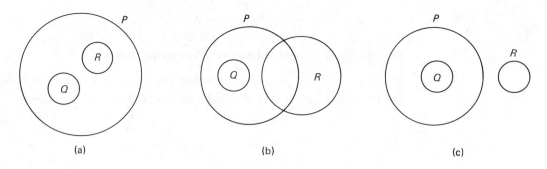

(a)   (b)   (c)

Fig. 1.6

Worked Example 1.4

If $\mathcal{E}$ = {quadrilaterals}, A = {rectangles with unequal sides}, B = {squares},
   C = {rhombuses} and D = {parallelograms},
draw a Venn diagram to show the relationship between the sets.

Solution

$A \cap B = \phi$.
A square is a special type of rhombus, hence $B \subset C$.
A rectangle cannot be a rhombus, hence $A \cap C = \phi$.
A, B and C are all subsets of D.
The relationship can then be shown as in Fig. 1.7.

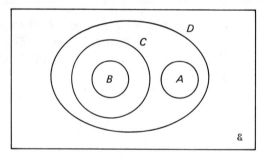

Fig. 1.7

Worked Example 1.5

In this question, P and Q are sets, and $P * Q$ means $P \cap Q'$. In a Venn diagram,
$P * Q$ could be shown by the shaded region of Fig. 1.8.

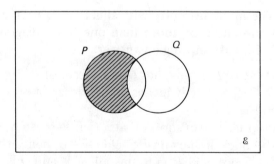

Fig. 1.8

Draw three separate Venn diagrams and shade the areas which represent
(a) $P' * Q$ (b) $P * Q'$ (c) $(P * Q) \cap P$ [L]

Solution (see Fig. 1.9(a)–(c).)

(a) $P' * Q = P' \cap Q' = (P \cup Q)'$.
(b) $P * Q' = P \cap (Q')' = P \cap Q$.
(c) $(P * Q) \cap P = (P \cap Q') \cap P$
$$= P \cap (Q' \cap P) = P \cap (P \cap Q')$$
$$= (P \cap P) \cap Q' = P \cap Q'.$$

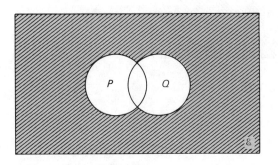

Fig. 1.9(a)

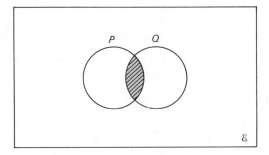

Fig. 1.9(b)

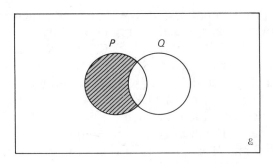

Fig. 1.9(c)

Exercise 1

1 If $A = \{x : 3 \leqslant 2x < 18\}$, then $n(A)$ equals:
    A 7   **B** 8   **C** 9   **D** none of these
2 If $A \cup (B \cup C) = B$, then it follows that:
    A $A \cap C = \phi$ **B** $B = C$ **C** $A \subset B$ **D** $A \subset C \subset B$
3 If $A \cap B' = \{3, 4, 5\}$, $B \cap A' = \{1, 6, 8\}$ and $\varepsilon = \{1, 2, 3, 4, 5, 6, 7, 8, 9, 10\}$,
    then $n(A \cap B)$ equals:
    A 3   **B** 4   **C** 6   **D** none of these
4 If $X \subset Y$ and $Y \cap Z = \phi$ then $Y \cup (X \cap Z)$ equals:
    A X **B** Y **C** Z **D** none of these
5 If $P = \{x : 1 < x + 4 \leqslant 8\}$ and $Q = \{x : x < 4\}$ then $P \cap Q$ equals:
    A $\{x : 1 < x < 4\}$ **B** $\{x : x \geqslant -3\}$ **C** $\{x : -3 < x < 4\}$
    D $\{x : -3 \leqslant x < 4\}$

6 If $n(A) = 9$, $n(B) = 8$ and $n(A \cap B') = 5$, then $n(A \cap B)$ equals:

    A 4   **B** 3   **C** 5   **D** none of these

7 In the Venn diagram in Fig. 1.10, the shaded area represents:

    A $P' \cup Q$ **B** $P' \cap Q$ **C** $P' \cup Q'$ **D** $P' \cap Q'$ [AEB 1980]

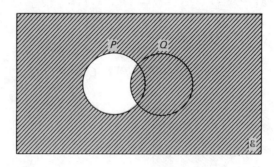

Fig. 1.10

8 A set S contains 8 elements and a set T contains 13 elements. The least possible number of elements in $S \cap T$ is:

    A 0   **B** 5   **C** 8   **D** 13   [AEB 1981]

9 Two sets P and Q are such that $P \cup Q = \&$ and $P \cap Q \neq \phi$. It follows that $P \cup Q'$ simplifies to:

    A Q' **B** Q **C** P **D** P'

10 If $R = \{$rich people$\}$ and $T = \{$teachers$\}$, then the statement, 'Some teachers are not rich people', can be represented by:

    A $T \subset R$ **B** $T \subset R'$ **C** $T \cap R' = \phi$ **D** $T \cap R' \neq \phi$

11 In the universal set $\{3, 5, 7, 9, 11, 13, 15\}$, the sets X and Y are given by $X = \{5, 9, 11\}$ and $Y = \{5, 9, 13, 15\}$. Find:

    (a) $X' \cap Y'$ (b) $(X \cup Y')'$

12 The universal set $\&$ is defined

    $\& = \{$even numbers from 2 to 60 inclusive$\}$,

and P, Q and R are subsets of $\&$ such that

    $P = \{$multiples of 3$\}$,

    $Q = \{$perfect squares$\}$,

    $R = \{$numbers, the sum of whose digits is 8$\}$.

    Find: (a) $P \cap Q$ (b) $P \cap Q'$ (c) $(R \cup Q) \cap P'$

13 In a survey of 149 households about an evening's television viewing, 25 watched BBC1 and ITV only, 53 watched BBC2 and BBC1 only, 26 watched BBC2 only and 27 watched ITV only. If 8 had not watched the television, and nobody watched all three, how many had watched ITV? Assume nobody had watched BBC1 only.

14 Newspapers are delivered to 40 houses. Each house receives either one copy of *The Times* or one copy of *The Gazette* or one copy of each. In all, 26 copies of *The Times* and 24 copies of *The Gazette* are delivered. Find the number of houses which receive *The Times* only.

15 Use set notation to describe the sets shaded in Fig. 1.11.

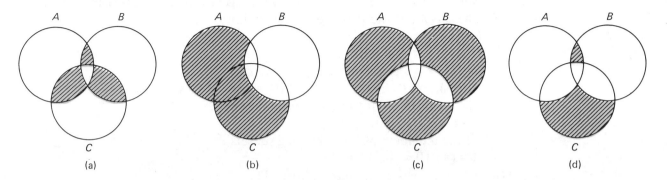

Fig. 1.11

16 The universal set is the set of all plane quadrilaterals.
The following subsets are defined:

A = {quadrilaterals with exactly one line of symmetry};

B = {quadrilaterals with four sides equal};

C = {quadrilaterals with exactly two internal angles of 90°};

D = {squares};

ϕ = the empty set.

(a) Which one of the above sets is equal to $A \cap B$?

(b) Draw a quadrilateral, q, for which $q \in A \cap C$. What is the name for this type of quadrilateral?

(c) Explain why a quadrilateral which belongs to set B cannot also belong to set C.

(d) Draw a Venn diagram to represent sets A, B and C, illustrating your answers to (a), (b) and (c).

(e) Illustrate set D in an appropriate position on your diagram.

(f) Draw a quadrilateral which belongs to $A' \cap C$. [OLE]

17 (a) Draw a single Venn diagram to illustrate the relations between the following sets:

P = {parallelograms},

Q = {quadrilaterals},

R = {rectangles},

S = {squares},

Z = {quadrilaterals having *one and only one* pair of parallel sides}.

State which one of the sets P, R, S, Z, ϕ is equal to

(i) $R \cap S$, (ii) $P \cap Z$.

(b) The 89 members of the fifth form all belong to one or more of the Chess Club, the Debating Society and the Jazz Club.

Denoting these sets by C, D and J respectively, it is known that 20 pupils belong to C only, 15 to J only and 12 to D only. Given that $n(C \cap J) = 18$, $n(C \cap D) = 20$ and $n(D \cap J) = 16$, calculate (a) $n(C \cap J \cap D)$, (b) $n(D')$. [L]

18 If $\& = \{$vehicles$\}$, $F = \{$fast cars$\}$, and $R = \{$red cars$\}$, express in good English (a) $R \cap F = \phi$, (b) $R \cap F \neq \phi$, (c) $R \cap F' \neq \phi$.

19 The universal set $\&$ consists of the positive integers less than 30. P and Q are subsets, P containing those members of $\&$ which are multiples of 5 and Q those members of $\&$ which are multiples of 3. List the members of the sets:

$$P, Q, P \cap Q', P' \cap Q, P \cup Q, P' \cup Q' \text{ and } (P \cap Q') \cup (P' \cap Q).$$

Represent the sets &, P and Q by a Venn diagram and shade in the region or regions representing $(P \cap Q') \cup (P' \cap Q)$.

20 The universal set is the set of positive integers which are less than or equal to 40. The sets M, N and P are defined as follows:

$M = \{x : x$ is a multiple of $3\}$,

$N = \{x : x$ is a factor of $36\}$,

$P = \{x : x$ is a prime number$\}$.

Find: (a) M, N, P (b) $M \cap N \cap P$ (c) $(M \cup N) \cap P'$

21 & is the set of the first twenty natural numbers,

i.e. & $= \{1, 2, \ldots, 20\}$

List the members of the following subsets:

(a) $A = \{t : 10 < 4t - 5 \leqslant 43\}$,

(b) $B = \{y : y$ is a prime number, $y > 1\}$,

(c) $C = \{z : z$ is a factor of 20, $z > 1\}$.

Draw a Venn diagram showing the relationship between &, A, B and C, writing each of the members of & in the appropriate region.

List the members of the following sets:

(d) $A' \cap B$ (e) $(A \cup B)'$ (f) $B' \cap C'$

22 Of the 125 members of a youth club, 46 like table tennis (T), 38 like darts (D) and 63 like snooker (S). 13 like table tennis and darts, 12 like darts and snooker and 16 like table tennis and snooker. All members like at least one of the three sports.

Illustrate this information in a Venn diagram and find:

(a) the number of members who like all three.

(b) the number of members who like only darts.

23 Some of the results of a survey amongst 70 fifth-year pupils are shown in the Venn diagram, Fig. 1.12.

& $= \{$pupils questioned in the survey$\}$,

$C = \{$pupils who went to the cinema$\}$,

$T = \{$pupils who went to the theatre$\}$,

$P = \{$pupils who went to a pop concert$\}$.

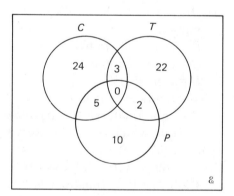

Fig. 1.12

Calculate the number of pupils

(a) who had been to the cinema,

(b) in $C \cup P$,

(c) in $C \cap T$, explaining the meaning of your answer,

(d) in $P \cup (C \cap T)$,

(e) in $(C \cup T \cup P)'$, explaining the meaning of your answer.

[AEB 1981]

24 The universal set is the set of positive integers less than or equal to N.
$A = \{x : x \text{ is even}\}$,
$B = \{y : y \text{ is exactly divisible by 7}\}$,
$C = \{z : z \text{ is a multiple of 5}\}$.
(a) Find $A \cap B \cap C$.
(b) If $n(A \cap B) = 5$, what is the largest possible value of N?

25 In a school where 80 students study sciences in the sixth form, 40 study chemistry, 46 study physics and 31 study biology. 20 study physics and biology, and the number who study physics and chemistry is three times the number who study chemistry and biology. If only 3 students take all three sciences, how many study only physics?

26 The Venn diagram, Fig. 1.13, concerns the numbers of players in a ladies' sports club.
$B = \{\text{ladies who play badminton}\}$,
$H = \{\text{ladies who play hockey}\}$,
$T = \{\text{ladies who play tennis}\}$.

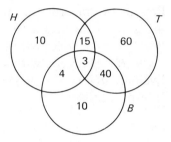

Fig. 1.13

The numbers shown indicate the number of ladies in each set. Find the number of ladies who play (a) badminton only; (b) all three games; (c) hockey and tennis but not badminton; (d) two of the three games but not all three.

[AEB 1980]

27 Given that X and Y are two subsets of $\mathscr{E}$ and that $n(X \cap Y) \neq 0$, draw Venn diagrams to illustrate:
(a) $(X \cup Y) \cap (X \cap Y')'$
(b) $(X' \cap Y') \cup (X' \cap Y)$

28 (a) $\mathscr{E}$ is the set of natural numbers $\{1, 2, 3, 4, 5, \ldots\}$.
List the members of the following sub-sets:
(i) $\{x : 3x - 1 = 8\}$ (ii) $\{y : 2y + 1 < 8\}$ (iii) $\{t : t - 1 \leqslant 4\}$
(b) $\mathscr{E}$ is the set of the first 50 natural numbers $\{1, 2, 3, \ldots, 50\}$.
A is the set $\{x : x \in \mathscr{E} \text{ and } x \text{ is an even number}\}$,
B is the set $\{y : y \in \mathscr{E} \text{ and } y \text{ is the square of a natural number}\}$,
C is the set $\{x : z \in \mathscr{E} \text{ and } z < 20\}$.
Write down the members of the sets
(i) $A \cap B$ (ii) $B \cap C'$ (iii) $A \cup B$ (iv) $(A \cap B) \cap (B \cap C')$

29 (a) In a survey of shoppers it was found that 60 per cent were pensioners and 30 per cent were male. If 60 per cent of the pensioners were female, what percentage of the shoppers were female non-pensioners? Show the information on a Venn diagram.
(b) A survey of cars in a car-park revealed that the most popular optional extras were radios, clocks and sunroofs.
6 of the cars had radios and sunroofs, 14 had radios and clocks and 5 had clocks and sunroofs but did not have radios.

20 had sunroofs, 60 had radios and 22 had clocks but neither radios nor sunroofs.

(i) If x cars had clocks, radios and sunroofs, complete a Venn diagram showing all the above information.

(ii) If there were 120 cars in the car-park, write down, on the Venn diagram, how many cars had none of these optional extras (answer in terms of x)?

(iii) If 19 cars had exactly 2 of these optional extras, write down an equation and solve it to find x. [SUJB]

30 A road safety officer reported to the head of a certain school as follows.

'I examined 100 bicycles of your pupils, looking for faults in brakes, steering and saddle heights. I found 9 cases of defective brakes, 4 of bad steering and 22 bicycles with saddles at the wrong height.

It is sad to reflect that although three-quarters of the bicycles had none of these faults, 4 had two faults and 3 failed on three counts. The 16 bicycles which had only saddle height faults, I have corrected straight away.'

(a) Present this information in a Venn diagram,
using B = {bicycles with faulty brakes},
S = {bicycles with bad steering}, and
H = {bicycles with saddles at the wrong height}.

(b) Evaluate $n\{B \cup S' \cup H'\}$.
Interpret this result. [NEA]

2 The Number System

2.1 The Number System

The numbers we use in mathematics can be classified into various sets, some of which are subsets of others. The definitions are as follows:

{Positive integers}   = {1, 2, 3, 4, 5, . . .} = {natural numbers}.
{Negative integers}   = {. . . −5, −4, −3, −2, −1}.
{Integers}   = {. . . −5, −4, −3, −2, −1, 0, 1, 2, 3, 4, . . .}.
{Rational numbers}   = {$x : x$ can be expressed as a fraction}.
{Irrational numbers} = {$x : x$ cannot be expressed as a fraction}.
{Prime numbers}   = {$x : x$ has only two different factors, 1 and itself}.
  = {2, 3, 5, 7, 11, 13, . . .}.
{Square numbers}   = {1, 4, 9, 16, 25, . . .}.

There are many others.

Notes: (1) A terminating decimal is rational, e.g.
$$3.12 = \frac{312}{100} = \frac{78}{25}.$$

(2) A non-terminating repeating decimal is rational, e.g.
$$3.\dot{1}\dot{2} = 3.121212 \ldots = 3\tfrac{4}{33}.$$

(3) An integer is rational, since it can be expressed as a fraction, e.g.
$$6 = \frac{6}{1}.$$

(4) π is irrational.

(5) Numbers such as $\sqrt{2}, \sqrt{3}$, which are not whole numbers, are irrational numbers. If left like this without working them out, they are referred to as *surds*. The manipulation of these is shown in section 2.18.

Worked Example 2.1

State whether the following values of x are rational or irrational:

(a) $x = 12.4$;   (b) $x^2 = 8$;   (c) $\pi x + 4\pi = 0$;   (d) $x^2 - 5x + 6 = 0$;
(e) $2.\dot{3}$.

Solution

(a) Since $12.4 = \frac{124}{10} = \frac{62}{5}$ then x is *rational*.
(b) If $x^2 = 8$, $x = \pm\sqrt{8}$. But this is not a fraction, hence x is *irrational*.
(c) Although π appears in this question, we can factorize the left-hand side.
    Hence $\pi (x + 4) = 0$, $\therefore x = -4$ and hence x is *rational*.
(d) The equation $x^2 - 5x + 6 = 0$ can be factorized as $(x - 3)(x - 2) = 0$. Hence
    $x = 2$ or $x = 3$, therefore x is *rational*.
(e) $0.\dot{3}$ as a fraction is $\tfrac{1}{3}$, hence $x = 2.\dot{3} = 2\tfrac{1}{3}$ and x is *rational*.

Worked Example 2.2

1   3   8   9   10

From these numbers, write down:
(a) the prime number,   (*Note*: 1 is *not* a prime number.)
(b) a multiple of 5,
(c) two square numbers,
(d) two factors of 32,
(e) Find two numbers m and n from the list such that

$$m = \sqrt{n} \quad \text{and} \quad n = \sqrt{81}.$$

(f) If each of the numbers in the list can be used once, find p, q, r, s, t such that
$(p + q)r = 2(s + t) = 36$.   [SEG]

Solution

(a) 3;   (b) 10;   (c) 1 and 9;
(d) A factor of 32 is any number that divides exactly into 32, hence in this case the answers will be 1 and 8.
(e) $n = \sqrt{81} = 9$; $m = \sqrt{9} = 3$.
(f) Any expression with a double equals sign is best split up.

$$\therefore \quad (p + q)r = 36 \qquad (1)$$
$$\text{or} \qquad 2(s + t) = 36. \qquad (2)$$

From equation (2), $s + t = 18$

$$\therefore s = 10, \qquad t = 8, \qquad \text{or} \qquad s = 8 \qquad \text{and} \qquad t = 10.$$

We are left with $(p + q)r = 36$.
r cannot be 1 because $p + q$ cannot equal 36.
If $r = 3$ $p + q = 12$ this is not possible,

hence $r = 9$, $\quad p + q = 4$, $\qquad p = 1$, $\quad q = 3$ $\quad$ or $\qquad p = 3$, $\quad q = 1$.

2.2   Number Sequences and Patterns

Consider the following *sequence* of numbers:

$$1, 3, 5, 7, 9, \ldots$$

It is easy to recognise that these are odd numbers, and the reader could easily continue the sequence. The following notation will be used for the *terms* in the sequence:

$$u_1 = 1, \quad u_2 = 3, \quad u_3 = 5, \quad u_4 = 7, \quad \text{etc.}$$

u_1 means the first term, u_2 the second term, etc. It is easier to use one letter.
    A slightly harder question would be, what is u_{100}? The answer is $u_{100} = 199$. Can you see a systematic way of getting this, without working them all out?

Number sequences and patterns are not really very helpful, unless the pattern can be predicted. Look at the sequence in a different way:

$$2 \times 1 - 1 \quad = 1 \quad = u_1$$
$$2 \times 2 - 1 \quad = 3 \quad = u_2$$
$$2 \times 3 - 1 \quad = 5 \quad = u_3$$
$$2 \times 4 - 1 \quad = 7 \quad = u_4$$
$$2 \times 5 - 1 \quad = 9 \quad = u_5$$

$$2 \times 100 - 1 = 199 \quad = u_{100}$$

$$2 \times n - 1 \quad = 2n - 1 = u_n.$$

We now have a formula for any term, e.g. $2n - 1$. Hence, if you were asked to find the sixty-seventh term, i.e. u_{67}, the answer is $u_{67} = 2 \times 67 - 1 = 133$.

A second example is as follows:

$$1, 0, 2, -1, 3, -2, 4, \ldots$$

Can you see the next two numbers in this sequence? There are two ways of looking at this sequence. Look at the differences between successive terms:

$$1 \quad 0 \quad 2 \quad -1 \quad 3 \quad -2 \quad 4 \quad \ldots$$

Differences: $\quad -1 \quad 2 \quad -3 \quad 4 \quad -5 \quad 6 \quad -7$

It can be seen that the differences increase by 1 each time and the sign changes. It is now easy to find the next term. You might however find it difficult to find u_{67}.

Look at the sequence again:

$$1 \quad 0 \quad 2 \quad -1 \quad 3 \quad -2 \quad 4 \quad \ldots$$

It is in fact two sequences put together, and u_{67} would be in the top path. Can you find u_{67} now? Can you find a formula for u_n? (It is not easy.)

There are many famous number patterns.

$$1, 1, 2, 3, 5, 8, 13, 21, \ldots$$

is called the Fibonacci sequence. Try to find out more about it. This is called Pascal's triangle:

```
                    1
                1       1
            1       2       1
        1       3       3       1
    1       4       6       4       1
1       5       10      10      5       1
```

can you see the pattern? It has a surprising number of uses.

There are also many obscure patterns. For example:

19

$$22 \times 22 \quad = (1 + 2 + 1) \times 121$$
$$333 \times 333 \quad = (1 + 2 + 3 + 2 + 1) \times 123\,21$$
$$4444 \times 4444 = (1 + 2 + 3 + 4 + 3 + 2 + 1) \times 1\,234\,321$$

Does it continue?

Check 2

Can you find the next two terms in the following sequences?

1 1, 4, 9, 16, . . ., ...
2 1, 3, 7, 15, 31, . . ., ...
3 1, $\frac{1}{2}$, 2, 1, 4, 2, 8, . . ., ...
4 1, 8, 27, 64, . . ., ...
5 40, 20, 10, 5, . . ., ...
6 1, −3, 5, −7, . . ., ...
7 2, 3, 5, 7, 11, 13, . . ., ...
8 1, $\frac{1}{2}$, $\frac{1}{4}$, $\frac{1}{8}$, . . ., ...
9 1, 3, 8, 19, . . ., ...
10 1, 5, 11, 19, . . ., ...

2.3 Decimal Places and Significant Figures

The importance of stating the correct number of digits in any calculation cannot be emphasized too much with the advent of the electronic calculator. Too many digits in any answer are usually irrelevant. All answers in this book are given correct to three significant figures unless stated otherwise. Also, unless stated otherwise, the digit 5 will be rounded up.

Examples using decimal places:

The following numbers are corrected to two decimal places (abbreviation d.p.):

$$84.739 \ = 84.74 \ (2 \ \text{d.p.})$$
$$6.104 \ = \ 6.10 \ (2 \ \text{d.p.}) \ \leftarrow \textbf{The zero must be included.}$$
$$0.0199 = \ 0.02 \ (2 \ \text{d.p.})$$
$$0.999 \ = \ 1.00 \ (2 \ \text{d.p.})$$

The following numbers are shown corrected to three significant figures (abbreviation s.f.):

$$128.4 \quad\quad = 128 \quad\quad (3 \ \text{s.f.})$$
$$6.093 \quad = \quad 6.09 \quad (3 \ \text{s.f.})$$
$$0.014\,98 = \quad 0.0150 \ (3 \ \text{s.f.})$$

Significant figures are not counted until the first non-zero digit is reached reading from the left. In this case the 1 is the first digit and the 9 is the third.

Check 3

1 Write the following numbers correct to 2 d.p.:
(a) 8.689   (b) 26.134   (c) 0.094   (d) 0.099   (e) 2.019
(f) 2.190   (g) 9.999

2 Write the following numbers correct to 3 s.f.:
(a) 86.41   (b) 186.9   (c) 0.09   (d) 1.999   (e) 169.86
(f) 3.004   (g) 8694   (h) 9999

*2.4   Number Bases

Written in full, the denary number 4186 would be four thousand, one hundred and eighty-six,

or $$4186 = 4 \times 1000 + 1 \times 100 + 8 \times 10 + 6$$
$$= 4 \times 10^3 + 1 \times 10^2 + 8 \times 10^1 + 6 \times 10^0.$$

The number 10 in this case is referred to as the *base* of the number.
  The number 69 can be written in two ways:

$$69 = 6 \times 10^1 + 9 \times 10^0,$$
or $$69 = 1 \times 2^6 + 0 \times 2^5 + 0 \times 2^4 + 0 \times 2^3 + 1 \times 2^2 + 0 \times 2^1 + 1 \times 2^0.$$

In the first case base 10 is used (denary); in the second, base 2 is used (binary).
  In binary, $69 = 1000101_2 \longleftarrow$ denotes the base.
  Clearly, any number can be used for the base.

Check 4

The following numbers should be converted into denary to refresh your mind:

(a) 136_8 (b) 214_8 (c) 2150_8 (d) 1011_2 (e) 111101_2
(f) 100011_2 (g) 3140_5 (h) 2415_6 (i) 6135_7 (j) 33333_5.

The process of changing the base of a number is illustrated by the following example:

Worked Example 2.3

(a) Change 683 into binary.
(b) Change 63_8 into base 3.
(c) Change 1011101_2 into base 8 (often referred to as octal).

Solution

The method usually involves a continuous division process writing down the remainders.

(a)

```
                          ┌──── Remainders
              2 ) 683        ▼
New base ───▶ 2 ) 341   r 1
              2 ) 170   r 1
              2 )  85   r 0
              2 )  42   r 1
              2 )  21   r 0
              2 )  10   r 1
              2 )   5   r 0
              2 )   2   r 1
              2 )   1   r 0
                   0    r 1
```

Stop when ──────▶ read upwards
this number   **Read upwards for the answer**
is zero

$\therefore$ $683 = 1010101011_2$.

(b) If changing from one base to another, usually you have to go via base 10.

$63_8 = 6 \times 8^1 + 3 \times 8^0 = 48 + 3 = 51$.

Change 51 to base 3:

$$\begin{array}{r} 3\,)\overline{51} \\ 3\,)\overline{17}\ \text{r}\ 0 \\ 3\,)\ \overline{5}\ \text{r}\ 2 \\ 3\,)\ \overline{1}\ \text{r}\ 2 \\ 0\ \text{r}\ 1 \end{array}$$

$\therefore \quad 63_8 = 1220_3$.

(c) Base 8 to base 2 can be changed in a quicker fashion.

$$1 \mid 011 \mid 101$$
$$\uparrow \qquad \uparrow \qquad \uparrow$$
$$1 \qquad 3 \qquad 5$$

Divide the binary number *into* groups of three digits reading from the *right*. Change each of these 3-digit (or less at the front) numbers into a denary number.

Hence $1011101_2 = 135_8$.

To change an octal number into a binary number, simply change each digit to binary reading from the right and write down the binary numbers in order.

Quickly try the following:

Check 5

1 Change the following numbers into binary:
   (a) 48   (b) 86   (c) 17   (d) 1496   (e) 212_3 (f) 543_6
   (g) 76_8 (h) 134_8.
2 Change the following binary numbers into octal numbers:
   (a) 1011   (b) 10111   (c) 11011011   (d) 1010101.

*2.5 Manipulation in Different Bases

Some knowledge of addition, multiplication etc. is assumed. The following example should clarify any problems.

Worked Example 2.4

Evaluate in the given bases:
(a) $10111_2 + 111_2$ (b) $4341_8 - 556_8$ (c) $210_3 \times 122_3$
(d) $10010000_2 \div 1100_2$.

Solution

(a)
```
  10111
+   111
  11110
   1 1 1
```

(b)
```
  1011
  3239
  4341
 − 556
  3563
```
Note: if 8 is carried this changes the 1 to a 9.

(c)
```
        210
      × 122
      21000
```
Here
$2 \times 2 = 11$
base 3
```
      11200
       1120
     111020
      1 1
```

(d)
```
1100   1012
      10010000
       1100
       1100
       1100
       1100
        000
```

You should now try the following:

Check 6

Evaluate the following questions in the stated bases:

1 $1101_2 + 111_2$ 2 $1011_2 \times 11_2$ 3 $212_3 + 122_3$
4 $650_8 + 573_8$ 5 $11011_2 − 111_2$ 6 $(47_8)^2 \times 12_8$
7 $24415_6 \div 35_6$ 8 $651_8 \div 21_8$ 9 $1331_8 \div 33_8$
10 $1000_2 − 1111_2$ 11 $1111_2 + 1111_2$ 12 $412_6 − 354_6$
13 $2201_3 − 222_3$ 14 $27_8 \times 63_8$ 15 $35_6 \times 21_6$

2.6   Fractions

The following example should refresh your memory about the rules of working with fractions.

Worked Example 2.5

Evaluate the following:
(a) $\frac{1}{4} + \frac{2}{3}$ (b) $4\frac{3}{5} − 2\frac{5}{6}$ (c) $\frac{4}{9} \times 1\frac{1}{4}$ (d) $3\frac{1}{2} \div 2\frac{1}{4}$

Solution

(a) $\frac{1}{4} + \frac{2}{3} = \frac{3}{12} + \frac{8}{12} = \frac{11}{12}$.

(b) $4\frac{3}{5} − 2\frac{5}{6} = \frac{23}{5} − \frac{17}{6} = \frac{138}{30} − \frac{85}{30} = \frac{53}{30}$
$$= 1\frac{23}{30}.$$

(c) $\frac{4}{9} \times 1\frac{1}{4} = \frac{\overset{1}{4}}{9} \times \frac{5}{\underset{1}{4}} = \frac{5}{9}$.

(d) $3\frac{1}{2} \div 2\frac{1}{4} = \frac{7}{2} \div \frac{9}{4} = \frac{7}{\underset{1}{2}} \times \frac{\overset{2}{4}}{9} = \frac{14}{9} = 1\frac{5}{9}$.

'Turn the second upside down'

23

Carry out the following check test *without* using a calculator and then check your answers *using* a calculator if it has a fractions key.

Check 7

1. $\frac{3}{5} + \frac{3}{4}$
2. $\frac{1}{3} + \frac{1}{5}$
3. $\frac{1}{2} + \frac{1}{3} + \frac{1}{4}$
4. $\frac{2}{5} - \frac{1}{4}$

5. $\frac{3}{5} - \frac{1}{2}$
6. $\frac{3}{8} - \frac{1}{6}$
7. $\frac{2}{5} \times \frac{5}{8}$
8. $\frac{3}{4} \times 1\frac{1}{2}$

9. $\frac{3}{5} \div \frac{2}{5}$
10. $1\frac{1}{2} \div 2\frac{1}{2}$
11. $2\frac{1}{3} + 4\frac{1}{2}$
12. $(\frac{3}{8} + \frac{1}{4}) \times 2\frac{1}{2}$

13. $(\frac{2}{5} \times \frac{1}{4}) \div \frac{1}{2}$
14. $\frac{\frac{2}{5} + \frac{1}{2}}{\frac{1}{10} + \frac{1}{4}}$
15. $(\frac{1}{3} - \frac{1}{4}) \times (2\frac{3}{4} - 1\frac{1}{5})$

16. $(4\frac{1}{2} \div 2\frac{1}{4}) \times 1\frac{1}{2}$
17. $(\frac{3}{4} + 2\frac{1}{5}) \div \frac{1}{10}$
18. $(\frac{3}{5})^2 \div \frac{1}{4}$

19. $3\frac{1}{3} \div (\frac{1}{4} + \frac{1}{8})$
20. $\frac{1}{5} \div (\frac{3}{4} \times \frac{4}{5})$

2.7 Fractions to Decimals

It was mentioned in section 2.1 that a fraction (rational number) could sometimes be expressed as an infinite repeating fraction. The following examples show how to change a fraction to a decimal, using the process of short division.

(a) $\frac{4}{25}$:
$$25 \overline{)\smash{4.00}^{\,0.16}}$$
$$= 0.16$$

(b) $\frac{5}{14}$:
$$14 \overline{)\smash{5.00000000}^{\,0.35714285\ldots}} \quad \xleftarrow{\text{\footnotesize 810264128}} \text{remainders}$$
$$= 0.3\dot{5}7142\dot{8}.$$

Now try the following:

Check 8

Convert the following fractions into decimals. Avoid using a calculator.

1. $\frac{3}{5}$
2. $\frac{3}{25}$
3. $\frac{5}{8}$
4. $\frac{5}{7}$
5. $\frac{2}{11}$
6. $\frac{13}{25}$
7. $\frac{5}{18}$
8. $\frac{7}{19}$
9. $\frac{7}{16}$
10. $\frac{17}{48}$

2.8 Fraction as a Ratio

If Jane has £5 and David has £8, we could express the amount of money that Jane has as a fraction of the amount David has; it would be $\frac{5}{8}$. However, more commonly we express the amounts as a ratio:

Jane : David = £5 : £8 or just 5 : 8.

Ratios behave much like fractions and can be simplified.

(a) 40 : 280 = 4 : 28 = 1 : 7;
(b) $2\frac{1}{2}$: $4\frac{1}{4}$ = 5 : $8\frac{1}{2}$ = 10 : 17.

Quantities can only be compared using ratios if they are measured in the same units.

2.9   Rate and Proportion

Material is priced at £8 per metre. This idea of some quantity per unit quantity is called a *rate*. Many rate problems are about speed and acceleration, where the unit is time. It follows that 2 m costs £16 and 3 m costs £24. The quantity of price is proportional to the length in metres. If you double the length you double the price. If you treble the length you treble the price.

We could express the cost £C of L m as

$$C = 8L.$$

In general, if y is *directly proportional* to x then y is a multiple of x,

$$\therefore y = kx;$$

k is called the *constant of proportionality*.

More examples of proportion will be given in later chapters. (See particularly section 3.18.)

2.10   Percentages

A percentage is really a fraction where the denominator equals 100. For example,

$$\tfrac{3}{4} = \tfrac{75}{100} = 75\% .$$

A less obvious example is

$$\frac{5}{12\frac{1}{2}} = \frac{5 \times 8}{12\frac{1}{2} \times 8} = \frac{40}{100} = 40\%.$$

To change a fraction to a percentage, simply multiply the fraction by 100.
To change a percentage to a fraction, divide the percentage by 100.

For example,
(a) $\tfrac{2}{5}$ becomes $\tfrac{2}{5} \times 100 = \tfrac{200}{5} = 40\%$.
(b) 28% becomes $\tfrac{28}{100} = \tfrac{7}{25}$.

Check 9

1 Change into percentages:
   (a) $\tfrac{2}{5}$ (b) 2.79   (c) $\tfrac{1}{6}$ (d) 0.0375   (e) $\tfrac{1}{200}$ (f) $\tfrac{11}{20}$
   (g) $\tfrac{3}{2}$ (h) $\tfrac{49}{500}$
2 Change into a fraction in its simplest form:
   (a) $33\tfrac{1}{3}\%$ (b) 72%   (c) $12\tfrac{1}{2}\%$ (d) 0.6%   (e) 12%
   (f) 36.5%

2.11   Using Percentages, Profit and Loss

To find a percentage of a quantity, proceed as in the following examples.

Find 8% of £25

Money problems are often simplified by the fact that 1 per cent of £1 is 1p.
In this case, 1 per cent of £25 is 25p.

$$\therefore 8\% \text{ is } 8 \times 25\text{p} = £2,$$

or 8% is $\tfrac{8}{100} \times £25 = £2$.

25

Express 7 cm as a Percentage of 3 m

Percentages can only be used to change ratios if the quantities have the same units.

$$7 \text{ cm} : 3 \text{ m} = 7 : 300$$

can be written as a percentage:

$$\frac{7}{300} \times 100 = 2\tfrac{1}{3}\%.$$

In problems on profit and loss, changes or errors, the formula used is

$$\text{Percentage profit (loss, change, error)} = \frac{\text{Profit (loss, change, error)}}{\text{Cost (original value)}} \times 100.$$

The danger in using this formula is shown in the following example.

Worked Example 2.6

A dealer buys a stamp collection and sells it for £2700, making a 35% profit. Find the cost of the collection.

Solution

Note that it is wrong to find 35 per cent of £2700 and subtract this amount from £2700.
  In fact, £2700 = 135% of the cost,

$$\therefore \ \frac{£2700}{135} \times 100 = 100\%,$$

$\therefore$ cost is £2000.

2.12 Exchange Rates

The ideas used in money changing are those of ratio or proportion.

For example, if £1 = $1.22, find
(a) how many dollars you would get for £8.40,
(b) how many pounds you would get for $8.40.

(a) Since £1 = $1.22,

multiplying each side by 8.4:

$$£1 \times 8.4 = \$1.22 \times 8.4$$
$$\therefore £8.40 = \$10.248.$$

(b) In the reverse process, reduce the number of dollars to one:

$$£1 = \$1.22.$$

Divide each side by 1.22:

$$£\frac{1}{1.22} = \$1,$$
$$\therefore £0.8197 = \$1.$$

Multiply each side by 8.4:

$$£0.8197 \times 8.4 = \$8.4 \times 1,$$
$$\therefore £6.885 = \$8.40.$$

2.13 Map Scales

(a) Lengths

The scale of a map is expressed as a ratio, for example 1 : 50 000. This means that any distance on the map represents 50 000 times that distance in reality. Hence 1 cm = 50 000 cm. Changed to km, 50 000 cm is 0.5 km. Hence, on the map, 1 cm = 0.5 km.

(b) Areas

In order to find the area represented by a map, the map ratio must be squared. (See section 8.11 on similar figures.)

In the above example, the ratio of areas is therefore $1^2 : 50\,000^2$, i.e. $1 : 2.5 \times 10^9$. Hence on the map 1 cm² represents 2.5×10^9 cm². To change to km², divide by $100\,000^2 = 10^{10}$.

$$\therefore 1 \text{ cm}^2 = 0.25 \text{ km}^2.$$

*2.14 Interest

(a) Simple Interest

If a sum of money called the *principal* is invested at a given interest rate per annum, it earns *interest* depending on the time invested.

If P = principal invested,
 I = interest earned,
 R = rate (percentage) per annum,
 T = time in years,

then $I = \dfrac{PRT}{100}$.

In practice, most interest is calculated as *compound* interest but *simple* interest is often used if the period invested is less than one year.

Worked Example 2.7

If £250 is invested at 12 per cent p.a. simple interest for 1 year 3 months, find the total amount of money at the end of this time.

Solution

Using the formula $I = \dfrac{PRT}{100}$,

$$P = 250, \qquad R = 12, \qquad T = 1\tfrac{1}{4},$$

$$I = \frac{250 \times 12 \times 1.25}{100} = 37.5.$$

∴ Total = £250 + 37.5 = £287.50.

(b) Compound Interest

If the interest is added at the end of each year, hence increasing the principal, the interest is compound.

Worked Example 2.8

If £800 is invested at $7\tfrac{1}{2}$ per cent compound interest for a period of 3 years, find the value of the investment at the end of that time.

Solution

The interest for each year is added to the principal at the beginning of each year, giving the new principal for the next year. We can proceed as follows:

First year:　principal = £800,

interest　$= £800 \times \dfrac{7.5}{100} = £60.$

Second year:　principal = £800 + 60 = £860,

interest　$= £860 \times \dfrac{7.5}{100} = £64.50.$

Third year:　principal = £860 + 64.50 = £924.50,

interest　$= £924.50 \times \dfrac{7.5}{100} = £69.34.$

∴ The value of the investment = £924.50 + 69.34 = £993.84.
　The formula

$$\text{Total} = P\left(1 + \frac{R}{100}\right)^{n}$$

can be used to find the capital at the end of n years.
　In the above example,

$$\text{Capital} = £800\left(1 + \frac{7.5}{100}\right)^{3} = £993.84.$$

2.15 Large and Small Numbers, Standard Form

(a) Large Numbers

You are no doubt aware that, using indices, we can write for example:

$$10\,000 = 10^4.$$

Using this notation enables large numbers to be written in a more convenient way, using standard form. For example:

(a) 4.8×10^3 means $4.8 \times 1000 = 4800$,
(b) 28.5×10^4 means $28.5 \times 10\,000 = 285\,000$.

In these two examples (a) *is* in standard form, (b) *is not*.

To write a number in standard form it is written as $A \times 10^n$ and we must have that
$$1 \leqslant A < 10.$$

To change a number into standard form, proceed as in the following example.

To Change 4 860 000 into Standard Form

Place a decimal point after the first digit (from the left), i.e. $4.860\,000$.
    Count the number of digits after the decimal point including the zeros; in this case there are six: $4.860\,000$.
$$\underbrace{}_{\text{6 digits}}$$

The answer is 4.86×10^6.

(b) Small Numbers

Now consider the situation for very small numbers.
    We can write
$$\tfrac{1}{10} = 10^{-1}, \tfrac{1}{100} = 10^{-2} \text{ etc.}$$

(See section 3.4 for more work on indices.)

Therefore, $0.086 = 8.6 \div 100 = 8.6 \times \tfrac{1}{100}$.

Hence $0.086 = 8.6 \times 10^{-2}$.
$$\underbrace{}_{\text{2 zeros}}$$

You should notice that the negative power of 10 is the number of zeros, including one in front of the decimal point, before the first non-zero digit.

(c) Using a Calculator

To enter a number in standard form on most calculators, proceed as follows.

To enter 3.95×10^4 :

Press: *Display:*
[3.95]   [EXP]   [4]   [3.95   04]

To enter 6.95×10^{-3} :

Press: *Display:*
[6.95]   [EXP]   [±]   [3]   [6.95 $-$ 03]

When a calculation gives an answer containing too many digits for the calculator, it automatically puts the answer into standard form.

Carry out the following simple questions without a calculator.

Check 10

1 Change into standard form:
   (a) 486   (b) 6930   (c) 857 000
   (d) 0.01   (e) 0.096   (f) 0.008 31   (g) 0.0909
2 Change from standard form:
   (a) 4.5×10^4 (b) 3.84×10^3 (c) 8.01×10^6 (d) 8.5×10^{-2}
   (e) 6.95×10^{-4} (f) 8.801×10^{-6}

2.16   Manipulation in Standard Form

(a) Addition or Subtraction

Numbers are better changed from standard form first.

$$2.86 \times 10^4 + 4.3 \times 10^2 = 28\,600 + 430 = 29\,030 = 2.903 \times 10^4.$$

(b) Multiplication

$$(3.9 \times 10^4) \times (4.6 \times 10^5) = 3.9 \times 4.6 \times 10^4 \times 10^5$$
$$= 3.9 \times 4.6 \times 10^9. \leftarrow (4 + 5; \text{see section 3.4.})$$
$$= 17.94 \times 10^9.$$

Note that this is not standard form; in standard form the answer would be 1.794×10^{10}.

(c) Division

$$(4.52 \times 10^5) \div (8.86 \times 10^{-2})$$
$$= \frac{4.52 \times 10^5}{8.86 \times 10^{-2}} = \frac{4.52}{8.86} \times \frac{10^5}{10^{-2}}$$
$$= 0.510\,(3\,\text{s.f.}) \times 10^7. \leftarrow (5 - -2 = 7; \text{see section 3.4.})$$

Once again, this is not in standard form; in standard form the answer would be 5.1×10^6.

Most calculators will carry out calculations directly on numbers entered in standard form, but answers will often be given in decimal form.

2.17 Approximations

The ability to approximate is a useful skill in that it enables you to check an answer quickly without working out the exact answer. Basic methods involve some form of guessing, or use of standard form. Consider the following example.

Find correct to one significant figure, the value of

(a) $\dfrac{84 \times 959}{63 \times 0.96}$
(b) $\dfrac{6.93 \times (0.87)^2}{4.23}$
(c) $\dfrac{869 \times 4965}{0.091 \times 9513}$

As a general rule, if you make a number on the top line smaller (or larger), make a number on the bottom line smaller (or larger).

(a) $\dfrac{84 \times 959}{63 \times 0.96} \approx \dfrac{80 \times 960}{60 \times 0.96}$ ($\approx$ means approximately equal)

$$\approx \dfrac{8\not0 \times 1000}{6\not0 \times 1} = \dfrac{8000}{6} \approx 1000.$$

The correct answer is 1332, therefore our approximation is correct to 1 s.f.

(b) $\dfrac{6.93 \times (0.87)^2}{4.23} \approx \dfrac{7 \times 1^2}{5} \approx 1.$

The correct answer is 1.24.

(c) $\dfrac{869 \times 4965}{0.091 \times 9513} \approx \dfrac{9 \times 10^2 \times 5 \times 10^3}{9 \times 10^{-2} \times 10^4}$

$$= \dfrac{45 \times 10^5}{9 \times 10^2} = 5 \times 10^3 = 5000.$$

The correct answer is 4984.

Try approximating the following calculations, correct to 1 s.f., checking your answer with a calculator.

Check 11

1 $\dfrac{86.3 \times (0.8)^2}{60}$

2 $\dfrac{4.3 \times 0.08}{6.5 \times 7.1}$

3 $\dfrac{(39)^2 \times 43^2}{81 \times 964}$

4 $7.3 \div (8.9 \times 2.7^2)$

5 $\dfrac{6.97 + 8.53}{4.21 + 7.35}$

6 $\dfrac{4395 \times (0.07)^2}{0.19}$

7 $\dfrac{63 \div (8.6 \times 10^{-5})}{6.47 \div 3.85}$

8 $\dfrac{(0.09)^2 \div (6.3 \times 10^{-5})}{7.4 \times 2951}$

*2.18 Surds

The fact that $\sqrt{3}$ is an irrational number was mentioned in section 2.1. It is often convenient to manipulate quantities like this called *surds*, without working them out.

(a) $\sqrt{3} \times \sqrt{3} = 3$.

(b) $\dfrac{1}{\sqrt{3}} = \dfrac{1}{\sqrt{3}} \times \dfrac{\sqrt{3}}{\sqrt{3}} = \dfrac{\sqrt{3}}{3}$.

(c) $\sqrt{12} = \sqrt{4 \times 3} = 2\sqrt{3}$ since $\sqrt{4} = 2$.

(d) $\sqrt{75} + \sqrt{12} = \sqrt{25 \times 3} + 2\sqrt{3} = 5\sqrt{3} + 2\sqrt{3} = 7\sqrt{3}$

(e) $\dfrac{1}{\sqrt{3} + \sqrt{2}} = \dfrac{1 \times (\sqrt{3} - \sqrt{2})}{(\sqrt{3} + \sqrt{2})(\sqrt{3} - \sqrt{2})}$

     (this is called rationalizing the denominator)

$$= \frac{\sqrt{3} - \sqrt{2}}{(\sqrt{3})^2 - (\sqrt{2})^2} \quad \text{(see section 3.7d)}$$

$$= \frac{\sqrt{3} - \sqrt{2}}{3 - 2} = \sqrt{3} - \sqrt{2}.$$

Check 12

1 Simplify the following:

  (a) $\sqrt{18} + 3\sqrt{2}$ (b) $\sqrt{24} + \sqrt{150}$ (c) $\sqrt{18} - \sqrt{8}$

  (d) $\sqrt{90} + \sqrt{40}$ (e) $2\sqrt{32} - \sqrt{128}$ (f) $\sqrt{63} - \sqrt{28}$

  (g) $\sqrt{99} - \sqrt{176}$ (h) $\sqrt{28} + \sqrt{7} + \sqrt{63}$

  (i) $\sqrt{12} - \sqrt{48} + \sqrt{98} + \sqrt{18}$ (j) $\sqrt{45} + \sqrt{20}$

2 Express the following with a rational denominator:

  (a) $\dfrac{1}{\sqrt{2}}$ (b) $\dfrac{1}{\sqrt{125}}$ (c) $\dfrac{1}{\sqrt{8} - \sqrt{2}}$ (d) $\dfrac{2}{\sqrt{8}}$ (e) $\dfrac{5}{\sqrt{10}}$

  (f) $\dfrac{3}{\sqrt{45}}$ (g) $\dfrac{1}{\sqrt{7} - \sqrt{2}}$

2.19 Rates

Every property is given a *rateable value* by the local authority. The *rate* is levied at so much in the £1 of rateable value. Rates are also levied separately for water.

Worked Example 2.9

The rateable value of a house used to be £260, and the annual amount paid in rates was £218.40. The new rateable value is £285 and the new rate is 91p in the pound. The old water rate was 8 per cent of the old rateable value and is now 9 per cent of the new rateable value.

(a) Find the yearly increase in rates payable, and the percentage increase in the rate per £1.

(b) Find the increased amount due for the water rate.

Solution

(a) The new rate payable is 285 × 91p
$$= £259.35.$$
The increase in rates = £259.35 − £218.40 = £40.95.
Since the old rate of £218.40 was obtained by a rate of x pence per £1 on £260, it follows that $260 \times x = 218.4$,

$$\therefore \quad x = \frac{218.4}{260} = 0.84.$$

The percentage increase in the rate $= \frac{(91 - 84)}{84} \times 100 = 8\frac{1}{3}\%.$

(b) The old water rate $= \frac{8}{100} \times £260 = £20.80.$

The new water rate $= \frac{9}{100} \times £285 = £25.65.$

The increase in water rate = £25.65 − £20.80
$$= £4.85.$$

If the total rateable value of an area is say £400 000, then an increase of 1p in the pound for rates would bring in £400 000 $\times \frac{1}{100} = £4000.$

This is called a *penny rate*.

2.20 Wages and Salaries

Some of the ideas are illustrated in the following examples.

Worked Example 2.10

An apprentice earns £1.80 an hour. His basic week is 35 hours. If he works over-time, he is paid 'time-and-a-half' except for weekends, when he is paid double time. Calculate the amount he earns in a week if he works 39 hours from Monday to Friday, Saturday 09.30 hours to 14.00 hours and $2\frac{1}{4}$ hours on Sunday.

Solution

In a basic week, the apprentice earns 35 × £1.80 = £63. Since he works 39 hours before Friday, we have 4 hours overtime at 'time-and-a-half', i.e. at £1.80 + 90p per hour:

$$4 \times £2.70 = £10.80.$$

On Saturday he works $4\frac{1}{2}$ hours, on Sunday $2\frac{1}{4}$ hours. The total is $6\frac{3}{4}$ at 'double time', i.e. at £3.60 an hour:

$$6\frac{3}{4} \times £3.60 = £24.30.$$

His total wage for the week is

$$£63 + 10.8 + 24.3 = £98.10.$$

Worked Example 2.11

National Westminster Bank issues this advice to people considering buying a house:

'You can calculate what your maximum potential mortage will be at the time you apply by multiplying your anticipated gross annual income by $2\frac{3}{4}$. In appropriate cases this can be increased by up to $1\frac{1}{2}$ times your partner's income.

'N.B. Remember, the actual mortgage available will always be limited to a maximum of 95% of the lower of valuation or purchase price of the property.'

Joy and Harry Black have seen a house they would like to buy. The purchase price is £41 000 but it is valued by the surveyor at only £38 000.

(a) What is the maximum mortgage that the bank would give on this house?

(b) Henry expects his gross annual income to be £10 200. The bank has agreed to consider Joy's income for mortgage purposes and will make the maximum allowance on it. What is the minimum gross income that Joy must earn in order for the Blacks to be able to ask for the maximum mortgage on this house? [NEA]

Solution

(a) The maximum mortgage will be 95% of the valuation figure, which is lower than the purchase price.

$$\tfrac{95}{100} \times £38\,000 = £36\,100.$$

(b) Henry would be allowed $2\frac{3}{4} \times £10\,200 = £28\,050$.
Henry and Joy still need $£36\,100 - £28\,050 = £8050$.
If Joy earns $£x$, then

$$x \times 1\tfrac{1}{2} = 8050,$$
$$\therefore \quad x = 8050 \div 1.5 = 5367.$$

Hence Joy needs to earn at least £5367 in a year.

Exercise 2

1 If x is a rational number and y is an integer, then:
   A xy cannot be an integer   B xy can be irrational
   C $x + y$ is rational   D $x + y$ is an integer
2 If $a : b = 2 : 5$ and $b : c = 7 : 9$, then $a : c$ equals:
   A   18 : 35   B $7 : 22\frac{1}{2}$ C   9 : 14   D   an indeterminate value
3 If $(2^x)^2 = 4$, then x equals:
   A   1   B   2   C   3   D   4
4 The scale of a map is 1 : 25 000. The ratio of the area of a field to its area on the map is:
   A $2.5 \times 10^4 : 1$ B $6.25 \times 10^{16} : 1$ C $1 : 6.25 \times 10^8$
   D $6.25 \times 10^8 : 1$

5 The next number in the sequence 1, 2, 4, 7, 11, . . . is

    A   14   **B**   16   **C**   22   **D**   18

6 The value of $\dfrac{18.1 \times 0.705}{630}$ estimated correct to one significant figure is:

    A   0.02   **B**   0.2   **C**   0.002   **D**   0.003

7 A dealer sold a television set for £88, and made a 10 per cent profit. It follows that he bought it for:

    A   £79.20   **B**   £80   **C**   £78   **D**   none of these

8 If $x = 2 \times 10^4$ and $y = 3 \times 10^3$, then $2x + 3y$ equals:

    A 1.3×10^8 **B** 9.4×10^4 **C** 1.3×10^4 **D** 4.9×10^4

9 The best estimate for $98 \times 99 \times 100 \times 101 \times 102$ is

    A 10^5 **B** 10^7 **C** 10^{10} **D** 10^{13} **E** 10^{15} [LEAG]

10 Which ONE of the following numbers is prime?

    A   57   **B**   61   **C**   63   **D**   65   **E**   69   [LEAG]

11 Which of the following has the largest numerical value?

    A $\sqrt{10}$ **B** $\sqrt{100}$ **C** $\dfrac{1}{\sqrt{0.01}}$ **D** $\dfrac{1}{0.01}$ [AEB 1982]

12 The average of $\frac{1}{4}$ and $\frac{1}{3}$ is:

    A $\frac{1}{6}$ **B** $\frac{2}{7}$ **C** $\frac{7}{24}$ **D** $\frac{7}{12}$

13 The scale of a map is 1 : 50 000. The distance, in km, represented by 40 cm on the map is:

    A   2   **B**   0.5   **C**   20   **D**   5

14 A tenant paid a monthly rent of £121 twelve times a year and a half-yearly rate of £58.40. Find to the nearest penny how much he paid for rent and rates per week (52 week year).

15 A town council have decided to increase the local rate by 6p in the pound. The total rateable value is £4 800 000. What will be the increase in income from the rates?

    A householder finds out that his yearly rates will increase from £246 to £264. What is the rateable value of the house, and what was the original rate before the 6p increase?

*16 (a) The following subtraction is not in base ten. Find the base, and determine the missing number x.

$$\begin{array}{r} 1324 \\ \underline{x42} \\ 572 \end{array}$$

    (b) The number 1234_n is divided by n^2. Write down the remainder in base n.

                                  [OLE]

17 Express the numbers 6286, 0.0104 and 2947 in standard form and use your answers, showing clearly your working, to find an approximation to $\dfrac{6286 \times 0.0104}{2947}$ correct to one significant figure.

18 In 26 hours, a car mechanic earns £67.08. Find out how much he will earn, at the same rate of pay per hour, in 34 hours.

*19 Calculate the following, giving your answers in each case as a binary number:

        (a) $2^5 + 2^3 + 2$ (b) $1001_2 - 11_2$

        (c) $657_8 + 24_8$ (d) $111_2 \times 101_2$

*20 Show that for all positive integers n,

    (a) 169_n is a perfect square,

    (b) 156_n cannot be a prime number.

*21 What base has been used in the following calculations?

        (a) $41 \times 35 = 2355$ (b) $33 + 123 = 222$

        (c) $1605 \div 65 = 21$

22 If $x = a + 3b$ and $y = 4a - 3b$, find a and b, given that when $x = 1.2 \times 10^5$, $y = 3.6 \times 10^6$.

23 (a) If the reciprocal of n is 400, calculate n.
   (b) (i) Use your calculator to find $\frac{1}{19}$ correct to 5 decimal places.
        (ii) Multiply your answer to (i) by 19.
       (iii) Subtract your answer to (ii) from 1.
      (iv) Use your answers to (i) and (iii) to find $\frac{1}{19}$ correct to 10 decimal places.
       (v) Describe, with reasons, how you could find $\frac{1}{19}$ correct to 15 decimal places. [SEG]

24 A line AB is divided into two parts, AC and CB, such that $AC : CB = 3 : 5$. A further point D divides CB into two parts such that $CD : DB = n : 1$. If $AD : DB = 19 : 5$, find n.

25 Given that $\sqrt{2} = 1.41$, $\sqrt{3} = 1.73$, $\sqrt{10} = 3.16$, evaluate as accurately as possible:
   (a) $\sqrt{6}$ (b) $\sqrt{0.02}$ (c) $\sqrt{500}$

26 Parvinda's dad runs Tali's Take-away. He buys his rice from Yaul's Cash and Carry. A 45 kg bag cost £28.50. He uses 150 g rice for a portion.
   (a) How many complete portions will he get from one bag?
   (b) How much does the rice for one portion cost to the nearest penny?
The foil trays he puts the rice in when he sells it cost £17.60 + VAT for 2000. VAT is 15%.
   (c) How much does it cost Parvinda's dad to sell 1 portion of rice?
He charges 35p for a portion of rice.
   (d) What is the cost to Parvinda's dad of the rice and container as a percentage of the selling price?
Parvinda's dad fixes all his prices so that the basic cost of the food and container is the same percentage of the selling price as the rice. His weekly expenses are:
     Rent £34.00   Water rates £12.50   Rates £23.00   Gas £49.00
     Electricity £19.60
   (e) One week he takes £407.50. How much profit does he make? [SEG]

27 In 1981, the owner of a coach business found that his running costs were £456 860 and his receipts from fares were £430 640. For 1982 he dispensed with uneconomic routes, which he hoped would reduce his costs by 14.5 per cent, and he estimated that the fall in receipts from fares would be 6.5 per cent. What trading profit did he expect in 1982? In fact, fuel price increases meant that the actual reduction in running costs was only 12 per cent and he made a trading loss of £10 154. Calculate the actual percentage fall in receipts from fares. (Give your answers correct to four significant figures.) [OLE]

28 The total rateable valuation of the property in a borough council area is £7 500 000.
   (a) How much is raised by levying a penny rate?

To provide for an increase in expenditure next year, the finance committee of the council estimates that an extra £240 000 will have to be demanded from the borough ratepayers.
   (b) (i) Calculate by how much the rate in the £ will have to be increased next year.
        (ii) Determine the increase in rates which will have to be paid by Mr Smith, whose property has a rateable valuation of £540.

This year's rate is 116.8p in the £. Next year Mr Jones will receive a rate demand for £276.
   (c) (i) What is the rateable valuation of his property?

(ii) What will be the percentage increase in the rates demanded of Mr Jones?

[NISEC]

29 A company which hires out caravans provides holidays in France. The table gives the total cost of caravan hire plus boat fares for two adults and their caravan:

	June	July/August
four-berth caravan		
1 week	£110	£122
2 weeks	£143	£160
3 weeks	£175	£199
six-berth caravan		
1 week	£121	£135
2 weeks	£161	£181
3 weeks	£203	£231

If more than two adults travel with the caravan, there is a charge of £16 for each extra adult and £8 for each child. This charge does not depend on the length of the holiday.

(a) (i) Mr and Mrs Morris hire a four-berth caravan for two weeks in June. Calculate the cost if they take Mrs Morris's mother with them on their holiday.

(ii) Mr and Mrs Jones hire a four-berth caravan for three weeks in August and take one child and his grandmother with them. Calculate the total cost.

(iii) Mr and Mrs Hill hire a six-berth caravan for two weeks in July and take their three children with them. Calculate the total cost.

(b) In addition to the cost in (a) (iii) the Hill family expect to spend £90 on petrol, £110 on entertainment, £140 on food, £40 on other items, and also to pay a camping charge of £3 for each of 13 nights. Calculate the total expected cost (including the fares and caravan hire) of their holiday.

(c) If the costs in (a) (ii) were increased by 10 per cent, calculate the new total cost for caravan hire and fares for the Jones family. [UCLES]

30 The cost, £6664, of making up a private road is shared between the council, the house-owners in the road and the house-owners in an adjoining road. The council pays one half of the total costs. The eight house-owners in the adjoining road each pay equal shares for access rights totalling one-eighth of the total costs. Each house-owner in the private road pays in proportion to the length of the frontage of the house owned. The seven houses in the road have frontages of 14, 15, 10.5, 12.5, 21.5, 24.5 and 49 metres. Calculate *exactly*:

(a) the amount paid by each owner in the adjoining road for access rights;

(b) the amount paid by the owner occupying the house with the shortest frontage;

(c) the percentage of the total costs paid by the owner of the house with the 24.5 m frontage.

The house owners in the private road agree to share equally the costs of extra work, tree planting etc. amounting to £385.

(d) Calculate the total amount now paid by the owner of the house with the 10.5 m frontage. [L]

31 An American woman spent a holiday in Paris, Rome and London. In each place, the total cost of her visit consisted of the payment of her hotel bill together with all other extra expenses.

In Paris: the cost at her hotel was 164 francs per day; she stayed for 9 days; the ratio of her extra expenses to her hotel bill was 3 : 5.

In Rome: her hotel bill was four times her extra expenses; the total cost of her visit was 425 000 lire.

In London: her total cost amounted to 100 dollars more than her total cost when visiting Rome; her hotel bill, in London, was equal to her extra expenses.

Use the above information to calculate:

(a) the total cost, in francs, of the woman's visit to Paris;

(b) her extra expenses, in lire, in Rome;

(c) the amount, in pounds, of her hotel bill in London;

(d) her overall total cost, in dollars, in visiting Paris, Rome and London.

(Assume that the rates of exchange were: 4.10 francs to the dollar, in Paris; 850 lire to the dollar, in Rome; 2.40 dollars to the pound, in London.)

[AEB 1982]

32 During the course of a year a motorist drove 28 000 km. For a quarter of this distance he drove in England and used a car with average petrol consumption of 14 litres per 100 km. For the remainder of this distance he drove in France and used a more economical car with an average petrol consumption of 8 litres per 100 km. Calculate:

(a) the total number of litres of petrol used;

(b) his average petrol consumption for the whole year giving the answer in litres per 100 km.

His total expenditure for the year on petrol was £630.

Given that the average price he paid for petrol in England was 20p per litre, calculate the total amount spent on petrol in France.

Assuming the average rate of exchange to be £1 = 8.4 francs, calculate the average price paid for petrol in France, giving the answer in francs per litre to the nearest tenth of a franc.

Calculate how much the motorist would have saved had he driven the more economical car in England as well as in France. [AEB 1980]

33

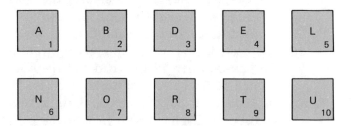

The ten tiles shown above are used in a game to make words and the scores shown on the tiles are added together. For example,

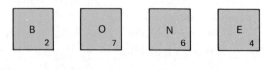

scores 2 + 7 + 6 + 4 = 19.

(a) Calculate the score for

(b) A player makes the word ABODE. Calculate the score for this word.

(c) Another player makes a five-letter word and scores a total of 23. Four of the letters in the word are A, E, L, N. What is the fifth letter?

(d) A third player makes a six-letter word using the letters A, E, L, N and two others. All the letters in the word are different and the score for the word is 34. What are the other two letters? [MEG]

34 The Morgan family buy a house costing £25 000 with the help of a £10 000 mortgage from a building society. The table shows the monthly repayments on mortgage loans.

Mortgage	10 years	15 years	20 years	25 years
£ 1 000	£ 12.95	£ 10.30	£ 9.00	£ 8.44
2 000	25.90	20.60	18.00	16.88
10 000	129.50	103.00	90.00	84.40
15 000	194.25	154.50	135.00	126.60
20 000	259.00	206.00	180.00	168.80

(a) How many monthly payments must be made in 25 years?

(b) What is the total amount repaid over 25 years on the £10 000 loan?

(c) The rateable value of the house is £235 and the rate in the pound is £1.7474. Calculate the annual rate bill (to the nearest penny). [NISEC]

35 The following examinations have to be timetabled.

Mathematics	$2\frac{1}{2}$ hours
English	$2\frac{1}{2}$ hours
History	2 hours
Spanish	$1\frac{1}{2}$ hours
Geography	2 hours
Physics	3 hours

There are two sessions each day. The morning session lasts up to 3 hours and the afternoon session up to 2 hours.

Everyone takes mathematics and English.

No one studies both history and Spanish.

No one takes both geography and physics.

(a) Explain why the examinations cannot be completely timetabled in 2 days.

(b) Draw up a possible timetable to complete the examinations within 3 days.

	Morning	Afternoon
Day 1		
Day 2		
Day 3		

[NISEC]

3 Algebra

3.1   Directed Numbers

There is always great confusion between the concept of a directed number, and the operations of addition and subtraction. The author will try to make it clearer in this section by writing all numbers negative or positive like $(+2)$ or (-5).

(a) Addition

$$(+2) + (+5) = (+7)$$

$$(+5) + (-3) = (+2)$$

$$(-5) + (-7) = (-12)$$

> Addition of any negative number to any other number always gives a smaller answer.
>   Addition of any positive number to any other number always gives a larger answer.

This is only helpful advice; the student still has to get the answer right! The following summarizes the above more accurately:

> Addition of a positive number p increases the original number by p.
>   Addition of a negative number n decreases the original number by n.

Note that in the third example above, if you decrease (-5) by 7 it becomes (-12).

(b) Subtraction

$$(+2) - (+5) = (-3)$$

$$(+5) - (-3) = (+8)$$

$$(-5) - (-7) = (+2)$$

> Subtraction of any positive number from any number always gives a smaller number.
>   Subtraction of any negative number from any number always gives a larger number.

Summary

Subtraction of a positive number p decreases the original number by p.
Subtraction of a negative number n increases the original number by n.

Note that in the third subtraction example above, if you increase $\left(-5\right)$ by 7 you get $\left(+2\right)$.

(c) Multiplication and Division

$$\left(+5\right) \times \left(+4\right) = \left(+20\right) \qquad \left(-8\right) \times \left(+3\right) = \left(-24\right)$$

$$\left(+3\right) \times \left(-6\right) = \left(-18\right) \qquad \left(-4\right) \times \left(-5\right) = \left(+20\right)$$

$$\left(+8\right) \div \left(+2\right) = \left(+4\right) \qquad \left(-14\right) \div \left(+2\right) = \left(-7\right)$$

$$\left(+12\right) \div \left(-3\right) = \left(-4\right) \qquad \left(-40\right) \div \left(-5\right) = \left(+8\right)$$

The results here are easier to follow.

If two positive or negative numbers are multiplied or divided the answer is positive.
If a negative and a positive number are multiplied or divided, the answer is negative.

3.2   Commutative, Associative, Distributive, Brackets

If a, b, c are any numbers,

$$\left. \begin{aligned} a + b &= b + a \\ a \times b &= b \times a \end{aligned} \right\} \text{commutative laws}$$

$$\left. \begin{aligned} (a + b) + c &= a + (b + c) \\ a \times (b \times c) &= (a \times b) \times c \end{aligned} \right\} \text{associative laws}$$

$$\left. \begin{aligned} a \times (b + c) &= a \times b + a \times c \\ (a + b) \times c &= a \times c + b \times c \end{aligned} \right\} \text{distributive laws}$$

Most of these rules will already be used quite competently by the student, but it is crucial to evaluate brackets correctly.

Worked Example 3.1

Evaluate without the use of a calculator:
(a) $(\frac{1}{2})^2 + (1 - \frac{2}{3})^2$,
(b) $(-\frac{2}{3} \times 1\frac{1}{2}) \div (\frac{1}{4} - (-\frac{1}{3})^2)$,
(c) $\frac{2}{3} \times (1\frac{1}{2} \times \{[\frac{2}{3} - (\frac{1}{2})^2] \div \frac{2}{5}\})$.

Solution

(a) $\frac{1}{4} + (\frac{1}{3})^2 = \frac{1}{4} + \frac{1}{9} = \frac{13}{36}$.

(b) $= (-\frac{2}{3} \times \frac{3}{2}) \div (\frac{1}{4} - \frac{1}{9}) = -1 \div \frac{5}{36}$
$= -1 \times \frac{36}{5} = -\frac{36}{5}$.

(c) Start with the inner brackets and work outwards:
$= \frac{2}{3} \times (\frac{3}{2} \times \{[\frac{2}{3} - \frac{1}{4}] \div \frac{2}{5}\})$
$= \frac{2}{3} \times (\frac{3}{2} \times \{\frac{5}{12} \div \frac{2}{5}\}) = \frac{2}{3} \times (\frac{3}{2} \times \frac{25}{24})$
$= \frac{2}{3} \times \frac{25}{16} = \frac{25}{24}$.

The following exercise is important; numbers have been chosen not to give too much heartache, and they should be evaluated without a calculator.

Check 13

1. $-8 - -2$
2. $-14 - -3 + -5$
3. $19 - -36 - 43$
4. $1\frac{3}{4} - 2\frac{7}{8}$
5. $1\frac{1}{12} - 1\frac{3}{4}$
6. $-8\frac{3}{8} - -3\frac{7}{8} + -2\frac{1}{2}$
7. $-\frac{3}{8} \div 2\frac{1}{2}$
8. $-\frac{1}{4} \times (\frac{1}{2} + -\frac{3}{8})$
9. $1\frac{3}{4} \times (-\frac{3}{8} - \frac{2}{5})$
10. $1\frac{1}{4} \times -1\frac{3}{4} \times -\frac{1}{2}$
11. $(-\frac{3}{4} \div -\frac{3}{5}) \div -\frac{1}{8}$
12. $(1\frac{1}{2} + 1\frac{1}{3}) \div (1\frac{1}{2} - 1\frac{1}{7})$
13. $(\frac{5}{8} - \frac{7}{16}) \div [1 - (\frac{5}{8} \times \frac{4}{15})]$
14. $\{[(3\frac{1}{4} + 1\frac{2}{5}) \div 3\frac{1}{10}] - 1\frac{1}{2}\}$
15. $[(6\frac{1}{2})^2 \div 4\frac{1}{3}] \times (-\frac{3}{5} + 4\frac{1}{4})$

3.3   Substitution

One of the most common applications of algebra is in the use of formulae. There are many pitfalls in substituting into such formulae and the following examples illustrate techniques to avoid these where possible.

Worked Example 3.2

In the following question, $a = 2$, $b = -3$, $c = -\frac{1}{2}$. In each case find the value of x given by each formula.
(a) $x = 2a + 3b + 4c$.
(b) $x = 3a - 5b$.
(c) $x = a^2 + b^2$.
(d) $x = 2b^2 + 4c^2$.
(e) $x = \dfrac{3ac}{b}$.
(f) $x = \dfrac{2}{a} + \dfrac{4}{c^2}$.
(g) $x = \sqrt{\dfrac{a + b}{c}}$.

Solution

(a)   In full, $x = 2 \times 2 + 3 \times -3 + 4 \times -\frac{1}{2}$;
with brackets, $x = (2 \times 2) + (3 \times -3) + (4 \times -\frac{1}{2})$
$= 4 + -9 + -2 = -7$.

(b)   In full, $x = 3 \times 2 - 5 \times -3$;
  with brackets, $x = (3 \times 2) - (5 \times -3)$
  $= 6 - -15 = 21$.

(c)   In full, $x = 2^2 + -3^2$;
  with brackets, $x = (2)^2 + (-3)^2$
  $= 4 + 9 = 13$.

(d)   In full, $x = 2 \times -3^2 + 4 \times -\frac{1}{2}^2$
  with brackets, $x = [2 \times (-3)^2] + [4 \times (-\frac{1}{2})^2]$
  $= [2 \times 9] + [4 \times \frac{1}{4}]$
  $= 18 + 1 = 19$.

(e)   In full, $x = \dfrac{3 \times 2 \times -\frac{1}{2}}{-3}$;
  with brackets, $x = (3 \times 2 \times -\frac{1}{2}) \div -3$
  $= -3 \div -3 = 1$.

(f)   In full, $x = \dfrac{2}{2} + \dfrac{4}{(-\frac{1}{2})^2}$;
  with brackets, $x = [2 \div 2] + [4 \div (-\frac{1}{2})^2]$
  $= 1 + [4 \div \frac{1}{4}]$
  $= 1 + 16 = 17$.

(g)   In full, $x = \sqrt{\dfrac{2 + -3}{-\frac{1}{2}}}$;
  with brackets, $x = \sqrt{(2 + -3) \div -\frac{1}{2}} = \sqrt{-1 \div -\frac{1}{2}} = \sqrt{2}$.

You should try to see that liberal use of brackets makes the substitution much clearer to understand, and also makes it much easier to use a calculator, especially one which has a bracket facility.

3.4   Indices

In Chapter 2, simple problems with indices were developed using standard form. The rules of indices in general are as follows:

(1) $a^m \times a^n = a^{m+n}$

(2) $a^m \div a^n = a^{m-n}$

(3) $(a^m)^n = a^{mn}$

(4) $a^{1/p} = \sqrt[p]{a}$

(5) $a^{q/p} = (\sqrt[p]{a})^q$ or $\sqrt[p]{a^q}$

(6) $a^0 = 1$

(7) $a^{-n} = \dfrac{1}{a^n}$

(8) $(ab)^n = a^n b^n$

The use of these rules is shown in the following example.

Worked Example 3.3

Simplify the following:
(a) $(2^3)^2 \div 2^{-4}$ (b) $(49^{1/3})^{3/2}$ (c) $16^{-3/4}$ (d) $(a^2 b)^3 \div 4ab^3$

Solution

(a) $(2^3)^2 \div 2^{-4} = 2^6 \div 2^{-4}$ Rule 3
  $= 2^{10}$.   Rule 2

(b) $(49^{1/3})^{3/2} = 49^{1/2}$ Rule 3

              $= 7.$ Rule 4

(c) $16^{-3/4} = \dfrac{1}{16^{3/4}}$ Rule 7

         $= \dfrac{1}{(16^{1/4})^3}$ Rule 5

         $= \dfrac{1}{2^3}$ Rule 4

         $= \dfrac{1}{8}.$

(d) $(a^2 b)^3 \div 4ab^3 = a^6 b^3 \div 4ab^3$ Rule 8

            $= \dfrac{a^6 b^3}{4ab^3} = \dfrac{a^5 b^0}{4}$ Rule 2

            $= \dfrac{a^5}{4}$ Rule 6.

A useful trick when working with indices is always to get rid of negative powers first if possible.

Now try the following:

Check 14

Simplify the following:

1 $\sqrt{10^4}$	2 $\sqrt[3]{27^2}$	3 $(0.09)^{1/2}$	4 $125^{-2/3}$
5 $27^{-1/3}$	6 $(2^{1/5})^{10}$	7 $(3^{2/3})^0$	8 $49^{1/2}$
9 $32^{2/5}$	10 $625^{-1/2}$	11 $4x^5 \div 2x^2$	12 $5p^{-3} \div 4p^5$
13 $3x^{-2} \times 4x^{-4}$	14 $(-3m)^3$	15 $\sqrt[3]{27x^6}$	16 $\sqrt{25y^{16}}$
17 $(8q^2)^{2/3}$	18 $\left(\dfrac{1}{u^{-2}}\right)^{1/2}$	19 $\left(-\dfrac{1}{3v^2}\right)^{-2}$	20 $1 \div (\tfrac{4}{9})^{-3/2}$

3.5   Like and Unlike Terms

The following examples indicate which terms in algebra are *like*, and which are *unlike*:

$4x + 7x = 11x.$
$2x^2 + 3x^2 = 5x^2.$

$4xy + 7x^2 y$ cannot be simplified (*unlike* terms).

$3xy + 7x^2 - 2xy = xy + 7x^2$ (first and last terms are *like*).

In an expression such as $11xy$, the number 11 is called the *coefficient* of xy.

3.6   Removal of Brackets

Worked Example 3.4

Remove brackets from the following expressions, and simplify answers where possible.

(a) $4x(a + x) + 3a(x + a)$

$\quad = 4xa + 4x^2 + 3ax + 3a^2 \qquad$ (using distributive law and indices rules)

$\quad = 4x^2 + 7ax + 3a^2$.

$\quad$ (*Note*: $4xa$ and $3ax$ are *like* terms.)

(b) $2y(x - y) - 3x(y - x)$

Subtraction of a negative quantity is the same as addition; see Chapter 2.

$\quad = 2yx - 2y^2 - 3xy \oplus 3x^2$.

(c) $(2x - 1)(3x + 1)$

$\quad = (2x \times 3x) + (2x \times 1) - (1 \times 3x) - (1 \times 1)$

$\quad = 6x^2 + 2x - 3x - 1 = 6x^2 - x - 1$.

3.7 Factors

The reverse process of putting brackets back into an algebraic expression is called *factorizing*.

(a) Two Terms

Basically this is the reverse of the distributive law:

(i) $8x + 16y = 8(x + 2y)$.

(ii) $4p^2 + 8pq = 4p(p + 2q)$. $\qquad \left[\begin{array}{l} p(4p + 8q) \text{ is correct but not completely} \\ \text{factorized.} \end{array}\right.$

(b) Four Terms

(i) $6a + 12 + 4ab + 8b$

$\quad = 6(a + 2) + 4b(a + 2) = (6 + 4b)(a + 2)$

$\quad\quad\quad\quad\quad\quad\quad\quad\quad\quad = 2(3 + 2b)(a + 2)$.

(ii) $a^2 - 3a - ab + 3b$

$\left[\begin{array}{l}\text{Note that this is negative, because} \\ -b \times -3 = +3b.\end{array}\right]$

$\quad = a(a - 3) - b(a - 3)$

$\quad = (a - b)(a - 3)$.

(c) Three Terms (Quadratic)

In Worked Example 3.4(c) we showed that

$$(2x - 1)(3x + 1) = 6x^2 - x - 1;$$

the expression $6x^2 - x - 1$ is called a *quadratic* expression.

The process of factorizing a quadratic is not easy and will be considered in stages.

(i) $x^2 + 5x + 6 \quad = x^2 + 2x + 3x + 6$

$\quad\quad\quad\quad\quad\quad\quad = x(x + 2) + 3(x + 2)$

$\quad\quad\quad\quad\quad\quad\quad = (x + 3)(x + 2)$.

(ii) $x^2 + x - 6 \quad = x^2 + 3x - 2x - 6$

$\quad\quad\quad\quad\quad\quad\quad = x(x + 3) - 2(x + 3)$

$\quad\quad\quad\quad\quad\quad\quad = (x - 2)(x + 3)$.

(iii) $x^2 - 7x + 10 = x^2 - 5x - 2x + 10$

$\quad\quad\quad\quad\quad\quad\quad = x(x - 5) - 2(x - 5)$

$\quad\quad\quad\quad\quad\quad\quad = (x - 2)(x - 5)$.

The process is really trial and error, and practice makes perfect.

(iv) $2x^2 - x - 6 = 2x^2 + 3x - 4x - 6$
$$= x(2x + 3) - 2(2x + 3)$$
$$= (x - 2)(2x + 3).$$

(v) $18x^2 + 45x - 8 = 18x^2 + 48x - 3x - 8$
$$= 6x(3x + 8) - (3x + 8)$$
$$= (6x - 1)(3x + 8).$$

When splitting up into four terms, notice that the product of the two middle terms equals the product of the two outside terms, e.g.:

(i) $x^2 \times 6 = 2x \times 3x = 6x^2$,

(iii) $x^2 \times 10 = -5x \times -2x = 10x^2$,

(v) $18x^2 \times -8 = 48x \times -3x = -144x^2$.

It is not always possible to put a quadratic expression into brackets; the following rule can save you a lot of time.

For the expression $ax^2 + bx + c$, work out $b^2 - 4ac$.

If it is a perfect square it factorizes, if not it doesn't.

For example:

(i) $x^2 + 6x + 8$ $a = 1, b = 6, c = 8$;
$b^2 - 4ac = 36 - 32 = 4$, which *is* a perfect square.
In fact $x^2 + 6x + 8 = (x + 4)(x + 2)$.

(ii) $x^2 - 4x - 12$ $a = 1, b = -4, c = -12$;
$b^2 - 4ac = 16 + 48 = 64$, which *is* a perfect square.

The alternative method which also involves trial and error is illustrated as follows:

Factorize $6x^2 + 19x - 20$.

Consider this   Consider this
number first.   number second.

$6x^2$ suggests $3x \times 2x$.
-20 suggests 5×-4 or 2×-10.
Try $(3x + 5)(2x - 4) = 6x^2 + 10x - 12x - 20$
$$= 6x^2 - 2x - 20. \qquad \times$$
Try $(2x - 10)(3x + 2) = 6x^2 + 4x - 30x - 20$
$$= 6x^2 - 26x - 20. \qquad \times$$
There are many possibilities.
In fact $(6x - 5)(x + 4) = 6x^2 - 5x + 24x - 20$
$$= 6x^2 + 19x - 20. \qquad \checkmark$$

(d) $a^2 - b^2$

This expression is known as a *difference of two squares*.
$a^2 - b^2 = (a - b)(a + b)$.
Example: $16x^2 - 25y^2 = (4x)^2 - (5y)^2 = (4x - 5y)(4x + 5y)$.

(e) $a^2 \pm 2ab + b^2$

This expression is a *perfect square*.
$a^2 + 2ab + b^2 = (a + b)(a + b) = (a + b)^2$.
$a^2 - 2ab + b^2 = (a - b)^2$.

Check 15

Factorize if possible the following:

1 $ay + 4y^2$	2 $3t^3 + 2t^2 + 5t$	3 $p^2q^3 - q^2p^3$
4 $7(p - 2) - 3(p - 2)$	5 $p(y - z) - q(z - y)$	6 $qr + rs - ps - pq$
7 $t^2 - 3t - tp + 3p$	8 $ax + bx + cx - ay - by - cy$	
9 $x^2 - 11x + 24$	10 $x^2 + 2x - 3$	11 $x^2 + 11x - 26$
12 $x^2 - 7x + 8$	13 $2x^2 + 13x + 15$	14 $4x^2 + 8x + 3$
15 $6x^2 - 5x + 1$	16 $9x^2 - 7x - 2$	17 $4x^4 - 3x^2 - 1$
18 $4x^2 - 25$	19 $1 - x^2$	20 $\pi R^2 - \pi r^2$
21 $(x - 3)^2 - 9$	22 $121x^2y^2 - 4$	23 $4x^2 - 12xy + 9y^2$
24 $25x^2 - 10xy + y^2$	25 $25 - 10b + b^2$	

3.8 LCM and HCF

The lowest common multiple (LCM) of two numbers is the smallest number that both numbers divide into exactly. It can be found by first expressing each number as the product of its prime factors. Consider the following example.

To find the LCM of 48 and 84:

```
2 ) 48        2 ) 84
2 ) 24        2 ) 42
2 ) 12        3 ) 21
2 )  6        7 )  7
3 )  3             1
     1
```

$\therefore \ 48 = 2^4 \times 3.$ $\therefore 84 = 2^2 \times 3 \times 7.$

Take the highest power of every prime number occurring in the two products and multiply these powers together. Hence,

$$\text{LCM} = 2^4 \times 3 \times 7 = 336.$$

The highest common factor (HCF) is the largest number that divides exactly into each number.

To find the HCF of these numbers, take the lowest power of each prime number occurring in both numbers, and multiply them together. Hence,

$$\text{HCF} = 2^2 \times 3 = 12.$$

3.9 LCM and HCF in Algebra

The method is slightly easier in algebra, because most of the work is done already.
For example, the LCM of $4a^3bc$ and $6a^2b^4c^2$ is

$$12 \times a^3 \times b^4 \times c^2 = 12a^3b^4c^2.$$

The HCF is $2 \times a^2 \times b \times c = 2a^2bc$.

*3.10   Algebraic Fractions

(a) Addition or Subtraction

$$\frac{4}{3ab} + \frac{1}{4a^2 b} = \frac{4 \times 4a}{12a^2 b} + \frac{1 \times 3}{12a^2 b} = \frac{16a + 3}{12a^2 b}$$

$$\uparrow$$

LCM of $3ab$ and $4a^2 b$

(b) Multiplication

$$\frac{3ab}{4c} \times \frac{6a^2 c}{5bt} \text{ in full } = \frac{3 \times a \times \cancel{b}}{\cancel{4} \times c} \times \frac{\overset{3}{\cancel{6}} \times a \times a \times \cancel{c}}{5 \times \cancel{b} \times t}$$

$$= \frac{9a^3}{10t}.$$

(c) Division

$$\frac{4xy^2}{9t} \div \frac{8x^2 y^3}{7t^2} = \frac{4xy^2}{9t} \times \frac{7t^2}{8x^2 y^3}$$

$$= \frac{\cancel{4} \times \cancel{x} \times \cancel{y} \times \cancel{y}}{9 \times \cancel{t}} \times \frac{7 \times \cancel{t} \times t}{\underset{2}{\cancel{8}} \times \cancel{x} \times x \times \cancel{y} \times \cancel{y} \times y}$$

$$= \frac{7t}{18xy}.$$

With practice, the 'in full' stage can be omitted.

* Check 16

Evaluate and simplify if possible the following:

1   (a) $\dfrac{1}{x} + \dfrac{1}{x^2}$ (b) $\dfrac{2}{a} + \dfrac{3}{ab}$ (c) $\dfrac{4}{t} - \dfrac{3}{2t^2}$

    (d) $\dfrac{x}{2} + \dfrac{x}{3} + \dfrac{x}{4}$ (e) $\dfrac{4}{y} - \dfrac{2}{3y} + \dfrac{5}{y}$ (f) $\dfrac{4x}{3y} - \dfrac{5y}{7x}$

    (g) $4x + \dfrac{1}{x}$ (h) $\dfrac{2a + 5b}{4} + \dfrac{3a + 2b}{8}$ (i) $\dfrac{x + 2}{3} - \dfrac{5}{6}$

    (j) $\dfrac{4}{(x - 1)} + \dfrac{3}{(x + 2)}$ (k) $\dfrac{1}{x} - \dfrac{1}{(x - 1)}$ (l) $\dfrac{1}{x^2 - 5x + 6} + \dfrac{x}{(x - 3)}$

    (m) $\dfrac{x + 1}{x - 1} - \dfrac{x - 1}{x + 1}$

2   (a) $\dfrac{x}{y^2} \times \dfrac{2y}{x}$ (b) $\dfrac{3pq}{t} \times \dfrac{4t^2}{9p}$ (c) $\dfrac{5t}{6q} \times \dfrac{18q^2}{25t^2}$

(d) $\dfrac{x}{y} \times \dfrac{2y}{3x} \times \dfrac{4x}{5y}$ (e) $\dfrac{p^2}{q} \times \dfrac{2q^2}{3p} \times \dfrac{4}{5pq}$ (f) $\dfrac{pq}{r} \div \dfrac{3p}{2r}$

(g) $\dfrac{a-b}{c} \times \dfrac{c^2}{a^2-b^2}$ (h) $\dfrac{5pq}{6t^2} \div \dfrac{3pq}{5t}$ (i) $\dfrac{16t^2}{5p} \div \dfrac{4t}{5p^2}$

(j) $\dfrac{a+b}{c} \div \dfrac{a-b}{c}$

3.11   Forming Expressions

The ability to write down an expression in terms of algebraic quantities is extremely important if problem solving is to be attempted. The following examples should illustrate the necessary techniques that need to be mastered.

(a) A number x is multiplied by 4, and 3 is subtracted from the answer. The result is divided by 4. What is the result?

Answer $= \dfrac{(4x-3)}{4}$.   Brackets are important in order to indicate that all of $4x - 3$ is divided by 4.

(b) Find the cost of p apples at t pence a dozen, and q pears at 6 pence each.

The cost of one apple is $\dfrac{t}{12}$ pence.

Hence the cost of p apples is $\dfrac{t}{12} \times p = \dfrac{tp}{12}$.

The cost of the pears is $6q$ pence.

The total cost is $\dfrac{tp}{12} + 6q$.

(c) A car travels at x m.p.h. for 30 min, and then travels a further k miles for $\frac{1}{4}$ hour. Find the average speed for the journey.

Since $\text{Average speed} = \dfrac{\text{Total distance}}{\text{Total time}}$,

We need to find the distance travelled in the first 30 min, i.e. in $\frac{1}{2}$ hour.

Distance = Speed × Time,
$\therefore$ distance $= \frac{1}{2}x$
$\therefore$ total distance $= \frac{1}{2}x + k$
    total time $= \frac{1}{2} + \frac{1}{4} = \frac{3}{4}$.
$\therefore$ Average speed $= \dfrac{\frac{1}{2}x + k}{\frac{3}{4}} = \frac{4}{3}(\frac{1}{2}x + k)$.

Answers should always be simplified as much as possible.

Check 17

Find in as simple a form as possible expressions for the following.
1 A number x is doubled, 5 is subtracted from this and the answer is divided in the ratio 2 : 1. What is the smallest part?
2 What is the total cost of p pencils at y pence for 20 and q pens at £k each. Give your answer in pounds.
3 What is the area of a rectangle in cm^2, if it measures x mm by y cm?

4 How many minutes are there between y min to 8.00 hours and x min after 10.30 hours?

5 A labourer earned £t a week for y weeks of the year, and £v a week for the remainder except for 2 weeks when he had no income. How much did he earn in the year?

6 I could buy p pens for £x. If the price is increased by 10 per cent, how many pens can I buy for the same amount?

7 A batsman scored f fours, s sixes and 9 singles in an innings. How many runs did he score?

8 A rectangle measures p cm by q cm. ($p < q$). If the shorter side is increased by 10 per cent, and the longer side is decreased by 8 per cent, find an expression for the percentage change in its area.

9 If income tax is charged at I pence in the pound, how much tax is paid by a person who earns £E, but is allowed deductions of £D before tax is calculated? Give your answer in pounds.

10 Telephone cable weighing W kg/m is wound on to a reel which weighs M kg. If the reel can hold 85 m, find the total weight of the reel and cable.

3.12 Linear Equations

You should be able to solve simple equations. The following examples, however, should refresh your memory and indicate simple procedures.

Remember, any number can be added or subtracted from either side of an equation without altering it. Similarly, either side of an equation can be multiplied or divided by any number without altering it.

(a) $7x - 5 = 4x + 11$;

add 5 to each side: $7x = 4x + 16$;

take $4x$ from each side: $3x = 16$;

divide each side by 3: $x = \dfrac{16}{3}$.

(b) $4 - (3x + 1) = 2(x - 5)$;

remove brackets first: $4 - 3x - 1 = 2x - 10$;

collect terms on the left: $3 - 3x = 2x - 10$;

add 10 to each side: $13 - 3x = 2x$;

add $3x$ to each side: $13 = 5x$;

divide each side by 5: $\dfrac{13}{5} = x$.

(c) $\dfrac{2x + 1}{4} - \dfrac{3x - 5}{2} = \dfrac{x}{3}$;

to avoid problems with signs, rewrite the equation with brackets inserted; i.e.

$$\frac{(2x + 1)}{4} - \frac{(3x - 5)}{2} = \frac{x}{3};$$

multiply the equation by the common denominator, i.e. the LCM of 2, 3, 4, which is 12:

$$\frac{\overset{3}{\cancel{12}}(2x + 1)}{\cancel{4}} - \frac{\overset{6}{\cancel{12}}(3x - 5)}{\cancel{2}} = \overset{4}{\cancel{12}} \times \frac{x}{\cancel{3}}; \qquad \text{cancel};$$

50

remove brackets: $\qquad 6x + 3 - 18x + 30 = 4x;$

collect terms: $\qquad -12x + 33 = 4x;$

add $12x$ to each side: $\qquad 33 = 16x;$

divide each side by 16: $\qquad \dfrac{33}{16} = x.$

(d) $\dfrac{7}{(x-1)} = \dfrac{4}{(x+1)}$;

the common denominator is $(x-1)(x+1)$;

multiply the equation by this:

$$\cancel{(x-1)}(x+1) \times \dfrac{7}{\cancel{(x-1)}} = \dfrac{4}{\cancel{(x+1)}} \times (x-1)\cancel{(x+1)}; \qquad \text{cancel;}$$

$\therefore \quad 7(x+1) = 4(x-1),$

$\qquad 7x + 7 = 4x - 4,$

$\qquad 3x = -11,$

$\therefore \qquad x = -\dfrac{11}{3} .$

3.13 Quadratic Equations

(a) By Factors

Consider $x^2 - 5x + 6 = 0$. In section 3.7 (c) we factorized quadratic expressions.

Hence $(x-3)(x-2) = 0$,

$\therefore$ either $x - 3 = 0$, or $x - 2 = 0$.

We get two solutions: $x = 3$ or $x = 2$.

A further example: $6x^2 - x - 2 = 0$;

factorizing, $(2x+1)(3x-2) = 0$

$\therefore 2x + 1 = 0 \quad$ or $\quad 3x - 2 = 0,$

$\qquad 2x = -1 \quad$ or $\quad 3x = 2,$

$\therefore \qquad x = -\frac{1}{2} \quad$ or $\quad x = \frac{2}{3}.$

*(b) By Formula

The equation $x^2 + x - 1 = 0$ cannot be solved by factors, because it does not factorize. The following formula can be used. A proof is given.

Consider the equation $ax^2 + bx + c = 0$.

Divide by a: $x^2 + \dfrac{bx}{a} + \dfrac{c}{a} = 0.$

Add $\dfrac{b^2}{4a^2}$ to both sides. This is part of the technique of completing the square.

$$\therefore x^2 + \dfrac{bx}{a} + \dfrac{b^2}{4a^2} + \dfrac{c}{a} = \dfrac{b^2}{4a^2} ,$$

$$\left(x + \dfrac{b}{2a}\right)^2 = \dfrac{b^2}{4a^2} - \dfrac{c}{a} \qquad \text{Check by squaring out the bracket.}$$

$$= \dfrac{b^2 - 4ac}{4a^2} .$$

Take the square root of each side, remembering that it could be positive or negative:

$$x + \frac{b}{2a} = \pm \frac{\sqrt{b^2 - 4ac}}{2a}.$$

Subtract $\frac{b}{2a}$ from both sides:

$$\boxed{x = \frac{-b \pm \sqrt{b^2 - 4ac}}{2a}.}$$

In the equation $x^2 + x - 1 = 0$, $a = 1$, $b = 1$, $c = -1$.

$$\therefore x = \frac{-1 \pm \sqrt{1 + 4}}{2} = \frac{-1 \pm \sqrt{5}}{2}.$$

Hence, $x = 0.618$ or -1.618.

3.14 Simultaneous Equations (Linear)

Linear simultaneous equations can be solved by elimination, as shown here, by graphs, see section 5.8, or by matrices, see section 9.8. See also section 3.19 for non-linear equations.

(a) Solve

$$3x + 4y = 2 \tag{1}$$
$$5x + 3y = 1. \tag{2}$$

Multiply (1) by 5: $\quad 15x + 20y = 10 \tag{3}$
multiply (2) by 3: $\quad 15x + \ 9y = 3. \tag{4}$

Each equation has the same number of x's. The equations can be subtracted:

$$(3) - (4): \quad 11y = 7, \quad \therefore y = \tfrac{7}{11}.$$

Substitute this value into any of the equations, i.e. (1):

$$3x + \tfrac{28}{11} = 2, \quad \therefore 3x = 2 - \tfrac{28}{11} = -\tfrac{6}{11}, \quad \therefore x = -\tfrac{2}{11}.$$

The solution to the equations is $x = -\tfrac{2}{11}$, $y = \tfrac{7}{11}$.

(b) A slightly harder example:

$$5x - 4y = 14 \tag{1}$$
$$7x + 9y = 18. \tag{2}$$

Multiply (1) by 9: $\quad 45x - 36y = 126 \tag{3}$
multiply (2) by 4: $\quad 28x + 36y = \ 72. \tag{4}$

This time, y can be eliminated by adding the equations:

$$(3) + (4): \quad 73x = 198, \quad \therefore x = \tfrac{198}{73} = 2.71 \ (2 \ \text{d.p.}).$$

Substitute in (2):

$$18.97 + 9y = 18, \quad \therefore 9y = -0.97, \quad \therefore y = -0.11.$$

The solution is $x = 2.71$, $y = -0.11$.

Notes:

(1) It may be possible to eliminate x or y without multiplying either equation (see the following example).

(2) It doesn't matter which variable is eliminated.

(c) Solve

$$4x = 5 + 3y, \tag{1}$$
$$3y - 5x = -4. \tag{2}$$

Before solving any simultaneous equations, the variables must be on the same side of the equation in the same order.

Rewrite (1): $\qquad 4x - 3y = 5.$ $\qquad\qquad$ (3)

Rewrite (2): $\qquad -5x + 3y = -4.$ $\qquad\qquad$ (4)

(3) + (4): $\quad -x = 1, \qquad \therefore x = -1.$

Substitute in (4): $\qquad 5 + 3y = -4$

$\qquad\qquad\qquad\qquad 3y = -9, \qquad \therefore y = -3.$

The solution is $x = -1$, $y = -3$.

Now practise solving the following equations:

Check 18

1 Solve for x:

(a) $2x + 3 = 7$; $\qquad\qquad$ (b) $8 - x = 4$;

(c) $4x - 1 = 7x + 3$; $\qquad\qquad$ (d) $4(x + 2) = 3 + (x - 5)$;

(e) $2(x + 1) + 3(x - 2) = 15$; $\qquad$ (f) $\frac{1}{2}x + 4 = 3x$;

(g) $2(x + 3) = 9$; $\qquad\qquad$ (h) $6 - 5(x + 1) = 9$;

(i) $\dfrac{x}{5} + \dfrac{2x}{3} = \dfrac{1}{2}$ $\qquad\qquad$ (j) $\dfrac{x + 1}{2} + \dfrac{x - 1}{2} = \dfrac{1}{2}$;

(k) $\dfrac{2x - 1}{5} + \dfrac{3x - 2}{4} = 1$; $\qquad$ (l) $\dfrac{(x + 2)}{5} - \dfrac{3x}{5} = 4$;

(m) $\dfrac{7}{x} = 9$; $\qquad\qquad$ (n) $\dfrac{2}{(x - 3)} = \dfrac{4}{(x + 2)}$;

(o) $\dfrac{1}{(x + 2)(x + 5)} = \dfrac{1}{(x + 3)(x - 1)}$.

2 Solve where possible the following quadratic equations:

(a) $x^2 - 2x - 3 = 0$; $\qquad\qquad$ (b) $x^2 - 10x + 16 = 0$;

(c) $2x^2 + x - 1 = 0$; $\qquad\qquad$ (d) $3x^2 - 10x + 3 = 0$;

(e) $x^2 - 2x + 1 = 0$; $\qquad\qquad$ (f) $x^2 - 9x = 0$;

(g) $x^2 + 3x - 9 = 0$; $\qquad\qquad$ (h) $x^2 + 2x - 1 = 0$;

(i) $x^2 + 8x = 3$; $\qquad\qquad$ (j) $4x^2 = 9x + 1$;

(k) $x + \dfrac{1}{3x} = 2$; $\qquad\qquad$ (l) $\dfrac{x + 2}{x + 5} = \dfrac{2x + 3}{x - 1}$;

(m) $4x^2 + x + 7 = 0$; $\qquad\qquad$ (n) $\dfrac{1}{x - 1} - \dfrac{1}{x + 1} = 6$;

(o) $\dfrac{1}{x} + x = 2$.

3 Solve the following simultaneous equations:

(a) $x + y = 7$, $2x - y = 8$; $\qquad$ (b) $3x - 2y = 4$, $5x - 2y = 0$;

(c) $4x - 3y = 5$, $7x - 5y = 9$; $\qquad$ (d) $2x + y = 8$, $5x - y = 6$;

(e) $x + 3y = 2$, $2x - 4y = 1$; $\qquad$ (f) $3x + 2y = 13$, $2x + 3y = 12$;

(g) $4x - 5y = 21$, $6x + 7y = -12$; $\quad$ (h) $3x + 2y = 17$, $4y - x = -8$;

(i) $3y = 2x - 7$, $3x = 13 + 2y$; $\qquad$ (j) $2x = 3y + 5$, $5x = 3y - 4$.

3.15 Forming Equations

The techniques of making algebraic expressions and solving equations can now be combined to solve simple problems.

Worked Example 3.5

The sum of £61 is divided between Arthur, Brenda and Catherine. Arthur has twice as much as Brenda, and Catherine has £5 less than Arthur and Brenda together. How much do all three have each?

Solution

Use a suitable letter to denote one unknown quantity.

Let Brenda have £M, then Arthur has £$2M$. Catherine has £$(M + 2M) - 5 =$ £$3M - 5$.

The total is £61, $\qquad \therefore M + 2M + 3M - 5 = 61$,

$$\therefore 6M = 66, \qquad \therefore M = 11.$$

$\therefore$ Arthur has £22, Brenda has £11 and Catherine £28.

*Worked Example 3.6

A machine produces two types of bolt. Bolt A is produced at the rate of x per minute, and bolt B is produced at the rate of $(x - 6)$ per minute.
(a) Write down an expression in seconds for the time taken to produce each bolt.
(b) If it takes $1\frac{1}{6}$ seconds longer to produce bolt B than bolt A, write down an equation in x and solve it.

Solution

(a) If x of bolt A are produced in 60 seconds, then one is produced in $\dfrac{60}{x}$ seconds. Similarly, one of B is produced in $\dfrac{60}{x - 6}$ seconds.

(b) Seeing that the difference is $1\frac{1}{6}$ seconds, and $\dfrac{60}{x - 6}$ is larger than $\dfrac{60}{x}$ (because less bolts are produced per minute), it follows that:

$$\frac{60}{x - 6} = \frac{60}{x} + \frac{7}{6};$$

multiply by common denominator $6x(x - 1)$:

$$\therefore 360x = 360(x - 6) + 7x(x - 6)$$

$$\therefore 360x = 360x - 2160 + 7x^2 - 42x$$

$$\therefore 7x^2 - 42x - 2160 = 0$$

$$\therefore (7x + 90)(x - 24) = 0.$$

x cannot be $-\dfrac{90}{7}$, $\qquad \therefore x = 24$.

Worked Example 3.7

(a) At the moment, Paul is six times as old as his daughter Jane.
 (i) If Jane's present age is x years, write down, in terms of x, the age Paul will be in 12 years' time.

(ii) In 12 years' time, Paul will be three times as old as Jane. Write down an equation for x and hence find Jane's present age.

(b) Solve the equation $(x - 1)^2 = 3$, giving your answers correct to two decimal places.

Solution

(a) (i) At present, since Paul is six times the age of Jane, Paul's age is $6x$.

∴ In 12 years' time, Paul's age $= 6x + 12$.

(ii) In 12 years' time, Jane will be $x + 12$ years old.
Paul will then be three times Jane's age.
Hence, $6x + 12 = 3(x + 12)$
∴ $\qquad 6x + 12 = 3x + 36$
∴ $\qquad 3x = 24$
∴ $\qquad x = 8$.
∴ Jane's present age is 8 years.

(b) Since $(x - 1)^2 = 3$,
$\qquad (x - 1) = +\sqrt{3} \qquad$ or $\qquad -\sqrt{3}$
∴ $\qquad x = 1 + \sqrt{3} = 2.73$
or $\qquad 1 - \sqrt{3} = -0.73$.

Worked Example 3.8

A bill of £355 was paid using £5 notes and £20 notes. If 35 notes were used altogether, find how many of each were used.

Solution

It is not possible to solve this problem with just one unknown.
Let the number of £5 notes be f.
Let the number of £20 notes be t.

For the money:	$5f + 20t = 355$.	(1)
For the notes:	$f + t = 35$.	(2)
Divide (1) by 5:	$f + 4t = 71$.	(3)
(3) − (2):	$3t = 36$, $\quad$ ∴ $t = 12$, $\quad f = 23$.	

Thus 23 £5 notes and 12 £20 notes were used.

3.16 Changing the Subject of Formulae

In a short space this is best illustrated by a number of examples.

Worked Example 3.9

Make x the subject of the following formulae:

(a) $t = ax + b$
(b) $t = a(x + b)$;
(c) $t = 2a\sqrt{x + y}$;

(d) $y = \dfrac{1}{t}(ax - k)$;
(e) $y = \dfrac{2t}{(1 + x)}$;
(f) $p = a\sqrt{x} + \dfrac{q}{t}$;

(g) $y = \dfrac{ax + b}{cx + d}$;
(h) $y = \dfrac{t}{1 - x^2}$.

Solution

It is important to realise that the following solutions are not the only ones, but are an attempt at a systematic approach. Short cuts are often possible with experience.

(a)
$$t = ax + b.$$

Subtract b from each side:
$$t - b = ax.$$

$\div a$:
$$\frac{t - b}{a} = x,$$

or, better,
$$x = \frac{(t - b)}{a}.$$

(b)
$$t = a(x + b).$$

Remove brackets:
$$t = ax + ab.$$

Subtract ab from each side:
$$t - ab = ax.$$

$\div a$:
$$x = \frac{(t - ab)}{a}.$$

(c)
$$t = 2a\sqrt{x + y}.$$

Square both sides (remember to square $2a$):
$$t^2 = 4a^2(x + y).$$

Remove brackets:
$$t^2 = 4a^2 x + 4a^2 y.$$

Subtract $4a^2 y$ from each side:
$$t^2 - 4a^2 y = 4a^2 x.$$

$\div 4a^2$:
$$x = \frac{t^2 - 4a^2 y}{4a^2}.$$

(d)
$$y = \frac{1}{t}(ax - k).$$

Remove brackets:
$$y = \frac{ax}{t} - \frac{k}{t}.$$

$\times t$:
$$yt = ax - k.$$

$+ k$ each side:
$$yt + k = ax.$$

$\div a$:
$$x = \frac{(yt + k)}{a}.$$

(e)
$$y = \frac{2t}{1 + x}.$$

$\times$ common denominator $(1 + x)$:
$$y(1 + x) = 2t.$$

Remove brackets:
$$y + xy = 2t.$$

$- y$ each side:
$$xy = 2t - y.$$

$\div y$:
$$x = \frac{(2t - y)}{y}.$$

(f)
$$p = a\sqrt{x} + \frac{q}{t}.$$

$-\dfrac{q}{t}$ each side: $\qquad p - \dfrac{q}{t} = a\sqrt{x}.$

Square both sides: $\qquad \left(p - \dfrac{q}{t}\right)^2 = a^2 x.$

Remove brackets: $\qquad p^2 + \dfrac{q^2}{t^2} - \dfrac{2pq}{t} = a^2 x$

$\times$ common denominator t^2:

$$p^2 t^2 + q^2 - 2pqt = a^2 t^2 x.$$

$\div\, a^2 t^2$: $\qquad x = \dfrac{p^2 t^2 + q^2 - 2pqt}{a^2 t^2}.$

(g) $$y = \dfrac{ax + b}{cx + d}.$$

Common denominator $cx + d$,

$$\therefore \quad y(cx + d) = ax + b.$$

Remove brackets: $\qquad ycx + yd = ax + b,$

$$\therefore \quad ycx - ax = b - yd.$$

Factorize side containing new subject x:

$$x(yc - a) = b - yd.$$

$\div\,(yc - a)$: $\qquad x = \dfrac{b - yd}{yc - a}.$

(h) $$y = \dfrac{t}{1 - x^2}.$$

Common denominator $(1 - x^2)$,

$$\therefore \quad y(1 - x^2) = t.$$

Remove brackets: $\qquad y - yx^2 = t,$

$$\therefore \quad y - t = yx^2$$

$\div\, y$: $\qquad x^2 = \dfrac{y - t}{y}.$

Take square root: $\qquad x = \sqrt{\dfrac{y - t}{y}} \qquad$ (remember x could be negative).

*3.17 Remainder Theorem

The remainder theorem states that if a polynomial function $f(x)$ (e.g. $x^3 + 2x + 1$, $3x^2 - 5x + 6$) is divided by $(x - a)$, the remainder is $f(a)$. Hence, if $f(a) = 0$, $(x - a)$ must be a factor of the original expression. This is extremely useful in factorizing higher-order polynomials than quadratics.

Worked Example 3.10

Factorize
(a) (i) $x^3 + x^2 - 10x + 8$,
   (ii) $2x^3 + 7x^2 + 2x - 3$.

Solution

(a) Let $f(x) = x^3 + x^2 - 10x + 8$.

By trial, $f(1) = 1 + 1 - 10 + 8 = 0$.

$\therefore (x - 1)$ is a factor.

By division,

$$
\require{enclose}
\begin{array}{r}
x^2 + 2x - 8 \\
x - 1 \enclose{longdiv}{x^3 + x^2 - 10x + 8} \\
\underline{x^3 - x^2 } \\
2x^2 - 10x \\
\underline{2x^2 - 2x } \\
-8x + 8 \\
\underline{-8x + 8} \\
0 \quad \longleftarrow \text{ no remainder}
\end{array}
$$

$\therefore f(x) = (x - 1)(x^2 + 2x - 8)$
         $= (x - 1)(x - 2)(x + 4)$.

(b) Let $f(x) = 2x^3 + 7x^2 + 2x - 3$.

This is less obvious:

$$f(1) = 2 + 7 + 2 - 3 = 8.$$
$$f(2) = 16 + 28 + 4 - 3 = 45.$$

This doesn't look too hopeful; try negative values:

$$f(-1) = -2 + 7 - 2 - 3 = 0.$$

$\therefore x + 1$ is a factor.

By division,

$$
\begin{array}{r}
2x^2 + 5x - 3 \\
x + 1 \enclose{longdiv}{2x^3 + 7x^2 + 2x - 3} \\
\underline{2x^3 + 2x^2 } \\
5x^2 + 2x \\
\underline{5x^2 + 5x } \\
-3x - 3 \\
\underline{-3x - 3} \\
0
\end{array}
$$

$f(x) = (x + 1)(2x^2 + 5x - 3)$
       $= (x + 1)(2x - 1)(x + 3)$.

Worked Example 3.11

The cubic function $x^3 + ax^2 + 7x + b$ leaves a remainder 2 when divided by $(x - 3)$ and a remainder 1 when divided by $x + 2$. Find a and b.

Solution

The remainder theorem can be used without having to do any division. The remainder when divided by $(x - 3)$ is given by f(3). Since this remainder is 2, it follows that:

$$f(3) = 2,$$

i.e. $\quad 3^3 + 9a + 21 + b = 2,$

$$\therefore \quad 9a + b = -46. \qquad (1)$$

Similarly, $\qquad\qquad f(-2) = 1,$

$$\therefore \quad (-2)^3 + 4a - 14 + b = 1,$$

$$\therefore \quad 4a + b = 23. \qquad (2)$$

(1) − (2): $\qquad\qquad 5a = -69.$

$$\therefore \quad a = -13.8, b = 78.2.$$

3.18   Variation and Proportion

In section 2.9, the idea of two quantities being proportional was introduced. The phrase 'varies (as)' can also be used. In general, if A varies as or is proportional to B, then $A = kB$, where k is the constant of proportionality. Other types of variation are possible.

If y is inversely proportional to x, then $y = \dfrac{k}{x}$.

If y varies as x^2, $\qquad\qquad y = kx^2$.
(y is proportional to x^2.)

This means that if x^2 is doubled, so is y. In order to double x^2, x would have to be multiplied by a factor $\sqrt{2}$.

A could be related to more than one quantity. See Worked Example 3.13. This is known as *joint variation*.

Worked Example 3.12

If y is proportional to x^2, and $y = 4$ when $x = 8$, find y when $x = 2$.

Solution

Let $\qquad\qquad\qquad\qquad y = kx^2.$

$y = 4, x = 8,$ $\qquad\qquad \therefore \quad 4 = k \times 8^2,$

$$\therefore \quad k = \tfrac{4}{64} = \tfrac{1}{16},$$

$$\therefore \quad y = \tfrac{1}{16}x^2.$$

$\therefore$ If $x = 2$, $y = \tfrac{1}{16} \times 4 = \tfrac{1}{4}.$

Worked Example 3.13

The lift, L, produced by the wing of an aircraft varies directly as its area, A, and as the square of the airspeed, V.

For a certain wing, $L = 1200$ when $A = 15$ and $V = 200$.

(a) Find an equation connecting L, A and V.

(b) If, for the same wing, the airspeed is increased by ten per cent, find the corresponding percentage increase in lift.

[SEB]

Solution

(a) If L varies directly as A, and as the square of V,

then $$L = kAV^2.$$

$L = 1200$ when $A = 15$, $V = 200$,

$$\therefore 1200 = k \times 15 \times (200)^2,$$

$$\therefore \quad k = \frac{1200}{15 \times 40\,000} = \frac{1}{500},$$

$$\therefore \quad L = \frac{AV^2}{500}.$$

(b) If V increases by 10 per cent, then $V = 220$.

$$\therefore L = \frac{15 \times (220)^2}{500} = 1452,$$

$$\therefore \text{Percentage increase} = \frac{\text{Increase}}{\text{Original}} \times 100$$

$$= \frac{252}{1200} \times 100 = 21\%.$$

3.19 Simultaneous Equations, One Linear, One Non-linear

This topic is illustrated by the following example.

Worked Example 3.14

Solve the simultaneous equations

$$2x + y = 5, \qquad 2x^2 + y^2 - xy = 7.$$

Solution

Since $2x + y = 5$, $\qquad\qquad y = 5 - 2x.$ (1)

Replace y in the second equation by $(5 - 2x)$:

$$\therefore \quad 2x^2 + (5 - 2x)^2 - x(5 - 2x) = 7,$$

$$\therefore \quad 2x^2 + 25 + 4x^2 - 20x - 5x + 2x^2 = 7,$$

$$\therefore \quad 8x^2 - 25x + 18 = 0,$$

$$\therefore \quad (x - 2)(8x - 9) = 0,$$

$\therefore$ $x = 2$; substitute in (1): $y = 1$;

or $x = \frac{9}{8}$, $y = \frac{11}{4}$.

Check 19

1 If y is proportional to the square of x, and $y = 2$ when $x = 4$, find y when $x = 3$.
2 If p varies inversely as the square of q and $p = 4$ when $q = 2$, find p when $q = 6$.
3 If y varies as the square of x, and inversely as the cube of H, and $y = 4$ when $H = 6$ and $x = 2$, find y when $H = 4$ and $x = 6$.
* 4 Use the remainder theorem to factorize:
    (a) $x^3 - 1$ (b) $x^3 + 2x^2 - x - 2$ (c) $x^3 + 7x^2 - 3x - 30$
    (d) $x^3 - 6x^2 + 11x - 6$ (e) $2x^3 - x^2 - 2x + 1$
    (f) $3x^3 + 8x^2 + 3x - 2$ (g) $x^3 - 6x^2 - x + 30$

* 5 If $x^3 + 2x^2 + ax + b$ leaves a remainder 2 when divided by $(x - 1)$ and a remainder 3 when divided by $(x + 1)$ find a and b.

3.20 Flowcharts and Iterative Methods

A flowchart is a useful device for representing any series of operations which have a logical pattern, or repeat.

Worked Example 3.15

Follow the flowchart shown in Fig. 3.1.
(a) What number does the flowchart give?
(b) How can you alter it to give $\frac{1}{3}$?

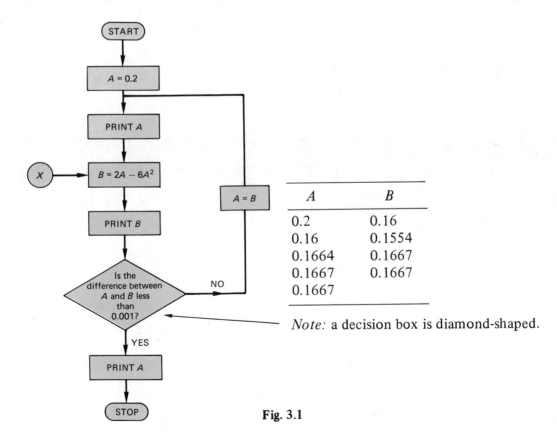

A	B
0.2	0.16
0.16	0.1554
0.1664	0.1667
0.1667	0.1667
0.1667	

Note: a decision box is diamond-shaped.

Fig. 3.1

61

Notes: (a) PRINT A means only print the value of A at that part of the loop.

(b) $A = B$ means change A to whatever value B has.

(c) The values calculated are shown in the table beside Fig. 3.1.

This flowchart which continually uses the same formula $B = 2A - 6A^2$ is called an *iteration*.

Since eventually A and B are equal, it must solve the equation

$$A = 2A - 6A^2;$$

i.e. $$6A^2 - A = 0, \therefore A (6A - 1) = 0$$

$\therefore$ $$A = 0 \text{ or } A = \tfrac{1}{6}.$$

As a decimal, $\tfrac{1}{6} = 0.166\dot{6}$.

(a) The flowchart gives $\tfrac{1}{6}$ as a decimal.

(b) In order to give a value of $\tfrac{1}{3}$, we need to change box X.

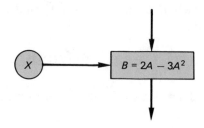

Using the notation of sequences in section 2.2 box X can be written

$$u_{n+1} = 2u_n - 3u_n^2.$$

The starting value would be called u_0.

$u_0 = 0.2,$
$u_1 = 2 \times 0.2 - 3 \times 0.2^2 = 0.16,$
$u_2 = 2 \times 0.16 - 3 \times 0.16^2 = 0.1664,$ etc.

Worked Example 3.16

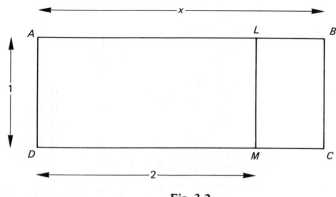

Fig. 3.2

The rectangle $ABCD$ is divided into two smaller rectangles by the line LM.
$AD = 1, DM = 2, AB = x$; see Fig. 3.2.

(a) Write down MC in terms of x.

(b) Rectangles $ABCD$ and $BCML$ are similar. Use this fact to write down two expressions that must necessarily be equal to each other and show that $x^2 - 2x - 1 = 0$.

(c) Show that the equation $x^2 - 2x - 1 = 0$ can be written in the form

$$x = 2 + \frac{1}{x}.$$

With $x_0 = 3$ use $x_{n+1} = 2 + \frac{1}{x_n}$ to calculate x_1 and x_2. Write down all the figures shown by your calculator.

(d) Continue the iteration and find a solution of the equation $x^2 - 2x - 1 = 0$, correct to three significant figures.   [LEAG]

Solution

(a) $MC = x - 2$.

(b) $\dfrac{BC}{AB} = \dfrac{MC}{BC}$. (See section 8.11 on similar figures.)

$\therefore \qquad BC^2 = MC \cdot AB$

$\therefore 1 = (x - 2)x = x^2 - 2x$

$\therefore x^2 - 2x - 1 = 0$ (1)

(c) Equation (1) can be written $x^2 = 2x + 1$.

Divide each side by x: $\qquad x = \dfrac{2x}{x} + \dfrac{1}{x}$

i.e. $\qquad\qquad\qquad\qquad x = 2 + \dfrac{1}{x}$.

Change this into an iteration formula:

$x_{n+1} = 2 + \dfrac{1}{x_n}$.

$x_0 = 3$,

$x_1 = 2 + \frac{1}{3} = 2.333\,333\,333$,

$x_2 = 2 + \dfrac{1}{2.333\,333\,333} = 2.428\,571\,429$.

(d) The change from x_1 to x_2 is too much to give an answer, so try again:

$x_3 = 2 + \dfrac{1}{2.428\,571\,429} = 2.411\,764\,706$,

$x_4 = 2 + \dfrac{1}{2.411\,764\,706} = 2.414\,634\,146$,

$x_5 = 2 + \dfrac{1}{2.414\,634\,146} = 2.414\,141\,414$.

Hence $x = 2.41$ (3 s.f.).

63

Exercise 3

1 The quadratic equation with solutions $2\frac{1}{2}$ and -3 is:

A $x^2 - 0.5x - 7.5 = 0$ **B** $x^2 + 0.5x + 7.5 = 0$

C $2x^2 - x + 15 = 0$ **D** $2x^2 + x - 15 = 0$

2 If $t = \dfrac{x}{y} + c$, then y equals:

A $\dfrac{x}{t + c}$ **B** $\dfrac{x}{t} - \dfrac{x}{c}$

C $\dfrac{x}{t - c}$ **D** $\dfrac{x}{t} + \dfrac{x}{c}$

3 The expression which must be added to $3x - y$ to make $7x + 4y$ is

A $10x + 3y$ **B** $4x + 3y$ **C** $4x + 4y$ **D** $4x + 5y$
E $-4x - 5y$ [LEAG]

4 If $x - 4$ is a factor of $x^2 - 3kx + 28$, then k equals:

A $-3\frac{2}{3}$ **B** $3\frac{2}{3}$ **C** $9\frac{1}{3}$ **D** $-9\frac{1}{3}$

5 If $1 \leqslant a \leqslant 4$ and $2 \leqslant b \leqslant 3$, then the smallest value of $\dfrac{a}{a + b}$ is:

A $\frac{2}{3}$ **B** $\frac{4}{7}$ **C** $\frac{1}{4}$ **D** $\frac{1}{3}$

6 If $x = 2y + 1$, then $x^2 - 2xy - y^2$ simplifies to:

A $-y^2 - 2y + 1$ **B** $-y^2 + 2y + 1$

C $-y^2 + 6y + 1$ **D** $-y^2 - 6y + 1$

7 If $\dfrac{1}{u} + \dfrac{1}{v} = \dfrac{1}{f}$, then if $u + v = 2$, f equals:

A 2 **B** $\frac{1}{2}$ **C** $\dfrac{uv}{2}$ **D** none of these

8 If $\dfrac{x - 2y}{x + 2y} = \dfrac{4}{5}$, then $\dfrac{x}{y}$ equals:

A 18 **B** $\dfrac{1}{18}$ **C** $4\frac{1}{2}$ **D** $\frac{1}{4}$

9 If $y = \dfrac{5x - 3}{2}$,

then I $x = \dfrac{2y}{5} + 3$ II when $y = 0$, $x = \frac{3}{5}$

III $x = \dfrac{2y + 3}{5}$ IV $x = (2y + 3) - 5$

A II only **B** IV only **C** II and III only **D** II and IV only
[OLE]

10 If the solution set of the equations $x + 4y = 6$ and $3x + ky = 9$ is ϕ, then k equals:

A 4 **B** 12 **C** $\frac{4}{3}$ **D** none of these

11 The table gives some values of u and the corresponding values of T:

u	2	4	5
T	10	2.5	1.6

Which of the following could be the relation connecting T and u?

A $T = \dfrac{78 - 14u}{5}$ **B** $T = \dfrac{20}{u}$ **C** $T = \dfrac{70 - 15u}{4}$ **D** $T = \dfrac{40}{u^2}$

[NISEC]

12 When a container is filled with water, the whole weighs 32 kg. When one-third of the water has been poured away, the weight becomes 24 kg. What will be the weight when one-half of the water is left?

A 20 kg **B** 18 kg **C** 16 kg **D** 12 kg [AEB 1982]

13 Solve the equation $\dfrac{x}{4} = \dfrac{9}{x}$.

14 If $ax = a + by^2$, express a in terms of b, x and y in its simplest form.

*15 One factor of the expression $2x^3 - 7x^2 + 2x + 3$ is $(x - 3)$. Factorize the expression completely.

16 Factorize $4a^2 + 16ab + 16b^2 - 25c^2$.

17 If $v = u + at$ and $s = ut + \frac{1}{2}at^2$, find a formula for a which does not contain t, simplifying your answer.

18 Given that $y = a^2 - b^2$ and a and b are positive, find:
    (a) a when $y = 17$, $b = 2\sqrt{3}$;
    (b) b when $a = \sqrt{\frac{1}{3}}$ and $y = \frac{2}{9}$.

19 A fraction $\dfrac{a}{b}$ is such that adding 1 to the numerator gives the same result as subtracting one from the denominator. What is the value of $a - b$?

20 Using the formula $T = 100n + \dfrac{k}{v^2}$,

    (a) find the value of T if $n = 2$, $k = 1000$ and $v = 250$;
    (b) find the value of n if $T = 200$ and $k = 4v^2$.
    (c) express v in terms of T, n and k.

21 Factorize completely:
    (a) $4(x + 1)^2 - 3(x + 1)$
    (b) $(2a + 3b)^2 - (4a - b)^2$
    (c) $x^3 + x^2 - 6x$

22 Write down those solutions, if any, of the equation

$$(x - \sqrt{2})(3x - 1) = 0$$

which are:
    (a) integers
    (b) rational
    (c) irrational
    (d) real [OLE]

23 Simplify:
    (a) $4p^2 - 2p^2$ (b) $(4x)^2 \div 2x$ (c) $2x^2 \times (3x)^2$

24 In the rectangle $ABCD$ in Fig. 3.3, $AB = x$ cm and $BC = 1$ cm. The line LM is drawn so that $ALMD$ is a square.

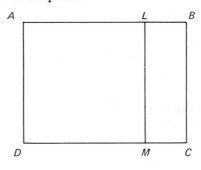

Fig. 3.3

Write down, in terms of x,
(a)   the length LB;

(b)   the ratios $\dfrac{AB}{BC}$ and $\dfrac{BC}{LB}$.

(c)   If $\dfrac{AB}{BC} = \dfrac{BC}{LB}$, obtain a quadratic equation in x. Hence find x correct to
two decimal places.
[London]

25 Make x the subject of the following formulae:

(a) $y = \sqrt{\dfrac{(4x^2 + 3)t}{q}}$ (b) $hx + ky + m = 0$ (c) $4x = yt - xk$.

26 (a)   Given that d varies directly as the square root of h and that $d = 7$ when
$h = 4$, find
(i)   the value of d when $h = 25$,
(ii) the value of h when $d = 14$.

(b)   Show that if $3^x \times 3^{2(x^2-2)} = 3^4$, then the values of x are given by:

$$2x^2 + x - 8 = 0.$$

Hence, calculate the positive value of x, correct to two decimal places.
[AEB 1982]

In questions 27–29 the equations are all based on examination questions.

27 Find x:
(a) $4(3 - 2x) = 5$;   (b) $2x^2 + x - 6 = 0$;

(c) $4x(3 + x) = 0$,   (d) $2x + \dfrac{x}{3} = 5$;

(e) $\dfrac{2 + x}{4} - \dfrac{2 - x}{4} = \frac{1}{2}$;   (f) $4x^2 - 100 = 0$;

(g) $\dfrac{3}{x + 1} = 4$;   (h) $3(x + 2) - (x - 2) = 6$;

(i) $(x - 2)(x + 2) = 5$;   (j) $\dfrac{4}{x^2} = \dfrac{x}{2}$.

28 Make x the subject:
(a) $q - x = 4y$;   (b) $T = \sqrt{\dfrac{4}{x + 2}}$;

(c) $y = \dfrac{4x + t}{x}$;   (d) $x^2 + y^2 = r^2$;

(e) $x - y = \dfrac{4}{x + y}$;   (f) $A = \dfrac{4\sqrt{x^2 + y^2}}{t}$;

(g) $ax + by + c = 0$;   (h) $E = \frac{1}{2}mx^2$;

(i) $F = \dfrac{1}{x} + \dfrac{1}{f}$.

29 Factorize:
(a) $2tq^2 - 18t$ (b) $4tq + 8t^2$
(c) $2tx + 2ty - 3x - 3y$ (d) $32x^2 - 28x - 99$
(e) $x^3 + x^2 - 2$

30 Evaluate the unknown quantity in each equation, using the values $a = 2$,
$b = -1, c = -4$:
(a) $A = 3a - 2b + c$;   (b) $B = 4a + 5b^2$;
(c) $C = a - b^2 - 2c$;   (d) $D = 5ab - 3bc + 2ac$.

31 (a) Solve the equations:
$$3x + 4y = 2,$$
$$5x - 3y = 13.$$

(b) Given that $\dfrac{1}{u} + \dfrac{1}{v} = \dfrac{1}{f}$, express u in terms of v and f.

(c) Express $x^2 + 8x + 25$ in the form $(x + k)^2 + t$, hence show that whatever the value of x, $x^2 + 8x + 25$ cannot equal 8.

32 Jane earned £y a week for the first w weeks of the year, and £r a week for the rest of the year. Write down an expression for her average weekly wage.

33 The pressure P at a point in a liquid is proportional to the depth h of the point below the surface. If $P = 460$ when $h = 5$, write down a relationship connecting P and h. Hence find the value of h when $P = 600$.

34 The force F between two objects is inversely proportional to the square of the distance d between them. If $F = 400$ when $d = 2$, write down a relationship connecting F and d. Use this to find
(a) the value of F when $d = 1$;
(b) the value of d when $F = 25$.

35 Kepler's third law states that the square of the time T (days) of a planet to complete one orbit of the Sun is proportional to the cube of the average distance D (km) from the Sun.

For the planet Venus, $T = 88$ days and $D = 58 \times 10^6$ km. Work out a formula connecting T and D. Assuming that the average distance of the Earth from the Sun is 1.5×10^8 km, find how many days the formula predicts that the Earth takes to travel round the Sun.

36 Two congruent rectangles $ABCD$ and $PQRS$ each of length l metres and breadth b metres are placed to form the capital letter 'T' as shown in Fig. 3.4.

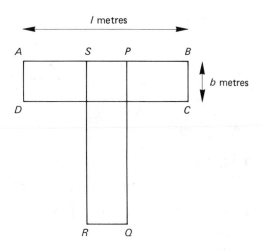

Fig. 3.4

(a) (i) Show, with an explanation using words or a diagram, that the area A square metres of the T-shape is given by the formula $A = b(2l - b)$.
(ii) Rearrange this formula to express l in terms of A and b.

(b) Find the formula for the perimeter p metres of the T-shape. [SEB]

1	2	3	4	5	6	7	8	9
10	11	12	13	14	15	16	17	18
19	20	21	22	23	24	25	26	27
28	29	30	31	32	33	34	35	36
37	38	39	40	41	42	43	44	45
46	47	48	49	50	51	52	53	54
55	56	57	58	59	60	61	62	63
64	65	66	67	68	69	70	71	72
73	74	75	76	77	78	79	80	81

Fig. 3.5

Figure 3.5 shows a number square with an outline 'T' on it. The number at the base of the outline is 20, so we say that the outline is 'based on 20'. Using a translation, the outline can be moved so that it is based on a different number, but it must always remain upright and completely within the number square.

(a) Find the total of the five numbers in the outline when it is based on 40.

(b) If the outline is based on x, write down (in terms of x) the other four numbers in the outline and show that the total of the five numbers in the outline is $5x - 63$.

(c) Find the five numbers in the outline, given that their total is 287.

(d) Explain why the total of the five numbers in the outline could not be
(i) 290,   (ii) 117.   [MEG]

38 (a) Copy Table 3.1, and use the flowchart in Fig. 3.6 to find the remaining values of P, Q, R and S.

Table 3.1

N	P	Q	R	S
1.234	123.4	123.9	123	1.23
0.4068				
0.007				
3.999				

(b) What is the relation between N and S?

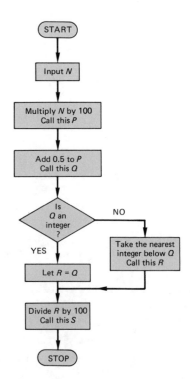

Fig. 3.6

[O & C]

39 (a) The flowchart in Fig. 3.7 will solve a certain equation by an iterative method.
  (i) Work through the flowchart, writing down each value of x. State the final value to the appropriate degree of accuracy.
  (ii) Find and simplify the equation which the flowchart solves.
(b) (i) Show algebraically that the iteration

$$u_{n+1} = \sqrt{\sqrt{12u_n}}$$

  also solves the same equation.
  (ii) Use this iteration, starting again with $x = 2$, to find the root to the same degree of accuracy.
(c) Comment on your results. [O & C]

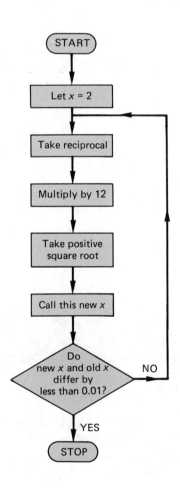

Fig. 3.7

40 (a) The flowchart in Fig. 3.8 gives a method of calculating approximately the area z under part of the graph of $y = 10x^2$.

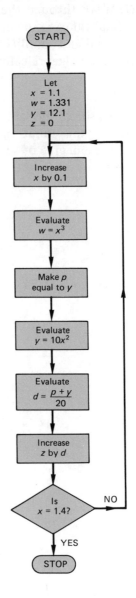

Fig. 3.8

Copy the table (allowing plenty of width) and complete it by using the chart, recording each new value as you obtain it.

x	w	p	y	d	z
1.1	1.331	—	12.1	—	0

(b) Using scales of 5 cm to a unit for w and 1 cm to a unit for z, draw axes for $0 \leqslant w \leqslant 3$ and $-5 \leqslant z \leqslant 5$, with the w-axis across the page.

Rounding the values in the table to one decimal place, plot the points (w, z).

(c) It is known that $z = hw + k$, where h and k are constant. Rule the best line for your plotted points and use it to find the values of h and k.   [O & C]

* **41** A solid cuboid of length p metres has a square cross-section of side $(p - 3)$ metres. Write down, in terms of p, expressions for:
(a) the surface area of the square cross-section;
(b) the surface area of one of the longer faces of the cuboid.
Given that the total surface area of the cuboid is 39 square metres, write down an equation in p and show that it reduces to

$$2p^2 - 8p - 7 = 0.$$

Find the two values of p which satisfy this equation, giving your answers correct to three significant figures.
Hence write down the dimensions of the cuboid. [UCLES]

* **42** An aeroplane travelled a distance of 500 km at an average speed of x km/h. Write down an expression for the number of hours taken.
On the return journey the average speed was increased by 10 km/h. Write down an expression for the number of hours taken on the return journey.
Given that the time taken for the return journey was 5 *minutes* less than that of the outward journey, form an equation in x and show that it reduces to

$$x^2 + 10x - 60\,000 = 0.$$

Given that $x^2 + 10x - 60\,000$ can be expressed in the form $(x + 250)(x - p)$, find the value of p.
Hence find the time taken on the outward journey. [UCLES]

43 A sequence is defined by $u_n = \frac{1}{2}n(n + 1)$.
(a) Work out u_0, u_1, u_2, u_3 and u_4.
(b) Work out $u_1 - u_0, u_2 - u_1, u_3 - u_2$ and $u_4 - u_3$.
(c) Write down u_{n-1}, and simplify $u_n - u_{n-1}$.
(d) Hence show that $1 + 2 + 3 + \ldots + n = u_n$.
(e) If the sum of the first n positive integers is 4950, show that $n^2 + n - 9900 = 0$, and hence find the value of n. [MEG]

44 (a) If p is the largest whole number which is a perfect square and which is also less than or equal to n, find p when
  (i) $n = 4.9$,
  (ii) $n = 49$,
  (iii) $n = 490$.
(b) The flow diagram in Fig. 3.9 can be used to find the approximate square root of 20, after first choosing an appropriate whole number x as an estimate of $\sqrt{20}$. [SEG]

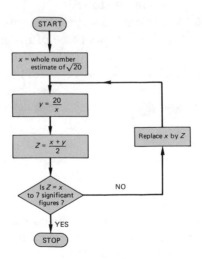

Fig. 3.9

Start with $x = 4$ and make out a table like the one here to show every stage in finding $\sqrt{20}$ to 7 significant figures. Show all the figures on your calculator at each stage.

x	y	Z	Difference between x and Z
4.0 4.5 4.472 222 2 etc.	5.0 4.444 444 4	4.5	0.5

45 A ring of 'stepping stones' has 14 stones in it, as shown in Fig. 3.10.

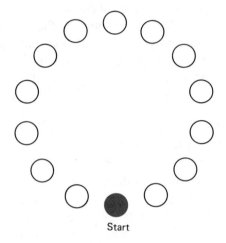

Start

Fig. 3.10

A girls hops round the ring, stopping to change feet every time she has made 3 hops. She notices that when she has been round the ring three times, she has stopped to change feet on each one of the 14 stones.
(a) The girl now hops round the ring, stopping to change feet every time she has made 4 hops. Explain why in this case she will not stop on each one of the 14 stones no matter how long she continues hopping round the ring.
(b) The girl stops to change feet every time she has made n hops. For which values of n will she stop on each one of the 14 stones to change feet?
(c) Find a general rule for the values of n when the ring contains more (or less) than 14 stones. [NEA]

46 A gardener always plants his white and red rose bushes in a special pattern. Fig. 3.11 shows three of his arrangements.

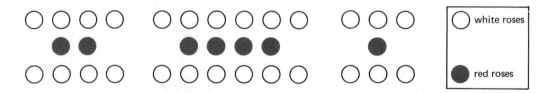

Fig. 3.11

(a) Draw another way he could plant bushes which still fits his pattern.
(b) How many white rose bushes would he need for an arrangement which used 27 red ones?
(c) How many red bushes would he need if he planted 100 white ones?

(d) If R stands for the number of red bushes used and W stands for the number of white ones used, write a formula connecting R and W for this pattern. (W =   )

(e) Another gardener always plants his rose bushes using the rule W = 3R + 4. Find the *total* number of bushes used if there are 10 red ones.

(f) Find the value of R given by the formula if W is 20.

(g) What does this tell you about a pattern using 20 white roses?

[SEG]

4 The Metric System

4.1   Units

The standard unit of length is the *metre* (m).
   1 kilometre (km)   = 1000 m
   1 millimetre (mm) = 0.001 m
   1 centimetre (cm) = 0.01 m
            1 cm = 10 mm
   1 square metre will be written 1 m^2
   1 cubic metre will be written 1 m^3
   1 hectare = 10 000 m^2
   1 litre = 1000 cm^3
The standard unit of mass is the kilogram (kg).
   1 kg   = 1000 grams
   1 gram (g)   = 0.001 kg
   1 milligram (mg) = 0.001 g
The standard unit of time is the second (s).
Speeds, for example 8 metres per second, are written 8 m/s in this book (rather than 8 m s^{-1}).

4.2   Changing Units in Area and Volume

How many mm^2 are there in 1 cm^2?
A very common but incorrect answer is 10.
   Figure 4.1 shows an enlarged centimetre square divided into square millimetres (shaded). It can be seen that the answer is $100 = 10^2$.

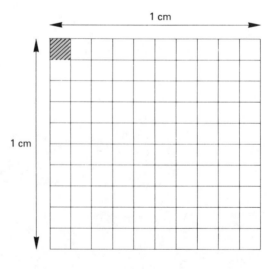

Fig. 4.1

74

When changing units of area, the multiplication factor is the square of the multiplication factor for the unit of length.

Similarly, when changing units of volume, we find that the multiplication factor is the cube of the multiplication factor for the unit of length.

4.3 Conversion of Units Involving Rates

How can we change 80 m/s into km/h?

Write 80 m/s as $\dfrac{80 \text{ m}}{1 \text{ s}}$.

But 1000 m = 1 km, $\therefore$ 1 m = $\frac{1}{1000}$ km.
    3600 s = 1 h, $\therefore$ 1 s = $\frac{1}{3600}$ h.

Hence $\dfrac{80 \text{ m}}{1 \text{ s}} = \dfrac{80 \times \frac{1}{1000} \text{ km}}{1 \times \frac{1}{3600} \text{ h}} = \dfrac{8\cancel{0}}{1\cancel{0}\cancel{0}\cancel{0}} \times \dfrac{36\cancel{0}\cancel{0} \text{ km/h}}{1}$

$$= 288 \text{ km/h}.$$

Another example: how can we change 80 g/cm³ into kg/m³?

Write 80 g/cm³ as $\dfrac{80 \text{ g}}{1 \text{ cm}^3}$.

1000 g = 1 kg, $\therefore$ 1 g = $\frac{1}{1000}$ kg.
1 m³ = (100)³ cm³, $\therefore$ 1 cm³ = $\frac{1}{100\,000}$ m³,

$$\therefore \dfrac{80 \text{ g}}{1 \text{ cm}^3} = \dfrac{80 \times \frac{1}{1000}}{1 \times \frac{1}{1\,000\,000}} = 80\,000 \text{ kg/m}^3.$$

Check 20

1 Express the following lengths in cm.
   (a) 4.3 m   (b) 684 mm   (c) 400 m   (d) 0.05 m
   (e) 2.5 mm   (f) 863 km   (g) 0.04 km   (h) 1255 mm
2 Express the following lengths in km:
   (a) 625 cm   (b) 8000 cm   (c) 9400 mm   (d) 895 m   (e) 86.9 cm
3 Express the following masses in g:
   (a) 8 kg   (b) 0.04 kg   (c) 685 mg   (d) 65 kg   (e) 1.8 mg   (f) 900 kg
4 Express the following areas in cm² :
   (a) 9.6 m²   (b) 2875 mm²   (c) 0.048 km²
5 Change the following volumes into litres:
   (a) 600 cm³   (b) 28 m³   (c) 2 km³
6 Carry out the following conversions:
   (a) 20 m/s into km/h   (b) 25 km/h into m/s   (c) 8 g/cm³ into kg/l

4.4 Area

A list of formulae for the areas of a number of useful shapes is given in Fig. 4.2. Proofs are not given as these can be found elsewhere.

Rectangle

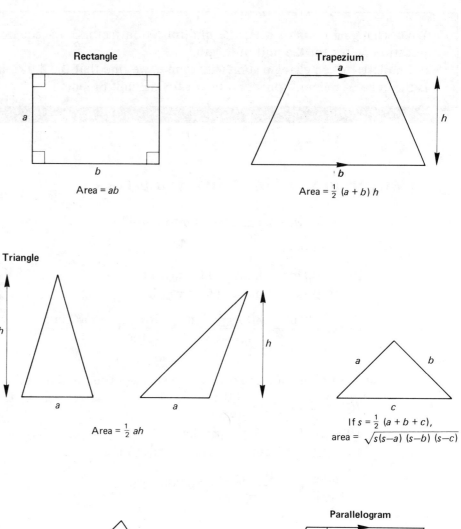

Trapezium

Triangle

Parallelogram

Circle

Rhombus

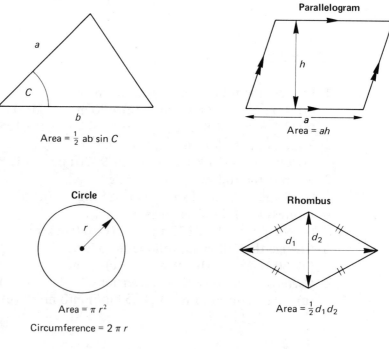

Fig. 4.2

Worked Example 4.1

Not to scale

Fig. 4.3

The faces of a round and a square clock have exactly the same area (Fig. 4.3). The round clock has a radius of 10 cm. How wide is the square clock?   [SEG]

Solution

This question contains some simple ideas of changing the subject of the formula.

The area of the round clock $= \pi \times 10^2$ cm^2
$= 314.2$ cm^2.

If d is the side of the square clock, then

$$d^2 = 314.2$$
$$\therefore d = \sqrt{314.2} = 17.7.$$

The square clock is 17.7 cm wide.

4.5 Volume

Formulae for finding volumes are given in Fig. 4.4.

Sphere

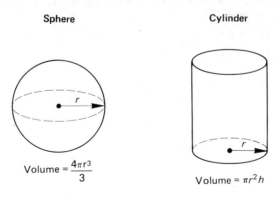

Volume $= \dfrac{4\pi r^3}{3}$

Cylinder

Volume $= \pi r^2 h$

Cone

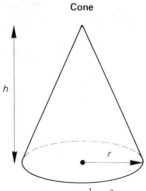

Volume $= \frac{1}{3}\pi r^2 h$

The point of the cone need not be above the centre of the base.

Fig. 4.4

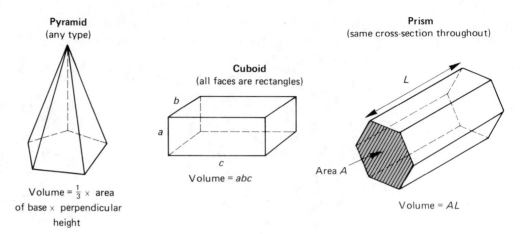

Pyramid
(any type)

Volume = $\frac{1}{3}$ × area
of base × perpendicular
height

Cuboid
(all faces are rectangles)

Volume = abc

Prism
(same cross-section throughout)

Area A

Volume = AL

Fig. 4.4 cont.

*4.6   Density

The mass of a unit volume of a given substance is called its *density*.

Density = $\dfrac{\text{Mass}}{\text{Volume}}$.

Units are kg/m³ etc.

See Worked Example 4.3.

4.7   Surface Area

Referring again to Fig. 4.4,

Sphere: surface area = $4\pi r^2$.
Cylinder: curved surface area = $2\pi rh$.
total surface area including the ends
$= 2\pi r^2 + 2\pi rh = 2\pi r(r + h)$.
Cuboid: surface area = $2ab + 2bc + 2ac$.
Cone: we need to assume that the vertex of the cone is above the centre of the base. If the slanting edge of the cone is of length l (Fig. 4.5), then the curved surface area of the cone = πrl.
Total surface area = $\pi r^2 + \pi rl$
$= \pi r(r + l)$.

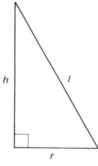

Note: $l^2 = h^2 + r^2$.

Fig. 4.5

When using any of the formulae for area and volume, it is important (in fact, necessary), that all measurements are in the same units.

Practise using the following check exercise.

Check 21

1 Find the area of the shapes in Fig. 4.6; all measurements are in cm ($\pi = 3.14$).

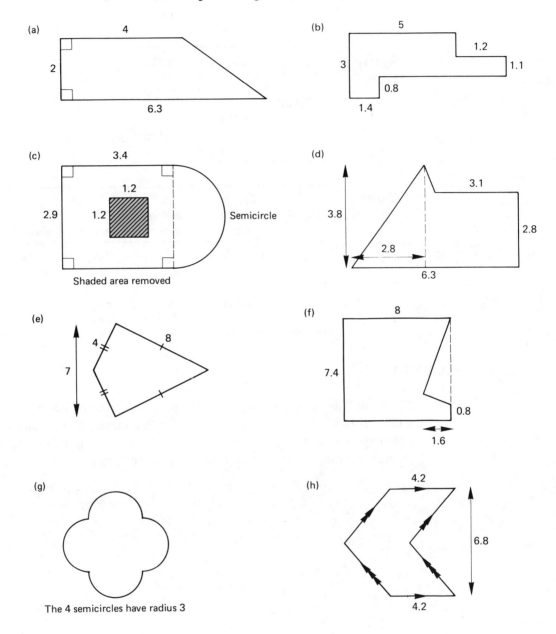

Fig. 4.6

2 A cuboid shaped box measuring 2 m x 85 cm x 1.6 m is packed with small $\frac{1}{2}$ cm cubes. How many can be packed into the box?

3 Find the area of a regular hexagon with sides of length 6 cm.

4 The sides of a rectangle are of length $3x$ and $4x$ cm. Given that the area of the rectangle is 147 cm², find x.

5 The following questions involve the use of $\pi = \frac{22}{7}$ in the calculations. All answers should be expressed as fractions if possible. Copy and complete the tables:

Cylinder:

Volume	Height	Radius	Total surface area
	4 cm	7 cm	
176 m³		2 m	
	70 cm	1 m	
		14 cm	1408 cm²

Sphere:

Volume	Surface	Radius
		21 cm
$33\frac{11}{21}$ m³		
	9856 cm²	
		1.4 cm
	98.56 m²	

Cone:

Volume	Curved surface area	Total surface area	Base radius	Height	Slant height
			7 cm	4 cm	
				12 cm	13 cm
154 cm³				3 cm	
	704 m²		8 m		
		1496 cm²	14 cm		

Worked Example 4.2

Figure 4.7 shows a horizontal rectangle *ABCD* where *AB* = 2 m and *AD* = 1 m, which forms the open top of a water container of semicircular cross-section. Calculate the capacity of the water container (a) in cubic metres; (b) in litres, giving your answer in each case to 3 significant figures.

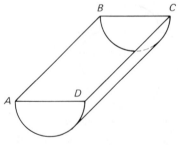

Fig. 4.7

The water container, including the ends, is to be made out of sheet metal. Calculate the area of sheet metal required in square metres, correct to three significant figures.

Calculate also the area of the surface of the water when the depth of the water at the deepest point is 0.2 m, giving your answer in square metres ($\pi = 3.14$).

[OLE]

Solution

(a)   The shape is best regarded as half a cylinder.

$\therefore$ Volume $= \frac{1}{2}\pi r^2 h = \frac{1}{2} \times 3.14 \times 0.5^2 \times 2$

Radius is $\frac{1}{2}AD$ AB is height

$= 0.785 \text{ m}^3$

(b)   1 litre $= 1000 \text{ cm}^3$.

$1 \text{ m}^3 = (100)^3 \text{ cm}^3 = 1\,000\,000 \text{ cm}^3 = 1000$ litres,

$\therefore$ capacity is 785 litres.

The surface area of the container is also half the total surface area of a cylinder.

$\therefore$ Area of metal $= \frac{1}{2} \times 2\pi r(r + h) = \pi r(r + h)$

$= 3.14 \times 0.5 \times 2.5 = 3.93 \text{ m}^2$.

To find the surface area of the water when the depth is 0.2 m, we need to find the distance XY shown in Fig. 4.8.

Since $PQ = 0.3$ m and $XP = 0.5$ m (radius),

$XQ = 0.4$ ($\triangle XPQ$ is a 3, 4, 5 triangle).

$\therefore$ Surface area $= 0.8 \times 2$

$= 1.6 \text{ m}^2$.

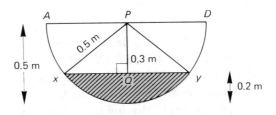

Fig. 4.8

Worked Example 4.3

A roll of copper wire is made of wire 200 m long with a circular cross-section of diameter 1.2 mm. Calculate the volume of the coil.

If the density of copper is 8.8 g/cm³, calculate the weight of the copper wire in kilograms.

Solution

Care must be taken with the units. Since the density is given per cubic centimetre, it is best to calculate the volume in cubic centimetres.

Using $V = \pi r^2 h$,

$V = 3.14 \times 0.06^2 \times 20\,000$

$= 226 \text{ cm}^3$.

$\therefore$ Weight $= \dfrac{226 \times 8.8}{1000}$ kg

$= 1.989 \text{ kg}$.

Worked Example 4.4

Figure 4.9 shows the vertical front face of a greenhouse. (The back face of the greenhouse is identical to the front face and the base of the greenhouse is rectangular.) $\triangle ABE$ is isosceles, with $AB = AE = 1.0$ m, and $BCDE$ is a trapezium with $BC = ED = 1.4$ m, $BE = 1.5$ m and $CD = 1.9$ m.

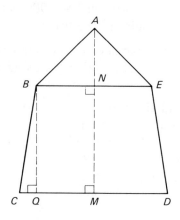

Fig. 4.9

Calculate, to two decimal places,
(a) the height AN of $\triangle ABE$ and the distance NM;
(b) the area of $\triangle ABE$ and the area of the trapezium $BCDE$. The length of the greenhouse from front to back is 2.5 m and the whole of each of its six faces (front, back, sloping sides and roof) is covered with glass.
   Find:
(c) the total area, in m², of glass;
(d) the volume, in m³, of air inside the greenhouse.   [L]

Solution

(a) By Pythagoras' theorem,

$$AB^2 = AN^2 + NB^2,$$

$$\therefore \quad 1^2 = AN^2 + (0.75)^2,$$

$$\therefore \quad AN = \sqrt{1 - 0.5625} = 0.66 \text{ m}.$$

BQ is a construction line, not on the original diagram.

$$\therefore \quad CB^2 = BQ^2 + CQ^2 = NM^2 + (0.2)^2,$$

$$\therefore \quad 1.4^2 - 0.2^2 = NM,$$

$$\text{hence} \quad NM = 1.39 \text{ m}.$$

(b) Area of $\triangle ABE = \frac{1}{2} \times 1.5 \times 0.66 = 0.5$ m².
   Area of trapezium $BCDE = \frac{1}{2}(1.9 + 1.5) \times 1.39 = 2.36$ m².
(c) The surface consists of two rectangles $1 \times 2.5 = 5$ m²
                       two rectangles $1.4 \times 2.5 = 7$ m².
   Two ends $2.36 + 0.5 = 5.72$ m².
   $\therefore$ Total area of glass $= 17.72$ m².
       To calculate the volume, the greenhouse can be regarded as a prism.

$$\text{Volume} = \text{Area of end} \times 2.5.$$
$$= 2.86 \times 2.5$$
$$= 7.15 \, \text{m}^3.$$

*4.8   Approximating Areas, Trapezium Rule

There are many occasions when an area (or volume) cannot be found exactly by formula.

The following technique, known as the *trapezium rule*, can be used in many situations (see section 4.12 on velocity- (speed-) time graphs).

In order to find the shaded area in Fig. 4.10 it has been divided into four trapezia (any number can be used). The width of each trapezium is h. The y values y_1, $y_2, \ldots$, give the length of the sides.

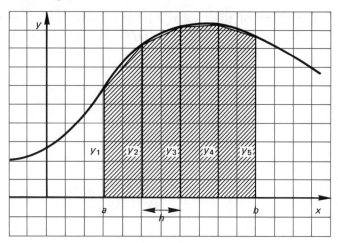

Fig. 4.10

$$\text{Total area} = \frac{h}{2}(y_1 + y_2) + \frac{h}{2}(y_2 + y_3) + \frac{h}{2}(y_3 + y_4) + \frac{h}{2}(y_4 + y_5).$$

$$\text{Factorizing:} \quad = \frac{h}{2}(y_1 + 2y_2 + 2y_3 + 2y_4 + y_5).$$

This formula is easily extended to any number of trapezia.
See Worked Example 4.6.

4.9   Sectors and Segments

Referring to Fig. 4.11,

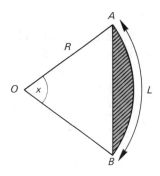

Fig. 4.11

length of arc $L = 2\pi R \times \dfrac{x}{360}$,

area of sector $OAB = \pi R^2 \times \dfrac{x}{360}$,

* area of segment (shaded) $= \dfrac{\pi R^2 x}{360} - \dfrac{1}{2}R^2 \sin x°$.

This is found from area of sector *minus* area of triangle.

Worked Example 4.5

The shape of the top of a table in a cafe is shown by the part of the circle, centre O, in Fig. 4.12. The angle $BOD = 90°$ and $BO = OD = 50$ cm.

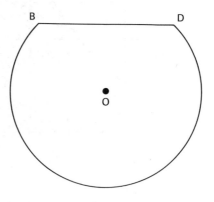

Fig. 4.12

The top of the table is made of laminate and a thin metal strip is fixed to its perimeter.
(a) Calculate
    (i) the length of the metal strip,
    (ii) the area of the laminate surface.
(b) If the table top is to be cut from a square of laminate of area 1 m², what percentage of laminate is wasted?   [SEG]

Solution

(a) (i) The perimeter of the table is found in two parts, the straight part BD, and the arc of a circle. Since triangle BOD is right-angled, Pythagoras' theorem states
$$BD^2 = BO^2 + OD^2$$
$\therefore BD^2 = 50^2 + 50^2 = 2500 + 2500 = 5000$
$\therefore BD = 70.7$

The arc of the circle corresponds to 270°, hence its length is given by:
$$\text{arc} = 2 \times \pi \times 50 \times \frac{270}{360} = 235.6 \text{ cm.}$$

Length of metal strip = 235.6 + 70.7 = 306.3 cm.

(ii) The area of the triangle $BOD = \frac{1}{2} \times 50 \times 50 = 1250$ cm^2.

The area of the rest $= \pi \times 50^2 \times \dfrac{270}{360} = 5890$ cm^2.

The area of the laminate = 1250 + 5890 = 7140 cm^2.

(b) 1 m^2 = 100 × 100 = 10 000 cm^2.

Amount of laminate wasted = 10 000 − 7140 = 2860.

The percentage wasted $= \dfrac{2860}{10\,000} \times 100 = 28.6\%$.

Check 22

1 Use the trapezium rule with 5 strips to find the area under the curve $y = x^2 + 1$ between $x = 1$ and $x = 2$.

2 The values in the table give the relationship between x and t:

t	0	1	2	3	4	5
x	0.8	1.3	1.8	2	1.4	0.8

Use the trapezium rule to find the area under the graph of x plotted against t.

3 Calculate the lengths of arcs of the following:

Radius	Angle subtended at centre
(a) 7 cm	70°
(b) 6370 km	130°
(c) 5.7 m	4° 30′
(d) 6400 km	22° 30′

4 Calculate the radii of the circles for the following:

Arc length	Angle subtended at centre
(a) 5 cm	20°
(b) 7.3 cm	13°
(c) 825 km	75°
(d) 400 km	112° 30′

5 Calculate the angle subtended by the following arcs to the nearest degree:

Radius	Length of arc
(a) 8 cm	12 cm
(b) 6370 km	6370 km
(c) 528 m	49 m
(d) 6370 km	150 km

4.10   Speed, Velocity and Acceleration

Speed is defined as $\dfrac{\text{distance travelled}}{\text{time taken}}$.

More specifically, *average* speed = $\dfrac{\text{total distance travelled}}{\text{total time taken}}$.

Units are m/s, km/h, etc.

Velocity is a *vector*. It describes both the speed and the direction of travel given.

Acceleration = $\dfrac{\text{change in velocity}}{\text{time taken}}$. Slowing down is called *retardation* (negative acceleration).

4.11   Displacement — Time (or Distance — Time) Graphs

If we plot a graph of displacement (distance from a point) against time, as in Fig. 4.13, it can be read as follows:

OA: Straight line means constant speed.
AB: Horizontal line means at rest.
BC: Gradually increasing and then decreasing gradient, means acceleration followed by retardation.
CD: At rest.
DEF: Constant speed returning to *O* and then going beyond *O* for *EF*.
FG: Return to *O* at constant speed.

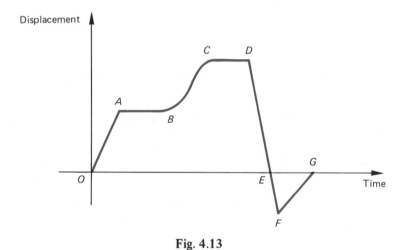

Fig. 4.13

4.12   Velocity (Speed) — Time Graphs

A velocity–time graph (see Fig. 4.14) is interpreted as follows:

OA: Straight line, constant acceleration.
AB: Horizontal line, constant speed (acceleration zero).
BC: Velocity decreasing, not straight, therefore non-uniform retardation.

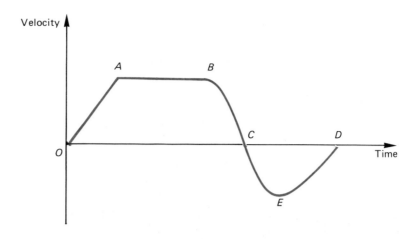

Fig. 4.14

CED: Stops at *C*, increases speed still on opposite direction until *E* is reached, then decreases until it stops at *D*. Non-uniform acceleration.

The area under a velocity–time graph gives the distance travelled. If the graph does not consist of straight lines, the trapezium rule can be used.

Worked Example 4.6

The table below gives the velocity v (m/s) of a body measured every 2 s over a 10 s period. Estimate the distance travelled in that time.

t	0	2	4	6	8	10
v	0	3	7	15	24	20

Solution

The graph would not be a straight line.
∴ Using the trapezium rule, with $h = 2$,

$$\text{Distance} = \frac{2}{2} \ (0 + 2 \times 3 + 2 \times 7 + 2 \times 15 + 2 \times 24 + 20)$$

$$= 118 \ \text{m}.$$

Worked Example 4.7

The diagram, Fig. 4.15, shows the speed–time graph for an underground train travelling between two stations. It starts from rest and accelerates at a constant rate for 10 seconds, then travels at constant speed for 30 seconds, and finally slows down at a constant rate. If the distance between the stations is 850 m, calculate:
(a) the maximum speed; (b) the acceleration; (c) the time it takes to reach the half-way point.

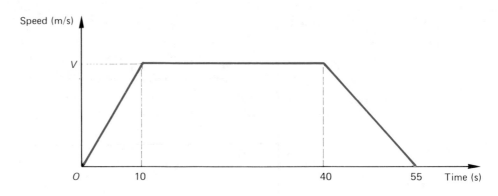

Fig. 4.15

Solution

Many questions on distance–time graphs can be solved on the basis that the area under the graph equals the distance travelled. Look out for triangles, trapeziums, etc.

(a) Area of the trapezium $= \frac{1}{2}(55 + 30)v$

$$= \frac{85v}{2}.$$

But distance = area, $\therefore \frac{85v}{2} = 850$;

this gives $v = 20$.

$\therefore$ Maximum speed = 20 m/s.

(b) The acceleration equals the gradient of the line.

$\therefore$ Acceleration $= \frac{20}{10} = 2$ m/s^2.

(c) To find how long it takes to reach the half-way point, we are trying to find the time T which divides the area under the graph into two equal parts; see Fig. 4.16. The shaded area must equal $\frac{850}{2} = 425$.

Since the triangle Ⓐ has area $= \frac{1}{2} \times 10 \times 20 = 100$, then rectangle Ⓑ has area $425 - 100 = 325$;

$\therefore (T - 10) \times 20 = 325$.

$T - 10 = \frac{325}{20} = 16.25$; $\quad \therefore T = 26.25$.

$\therefore$ It takes 26.25 seconds.

Note: This is not one-half of 55 seconds.

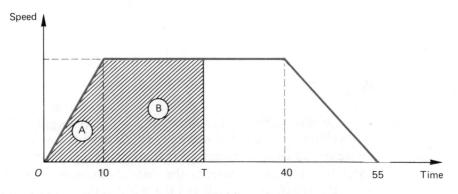

Fig. 4.16

Worked Example 4.8

A particle is moving with an initial speed of 4 m/s. In the next four seconds its speed increases uniformly to 10 m/s and then the speed decreases uniformly until the particle stops moving after a further eight seconds.
(a) Show this information on a speed–time graph.
(b) Find
   (i) the acceleration in the last eight seconds of the motion,
   (ii) the total distance travelled by the particle.   [LEAG]

Solution

(a) The speed–time graph is shown in Fig. 4.17. Always label axes carefully.

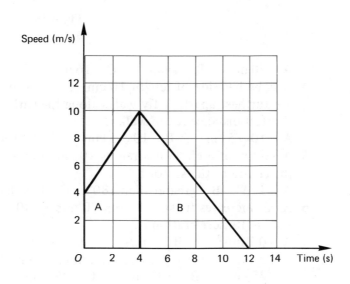

Fig. 4.17

(b) (i) Since the particle is slowing down, the acceleration will be negative.

$$\text{Hence acceleration = gradient of the line} = \frac{-10}{8}$$

$$= -1.25 \text{ m/s}^2.$$

   (ii) Distance travelled equals the area under the graph, which consists of a trapezium A and a triangle B.

$$\text{Distance = area} = \tfrac{1}{2}(4 + 10) \times 4 + \tfrac{1}{2} \times 10 \times 8$$

$$= 28 + 40 = 68 \text{ m.}$$

Exercise 4

1 A piece of wire 4 m long has a volume of 0.4 cm^3. Its cross-sectional area is:
   A   0.01 cm^2 B   0.1 mm^2 C   0.4 mm^2 D   none of these
2 A bucket is in the form of a cylinder of radius 20 cm, and height 40 cm. If the mass of 1 litre of water is 1 kg, then the mass of water in the bucket is:
   A 16π kg   B 160π kg   C 1.6π kg   D   16 kg
3 The diagram (Fig. 4.18) shows the speed-time graph of an object. The total distance travelled is:

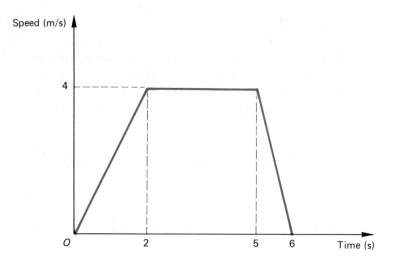

Fig. 4.18

A 20 m   **B** 24 m   **C** 16 m   **D** 18 m

4 A cube has side of length 10 cm. *A* and *B* are two vertices of the cube which are furthest apart. A fly walks along the surface of the cube from *A* to *B*. The shortest distance it can walk is:

A $10\sqrt{5}$ cm   **B** $10\sqrt{3}$ cm   **C** 30 cm   **D** $20\sqrt{2}$ cm

5 A sector of a circle has radius 10 cm, and length of arc 20 cm. The angle at the centre of the sector is:

A 120°   **B** greater than 180°   **C** less than 120°   **D** greater than 120°

6 A car increases its speed from 20 m/s to 40 m/s while travelling a distance of 100 m. Its acceleration is:

A 0.2 m/s²   **B** 6 m/s²   **C** 6 m/s   **D** none of these

7 The radius of a circle whose circumference is 50π cm is

A 25 cm   **B** $12\frac{1}{2}$ cm   **C** 25π cm   **D** $12\frac{1}{2}\pi$ cm

8 The total surface area of a solid hemisphere of radius 7 cm is:

A 245 cm²   **B** 770 cm²   **C** 245π cm²   **D** none of these

9 72 km/h expressed in m/s is:

A 2   **B** 20   **C** 200   **D** 2000

10 The total surface area of a solid cylinder of radius 6 cm and height 2 cm is:

A 144π cm   **B** 108π cm²   **C** 144π cm²   **D** none of these

11 A car covers 84 km in 1 hour 45 minutes. The average speed of the car, in km/h, is

A 132   **B** 84   **C** 63   **D** 48   **E** 24   [LEAG]

12 The length of the semicircular arc *BEC* in Fig. 4.19 is 4π cm. Calculate the area of the square *ABCD*.   [OLE]

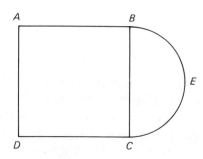

Fig. 4.19

90

13 A rectangular cuboid measures 8 cm by 40 cm by 85 cm. Find, giving your answers in standard form:
(a) its surface area in mm^2 ;
(b) its volume in m^3 .

14 In Fig. 4.20, the radius of the larger circle is twice that of the smaller concentric circle and θ is the angle between two radii of the larger circle.

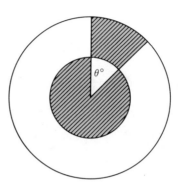

Fig. 4.20

(a) Find the value of θ for which the two shaded regions have equal areas.
(b) Find the value of θ for which the two shaded regions have equal perimeters.

[NISEC]

15 A county council surveyor calculating the costs of road construction determines the costs from the following:
(a) preparation, etc.   £9 000 per km;
(b) excavation: £300 000 per km;
(c) materials: hardcore   £310 per m^3 ;
      base sealer   £150 per m^3 ;
      final surface   £170 per m^3 .

Construction regulations require the hardcore to be 20 cm thick, the base sealer to be 8 cm thick and the final surface to be 6 cm thick.

Find the total costs involved in constructing each km of a new road 8 m wide.

For resurfacing roads of the same width, no other costs apart from the final surfacing costs are incurred. If, in a year, the County Council decides to spend £42 432 000 on this task, calculate the total length of roads of this width which may be resurfaced.   [L]

16 In a certain year a factory producing coats had a total wage bill of £1 500 000. Of this bill, 20 per cent was paid for overtime and the remainder for normal working. The total amounts paid for normal working to each of three groups of employees, namely management, skilled workers and semi-skilled workers, were in the ratios 1 : 6 : 3. Calculate the yearly wages bill for normal working for each of the three groups of workers.

The average payments for normal work to employees in each of the three groups were in the ratio 5 : 3 : 2, and the factory employed 20 persons in the management group. Using the wages bill as calculated above, calculate:
(a) the average yearly wage, for normal working, for an employee in each of the three groups;
(b) the total number of persons employed in the factory.

The payments for overtime were distributed between the three groups of employees in the ratio 0 : 3 : 2. Calculate the *total* average yearly wage of a person in the skilled worker group and express this as a percentage of the *total* average yearly wage of a person in the management group. [L]

17 The diagram in Fig. 4.21, not drawn to scale, shows the uniform vertical cross-section *PQRST* of a swimming pool of length 50 m and width 12 m. The deepest point *S* of the cross-section is vertically below the point *V*. The areas of the cross-section *PVST* and *VQRS* are equal and *PT* = 1 m, *VS* = 6 m and *QR* = 2 m. Given that *VQ* = *x* m, show that $x = 23\frac{1}{3}$.

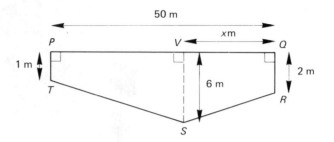

Fig. 4.21

Calculate the volume of water in the pool:
(a) when it is completely full;
(b) when the whole of the surface of the base of the pool is just covered with water.
(c) The pool is empty and is then filled by water flowing at a rate of $2\frac{3}{4}$ m/s through a system of 10 cylindrical pipes. Given that the radius of the cross-section of each of the pipes is *r* cm, and taking π as $\frac{22}{7}$, write down an expression in terms of *r* for the volume, in m³, of water flowing into the pool each hour through the system of pipes. Given that it takes 16 hours to fill the pool completely, calculate the value of *r*. [L]

18 To estimate the cost of providing windows, glazing suppliers measure the perimeter of the window spaces in millimetres and charge the following rates per mm:
1.25p per mm for glazing with a single piece of glass;
1.5p per mm for glazing with two sliding pieces of glass;
1.75p per mm for glazing with three sliding pieces of glass.
I have four windows which each measure 1200 mm by 1780 mm.
(a) Calculate the perimeter of one window.
I decide to fit two sliding pieces of glass to each of two of the windows.
(b) Calculate the cost of glazing these two windows.
I decide to fit three sliding pieces of glass to each of the other two windows.
(c) Calculate the cost of glazing these two windows.
In addition, I decide that a single pane of glass will be adequate for the small hall window which measures 1050 mm by 840 mm.
(d) Calculate the cost of glazing this window.
(e) Find the total cost of all five windows.
An extra 10 per cent is added to this total for fitting the windows.
(f) Calculate the fitting charge.
A discount of 5 per cent of the total price (including the fitting charge) is allowed for a cash payment.
(g) Find, to the nearest penny, what saving this would represent on this order. [L]

19 A body starts from rest, and moves with constant acceleration for 3 s. It then moves with constant speed *x* m/s for 6 s, and finally comes to rest with

constant retardation. The complete journey takes 13 s.

(a) Draw the velocity–time graph for the journey.

(b) Find the total distance travelled in terms of x.

(c) Find x, if the average speed for the journey is 38 m/s.

20 Calculate the amount of liquid that can be stored in a rectangular tank measuring 4 m by 8 m by 1.5 m.

    The tank is filled using a pipe of cross-sectional area 0.08 m^2, at a constant speed of 2 m/s. Calculate the time it takes to fill the tank.

    The tank is then emptied into a similar tank, the smallest dimension being 3 m. Find the volume of this second tank, and the depth of the liquid, assuming that 3 m is the height of the second tank.

21 The speed v m/s of an experimental trolley is measured running along a straight track after t seconds, and found to satisfy the equation $v = 16t - t^2$.

(a) Draw up a table of values for $0 \leqslant t \leqslant 16$ at intervals of 2 seconds.

(b) Using the scales of 1 cm to represent 5 m/s vertically and 1 cm to represent 2 seconds horizontally, draw the graph for $0 \leqslant t \leqslant 16$.

(c) Using your graph, (i) find the maximum speed of the trolley; (ii) find the acceleration of the trolley when $t = 4$ seconds; (iii) estimate the distance travelled in the 16 seconds, using the trapezium rule. Show your working clearly.

22 The diagram in Fig. 4.22 shows the speed–time graph of a car starting from rest, and travelling for 16 seconds with constant acceleration. Its speed at the end of this time is v m/s. If the total distance travelled is 480 m, calculate:

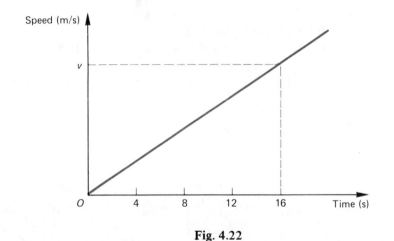

Fig. 4.22

(a) the value of v;

(b) the time it took to cover the first 240 m;

(c) the acceleration of the car.

23 A train travels between two towns A and B, 60 km apart. The scheduled time for the journey is 1 hour. The first two-thirds of the journey is travelled non-stop at an average speed of 80 km/h. There are three stations in the last one-third of the journey, and the average stop at each station is x min. If the average speed for the last part of the journey is 60 km/h, find x. If the maximum amount that x can be reduced by is 1 min and the train is 10 min late after the first two-thirds of the journey, what is the earliest time the train can arrive at B, assuming that the average speed for the last part of the journey is the same as before?

24 A family man wishes to hire a car for a day. Three car-hire firms quoted their prices as follows:

Alpha Agency charged £20 per day irrespective of the distance travelled.

Betta Travel charged £10 for any distance up to, and including 200 km, and then 6p for every kilometre over the initial 200 km.

Cruiser Car charged a basic £5 plus 4p for every kilometre travelled.

(a) Draw up a table that shows the cost of hiring a car for one day from each firm and using it to travel 0, 200 and 400 km in that day.

(b) Use your table to draw graphs on the same axes showing the cost of hiring a car from each firm for all distances up to 400 km in one day.

(Scales: take 2 cm to represent 50 km on the distance axis and 2 cm to represent £2 on the cost axis.)

Use your graphs to estimate:

(c) the range of distances for which Betta Travel is cheaper than Cruiser Cars;

(d) the range of distances for which Alpha Agency is cheaper than either of the other two firms;

(e) the maximum cost per kilometre that Cruiser Cars would have charged if the firm kept its basic £5 charge and was cheaper than both the other two firms up to distances of 400 km.   [AEB]

25 The distance–time graph in Fig. 4.23 shows the progress of David in a cross-country race between two points A and B shown on the map in Fig. 4.24. The first part of the race is from A in a straight line towards Dane Hill (centre of 448). The runners are then allowed a short stop before continuing on to B.

(a) Mark the point S where David stops.

(b) What is the bearing of B from S?

(c) How far is the race?

(d) How far is David from the finish at 1048?

(e) How long is David actually running?

(f) What is David's average speed for the race?

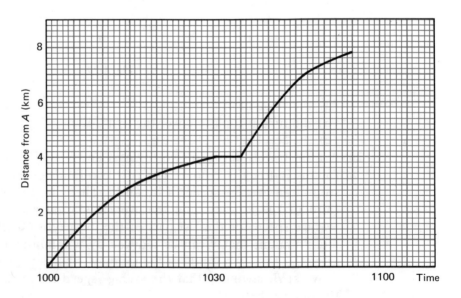

Fig. 4.23

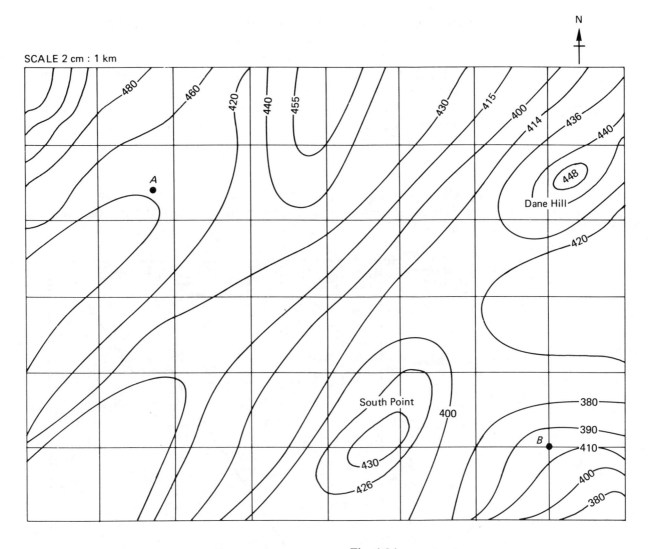

SCALE 2 cm : 1 km

Fig. 4.24

26 At 10.00 a.m. George set out from home to ride his cycle to a friend's home 12 km away. He rode at a steady speed of 18 km/h but, after 20 minutes, one of his tyres was punctured. After spending 5 minutes trying to repair it, George walked the rest of the way at 6 km/h.

(a) Using a scale of 2 cm to represent 10 minutes on the time axis and 2 cm to represent 2 km on the distance axis, draw a distance–time graph for George's journey.

(b) Find the time at which George arrived at his friend's home.

27

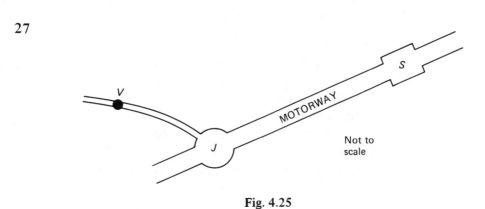

Fig. 4.25

In the diagram (Fig. 4.25), V represents a village, J represents a motorway junction and S represents a service station.

(a) A car started at V and travelled along the road from V to J, a distance of 24 km, at an average speed of 48 km/h. Find the time taken, in hours, to travel from V to J.

(b) The car then travelled along the motorway from J to S, a distance of 156 km at an average speed of 104 km/h. Find the time taken, in hours, to travel from J to S.

(c) Calculate the total distance travelled from V to S.

(d) Calculate the total time taken for the journey from V to S.

(e) Calculate the average speed of the car for the journey from V to S.

(f) The car started at V at a quarter past eleven. At what time did it arrive at S?

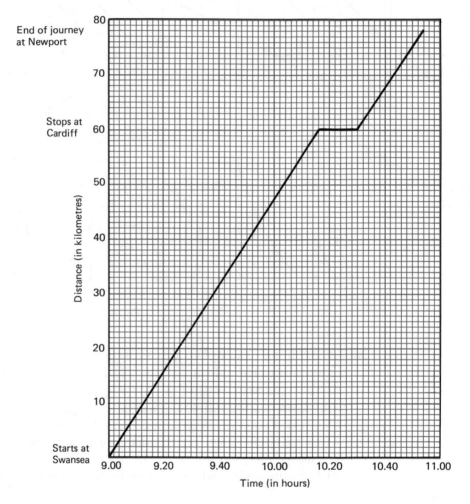

Fig. 4.26

28 The graph in Fig. 4.26 represents the journey by car from Swansea to Cardiff on to Newport. Use your graph to find

(a) the time the car arrives at Newport;

(b) how long the journey takes;

(c) how long the car stops at Cardiff;

(d) how far the car is from Swansea at 10.00;

(e) the car's average speed on the journey from Swansea to Cardiff;

(f) the distance travelled by the car on the journey from Cardiff to Newport.

[WJEC]

5 Functions and Graphs

5.1   Definition

Figure 5.1 shows the relationship between the elements of a set Y, and those of a set X. It can be seen that if $y \in Y$ and x is the value it is related to in X (shown by an arrow), then $y = x + 2$. This mathematical 'rule' which changes a value of x into a value of y is called a *function* or *mapping*. It can also be written $f : x \longmapsto x + 2$.

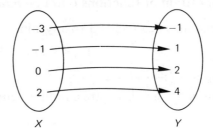

Fig. 5.1

The function f maps x onto $x + 2$. The letter f is not important, and a different letter should be used for a different function. The effect of f on a particular value of x, say $x = 3$, would be written $f(3)$ and (read as 'function of 3'). It follows that: $f(3) = 3 + 2 = 5$.

We can also write f as $f(x) = x + 2$. Since f describes a rule, the variable x is not important, and is called a *dummy* variable. f could also be written as $f : t \longmapsto t + 2$ or $f(y) = y + 2$.

5.2   Domain, Codomain, Range, Image

The above terms are illustrated by Fig. 5.2. The set of values used for x is called

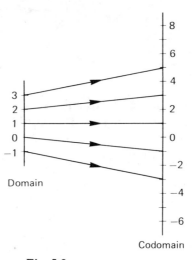

Fig. 5.2

the *domain* of the function. In this case, the domain = {−1, 0, 1, 2, 3}. The *co-domain* of a function is any set which contains all the answers. In this case, {−6, 5, . . ., 7, 8} was used. The set of answers is called the *range* of the function. Hence, the range = {−3, −1, 1, 3, 5}. The value that any given element of the domain is mapped onto is called its *image*. For example, since f(2) = 3, then 3 is the image of 2.

5.3 Composition of Functions

If $f : x \longmapsto x + 3$ and $g : x \longmapsto x^2 + 1$, then fg is called the *product* or *composition* of f and g. It is used to denote g applied first, followed by f applied to the answer. Since $g(2) = 5$ and $f(5) = 8$, it follows that fg(2) = 8.
Also, $f(2) = 5$ and $g(5) = 26$, hence gf(2) = 26.
We can see that, in general, fg ≠ gf.

Composition of functions is *not commutative*.

In general, since f adds 3 to anything,

$$f(x^2 + 1) = (x^2 + 1) + 3 = x^2 + 4,$$

hence fg : $x \longmapsto x^2 + 4$.
  But, since g will square a number and add 1,

$$\begin{aligned} g(x + 3) &= (x + 3)^2 + 1 \\ &= x^2 + 6x + 9 + 1 \\ &= x^2 + 6x + 10, \end{aligned}$$

hence gf : $x \longmapsto x^2 + 6x + 10$.

5.4 Inverse

Referring back to Fig. 5.1, we could also argue that the values of *x* are related to the values of *y*. We can show this (see Fig. 5.3) simply by reversing the arrows.

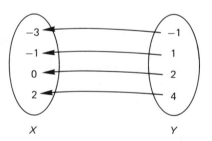

Fig. 5.3

The 'rule' is clearly to subtract 2. This rule is called the inverse of f, written f^{-1}. Hence, $f^{-1} : y \longmapsto y - 2$. It could also be written $f^{-1} : x \longmapsto x - 2$. The inverse relation can usually be found by changing the subject of the original function. See 3.16. For example, if g : $x \longmapsto 2x + 1$, then, writing this as

$$y = 2x + 1,$$
$$y - 1 = 2x,$$
$$\therefore \quad \frac{y - 1}{2} = x.$$

Hence,
$$g^{-1} : y \longmapsto \frac{y - 1}{2}.$$

Worked Example 5.1

If $g(x)$ denotes the sum of all the prime numbers which are less than x, find (a) $g(16)$; (b) a value of x such that $g(x) = 77$; (c) the solution of the equation $g(x) = g(10)$.

Solution

(a) $g(16) = 2 + 3 + 5 + 7 + 11 + 13 = 41$.
(b) This is basically trial and error.
   Since $2 + 3 + 5 + 7 + 11 + 13 + 17 + 19 = 77$, then any number greater than 19 and less than the next prime number which is 23 works.
   Hence $x = 20$ will do.
(c) If $g(x) = g(10)$, then $x = 10$ is an obvious solution.
   However,

$$g(10) = 2 + 3 + 5 + 7 = 17, \quad \text{also} \quad g(8) = 17, g(9) = 17 \quad \text{and} \quad g(11) = 17.$$

Hence the solution is $\{8, 9, 10, 11\}$.

Worked Example 5.2

For any positive integer n, $T(n)$ is defined as the smallest multiple of 3 which is larger than or equal to n, e.g. $T(5) = 6$.
(a) Write down the value of $T(9)$ and that of $T(10)$.
(b) Give the solution set of the equation $T(n) = 12$.
(c) State whether each of the following equations is satisfied by all values of n, by some values of n, or by no values of n. Give the solution set of each equation which is satisfied by some values of n.
   (i) $T(n + 1) = T(n) + 1$; (ii) $T(n + 3) = T(n) + 3$; (iii) $T(2n) = 2T(n)$.   [L]

Solution

This example illustrates a function which cannot easily be represented by formulae.
(a) $T(9) = 9$, $T(10) = 12$.
(b) **Try to express in words what this says**: the smallest multiple of 3 which is larger than or equal to n is 12. Hence $n = 10$, 11 or 12. The solution set is 10, 11, 12.
(c) (i) Since $T(n)$ is a multiple of 3, $T(n) + 1$ is not a multiple of 3, therefore it cannot be $T(n + 1)$. Therefore (i) is not satisfied by any values of n.
    (ii) This is true for all values of n. (Convince yourself with a few examples.)
    (iii) This is not always true, since $T(10) = 2T(5)$ but $T(14) \neq 2T(7)$.
       It is true, however, for $n \in \{1, 4, 7, 10, \ldots\}$.

5.5   Graphical Representation

The reader should have some knowledge of graph plotting. A graph can be used to represent a function or mapping. The values of the domain and function are tabulated in a *table of values*.
(a) Consider the function $f : x \longmapsto 3x - 2$ for the domain $\{x \in \mathbb{R} : -3 \leqslant x \leqslant 3\}$.

The following is the table of values:

x	-3	-2	-1	0	1	2	3	Domain
$y = 3x - 2$	-11	-8	-5	-2	1	4	7	Image (range)

These points can now be plotted on a graph. If all values of the domain had been used, a continuous straight line would have resulted: see Fig. 5.4.

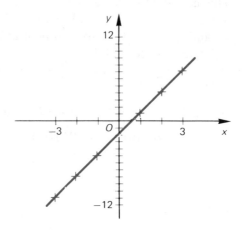

Fig. 5.4

Note that by changing the scale for the y-values, a better-shaped graph is created.

(b) Now a more complicated example. Consider the function

$$f : x \longmapsto x^3 + x^2 - 4x - 4$$

for the domain $\{x : -3 \leqslant x \leqslant 3\}$.

It is often helpful to split the function up into different parts when forming the table.

This has been done in Table 5.1.

Table 5.1

x	-3	-2	-1	0	1	2	3
x^3	-27	-8	-1	0	1	8	27
x^2	9	4	1	0	1	4	9
$-4x$	12	8	4	0	-4	-8	-12
-4	-4	-4	-4	-4	-4	-4	-4
$y = x^3 + x^2 - 4x - 4$	-10	0	0	-4	-6	0	20

The graph is shown plotted in Fig. 5.5. Note that between $x = -2$ and $x = -1$, the curve must not be drawn flat. To be sure, extra values of x should be tried. If $x = -1.5$, $y = 0.875$. The trough of the curve is in fact at $x = 0.87$.

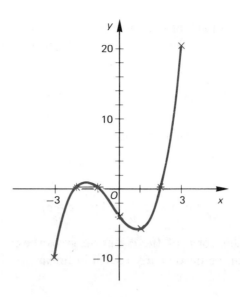

Fig. 5.5

5.6   The Equation of a Straight Line

(a) The simplest form of the equation of a straight line is $y = mx + c$. When $x = 0$, $y = c$.

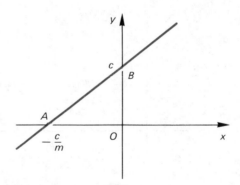

Fig. 5.6

When $y = 0$, $\qquad\qquad 0 = mx + c$

$$\therefore \quad mx = -c$$

$$\therefore \quad x = -\frac{c}{m}.$$

The gradient of the line is $\dfrac{OB}{OA}$; see Fig. 5.6.

Hence gradient $= \dfrac{c}{\dfrac{c}{m}} = m$.

(b) Other forms:

$$ax + by + c = 0, \tag{1}$$

$$\frac{x}{a} + \frac{y}{b} = 1. \tag{2}$$

(1) Consider the equation $3x + 5y + 4 = 0$;
make y the subject of this formula;

$$\therefore \ 5y = -3x - 4.$$

$\div 5$: $\qquad y = -\dfrac{3x}{5} - \dfrac{4}{5}.$

Hence the gradient of the line is $-\frac{3}{5}$, and it cuts the y-axis at $(0, -\frac{4}{5})$.

(2) Put $x = 0$, $\dfrac{y}{b} = 1$; $\therefore \ y = b$.

Put $y = 0$, $\dfrac{x}{a} = 1$; $\therefore \ x = a$.

This form of the equation gives the points where it cuts the axes straight away. It can be particularly useful in linear programming problems.

5.7 Simple Coordinate Geometry (Distance, Mid-point)

If we want to find the distance between two points $P\,(x_1, y_1)$ and $Q\,(x_2, y_2)$, then a simple right-angled triangle can be constructed with sides parallel to the axes (see Fig. 5.7).

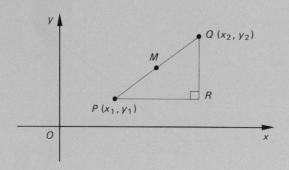

Fig. 5.7

$$PQ = \sqrt{QR^2 + PR^2}$$
$$= \sqrt{(y_1 - y_2)^2 + (x_1 - x_2)^2}.$$

The mid-point M of PQ is a simple average of the coordinates of P and Q.

$$\therefore \ M \text{ is } \left(\frac{x_1 + x_2}{2}, \ \frac{y_1 + y_2}{2}\right).$$

5.8 Graphical Solution of Equations

In section 3.14, it was stated that simultaneous equations can be solved graphically. For example, to solve $3x + 2y = 5$ and $4x - 2y = 7$, simply plot the two straight lines in the form $y = \dfrac{-3x}{2} + \dfrac{5}{2}$ and $y = 2x - \dfrac{7}{2}$. Where the two lines intersect (x, y) gives the solution of the equations. We can, however, tackle more complicated examples.

Worked Example 5.3

Solve by a graphical method the equation $x^3 = 2x + 1$. Without too much extra work, how could you solve the equation $2x^3 - 3 = 4x$?

Solution

To solve $x^3 = 2x + 1$ is fairly easy. If you plot $y = x^3$ and $y = 2x + 1$, when the lines cross, the two y values are equal, hence $x^3 = 2x + 1$. The values of x where the curves cross will be the solution of the equation.

The most difficult part of this is plotting $y = x^3$. It is worth seeing if this can be used again.

Consider $2x^3 - 3 = 4x$;

$$2x^3 = 4x + 3; \quad \therefore \; x^3 = 2x + \frac{3}{2}.$$

Hence, by just drawing the straight line $y = 2x + \dfrac{3}{2}$, the second equation can be solved.

Worked Example 5.4

(a) Copy and complete Table 5.2, calculating, for values of x from 1 to 6, the value of y, where

$$y = 2 + \frac{4}{x^2}.$$

Table 5.2

x	1	1.5	2	2.5	3	4	5	6
x^2		2.25		6.25	9			36
$\dfrac{4}{x^2}$		1.78		0.64	0.44			0.11
$y = 2 + \dfrac{4}{x^2}$		3.78		2.64	2.44			2.11

(b) Using a scale of 2 cm to represent one unit on the x-axis and 4 cm to represent one unit on the y-axis, draw the graph of the curve whose equation is $y = 2 + \dfrac{4}{x^2}$, for values of x from $x = 1$ to $x = 6$.

(c) Using the same axes and the same scales, draw a graph of the straight line whose equation is $y = \frac{1}{3}x + 1$.

(d) Write down, but do not simplify, the equation in x satisfied by the value of x at the point of intersection of the curve and the straight line.

(e) Show that the equation you have written in (d) can be simplified to
$x^3 - 3x^2 - 12 = 0$.

(f) Read off, from your graphs, an approximate solution of the equation in (e).

[AEB 1981]

Solution

This question is slightly more difficult numerically but this should not deter you.

(a) Table 5.3 shows only the *missing values:*

Table 5.3

x	1	1	4	5
x^2	1	4	16	25
$\dfrac{4}{x^2}$	4	1	0.25	0.16
y	6	3	2.25	2.16

(b) The graph of the function is shown in Fig. 5.8.

(c) If you can *safely* recognize $y = \frac{1}{3}x + 1$ is a straight line, only **three** points need be plotted:

$$x = 0, y = 1; \quad x = 3, y = 2; \quad x = 6, y = 3.$$

Choose values of x to get a good spread.

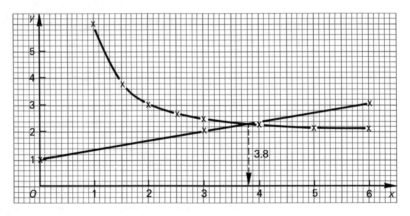

Fig. 5.8

(d) When the two graphs meet, both y-values are equal,

$$\therefore \quad \tfrac{1}{3}x + 1 = 2 + \frac{4}{x^2}.$$

(e) Multiply by $3x^2$:

$$3x^2 \times \frac{1}{3}x + 3x^2 \times 1 = 3x^2 \times 2 + 3x^2 \times \frac{4}{x^2}$$

$$\therefore \quad x^3 + 3x^2 = 6x^2 + 12.$$

Collect terms on left-hand side:

$$x^3 - 3x^2 - 12 = 0.$$

(f) The value of x where the two lines meet is $x = 3.8$.

Worked Example 5.5

(a) The point A (2, 5) is mapped onto the point B (2, -4) under reflection in the line $y = mx + c$. Find m and c.

(b) The lines $2y - x = 8$ and $y + mx = 4$ are parallel; find m.

(c) Find the coordinates of the point C (3, 4) after a rotation of $180°$ about the point D (5, -1).

Solution

A reasonably accurate diagram is often helpful in questions like this.

(a) Since the x-coordinate is unchanged, the mirror line must be parallel to the x-axis (Fig. 5.9).

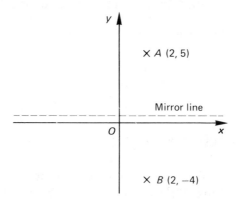

Fig. 5.9

$$\therefore \quad m = 0, \quad \therefore \text{ line is } y = c.$$

The distance between A and B is 9. Mirror line is halfway.

$$\therefore \ c = 5 - 4\tfrac{1}{2} = \tfrac{1}{2}.$$

(b) **Questions on gradients of lines are often much easier if the equation of the line is written in the form $y = mx + c$.**

$$2y - x = 8 \quad \Rightarrow \quad 2y = x + 8 \quad \Rightarrow \quad y = \tfrac{1}{2}x + 4;$$

$$y + mx = 4 \quad \Rightarrow \quad y = -mx + 4.$$

Lines are parallel if the gradients are equal,

$$\therefore \ \tfrac{1}{2} = -m, \quad \therefore \ m = -\tfrac{1}{2}.$$

(c) Since CD rotates by $180°$, CDE is a straight line, and $CD = DE$ (Fig. 5.10).

$$\therefore \quad \overrightarrow{CD} = \begin{pmatrix} 2 \\ -5 \end{pmatrix},$$

$$\text{hence } \overrightarrow{DE} = \begin{pmatrix} 2 \\ -5 \end{pmatrix}.$$

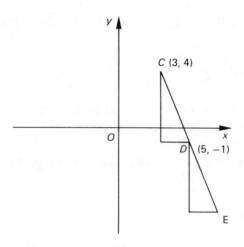

Fig. 5.10

Starting at D (5, −1) and using the translation $\begin{pmatrix} 2 \\ -5 \end{pmatrix}$, we find that E is (7, −6).

5.9 Curve Sketching

It is often useful to have some idea of what a curve looks like without accurate plotting. We have looked at the straight line. Other types are shown in Fig. 5.11.

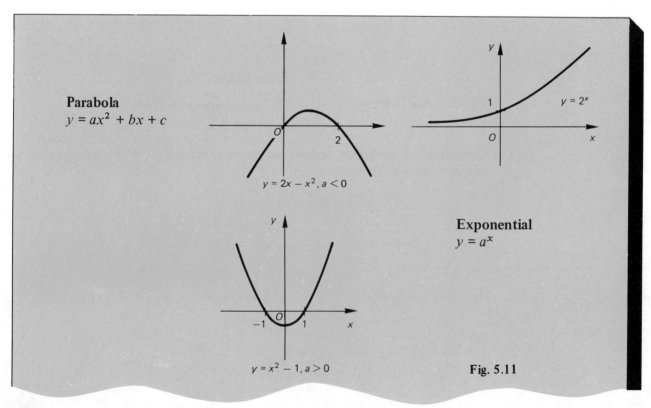

Parabola
$y = ax^2 + bx + c$

$y = 2x - x^2, a < 0$

$y = 2^x$

Exponential
$y = a^x$

$y = x^2 - 1, a > 0$

Fig. 5.11

Continued on page 107

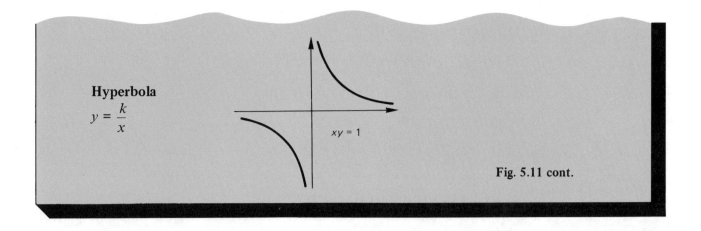

Hyperbola

$$y = \frac{k}{x}$$

$xy = 1$

Fig. 5.11 cont.

5.10   Variation and Proportion

If y is proportional to x, the graph of y against x will be a straight line. Conversion graphs are examples.

Worked Example 5.6

A cylinder of height h and radius r has volume V. Sketch the graph of the variation in V with r, if h remains constant.

Solution

Always write down an equation which describes the problem.

In this case $V = \pi r^2 h$.
Replace any quantities by k which are not varying.
$\therefore V = kr^2$.

The graph will look like that shown in Fig. 5.12. Note that you cannot have a negative radius.

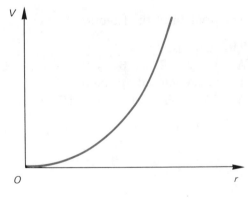

Fig. 5.12

Check 23

1 State the range of the following functions:
   (a) f : $x \longmapsto 2x - 1, \{-3 \leqslant x \leqslant 3\}$
   (b) g : $x \longmapsto x^2, x \in \{-3, -2, -1, 0, 1\}$

(c) $h : x \longmapsto \dfrac{1}{x-1}$, $x \in \mathbb{R}$, $x \neq 1$

(d) $m : x \longmapsto \sin x°$, $\{0 \leqslant x \leqslant 360\}$

2 If $f : x \longmapsto 2x + 1$, $g : x \longmapsto x^2$ and $h : x \longmapsto 2x - 3$, find:

(a) fg   (b) gh   (c) h^2 (d) (fg)h

3 If $f(x) = \dfrac{2x + 1}{3x}$, find:

(a) $f(1)$ (b) $f(-\frac{1}{2})$ (c) $f(4)$

4 Given that $f : x \longmapsto x^2 - 14x + 33$, find:

(a) x if $f(x) = 0$

(b) a value of x such that $f(x) < 0$

5 $G(x)$ denotes the sum of all positive integers less than x which are perfect squares. Find:

(a) $G(25)$ (b) $G(26)$

6 The function g is defined on the domain $\{-2, -1, 0, 1, 2, 3\}$ by

$$g : x \longmapsto \text{units digit of } x^3.$$

Draw a mapping diagram for this function.

7 Plot the function $f : x \longmapsto x^3 - 2x^2 + 1$ for the domain $\{-3 \leqslant x \leqslant 3\}$.

8 Choose a suitable domain in order that the range of the function

$$g : x \longmapsto 2x^2 - 4$$

should not be outside the limits of -6 to 10. Using this domain, plot the graph. What is the minimum value of $g(x)$ for this domain?

9 Find the equations of the straight lines joining the following pairs of points:

(a) $(0, 4)$ and $(3, 6)$ (b) $(0, -2)$ and $(1, 1)$

(c) $(2, 0)$ and $(0, -3)$ (d) $(3, 1)$ and $(2, 4)$

10 Find the mid-points of the join of the pairs of points given in question 9.

Exercise 5

1 If $f : x \longmapsto -2x$ and $g : x \longmapsto x - 1$,

then $gf^{-1}(2) =$

A   1   B   2   C -1 D -2

2 The domain of the function $f : x \longmapsto \dfrac{1 - x^2}{1 + x}$ is $0 \leqslant x \leqslant \frac{1}{2}$.

The range is:

A $1 \leqslant y \leqslant 2$ B $\frac{1}{2} \leqslant y \leqslant 1$ C $0 \leqslant y \leqslant \frac{3}{4}$ D $\frac{3}{4} \leqslant y \leqslant 1$

3 The area enclosed by the line $2x - 5y + 20 = 0$ and the x- and y-axes is:

A   40   B   20   C   10   D   none of these

4 Given that $f : x \longmapsto \dfrac{1 - x}{1 + x}$, then f^{-1} can be expressed as:

A $x \longmapsto \dfrac{1 - x}{1 + x}$ B $x \longmapsto \dfrac{1 + x}{1 - x}$ C $x \longmapsto \dfrac{x + 1}{x - 1}$ D $x \longmapsto \dfrac{x - 1}{x + 1}$

5 The equation of the line through the point $(4, 3)$ parallel to $y = 2x - 7$ is:

A $y = 2x + 3$ B $y = 2x - 4$ C $y = 2x - 5$ D $y = 2x + 5$

6 Which line is perpendicular to $2y = 3x - 7$?

A $2y + 3x + 5 = 0$ B $2y - 3x + 5 = 0$ C $3y - 2x + 5 = 0$

D $3y + 2x - 5 = 0$

7 The gradient of the line $\dfrac{x}{5} + \dfrac{y}{3} = 1$ is:

A $\frac{5}{3}$ B $-\frac{3}{5}$ C $\frac{3}{5}$ D $-\frac{5}{3}$

8 The line $y = x + 5$ passes through the point

    A (1, 5)   **B** (5, 0)   **C** (0, 5)   **D** (5, 5)

9 A function f is defined by $f : x \longmapsto x^2 - 2$.

    If $f(t) = t$, then t equals:

    A 1   **B** 0   **C** -2 or 1   **D** 2 or -1

10 Given that $f(x) = \dfrac{k}{x^2} + 1$, $x \neq 0$, and $f(3) = 5$,

    then k equals:

    A $\frac{2}{3}$ **B** $\frac{14}{9}$ **C** 24   **D** 36   **E** 44   [SEB]

11 The quadratic function whose graph is symmetrical about $x = 0$ is:

    A $f(x) = (x - 3)^2 - 4$ **B** $f(x) = (x - 3)^2$

    C $f(x) = x^2 - 3$ **D** $f(x) = (x - 2)(x + 3)$

12 Draw sketches to illustrate the following equations:

    (a) $y = 2x^2$;   (b) $y = x^3 - 2$;   (c) $y = 3^x$;   (d) $y = \dfrac{-4}{x^2}$.

13 A cylinder of variable radius r has constant height h. Its volume is denoted by V. Draw a sketch graph to show the relationship between V and r as r varies.

14 The line L has equation $2x - y + 6 = 0$ and intersects the x-axis at P and y-axis at Q. The midpoint of PQ is M.

   Find:

   (a) the gradient of L; (b) the coordinates of M; (c) the coordinates of the image of M under an enlargement with centre the origin and scale factor -2.   [UCLES]

15 (a) (i) Write down an expression for the gradient of the line joining the points (6, k) and (4, 1).

       (ii) Find the value of k if this gradient is $\frac{3}{5}$.

   (b) Find the equation of the line through the point $(-4, 5)$ with gradient -2.

16 (a) Given that $y = 2x^2\,(1.6 + x)$, copy and complete the following table:

x	-3	-2.5	-2	-1.5	-1	-0.5	0	1
$y = 2x^2\,(1.6 + x)$	-25.2		-3.2					5.2

   (b) Using suitable scales to use as much of a sheet of graph paper as possible, plot the graph for x between -3 and 1 inclusive.

   (c) On the same axes, plot the graph of the straight line $y + 2x + 2 = 0$.

   (d) Write down the equation in the form $f(x) = 0$ whose solutions are the values of x where your two lines meet. Use your graph to solve $f(x) = 0$.

17 Prepare a table of values of $y = x + \dfrac{5}{x}$ for the values $x = 1, 1.5, 2, 2.5, 3, 3.5,$ 4, 4.5, 5. Draw the graph over this range using a scale of 4 cm for 1 unit on both axes. From your graph determine, in the range $1 \leqslant x \leqslant 5$,

   (a) the least value of $x + 5/x$ and the value of x at which this occurs;

   (b) two solutions of the equation $x^2 - 4.8x + 5 = 0$.   [OLE]

18 (a) Copy and complete the following table of values of $y = 2^{-x}$ for values of x from -4.5 to 2:

x	-4.5	-4	-3	-2	-1	0	1	2
y	22.6		8				0.5	

   (b) Using a scale of 2 cm to represent one unit on the horizontal x-axis and two units on the vertical y-axis, draw the graph of $y = 2^{-x}$.

   (c) From your completed graph estimate:

     (i) the value of $2^{-0.3}$;

(ii) the value of x for which $2^{-x} = 17$;

(iii) the square root of 2^7, showing clearly on the diagram how your answer was obtained.

(d) Draw on your diagram the straight line which enables you to solve the equation

$$2^{-x} - 2x = 10.$$

Hence find the solution to this equation.

(e) The solutions to the equation $2^{-x} = a + bx$, where a and b are constants, are 0 and -3. Determine the values of a and b.

19 A function f is defined by the formula

$$f(x) = 6 \tan (x + 15)°, \text{ where } x \text{ is a real number.}$$

(a) Evaluate $f(30)$.

(b) Write down the exact values of $f(45)$ and $f(15)$ in terms of surds.
Without using approximations, show that

$$f(45) - f(15) = 4\sqrt{3}.$$

[SEB]

20 The line $2y + x = 10$ cuts the axes of x and y at A and B respectively. Find:

(a) the coordinates of the points A and B;

(b) the gradient of AB;

(c) the equation of the line L which passes through the origin, O, and is perpendicular to AB;

(d) the coordinates of the point of intersection of the line L with AB;

(e) the coordinates of the point D, given that the quadrilateral $OBDA$ is a kite;

(f) the coordinates of the centre of the circle which passes through the points O, B, D and A;

(g) the radius of this circle.

[NISEC]

21 The functions f, g and h map the set of all rational numbers to itself and

$$f : x \longmapsto 2, \quad g : x \longmapsto \frac{x}{3} + 1, \quad h : x \longmapsto x^2.$$

(a) Write down a formula for the mapping obtained:
(i) by using g followed by f; and (ii) by using f followed by h.

(b) Express the function $x \longmapsto \dfrac{x^2 + 3}{3}$ (with domain the same as f, g and h) in terms of f, g and h.

(c) Find a function m such that $m(g(x)) = x$.

22 $R(x)$ denotes the remainder when x is divided by 3. Find:

(a) $R(20)$ (b) $R(20m)$ (c) $R(21n)$

where m and n are integers.

23 Find the inverse of the following functions:

(a) $f : x \longmapsto 3 - 2x$ (b) $g : x \longmapsto \dfrac{2}{3x}$

(c) $h : x \longmapsto x^3$ (d) $m : x \longmapsto 2 + x^3$

(e) $n : x \longmapsto \dfrac{1}{2x + 1}$ (f) $q : x \longmapsto \dfrac{ax + b}{cx + d}$

24 Using the domain $-4 \leqslant x \leqslant 4$, plot the graphs of the following functions. In each case:

(a) state the greatest and least values of the function in the range;

(b) by drawing a suitable straight line, solve if possible the equation $f(x) = x - 1$, giving the equation that you have solved in its simplest form.

(i) $f : x \longmapsto x^2$ (ii) $f : x \longmapsto 2x^2 - 3$

(iii) $f : x \longmapsto \dfrac{1+x}{x}$ $(x \neq 0)$ (iv) $f : x \longmapsto x^3$

(v) $f : x \longmapsto 1 - \dfrac{x^2}{x-5}$

25 $|x|$ denotes the numerical value of x, e.g. $|-4| = 4$, $|8| = 8$.

On the same diagram, for values of x between -3 and 3 inclusive, plot the graphs of the functions:

$$f : x \longmapsto |x^2 - 4| \quad \text{and} \quad g : x \longmapsto 3.$$

How many solutions are there to the equation $|x^2 - 4| = 3$ for this domain? Read off the largest value as accurately as possible.

26 The function f maps x onto $f(x)$ where $f(x) = x^2 - 5x - 36$ and the function g maps x onto $g(x)$ where $g(x) = 3x - 17$. Find:
(a) $f(-2)$ (b) $g(5)$ (c) $f(g(5))$
(d) the values of x if f maps x onto 0
(e) the values of x, correct to two decimal places, if $f(x) = g(x)$.   [WJEC]

27 The function f is defined on the domain of real numbers by $f : x \longmapsto x^2 + 6$.
(a) Calculate $f(-3.58)$, giving your answer correct to three significant figures.
(b) Calculate two values of x such that $f(x) = 34$, giving your answers correct to three significant figures.
(c) Solve the equation $f(2x) = f(2x + 7)$.
(d) Sketch the graph of f.
(e) State the range of f.
    The operation $*$ is defined on the set of real numbers by $a * b = f(a - b)$, where f is the function defined above.
(f) Give a numerical example to illustrate that the operation $*$ is commutative.
(g) Give a numerical example to illustrate that the operation $*$ is not associative.   [JMB]

28 Using a scale of 2 cm to 1 unit on each axis, draw the graph of $y = x - \dfrac{2}{x}$ for values of x from 1 to 6.

Using the same axes and scales, draw the graph of $y = \frac{2}{3}(5 - x)$. From your graphs, find:
(a) one root of the equation $x - \dfrac{2}{x} = \frac{2}{3}(5 - x)$;

(b) one root of the equation $x - \dfrac{2}{x} = 3$;

(c) the set of values of x for which

$$0 < \left(x - \frac{2}{x}\right) - \frac{2}{3}(5 - x) < 3,$$

giving your answer in the form $a < x < b$, where the values of a and b are to be found.   [O & C]

29 In this question state any assumptions you make.

Jason is arrested for drunken driving at 10.30 p.m. on Saturday. At the police station his alcohol level is taken every hour (it is measured in milligrams per 100 millilitres of blood). A record of the measurements is kept.

Time after arrest (hours)	1	2	3	4	5
Level (milligrams)	160	152	139	131	120

(a) Plot these results on a graph.
(b) What would you expect Jason's alcohol level to be 7 hours after his arrest?

(c) By considering a line of best fit, find a formula connecting Jason's alcohol level and the time since his arrest.

He is released from the police station when he has a level below 80. Predictions are liable to 12% error.

(d) What time can Jason expect to leave the police station? [SEG]

30 (a) Given that $y = (x - 1)^2$, copy and complete the table.

x	-1	-0.5	0	0.5	1	1.5	2	2.5	3
y		2.25	1	0.25		0.25	1		4

(b) (i) Using a scale of 4 cm to represent 1 unit on each axis, draw the graph of $y = (x - 1)^2$ for values of x from -1 to 3 inclusive.

(ii) By drawing a tangent, estimate the gradient of the graph $y = (x - 1)^2$ at the point (2, 1).

(c) Use your graph to find the values of x for which $(x - 1)^2 = 3$. [MEG]

31 The information in Fig. 5.13 on stopping distances is reproduced from the Highway Code.

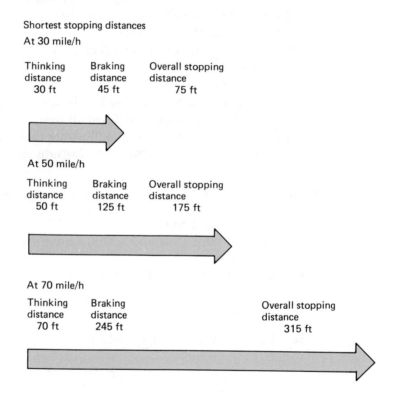

Fig. 5.13

It is known that the overall stopping distance d and the speed v are related by the formula

$$d = av + bv^2,$$

where a and b are constants.

(a) Complete the table showing values of d and v.

v (mile/h)	30	50	70
d (feet)	75		

(b) Use your completed table to show that the formula relating d and v is

$$d = v + \frac{v^2}{20}.$$

(c) On graph paper draw the graph of d against v, for values of v from 10 to 90.

If the road surface is wet then twice the normal overall stopping distance should be allowed. Use your completed graph to estimate the maximum speed at which a car should travel if visibility is limited to 150 feet

(d) on a dry road,

(e) on a wet road. [NISEC]

32 (a) Factorise $x^2 - 5x + 6$.

(b) Solve the equation $x^2 - 5x + 6 = 0$.

(c)

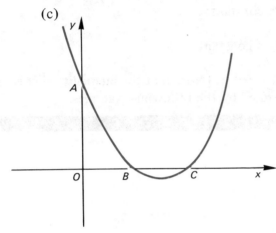

Fig. 5.14

Fig. 5.14 shows the graph of $y = x^2 - 5x + 6$.

Write down the coordinates of the points marked A, B and C.

(d)

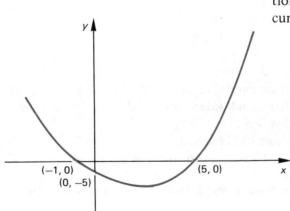

Fig. 5.15

Find the values of p and q in the equation $y = x^2 + px + q$ of the quadratic curve shown in Fig. 5.15.

[WJEC]

113

6 Inequalities

6.1 Properties of $<$ and $\leqslant$

$a < b$ means a is less than b or b is greater than a.
$a \leqslant b$ means a is less than or equal to b, etc.
(a) Addition or subtraction of a constant:
  $a < b \Rightarrow a \pm k < b \pm k$.
(b) Multiplication or division by a constant:
  If $k > 0, a < b \Rightarrow ka < kb$,
  $k < 0, a < b \Rightarrow ka > kb$. ⟵ [**Note that the inequality sign is reversed.**]
These rules will be demonstrated by the following examples.

6.2 Inequations

(a) Solve $x + 5 < 9$.
   First, subtract 5 from each side: $\qquad x < 4$.
   There are an infinite number of solutions; the *solution set* is $\{x : x < 4\}$.
(b) Solve $2x - 3 \geqslant 8$.
   Add 3 to each side: $2x \geqslant 11$.
   Divide by $+2$. $\qquad x \geqslant 5\frac{1}{2}$.
(c) Solve $3(x + 4) < 5x + 9$.
   $3x + 12 < 5x + 9$.
   Subtract 12 from each side: $3x < 5x - 3$.
   Subtract $5x$ from each side: $-2x < -3$.
   Divide by -2 $x > \frac{3}{2}$;
   note that the sign has changed.
(d) Solve $3 < 2x - 10 < 7$, given that x is an integer.

A problem of this type is best solved by splitting it into two inequations.

The left-hand side is: $3 < 2x - 10$;
$\qquad \therefore 13 < 2x$;
$\qquad \therefore 6\frac{1}{2} < x$.
The right-hand side is: $2x - 10 < 7$;
$\qquad \therefore 2x < 17$;
$\qquad \therefore x < 8\frac{1}{2}$;
$\qquad \therefore 6\frac{1}{2} < x < 8\frac{1}{2}$.
But x is an integer, $\qquad \therefore x \in \{7, 8\}$.

*(e) Solve $\frac{4}{x} > 3$.

We do not know whether x is positive or negative; therefore you have to be careful when multiplying each side by x.

If $x > 0, 4 > 3x$.

Divide by 3: $\frac{4}{3} > x$.

Since $x > 0$ the solution is $0 < x < \frac{4}{3}$.

If $x < 0, 4 < 3x$.

Divide by 3: $\frac{4}{3} < x$.

This is impossible because x cannot be both negative and greater than $\frac{4}{3}$.
The only solution is $\{x : 0 < x < \frac{4}{3}\}$.

*(f) Solve the quadratic inequation $x^2 - 5x + 4 > 0$.

Factorizing gives $(x - 1)(x - 4) > 0$.

Look at the number line in Fig. 6.1 divided into three regions by the points $x = 1$ and $x = 4$.

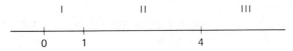

Fig. 6.1

Take any value in region I, $x = -2$;
substitute into $x^2 - 5x + 4 = (-2)^2 - 5(-2) + 4 = 18 > 0$.

Take any value in region II, $x = 3$;
substitute into $x^2 - 5x + 4 = 3^2 - 5(3) + 4 = -2 < 0$.

Take any value in region III, $x = 6$;
substitute into $x^2 - 5x + 4 = 6^2 - 5(6) + 4 = 10 > 0$.

Since we want $x^2 - 5x + 4$ to be positive, this happens in regions I and III.
The solution can be written: $\{x : x < 1 \text{ and } x > 4\}$.

Check 24

Find the solution sets of the following inequations:

1 $18 - x > 2x + 7$.
2 $3 - 2x < 4 - 3x$.
3 $3x - 5 \leqslant x + 15$ (x is a positive integer).
4 $3 - x < 14 + 5x$ (x is a negative integer).
5 $4 < x + 6 < 18$.
6 $3 < 2(x - 5) < 7$ (x an integer)
7 $-14 < 3x - 5 < 7$.
8 $-3 < 5(x + 4) < 9$.
9 $-2 \leqslant 5 - x \leqslant 3$ (x is an integer).
*10 $x^2 - 3x - 4 < 0$.
*11 $x^2 - 5x + 3 < -3$.
*12 $x^2 - 12 < 3$.
*13 $6 - x - x^2 > 0$.
*14 $\frac{2}{5} < \frac{1}{x}$.
*15 $\frac{1}{2 - x} < \frac{1}{4}$ ($x \neq 2$).

*6.3 **Errors**

v, u, a and t are related by the equation $v = u + at$. If u, a and t cannot be measured exactly, then there is uncertainty in the value of v. If u, a and t can be guaranteed to the nearest whole number, what can be said about v when $u = 40$, $a = 4$ and $t = 15$? Since the values are only correct to the nearest whole number, then $39.5 \leqslant u \leqslant 40.5$, $3.5 \leqslant a \leqslant 4.5$ and $14.5 \leqslant t \leqslant 15.5$.

Although 40.5 would be rounded up to 41, it is included to keep the working simple.

If the smallest values of u, a and t are taken, then $v = 39.5 + 3.5 \times 14.5 = 90.25$.
If the largest values of u, a and t are taken, then $v = 40.5 + 4.5 \times 15.5 = 110.25$.
Hence $90.25 \leqslant v \leqslant 110.25$.
Clearly, if this were a scientific experiment, we could be in trouble.

Worked Example 6.1

It is given that $H = \dfrac{4a}{2 + 4t}$, with a and t measured in centimetres to the nearest centimetre. If $a = 6$ and $t = 4$, find the range of possible values of H.

Solution

Since a and t are measured to the nearest whole number, a can be anywhere between 5.5 and 6.5,

i.e. $\qquad\qquad\qquad\qquad\qquad 5.5 \leqslant a \leqslant 6.5$.
Similarly, $\qquad\qquad\qquad\qquad\quad 3.5 \leqslant t \leqslant 4.5$.

Strictly speaking, we should exclude 6.5, as this would normally be rounded up. But this leads to complications, and does not really affect the result. Since H is a fraction, the largest value of H will have the largest numerator, and the smallest denominator. The smallest value of H will have the smallest numerator and the largest denominator.

Hence $\qquad\qquad \dfrac{4 \times 5.5}{2 + 4 \times 4.5} \leqslant H \leqslant \dfrac{4 \times 6.5}{2 + 4 \times 3.5}$

and hence $\qquad\qquad\qquad 1.1 \leqslant H \leqslant 1.625$.

6.4   Regions

We can use set notation to describe regions in the Cartesian plane in quite a neat way. Consider the following example:

Worked Example 6.2

Draw a sketch to illustrate the following regions:
(a) $A = \{(x, y) : y \geqslant 1, x + y \leqslant 5, 3y - 2x < 6\}$;
(b) $B = \{(x, y) : y \geqslant x^2, y \leqslant x + 2\}$.

Solution

(a) We will generally operate the convention of shading the *unwanted* region.
   Step 1 is to plot the lines without the inequalities (see Fig. 6.2);

i.e. $\qquad\qquad\qquad y = 1, \qquad x + y = 5, \qquad 3y - 2x = 6$.

The last will be drawn dotted because the inequality does not include the equal part.
$y \geqslant 1$ means shade below $y = 1$.

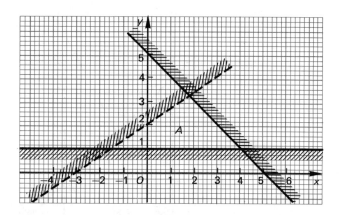

Fig. 6.2

$x + y \leqslant 5$ means shade above line $x + y = 5$.

$3y - 2x < 6$:   it is easier to rewrite this $y < \dfrac{2x}{3} + 2$ (careful with the sign);

∴ shade above this line.

(b) Step 1: plot $y = x^2$, $y = x + 2$.

$y \geqslant x^2$, ∴ shade below the curve.

$y \leqslant x + 2$, ∴ shade above the line.

The region is shown in Fig. 6.3.

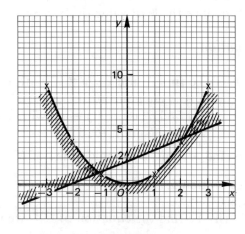

Fig. 6.3

*6.5   Linear Programming

The techniques of linear programming are built around finding the maximum or minimum values of an expression $Ax + By$ in a given region. It is always worth looking at the value of $Ax + By$ at the vertices of the region first. The following worked examples should illustrate the ideas involved.

Worked Example 6.3

In Fig. 6.4 the line with equation $x + y = 12$ crosses the y-axis at A and meets the line $x = 6$ at B. C is the point $(0, 3)$ and M is the mid-point of AB.

(a) Find:

(i) the coordinates of A, B and M;

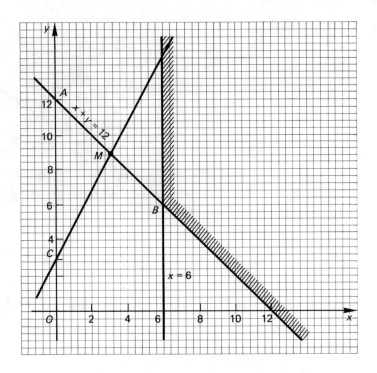

Fig. 6.4

    (ii) the equation of the line *CM*.

(b) If *x* and *y* are subject to the restrictions

$$y \geqslant 0, \qquad x \geqslant 6 \qquad \text{and} \qquad x + y \geqslant 12,$$

deduce the least value of $2x + 3y$.   [SEB]

Solution

(a) (i) To find *A*, use $x + y = 12$ with $x = 0$, i.e. $y = 12$.
            ∴ *A* is the point (0, 12).
            To find *B*, use $x + y = 12$ with $x = 6$, i.e. $y = 6$.
            ∴ *B* is the point (6, 6).

To find *M*, this is the mid-point of (0, 12) and (6, 6). Using $\left(\dfrac{x_1 + x_2}{2} , \dfrac{y_1 + y_2}{2} \right)$

(see section 5.7),
M is (3, 9).

      (ii) To find the equation of *CM*, we need its gradient,

        i.e. $\dfrac{9 - 3}{3 - 0} = 2$.

        It passes through (0, 3).
        ∴ Equation of line is $y = 2x + 3$.

(b) To satisfy $y \geqslant 0$, $x \geqslant 6$ and $x + y \geqslant 12$, the point (x, y) lies *in* the shaded region. The least value of $2x + 3y$ is bound to occur at $B(6, 6)$;
    ∴ least value $= 2 \times 6 + 3 \times 6 = 30$.

Worked Example 6.4

A man has 12 acres of land available for growing peas and beans. Each acre of peas that he plants costs him £70 and involves him in 18 hours of labour, while each acre of beans that he plants costs him £150 and involves him in 5 hours of labour. He has £1050 and 90 hours of labour available.

    Let *x* acres and *y* acres be the areas that he uses to grow peas and beans respectively and write down three inequalities other than $x \geqslant 0$ and $y \geqslant 0$. Using 1 cm to denote 1 acre on both the x- and y-axes, draw a graph to illustrate these inequalities.

Show that the man cannot use all the land that he has available, and use your graph to estimate the largest amount of land that he can use for growing peas and beans. [OLE]

Solution

The three inequalities are determined by the number of acres, the number of hours, and the cost.

The number of acres cannot exceed 12,

$$\therefore x + y \leqslant 12. \tag{1}$$

The number of hours cannot exceed 90,

$$\therefore 18x + 5y \leqslant 90 \tag{2}$$

The cost cannot exceed £1050,

$$\therefore 70x + 150y \leqslant 1050.$$

Always simplify if possible; in this case, ÷ 10:

$$\therefore 7x + 15y \leqslant 105. \tag{3}$$

The region within which x and y must lie is denoted by R in Fig. 6.5.

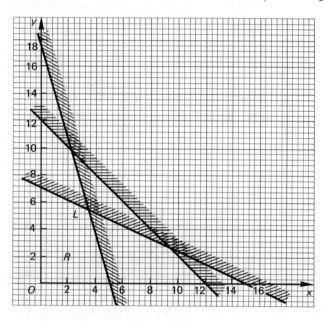

Fig. 6.5

Since the line $x + y = 12$ does not pass through the region R, there is no solution for which all the acreage is used. The largest value of $x + y$ occurs at the point L (3.5, 5.4) (answers to 1 d.p.).

The largest area = 3.5 + 5.4 = 8.9 acres.

Worked Example 6.5

A depot for famine relief has 20 sacks of rice and 35 sacks of maize. The weight, volume and number of meal rations *for each sack* are as shown:

	Weight (kg)	Volume (m³)	No. of meals
Sack of			
rice	25	0.05	800
maize	10	0.05	160

A delivery van is to carry the largest possible total number of meals. It can carry up to 600 kg in weight and 2 m³ in volume.

(a) If a load is made up of x sacks of rice and y sacks of maize, say why $x \leqslant 20$ and write down three other inequalities (other than $x \geqslant 0$, $y \geqslant 0$) which govern x and y.

(b) Illustrate these inequalities on a graph and indicate the area in which the point (x, y) must lie.

(c) Write down an expression for the number of meals that can be provided from x sacks of rice and y sacks of maize. Using the graph, find the best values to take for x and y. [NISEC]

Solution

(a) Since only 20 sacks of rice are available, we must have $x \leqslant 20$. Similarly, $y \leqslant 35$.

The total weight of rice is $25x$ kg.
The total weight of maize is $10y$ kg.
Since the lorry cannot carry more than 600 kg, it follows that

$$25x + 10y \leqslant 600.$$

$\div 5$: $\qquad\qquad 5x + 2y \leqslant 120.$

The total volume of rice is $0.05x$ m³.
The total volume of maize is $0.05y$ m³.
Since the lorry cannot carry more than 2 m³, it follows that

$$0.05x + 0.05y \leqslant 2.$$

$\times 20$: $\qquad\qquad x + y \leqslant 40.$

(b) The region is shown in Fig. 6.6. The points which will be needed can be found

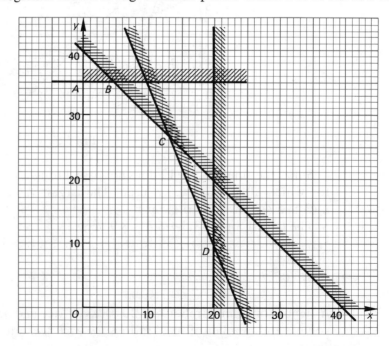

Fig. 6.6

either by drawing or by simultaneous equations. They are A (0, 35), B (5, 35), C $(\frac{40}{3}, \frac{80}{3})$, D (20, 10) and E (20, 0).

(c) The number of meals is

$$800x + 160y = 160 (5x + y).$$

This will be greatest when $5x + y$ is greatest. The values of $5x + y$ at the points found in (b) are A (35), B (60), C $(93\frac{1}{3})$, D (110) and E (100). The best value is at D, i.e. $x = 20$, $y = 10$.

6.6   Locus

The path or region traced out by a point is called its *locus*. Some locus problems can be stated using the inequality signs; consider the following example.

Worked Example 6.6

In Fig. 6.7, $ABCD$ is a square; a point P moves inside the square so that $PA \geqslant PB$, and $PC \leqslant PA$. Shade the region in which P must lie.

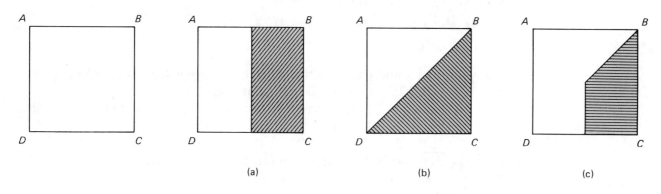

Fig. 6.7

Solution

$PA \geqslant PB$ means P is nearer to B than A. This means that P lies in the shaded region in (a).

$PC \leqslant PA$ means P is nearer to C than A. Hence P lies in the shaded region in (b). The final region is the intersection of these, shown in (c).

Exercise 6

1 Given that $p = \frac{1}{3}$, $q = \frac{2}{7}$ and $r = \frac{3}{10}$, it follows that:

    A $p < q < r$ **B** $p < r < q$ **C** $p > q > r$ **D** $p > r > q$

                                                      [AEB 1981]

2 p is a negative integer and q is a positive integer. Which of the following is (are) true?

    I $pq > 0$ II $\dfrac{p}{q} < 0$ III $\dfrac{q}{p} < 0$ IV $pq < 0$

    A I and II only   **B** II and IV only   **C** II, III and IV only

    D III and IV only   **E** IV only   [SEB]

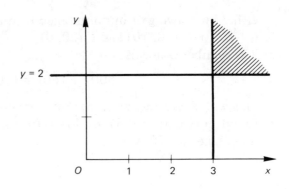

Fig. 6.8

3 The shaded area shown in Fig. 6.8 represents the set:

A $\{(x, y) : x \geqslant 3\} \cap \{(x, y) : y \geqslant 2\}$

B $\{(x, y) : x \geqslant 3\} \cup \{(x, y) : y \geqslant 2\}$

C $\{(x, y) : x \leqslant 3\} \cup \{(x, y) : y \leqslant 2\}$

D $\{(x, y) : x \leqslant 3\} \cap \{(x, y) : y \leqslant 2\}$

E none of these

4 If $S = \{(x, y) : x$ and y are positive integers and $x + y \leqslant 5\}$, then n(S) equals:
A 36   B 25   C 16   D none of these

5 If $a = 0.32$ and $b = 5.71$ are correct to two decimal places, the maximum value of $b - a$ is:
A 5.4   B 5.5   C 5.39   D 5.335

6 If $n^2 \leqslant \sqrt{300} \leqslant (n + 1)^2$ and n is an integer, then n equals:
A 17   B 18   C 3   D 4

7 If $\dfrac{1}{\sqrt{3}} < \dfrac{p}{q} < \dfrac{1}{\sqrt{2}}$, then $\dfrac{p}{q}$ could equal:
A $\frac{4}{5}$ B $\frac{1}{2}$ C $\frac{2}{3}$ D $\frac{5}{6}$

8 If $E = \dfrac{2b}{c + 2}$, and $3 \leqslant b \leqslant 7$, $2 \leqslant c \leqslant 5$, the minimum value of E is:
A 2   B $\frac{6}{7}$ C $\frac{4}{5}$ D $\frac{14}{4}$

9 If $x^a > x^b$, it follows that:
A $x > 0$ B $a > b$ C $a < b$ D none of these

10 The largest prime number x which satisfies $2x + 1 < 48$ is
A 47   B 24   C 23   D 22

11 List the integer values of x which satisfy $3x - 4 < 27 \leqslant 4x - 5$.   [UCLES]

12 Given that $1 \leqslant x \leqslant 4$ and $3 \leqslant y \leqslant 5$, find:
(a) the largest possible value of $y^2 - x$;
(b) the smallest possible value of (i) $\dfrac{y^2}{x}$; (ii) $(y - x)^2$.   [UCLES]

13 Mrs Jones is baking two kinds of cake for a local fête. Each cake of type A requires 150 g flour, 120 g fat and 60 g sugar, while each cake of type B requires 160 g flour, 75 g fat and 100 g sugar. She has 2.4 kg flour, 1.8 kg fat and 1.2 kg sugar available for baking the cakes.

She makes x cakes of type A and y cakes of type B. Write down three inequalities, apart from $x \geqslant 0$ and $y \geqslant 0$, which govern the possible values of x and y. Draw a graph to illustrate these inequalities, taking 1 cm to represent

1 unit on each axis. Indicate clearly the region of points whose coordinates satisfy all the conditions.

Cakes of type *A* sell at a profit of 25 pence each and those of type *B* at a profit of 40 pence each. Write down an expression, in terms of *x* and *y*, for the total profit she makes if she sells all the cakes that she bakes. What is the largest profit she could make? [OLE]

14 A shopkeeper stocks two brands of drinks called Kula and Sundown, both of which are produced in cans of the same size. He wishes to order fresh supplies and finds that he has room for up to 1000 cans. He knows that Sundown is more popular and so proposes to order at least twice as many cans of Sundown as of Kula. He wishes, however, to have at least 100 cans of Kula and not more than 800 cans of Sundown. Taking *x* to be the number of cans of Kula and *y* to be the number of cans of Sundown which he orders, write down the four inequalities involving *x* and/or *y* which satisfy these conditions.

The point (x, y) represents *x* cans of Kula and *y* cans of Sundown. Using a scale of 1 cm to represent 100 cans on each axis, construct and indicate clearly, by shading the unwanted regions, the region in which (x, y) must lie.

The profit on a can of Kula is 3p and on a can of Sundown is 2p. Use your graph to estimate the number of cans of each that the shopkeeper should order to give the maximum profits. [UCLES]

15 A new book is to be published in both a hardback and a paperback edition.
A bookseller agrees to purchase:
(a) 15 or more hardback copies;
(b) more than 25 paperback copies;
(c) at least 45, but fewer than 60, copies altogether.

Using *h* to represent the number of hardback copies and *p* to represent the number of paperback copies, write down the inequalities which represent these conditions.

The point (h, p) represents *h* hardback copies and *p* paperback copies. Using a scale of 2 cm to represent 10 books on each axis, construct, and indicate clearly by shading the *unwanted* regions, the region in which (h, p) must lie. Given that each hardback copy costs £5 and each paperback costs £2, calculate the number of each sort that the bookseller must buy if he is prepared to spend between £180 and £200 altogether and he has to buy each sort in packets of five. [UCLES]

7 Vectors

7.1 Definition

A vector is a quantity which has length (magnitude) and direction. A simple translation (or displacement) is a vector quantity. The notation **AB**, $\vec{AB}$, **a** will be used. In this book, a vector will be represented by a simple column vector,

e.g. $$\vec{OA} = \begin{pmatrix} 3 \\ 2 \end{pmatrix}$$

represents the vector $\vec{OA}$ shown in Fig. 7.1. Note that 3 and 2 are called the *components*.

The direction of the arrow is important: it means 'from O to A'.
a = $\vec{OA}$ is the *position vector* of A with respect to O.

7.2 Multiplication by a Scalar

An ordinary number is called a *scalar*.

If $\mathbf{a} = \begin{pmatrix} 3 \\ 2 \end{pmatrix}$, then to get from O to C (Fig. 7.1), we apply **a** followed by **a**, i.e. 2**a**.

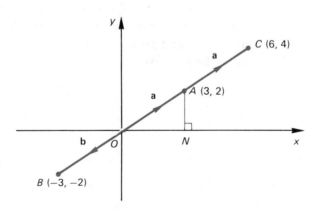

Fig. 7.1

But since $\vec{OC} = \begin{pmatrix} 6 \\ 4 \end{pmatrix}$, then $2\mathbf{a} = \begin{pmatrix} 6 \\ 4 \end{pmatrix} = 2\begin{pmatrix} 3 \\ 2 \end{pmatrix}$. Hence, to multiply a vector by a scalar, we multiply each component by the scalar.

Also, $\mathbf{b} = \begin{pmatrix} -3 \\ -2 \end{pmatrix} = -\begin{pmatrix} 3 \\ 2 \end{pmatrix} = -\mathbf{a}$.

Hence the negative of a vector is the same length in the opposite direction.

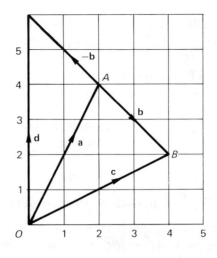

Fig. 7.2

7.3   Addition and Subtraction

In Fig. 7.2,

$$\overrightarrow{OA} = \begin{pmatrix} 2 \\ 4 \end{pmatrix} = \mathbf{a}, \quad \overrightarrow{AB} = \begin{pmatrix} 2 \\ -2 \end{pmatrix} = \mathbf{b}.$$

If we start at O and apply the translation $\mathbf{a}$ followed by $\mathbf{b}$, we arrive at the point $B\,(4, 2)$. We could also have arrived at B by the translation $\mathbf{c} = \begin{pmatrix} 4 \\ 2 \end{pmatrix}$.

We say that $\mathbf{c}$ is the *sum* or *resultant* of $\mathbf{a}$ and $\mathbf{b}$,

$$\therefore \mathbf{a} + \mathbf{b} = \mathbf{c}, \text{ i.e. } \begin{pmatrix} 2 \\ 4 \end{pmatrix} + \begin{pmatrix} 2 \\ -2 \end{pmatrix} = \begin{pmatrix} 4 \\ 2 \end{pmatrix}.$$

Hence to add two vectors, we simply add the components:

$$\mathbf{a} - \mathbf{b} = \mathbf{a} + (-\mathbf{b}) = \begin{pmatrix} 2 \\ 4 \end{pmatrix} + \begin{pmatrix} -2 \\ 2 \end{pmatrix} = \begin{pmatrix} 0 \\ 6 \end{pmatrix} = \mathbf{d}.$$

Hence to subtract two vectors, we subtract the components.

7.4   Length

The length or *modulus* of a vector is denoted by $|\mathbf{a}|$, $|\mathbf{OA}|$ or $|\overrightarrow{OA}|$.
In Fig. 7.1, applying Pythagoras' theorem to triangle ONA gives

$$|\mathbf{a}| = \sqrt{3^2 + 2^2} = \sqrt{13}.$$

In general, if $\mathbf{a} = \begin{pmatrix} x \\ y \end{pmatrix}$, then $|\mathbf{a}| = \sqrt{x^2 + y^2}$.

Check 25

1 If $\mathbf{a} = \begin{pmatrix} 3 \\ 1 \end{pmatrix}$, $\mathbf{b} = \begin{pmatrix} -2 \\ 1 \end{pmatrix}$ and $\mathbf{c} = \begin{pmatrix} 4 \\ -2 \end{pmatrix}$, find:

(a) $\mathbf{a} + \mathbf{b}$ (b) $\mathbf{b} - \mathbf{c}$ (c) $2\mathbf{a} - \mathbf{b}$

(d) $\mathbf{a} + \mathbf{b} + \mathbf{c}$ (e) $3\mathbf{a} - \mathbf{b} - \mathbf{c}$ (f) $|\mathbf{a}|$

(g) $|\mathbf{a} + \mathbf{b}|$ (h) $|\mathbf{a}| + |\mathbf{b}|$

2 $OABC$ is a quadrilateral $\overrightarrow{OA}$ = **a**, $\overrightarrow{AB}$ = **b**, and $\overrightarrow{BC}$ = **c**.
  Write down the following vectors in terms of **a**, **b** and **c**:
  (a) $\overrightarrow{AC}$　　(b) $\overrightarrow{OC}$　　(c) $\overrightarrow{OB}$
3 $RSTU$ is a rectangle. The diagonals of the rectangle meet in M. If $\overrightarrow{MR}$ = **a** and $\overrightarrow{MS}$ = **b**, write down in terms of **a** and **b**:
  (a) $\overrightarrow{RS}$　　(b) $\overrightarrow{ST}$　　(c) $\overrightarrow{US}$
4 X is the point (4, 1), Y is the point (−2, −1) and Z is the point (5, −3).
    Express, as a 2 × 1 column vector, the following:
  (a) $\overrightarrow{XY}$　　(b) $\overrightarrow{YZ}$　　(c) $\overrightarrow{XZ}$
5 O (0, 0), A (3, 1) and B (2, −1) are three vertices of a quadrilateral $OABC$. If $\overrightarrow{BC}$ = $\begin{pmatrix} 3 \\ -2 \end{pmatrix}$, what are the coordinates of C? Find $\overrightarrow{AC}$.
6 $ABCD$ is a quadrilateral, A, B, D have coordinates (0, 2), (2, 5), (8, 0) respectively. If $\overrightarrow{AD}$ = $2\overrightarrow{BC}$, find the coordinates of C.
    AC is produced to P so that $\overrightarrow{CP}$ = $2\overrightarrow{AC}$. Find the coordinates of P, and $|\overrightarrow{BP}|$.

7.5　Equations

> 1 If **a** and **b** are parallel vectors, then **a** = k**b** where k is a scalar.
> 2 If **a** and **b** are not parallel vectors, and h**a** = k**b**, then $h = k = 0$.

Both of these results will be used in the section on geometrical proofs.
(*Note:* See Worked Example 7.2.)

7.6　Geometrical Proofs

The following three examples should indicate how vectors can be used to prove results in geometry.

Worked Example 7.1

ABC is a triangle. X is the mid-point of AB, and Y is the mid-point of BC. XY is produced to T so that $XY = YT$. Prove that $XBTC$ is a parallelogram.

Solution

Referring to Fig. 7.3, let $\overrightarrow{BX}$ = **a**, and $\overrightarrow{BY}$ = **b**. There are several other vectors that could have been used for **a** or **b**. Try and choose those which give the simplest answers.

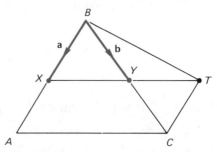

Fig. 7.3

$\overrightarrow{XY} = -\mathbf{a} + \mathbf{b}, \therefore \overrightarrow{XT} = 2(-\mathbf{a} + \mathbf{b}) = -2\mathbf{a} + 2\mathbf{b}.$
$\overrightarrow{BC} = 2\mathbf{b}, \therefore \overrightarrow{XC} = -\mathbf{a} + 2\mathbf{b}.$
$\overrightarrow{TC} = \overrightarrow{TX} + \overrightarrow{XC} = -\overrightarrow{XT} + \overrightarrow{XC} = 2\mathbf{a} - 2\mathbf{b} - \mathbf{a} + 2\mathbf{b} = \mathbf{a}.$
Hence $\overrightarrow{TC} = \overrightarrow{BX}$. It follows that BX is parallel to TC and the same length.
$\overrightarrow{BT} = \overrightarrow{BC} + \overrightarrow{CT} = 2\mathbf{b} - \mathbf{a} = \overrightarrow{XC}.$
Hence BT is parallel to XC and of equal length.
$\therefore XBTC$ is a parallelogram.

When trying to find an expression for, say, $\overrightarrow{XY}$, look at a route which takes you from X to Y, i.e. $X \rightarrow B \rightarrow Y$.
$\therefore \overrightarrow{XY} = \overrightarrow{XB} + \overrightarrow{BY} = -\mathbf{a} + \mathbf{b}.$

Worked Example 7.2

In the triangle OAB, $\overrightarrow{OA} = \mathbf{a}$ and $\overrightarrow{OB} = \mathbf{b}$. L is a point on the side AB. M is a point on the side OB, and OL and AM meet at S. It is given that $AS = SM$ and $OS/OL = \frac{3}{4}$; also that $OM/OB = h$ and $AL/AB = k$.
(a) express the vectors $\overrightarrow{AM}$ and $\overrightarrow{OS}$ in terms of a, b and h;
(b) express the vectors $\overrightarrow{OL}$ and $\overrightarrow{OS}$ in terms of a, b and k.
Find h and k, and hence find the values of the ratios OM/MB and AL/LB.

Solution (Fig. 7.4)
Referring to Fig. 7.4, since

Since $\dfrac{OS}{OL} = \frac{3}{4}, \overrightarrow{OS} = \frac{3}{4}\overrightarrow{OL}.$

$\dfrac{OM}{OB} = h, \therefore OM = hOB$

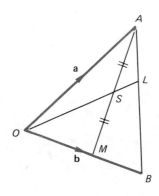

Fig. 7.4

Using vectors, therefore,

$$\overrightarrow{OM} = h\mathbf{b}$$

also $$\overrightarrow{AL} = k\overrightarrow{AB}$$

Now $$\overrightarrow{AB} = -\mathbf{a} + \mathbf{b} = \mathbf{b} - \mathbf{a},$$
$\therefore$ $$\overrightarrow{AL} = h(\mathbf{b} - \mathbf{a}).$$

(a) $\overrightarrow{AM} = \overrightarrow{AO} + \overrightarrow{OM} = -\mathbf{a} + h\mathbf{b}$
    $\overrightarrow{OS} = \overrightarrow{OA} + \overrightarrow{AS}$
    $= \overrightarrow{OA} + \frac{1}{2}\overrightarrow{AM}$
    $= \mathbf{a} + \frac{1}{2}(-\mathbf{a} + h\mathbf{b}).$

127

Before we can use the results of section 7.5, this must be simplified.

$$\vec{OS} = \tfrac{1}{2}\mathbf{a} + \tfrac{1}{2}h\mathbf{b}.$$

(b) $\vec{OL} = \vec{OA} + \vec{AL} = \mathbf{a} + k(\mathbf{b} - \mathbf{a}) = (1 - k)\mathbf{a} + k\mathbf{b},$

$$\vec{OS} = \tfrac{3}{4}\vec{OL} = \tfrac{3}{4}(1 - k)\mathbf{a} + \tfrac{3}{4}k\mathbf{b}.$$

Since both expressions for $\vec{OS}$ must be the same,

$$\tfrac{1}{2}\mathbf{a} + \tfrac{1}{2}h\mathbf{b} = \tfrac{3}{4}(1 - k)\mathbf{a} + \tfrac{3}{4}k\mathbf{b},$$

$$\therefore \ [\tfrac{1}{2} - \tfrac{3}{4}(1 - k)]\,\mathbf{a} = (\tfrac{3}{4}k - \tfrac{1}{2}h)\,\mathbf{b}.$$

Since $\mathbf{a}$ and $\mathbf{b}$ are not parallel,

$$\tfrac{1}{2} - \tfrac{3}{4}(1 - k) = 0$$

and

$$\tfrac{3}{4}k - \tfrac{1}{2}h = 0.$$

The solutions of these are $k = \tfrac{1}{3}$, $h = \tfrac{1}{2}$.

$\therefore$ The ratios $\dfrac{OM}{MB} = 1,\qquad \dfrac{AL}{LB} = \tfrac{1}{2}.$

Worked Example 7.3

Y and X are points with position vectors $\mathbf{y}$ and $\mathbf{x}$ referred to an origin O. OY is produced to a point Z where $OY : YZ = 1 : 3$. V is a point on YX such that $YV : VX = 1 : 2$ and W is a point on XZ such that $XW : WZ = 1 : 2$.

Show that O, V and W lie on a straight line.

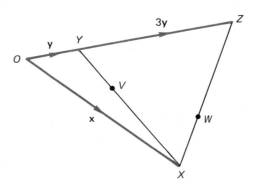

Fig. 7.5

Solution

To show that the three points lie on a straight line, try and show that $\vec{OW}$ is a multiple of $\vec{OV}$.

The positions of the points are shown in Fig. 7.5. To express $\vec{OV}$ in terms of $\mathbf{x}$ and $\mathbf{y}$, try to write $\vec{OV}$ in a different way.

$$\vec{OV} = \vec{OX} + \vec{XV} = \vec{OX} + \tfrac{2}{3}\vec{XY}$$

$$= \mathbf{x} + \tfrac{2}{3}(-\mathbf{x} + \mathbf{y}) = \tfrac{2}{3}\mathbf{y} + \tfrac{1}{3}\mathbf{x}.$$

Similarly, $\qquad \overrightarrow{OW} = \overrightarrow{OX} + \overrightarrow{XW} = \mathbf{x} + \frac{1}{3}\overrightarrow{XZ}$

$$= \mathbf{x} + \frac{1}{3}(-\mathbf{x} + 4\mathbf{y})$$

$$= \frac{4}{3}\mathbf{y} + \frac{2}{3}\mathbf{x}.$$

Hence $\overrightarrow{OW} = 2\overrightarrow{OV}$.

It follows that OVW is a straight line, and also V is the mid-point of OW.

Exercise 7

1 If $\mathbf{x} = \begin{pmatrix} 3 \\ 4 \end{pmatrix}$ and $4\mathbf{x} - 3\mathbf{y} = \begin{pmatrix} 2 \\ -1 \end{pmatrix}$, then $\mathbf{y}$ equals:

  A $\begin{pmatrix} 10 \\ 17 \end{pmatrix}$ B $\begin{pmatrix} 14 \\ 15 \end{pmatrix}$ C $\begin{pmatrix} 4\frac{2}{3} \\ 5 \end{pmatrix}$ D $\begin{pmatrix} 3\frac{1}{3} \\ 5\frac{2}{3} \end{pmatrix}$

2 If $\mathbf{x} = \begin{pmatrix} -4 \\ -3 \end{pmatrix}$, then $|\mathbf{x}|$ equals:

  A −5   B 5   C 7   D undefined

3 If $\mathbf{a} = \begin{pmatrix} 2 \\ 5 \end{pmatrix}$ and $\mathbf{b}$ is perpendicular to $\mathbf{a}$, then $\mathbf{b}$ could equal:

  A $\begin{pmatrix} 2 \\ -5 \end{pmatrix}$ B $\begin{pmatrix} -10 \\ -4 \end{pmatrix}$ C $\begin{pmatrix} 10 \\ -4 \end{pmatrix}$ D $\begin{pmatrix} 5 \\ 2 \end{pmatrix}$

4 If $\mathbf{a}$ and $\mathbf{b}$ are non-parallel vectors, and $(2 - h)\mathbf{a} + (3 + k)\mathbf{b} = 0$, where h and k are numbers, then $h + k$ equals:

  A 0   B −1   C 1   D 5

5 $ABCDEF$ is a regular hexagon. $\overrightarrow{AB} = \mathbf{a}$ and $\overrightarrow{BC} = \mathbf{b}$. $\overrightarrow{DF}$ equals:

  A $\mathbf{b} - \mathbf{a}$ B $\mathbf{a} - \mathbf{b}$ C $-\mathbf{a} - \mathbf{b}$ D $\mathbf{b} + \mathbf{a}$

6 $OPQR$ is a parallelogram. $\overrightarrow{OP} = 3\mathbf{a} + \mathbf{b}$, $\overrightarrow{OR} = 4\mathbf{a} + 5\mathbf{b}$. It follows that $\overrightarrow{RP}$ equals:

  A $7\mathbf{a} + 6\mathbf{b}$ B $\mathbf{a} + 4\mathbf{b}$ C $-\mathbf{a} - 4\mathbf{b}$ D $-7\mathbf{a} - 6\mathbf{b}$

7 $\mathbf{p}$ and $\mathbf{q}$ are two vectors, such that $\mathbf{p}$ is perpendicular to $(\mathbf{p} + \mathbf{q})$. If $|\mathbf{p}| = 5$, and $|\mathbf{q}| = 8$, then $|\mathbf{p} + \mathbf{q}|$ equals:

  A 3   B 13   C $\sqrt{39}$ D none of these

8 $\overrightarrow{AB} = \mathbf{e} + 4\mathbf{n}$, where $|\mathbf{e}| = |\mathbf{n}| = 1$, $\mathbf{e}$ is due east and $\mathbf{n}$ is due north. The bearing of A from B to the nearest degree is:

  A 14°   B 194°   C 76°   D 346°

9 $OABC$ is a rectangle. $\overrightarrow{OA} = \mathbf{a}$ and $\overrightarrow{OC} = \mathbf{c}$. If $|\mathbf{a}| = 12$ and $|\mathbf{c}| = 5$, then $\angle OMA$, where M is the mid-point of OB, equals (to the nearest degree):

  A 135°   B 134°   C 136°   D 45°

10 $ABCDEF$ is a regular hexagon. If $AB = \mathbf{x}$ and $AF = \mathbf{y}$, then $\overrightarrow{AD}$ equals

  A $\mathbf{x} + \mathbf{y}$ B $2\mathbf{x}$ C $2\mathbf{y}$ D $2\mathbf{x} + 2\mathbf{y}$

*11 $\mathbf{r}$ and $\mathbf{s}$ are two perpendicular vectors, such that $|\mathbf{r}| = 5$ and $|\mathbf{s}| = 12$. Find:
  (a) $|2\mathbf{r}| + |2\mathbf{s}|$ (b) $2|\mathbf{r} + \mathbf{s}|$

12 $\mathbf{x}$ and $\mathbf{y}$ are non-parallel vectors and $4\mathbf{x} + (h - 3)\mathbf{y} = k\mathbf{x} + 4\mathbf{y}$; find h and k.

13 $PQRST$ is a plane five-sided figure. Express as a single vector

$$\overrightarrow{PQ} + \overrightarrow{QR} + \overrightarrow{RS} + \overrightarrow{ST} + 4\overrightarrow{PT}$$

14 If $\mathbf{a} = \begin{pmatrix} 3 \\ y \end{pmatrix}$, $\mathbf{b} = \begin{pmatrix} 2x \\ -4 \end{pmatrix}$ and $2\mathbf{a} + 3\mathbf{b} = \begin{pmatrix} y \\ x \end{pmatrix}$, find y and x.

15 In the parallelogram $WXYZ$ shown in Fig. 7.6, M and N are the mid-points of WX and ZY respectively. P and Q divide WZ and XY respectively in the ratio $1 : 2$. WM represents the vector $\mathbf{u}$ and WP represents the vector $\mathbf{v}$.

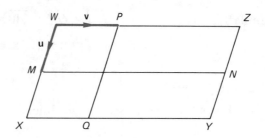

Fig. 7.6

(a) Express in terms of **u** and **v** the vectors represented by (i) $\overrightarrow{PZ}$ (ii) $\overrightarrow{WY}$ (iii) $\overrightarrow{YP}$

(b) Using only the letters in the diagram, write down the directed line segment which represents the vector $2\mathbf{v} - \mathbf{u}$. [SEB]

16 Given that $\overrightarrow{OP} = \mathbf{p}$, $\overrightarrow{OQ} = \mathbf{q}$ and M is the mid-point of PQ,

(a) express, in terms of **p** and **q**, the vectors $\overrightarrow{PQ}$, $\overrightarrow{PM}$ and $\overrightarrow{OM}$.

Given also that G is the point on OM such that $OG = \frac{2}{3}OM$,

(b) express $\overrightarrow{OG}$ and $\overrightarrow{PG}$ in terms of **p** and **q**.

Given, further, that N is the mid-point of OQ,

(c) express $\overrightarrow{PN}$ in terms of **p** and **q**.

(d) Hence show that $\overrightarrow{PG} = k\overrightarrow{PN}$, where k is a constant, and find the numerical value of k.

(e) State the geometrical meaning of your answer to (d). [L]

17 The position of a ship with respect to a fixed origin O is given by

$$\mathbf{r} = \begin{pmatrix} 0 \\ 10 \end{pmatrix} + t \begin{pmatrix} 0.4 \\ -0.3 \end{pmatrix},$$ where t is the time in minutes after noon, and distances are measured in kilometres.

(a) Calculate the position of the ship when $t = 0, 5, 10, 15, 20$.

(b) Using a scale of 2 cm to 1 km on both the x- and y-axes, draw a diagram to show the path of the ship during the period between noon and 12.20 p.m.

(c) A torpedo has a position given by

$$\mathbf{r} = \begin{pmatrix} 2 \\ 0 \end{pmatrix} + t \begin{pmatrix} 0.5 \\ 0.8 \end{pmatrix}.$$

Using the same set of axes as in part (b), draw a diagram to show the path of the torpedo.

(d) Measure the distance between the ship and the torpedo at 12.05 p.m.

(e) At what time does the ship cross the path of the torpedo? [OLE]

18 $OABCDE$ is a regular hexagon. Let $\overrightarrow{OA} = \mathbf{a}$ and $\overrightarrow{OB} = \mathbf{b}$. Write the following vectors in terms of **a** and **b**:

(a) $\overrightarrow{AB}$; (b) $\overrightarrow{OC}$; (c) $\overrightarrow{BC}$; (d) $\overrightarrow{OD}$; (e) $\overrightarrow{OE}$; (f) $\overrightarrow{AE}$.

Given that $h\mathbf{b} = \mathbf{a} + k(\mathbf{b} - 3\mathbf{a})$, where h and k are numbers, find h and k.

AE meets OB at X. Calculate $OX : OB$. [OLE]

19 In the triangle OAB (Fig. 7.7), $\overrightarrow{OA} = \mathbf{a}$ and $\overrightarrow{OB} = \mathbf{b}$. The points P on OA, Q on AB and R on OB produced are such that $OP = \frac{3}{4}OA$, $AQ = \frac{7}{12}AB$ and $OR = \frac{21}{16}OB$.

(a) Express (i) $\overrightarrow{OP}$ in terms of **a**;

(ii) $\overrightarrow{OR}$ in terms of **b**;

(iii) $\overrightarrow{AB}$ in terms of **a** and **b**;

(iv) $\overrightarrow{AQ}$ in terms of **a** and **b**.

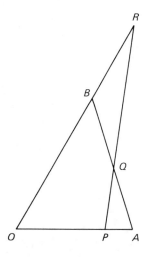

Fig. 7.7

(b) By considering the triangle PAQ, show that $\vec{PQ} = \frac{7}{12}\mathbf{b} - k\mathbf{a}$, and state the value of k.

(c) By considering the triangle POR, show that $\vec{PR} = m\mathbf{b} - \frac{3}{4}\mathbf{a}$, and state the value of m.

(d) Find the value of $\dfrac{PQ}{PR}$.   [EAUCJ]

20 In Fig. 7.8, $\vec{OA} = \mathbf{a}$, $\vec{OB} = \mathbf{b}$, $\vec{OC} = \mathbf{c}$ and $\vec{OD} = \mathbf{d}$. X is the mid-point of AB and Y is the mid-point of CD.

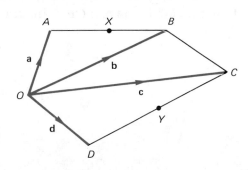

Fig. 7.8

(a) Find, in terms of $\mathbf{a}$ and $\mathbf{b}$: (i) $\vec{AB}$; (ii) $\vec{AX}$; (iii) $\vec{OX}$.

(b) Similarly, find $\vec{OY}$ in terms of $\mathbf{c}$ and $\mathbf{d}$.

(c) If M is the mid-point of XY (not shown in the figure), write down an expression for $\vec{OM}$ in terms of $\mathbf{a}$, $\mathbf{b}$, $\mathbf{c}$, and $\mathbf{d}$.

(d) Describe exactly the position of P if $\vec{OP} = \frac{1}{2}(\mathbf{a} + \mathbf{d})$.   [EAUCJ]

21 In Fig. 7.9, E is the point on the side BD of the triangle ABD such that $DE = kDB$. The lines AB and DC are parallel and $DC = mAB$.

It is given that $\vec{AB} = 10\mathbf{a}$ and $\vec{AD} = 2\mathbf{b}$.

(a) Express $\vec{DB}$ in terms of $\mathbf{a}$ and $\mathbf{b}$.

(b) Express $\vec{AE}$ in terms of $\mathbf{a}$, $\mathbf{b}$ and k.

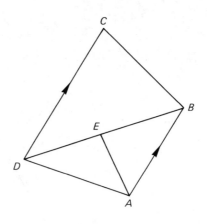

Fig. 7.9

(c) Express $\overrightarrow{BC}$ in terms of **a**, **b** and m.

(d) If BC is parallel to AE, show that $m - 1 - km = 0$.

22 $ABCDEF$ is a regular hexagon. The displacements $\overrightarrow{AB}$ and $\overrightarrow{BC}$ are denoted by **x** and **y** respectively.

(a) Express each of the following displacements in terms of **x** or **y** or both:
   (i) $\overrightarrow{DE}$ (ii) $\overrightarrow{FC}$ (iii) $\overrightarrow{AF}$ (iv) $\overrightarrow{FD}$ (v) $\overrightarrow{EC}$

(b) If EC and AB are produced to meet at G, explain why $BFCG$ is a parallelogram.

   Hence, or otherwise, express in terms of **x** or **y** or both:
   (i) $\overrightarrow{AG}$ (ii) $\overrightarrow{EG}$

(c) The area of the hexagon is 6 units. Find the areas of:
   (i) triangle BCG (ii) quadrilateral $AGEF$ [NISEC]

23 The square $OACB$ (Fig. 7.10) is divided into 16 equal squares of side 1 cm. Given that $\overrightarrow{OA} = 4\mathbf{a}$ and $\overrightarrow{OB} = 4\mathbf{b}$, draw a diagram and mark clearly

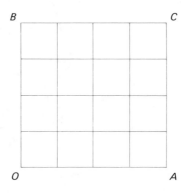

Fig. 7.10

(a) the point X such that $\overrightarrow{OX} = \mathbf{a} + 3\mathbf{b}$;

(b) the point Y such that $\overrightarrow{YA} = 2\mathbf{a} - \mathbf{b}$;

(c) a point Z, at one of the intersections, such that $|\overrightarrow{OZ}|$ 5 cm.

24 (a) The vectors **e** and **n** represent velocities of 1 km/h due east and 1 km/h due north respectively. A man rows a boat on a river in such a way that, if there were no current, its velocity would be $2\mathbf{n} - \mathbf{e}$. On a river flowing with velocity $3\mathbf{e}$ the boat's actual velocity is **v**.

   (i) Express **v** in the form $a\mathbf{e} + b\mathbf{n}$.

   (ii) Calculate $|\mathbf{v}|$.

(b) In the triangle ABR (Fig. 7.11), T is the mid-point of AB and S is the mid-point of BR. Given that $\mathbf{AS} = \mathbf{s}$ and $\mathbf{AT} = \mathbf{t}$, express in terms of $\mathbf{s}$ and/or $\mathbf{t}$, as simply as possible, the vectors

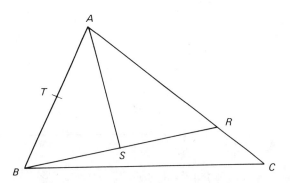

Fig. 7.11

(i) **TS** (ii) **AB** (iii) **BR** (iv) **AR**.

Given also that C is the point such that $\mathbf{AR} = 5\mathbf{RC}$ and $\mathbf{TS} = k\mathbf{RC}$, find the value of k.   [UCLES]

25 (a) Given that $\mathbf{OK} = \begin{pmatrix} 16 \\ 2 \end{pmatrix}$, $\mathbf{OL} = \begin{pmatrix} 4 \\ -3 \end{pmatrix}$ and that M and N are the mid-points of OK and OL respectively,

(i) express **MN** as a column vector;

(ii) find the value of $|\mathbf{KL}|$.

(b) Referring to Fig. 7.12, $\mathbf{OA} = 4\mathbf{a}$, $\mathbf{OB} = 4\mathbf{b}$ and $\mathbf{BP} = 3\mathbf{a} - \mathbf{b}$. Express as simply as possible, in terms of $\mathbf{a}$ and $\mathbf{b}$:

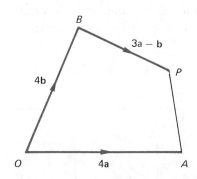

Fig. 7.12

(i) **OP** (ii) **AP**.

The lines OA produced and BP produced meet at Q. Given that $\mathbf{BQ} = m\mathbf{BP}$ and $\mathbf{OQ} = n\mathbf{OA}$, form an equation connecting m, n, $\mathbf{a}$ and $\mathbf{b}$. Hence deduce the values of m and n.   [UCLES]

26 In the triangle OAB shown in Fig. 7.13,

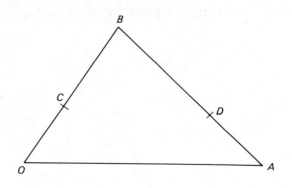

Fig. 7.13

$$OC = \frac{2}{5}OB, \qquad \overrightarrow{OA} = \mathbf{a}, \qquad \overrightarrow{OB} = \mathbf{b}.$$

(a) Express the vectors $\overrightarrow{OC}$, $\overrightarrow{CB}$ and $\overrightarrow{BA}$ in terms of $\mathbf{a}$, or $\mathbf{b}$, or $\mathbf{a}$ and $\mathbf{b}$. The point D divides BA in the ratio 3 : 2.

(b) Find $\overrightarrow{BD}$ and $\overrightarrow{CD}$ in terms of $\mathbf{a}$, or $\mathbf{b}$, or $\mathbf{a}$ and $\mathbf{b}$.

(c) Give the special name of the quadrilateral $OCDA$.

(d) Calculate the value of $\dfrac{\text{area of triangle } OAB}{\text{area of triangle } CDB}$.

(e) Given that the area of the quadrilateral $OCDA$ is 48 cm², find the area of the triangle CBD.

[LEAG]

27 In a video game, a spot on the screen bounces off the four sides of a rectangular frame. The spot moves from A to B to C to D, as shown in Fig. 7.14.

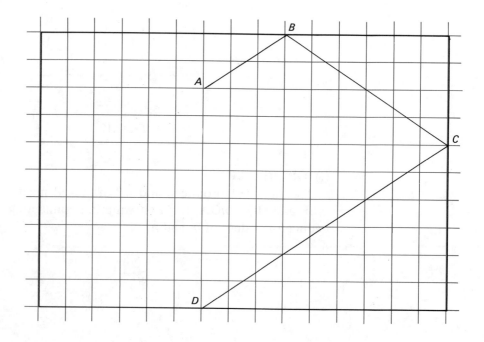

Fig. 7.14

(a) What can you say about the angle at which the spot bounces off each side, compared with the angle at which it approached that side?

(b) The column vector describing the part **AB** of the movement is $\begin{pmatrix} 3 \\ 2 \end{pmatrix}$. Write down the column vectors describing **BC** and **CD**.

(c) What do you notice about the parts of the path **AB** and **CD**? Justify your answer using the column vectors.

From D, the spot moves to a point E on the fourth side of the frame.

(d) Given that the spot continues in the same way, write down the vector **ED**.

(e) Given that the spot bounces off the fourth side at E and continues to move, describe its subsequent path. [WJEC]

8 Transformation Geometry

8.1 Translation

In Fig. 8.1, each point of P has been mapped onto Q, by a simple *displacement* or *translation*. A translation can be represented by a vector.

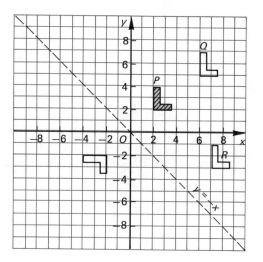

Fig. 8.1

We write $P \rightarrow Q$ under the translation $\mathbf{T}_1 = \begin{pmatrix} 4 \\ 3 \end{pmatrix}$. Similarly, $Q \rightarrow R$ under the translation $\mathbf{T}_2 = \begin{pmatrix} 1 \\ -8 \end{pmatrix}$.

If we wish to carry out one transformation followed by another, i.e. $\mathbf{T}_1$ followed by $\mathbf{T}_2$, it is denoted by $\mathbf{T}_2\mathbf{T}_1$. Note the order of letters.

Now $P \rightarrow R$ under the translation $\mathbf{T}_3 = \begin{pmatrix} 5 \\ -5 \end{pmatrix}$ but $\mathbf{T}_3$ is the same as $\mathbf{T}_2\mathbf{T}_1$. It can be seen that combining translations is the same as adding vectors.

$$\therefore \ \mathbf{T}_2\mathbf{T}_1 = \begin{pmatrix} 1 \\ -8 \end{pmatrix} + \begin{pmatrix} 4 \\ 3 \end{pmatrix} = \begin{pmatrix} 5 \\ -5 \end{pmatrix} = \mathbf{T}_3.$$

8.2 Reflection

Referring again to Fig. 8.1, $P \rightarrow S$ by a *reflection* in the line $y = -x$. This line is called the *mirror line*. Reflection in a line through the origin can be represented by using a 2×2 matrix; see section 9.13.

8.3　　**Rotation**

In Fig. 8.2, the flag motif $X \rightarrow Z$ by a rotation $\mathbf{R_1}$, centre (1, 1), angle $-90°$. (**Note that a clockwise rotation is negative.**)

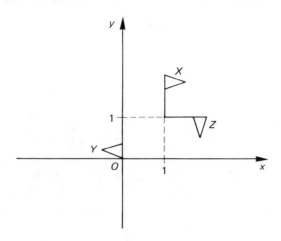

Fig. 8.2

Also, $X \rightarrow Y$ by a rotation $\mathbf{R_3}$, centre $(\frac{1}{2}, 1)$, angle $180°$, and $Z \rightarrow Y$ by a rotation $\mathbf{R_2}$, centre $(\frac{1}{2}, 1\frac{1}{2})$, angle $-90°$. (Check this by accurate drawing.)

$$\therefore \mathbf{R_3} = \mathbf{R_2} \mathbf{R_1}.$$

In most cases, a _rotation_ followed by a _rotation_ is a _rotation_.
Try to find an example of when this is not true.

A rotation about O can be represented by a 2 x 2 matrix; see section 9.13.

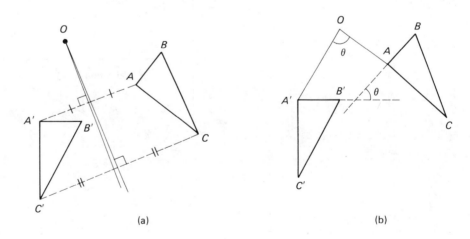

Fig. 8.3

To find the centre of rotation by construction (see Fig. 8.3(a)):

Join two pairs of corresponding points AA' and CC'. Bisect each line at right angles, and where these bisectors meet is the centre of rotation O. Note also in Fig. 8.3(b) all lines in the shape are rotated by the angle of rotation.

A reflection followed by a reflection can often be represented by a rotation.

In Fig. 8.4 a reflection in m_1 followed by a reflection in m_2 is equal to a rotation of $2x°$ twice the angle between the mirror lines about O (the point of intersection of the mirror lines).

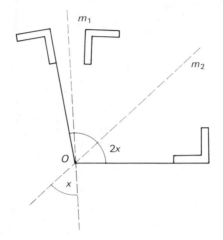

Fig. 8.4

8.4   Glide Reflection

A *glide reflection* is the name given to a simple transformation which consists of a reflection followed by a translation, or vice versa. See Fig. 8.5.

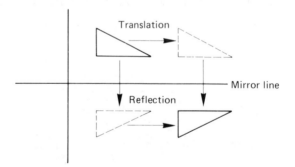

Fig. 8.5

*8.5   Isometries

The transformations: reflection, rotation, translation and glide reflection all leave the shape of the transformed figure unchanged. For this reason, they are called *isometries*.

8.6   Dilatation

Figure 8.6 shows two examples of a dilatation, one an enlargement, the other a reduction.

138

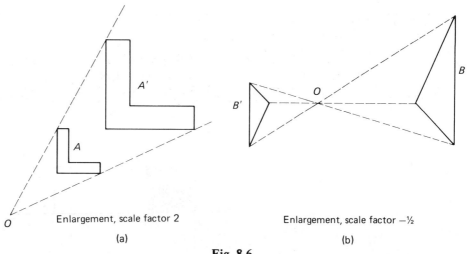

Enlargement, scale factor 2

(a)

Enlargement, scale factor −½

(b)

Fig. 8.6

All corresponding lengths in Fig. 8.6(a) are multiplied by 2, including distances from the centre of enlargement *O*. All corresponding lengths in Fig. 8.6(b) are multiplied by $\frac{1}{2}$. The negative sign indicates that the centre of enlargement is between the object and the image. If the scale factor is −1, the figure has *point symmetry*.

8.7   Shear

Students often find it difficult to grasp the concept of a shear. In Fig. 8.7(a), $A \to A'$ by a shear parallel to the *x*-axis, and the *x*-axis is *invariant*. The further a point is from the invariant line, the greater the shift of the point. In order to define a shear, specify where one point moves, and the invariant line.

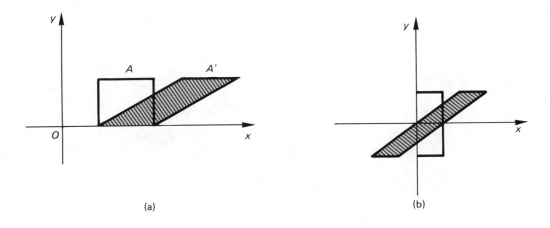

(a)

(b)

Fig. 8.7

The distance moved by any point in the direction of the invariant line is proportional to the distance from the invariant line. The constant of proportionality is called the *shear factor*.

In Fig. 8.7(b) the same shear has been applied to a shape part of which lies *below* the invariant line. It can be seen that the part below moves backwards, because the distance from the invariant line is negative. A shear can be represented by a 2 x 2 matrix. **Shearing preserves the area of a shape.**

8.8   Stretch

In Fig. 8.8, the square *OABC* has been stretched by a factor 3 in a direction parallel to the *x*-axis. All *x*-coordinates are multiplied by 3.

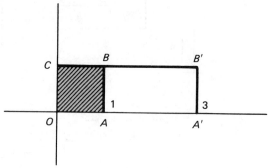

Fig. 8.8

Note: It is possible to have a negative stretch factor.

8.9   Similarity and Congruence

If two shapes are *exactly* the same but have a different orientation, they are said to be *congruent*.

If one shape is a simple enlargement of another, in two or three dimensions, they are said to be *similar*.

Situations where similar shapes occur are shown in Fig. 8.9.

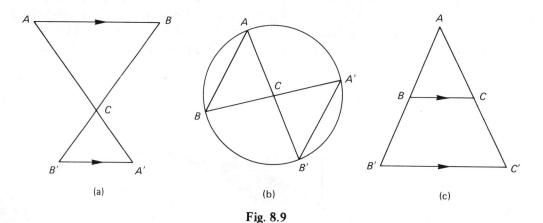

(a)   (b)   (c)

Fig. 8.9

8.10   Geometrical Problems

Modern geometry uses the ideas of transformation geometry to prove geometrical theorems, and to carry out calculations. See section 12.2 for a proof of Pythagoras' theorem. We illustrate these ideas with the following examples; a full treatment is beyond the scope of this book.

Worked Example 8.1

The points *A* and *B* have coordinates (2, 3) and (4, 4) respectively. Their images under a rotation are *A'* (3, −4) and *B'* (4, −6). Plot *A* and *B* and their images on graph paper and by construction or calculation determine the centre and angle of the rotation.

It is also possible to transform A and B to A' and B' by reflection in $y = x$, followed by reflection in a second line. Find the equation of the second line.

[OLE]

Solution

The centre of rotation lies on the line $y = -1$. This is the perpendicular bisector of BB'; see Fig. 8.10. The perpendicular bisector of AA' meets this at the point $(-1, -1)$.

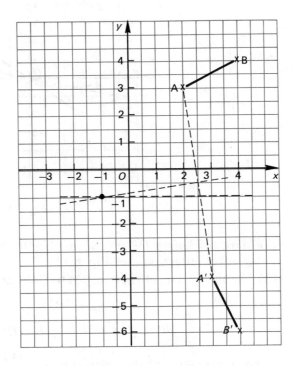

Fig. 8.10

The centre of rotation is $C(-1, -1)$.
The angle of rotation is the angle between AC and $A'C$ by measurement = $90°$.
If B is reflected in the line $y = x$ it maps onto $(4, 4)$ (i.e. it stays put).

$$\therefore \text{ Since } (4, 4) \rightarrow (4, -6).$$

The other line of reflection must be $y = -1$.

Worked Example 8.2

Using a scale of 1 cm to 1 unit on both axes, plot the points $P\,(-5, -1)$, $Q\,(-3, -2)$, $R\,(6, 4)$ and $S\,(5, 1)$. Draw the triangles OPQ and ORS.

A transformation, T, consists of a reflection in a line through O followed by an enlargement, centre O, such that triangle OPQ is transformed by T onto triangle ORS.

(a) Use ruler and compasses only to construct a suitable axis of reflection.
(b) The equation of that axis of reflection may be written in the form $y = kx$.
Estimate from your graph the value of k to two significant figures.

(c) Calculate the lengths of *OP* and *OR* and hence deduce the linear scale factor of the enlargement.

(d) Write down the coordinates of the images of points *P* and *Q* when triangle *OPQ* is transformed by T^2. [OLE]

Solution

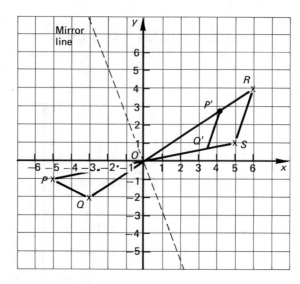

Fig. 8.11

(a) Mark off length *OP* on *OR* and length *OQ* on *OS*. This gives the images *P′* and *Q′* after reflection. See Fig. 8.11.

(b) The mirror line at right angles to *QQ′* can be drawn in. Its gradient is −2.4

$$\therefore k = -2.4.$$

$$OP = \sqrt{5^2 + 1^2} = \sqrt{26}, \; OR = \sqrt{6^2 + 4^2} = \sqrt{52}.$$

The scale factor of the enlargement is $\dfrac{OR}{OP} = \dfrac{\sqrt{52}}{\sqrt{26}} = \sqrt{2}.$

After T^2, the enlargement is by a factor 2, and the triangle has been reflected back to the third quadrant.

$$\therefore \text{Image of } P \text{ is } (-10, -2),$$
$$\text{image of } Q \text{ is } (-6, -4).$$

Worked Example 8.3

In Fig. 8.12 *M* and *N* are the mid-points of the sides *AB* and *AC* respectively of

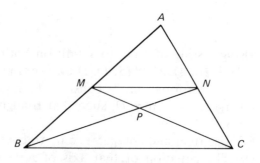

Fig. 8.12

triangle ABC, which is not isosceles. BN and CM meet at P. An enlargement has centre A and scale factor 2.

(a) Under this enlargement, which point is the image of (i) M, (ii) N?

(b) Let the images of B, C and P under this enlargement be B', C' and P' respectively. Draw a neat copy of the diagram and mark the positions of B', C' and P'.

(c) Which triangle in your figure is similar to triangle ABC'?

(d) Describe the shape of the quadrilateral $BPCP'$.

(e) L is the point at which AP produced meets BC. Give a reason why L is the mid-point of BC.

(f) Find the ratios of $AP : PL$ and $BC : MN$, giving reasons for your answers.

(g) Complete the following:

$$\frac{BC}{MN} = \frac{}{MP} = BP.$$

(h) State the ratio of $BP : PN$.

[OLE]

Solution

(a) (i) B;   (ii) C since $AB = 2AM$ and $AC = 2AN$.

(b) See Fig. 8.13.

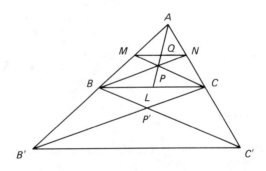

Fig. 8.13

(c) $\triangle AMC$ is similar to ABC', because $AB = 2AM$, $AC' = 2AC$ and angle BAC is common to both triangles.

(d) $MC \parallel BC'$ and $BN \parallel B'C$
Hence $BPCP'$ is a parallelogram.

(e) This is a little awkward at first sight. The reason is that the medians of a triangle (lines joining vertices to the mid-points of the opposite sides) all meet at a point. Since CM and BN are medians, AP must be a median, therefore L is the mid-point.

(f) If AL meets MN at Q, and if we let $AQ = x$, then $QL = x$.
$\triangle BPC$ is an enlargement of $\triangle NPM$, scale factor 2, therefore

$$PL = \frac{2x}{3}, \quad QP = \frac{1}{3}x$$

$$\therefore \ AP = AQ + QP = x + \frac{1}{3}x = \frac{4x}{3}.$$

Hence $AP : PL = \frac{4x}{3} : \frac{2x}{3} = 2 : 1$

$BC : MN = 2 : 1$ enlargement, centre A, scale factor 2.

(g) $\dfrac{BC}{MN} = \dfrac{BP'}{MP} = \dfrac{BP}{PN}$. All ratios are equal to 2.

(h) $BP : PN = 2 : 1$.

Worked Example 8.4

In Fig. 8.14, OL and OM are two lines inclined to one another at an angle $\beta°$, and P is a point such that angle $POL = \alpha°$. P' is the image of P on reflection in OL, and P'' is the image of P' on reflection in OM. The angle POP'', in degrees, is

A $\alpha + \tfrac{3}{2}\beta$ **B** $\beta - \alpha$ **C** $\alpha + 2\beta$ **D** 2β **E** $2\alpha + \beta$ [OLE]

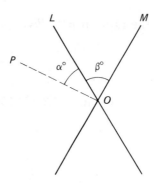

Fig. 8.14

Solution

If α is less than β, then P' lies between OL and OM. See Fig. 8.15(a).
    The angle $POP'' = \alpha + \alpha + \beta - \alpha + \beta - \alpha = 2\beta$.
    If α is greater than β, then P' lies outside OL and OM. See Fig. 8.15(b).
    The angle $POP'' = \alpha + \beta - (\alpha - \beta) = \alpha + \beta - \alpha + \beta = 2\beta$.

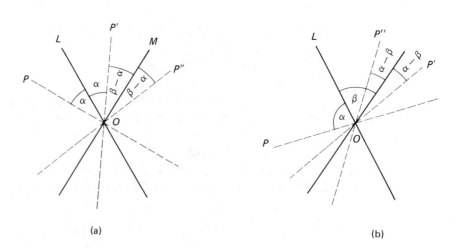

(a)   (b)

Fig. 8.15

In each case the correct answer is **D**.

8.11   Area and Volume of Similar Figures

If a shape is enlarged by a scale factor k, its area is enlarged by a scale factor k^2.

If a three-dimensional shape is enlarged by a scale factor k, its volume is enlarged by a scale factor of k^3.

Note also that its surface area is enlarged by a scale factor of k^2.

The next three examples illustrate quite popular examination questions.

Worked Example 8.5

Figure 8.16 shows a parallelogram $PQRS$, and T is the mid-point of PQ. Find the following ratios:

(a) $\dfrac{\text{Area of triangle } TQU}{\text{Area of triangle } SUR}$;

(b) $\dfrac{\text{Area of triangle } TQU}{\text{Area of quadrilateral } PTUS}$.

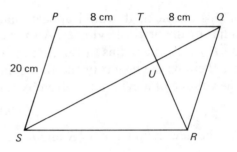

Fig. 8.16

Solution

Since no angles are given, it is not possible to work out any of the individual areas. The methods of similar figures must be used.

(a) $\triangle SUR$ is an enlargement of $\triangle QUT$ centre U and scale factor -2 ($SR = 16$ cm, $TQ = 8$ cm);

hence $\dfrac{\text{Area } \triangle TQU}{\text{Area } \triangle SUR} = \dfrac{1}{(-2)^2} = \tfrac{1}{4}$.

(b) There is no direct enlargement from $\triangle TQU$ to the quadrilateral $PTUS$, hence a different technique must be used. Although the following method is not the only one, it has the advantage of being easily seen diagrammatically. In Fig. 8.17 the area of $\triangle TQU$ is denoted by A. Hence the area of $\triangle SUR$ is $4A$.

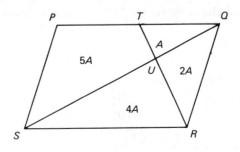

Fig. 8.17

$UR = 2TU$, hence if you regard TU as the base of $\triangle TUQ$ and UR as the base of $\triangle URQ$, they have the same height, but the base has been doubled. Hence the area has been doubled. The area of $\triangle UQR$ is therefore $2A$. Since the diagonal SQ divides the area of the area of the parallelogram into two equal parts, the area of quadrilateral $PTUS$ must be $5A$.

Hence
$$\frac{\text{Area } \triangle TQU}{\text{Area } PTUS} = \frac{A}{5A} = \frac{1}{5}.$$

Worked Example 8.6

A cylinder has a volume of 100 cm³. If another cylinder of the same material is made with half the radius, and three times the height of the original cylinder, find the volume of the second cylinder.

Solution

In this problem, it would appear that there are two unknowns, the height and radius of the original cylinder. Also, we are not given a value for π.
Let R cm be the radius of the first cylinder.
Let H cm be the height of the first cylinder.
The volume of a cylinder is given by the formula $V = \pi r^2 h$,

$$\therefore \ 100 = \pi R^2 H. \tag{1}$$

For the new cylinder, $r = \frac{1}{2}R$ and $h = 3H$.

The new volume
$$V = \pi(\tfrac{1}{2}R)^2(3H) = \frac{3\pi R^2 H}{4}. \tag{2}$$

Using equation (1), however,

$$V = \tfrac{3}{4} \times 100 = 75.$$

The new volume is 75 cm³.

Worked Example 8.7

A balloon is filled with hydrogen, so that its volume is V cm³. The radius of the balloon is then 6 cm. The balloon is then further inflated so that its volume increases by 40 per cent. Find the new radius of the balloon. Assume the shape of the balloon is a sphere at all times.
   The method of enlargements is always easier to use in this type of problem. Find the scale factor for the quantities that you know.

Solution

Original volume = V cm³.

New volume = $V + \dfrac{40V}{100} = 1.4V$ cm³.

$$\frac{\text{New volume}}{\text{Old volume}} = \frac{1.4V}{V} = 1.4.$$

But $\left(\dfrac{\text{New radius}}{\text{Old radius}}\right)^3 = \dfrac{\text{New volume}}{\text{Old volume}} = 1.4.$

Take the cube root of each side:

$$\dfrac{\text{New radius}}{\text{Old radius}} = \sqrt[3]{1.4} = 1.12.$$

$$\text{New radius} = 6 \times 1.12$$

$$= 6.72 \text{ cm}.$$

Worked Example 8.8

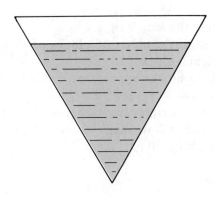

Fig. 8.18

A sealed hollow cone with vertex downwards is partially filled with water. The volume of water is 200 cm^3 and the depth of the water is 50 mm. Find the volume of the water which must be added to increase the depth to 70 mm.   [NISEC]

Solution

This is a question involving similar shapes. If the new depth of water is 70 mm, the ratio of the depths is 50 : 70 = 5 : 7.

The scale factor   = 5 : 7.
The ratio of the volumes = $5^3 : 7^3$
                         = 125 : 343.
The smallest volume has to be made 200 cm.

$\div 5$:   ratio $= 25 : \dfrac{343}{5};$

$\times 8$:   ratio $= 200 : \dfrac{343}{5} \times 8 = 548.8.$

Extra volume needed $= 548.8 - 200 \text{ cm}^3 = 348.8 \text{ cm}^3.$

Worked Example 8.9

A rectangular block of ice cream measures 80 cm by 40 cm by 20 cm. It is to be cut into smaller blocks of the same shape as (i.e., similar to) the original block.

One possible cut is shown shaded in Fig. 8.19 and the resulting block is *ABCDEFGH*.

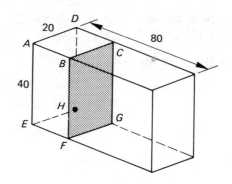

Fig. 8.19

(a) State the length of *AB*.
(b) State the number of blocks of this new size which can be produced from the original block.
   These blocks are further divided into similar blocks each with a longest edge of 5 cm.
(c) State the other two dimensions of such a block.
(d) Calculate how many blocks of this size can be cut from the block 80 cm by 40 cm by 20 cm.   [NEA]

Solution

It is important to realise that this is a question on similar figures.
(a) *AE* is the longest side of the smaller block and is of length 40 cm. The longest side of the large block is of length 80 cm, hence measurements have been halved.
   AB is the shortest side, and hence its length is half of 20 cm, ∴ *AB* = 10 cm.
(b) Clearly 8 blocks can be cut (80 ÷ 10).
(c) 5 cm is one-sixteenth of the original block's longest side.
   The other two lengths are 40 ÷ 16 = 2.5 cm
   and 20 ÷ 16 = 1.25 cm.
(d) The number of smaller blocks can be calculated using the ideas of similar volumes stated in section 8.11.
   The scale factor is 16 : 1.
   The number of blocks is 16^3 = 4096.

Exercise 8

1 Given that two triangles are similar, it then follows that:
   I the areas of the triangles are in the same ratio as the squares of corresponding sides;
   II the three sides of one triangle are equal in length to the lengths of the corresponding sides of the other;
   III the three interior angles of one triangle are equal to the corresponding angles in the other.
   A   I and II only   B   I and III only
   C   II and III only   D   I, II and III   [AEB 1980]

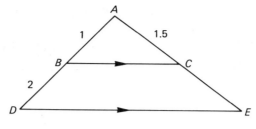

Fig. 8.20

2 In Fig. 8.20, AE equals:
   A 3   **B** 3.5   **C** 4   **D** 4.5

3 ABC is a triangle and E is a point on AB such that $AE : EB = 2 : 5$. F is on AC and EF is parallel to BC. It follows that the ratio of the area of trapezium $BEFC$ to the area of the triangle AEF is:
   A $4 : 25$ **B** $21 : 25$ **C** $45 : 4$ **D** $2 : 5$

4 A metal sphere of diameter 150 mm has a mass of 120 g. A metal sphere of the same material, which weighs 60 g, will have a diameter of approximately:
   A 119 mm   **B** 75 mm   **C** 37.5 mm   **D** 18.8 mm

5 Sphere X has diameter 5 cm and sphere Y has radius 6 cm. The ratio of their surface areas is:
   A $25 : 36$ **B** $36 : 25$ **C** $25 : 24$ **D** $25 : 144$

6 A translation followed by a reflection will always be:
   A a reflection   **B** a rotation
   C a translation   **D** none of these

7 The coordinates of the point P (3, 1) after reflection in the line $y + x = 0$, followed by reflection in the line $y = 0$, are:
   A $(3, -1)$ **B** $(-1, 3)$ **C** $(1, -3)$ **D** $(-1, -3)$

8 In Fig. 8.21, BOC and AOD are straight lines, $2OC = OB$ and $2OD = AO$, E is the mid-point of OC and F the mid-point of OB. Describe the transformation

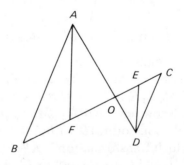

Fig. 8.21

which maps AF into DE. What is the ratio of the area of $\triangle OED$ to that of $\triangle OAB$?

9 A square $ABCD$ has sides of length 2 cm. M_1 denotes a reflection in AB, M_2 a reflection in BC, M_3 a reflection in CD and M_4 a reflection in DA. A small equilateral triangle of side about $\frac{1}{2}$ cm is placed with one side parallel to AB and about $\frac{1}{2}$ cm from AB outside the square with the opposite vertex of the triangle pointing away from the square. Draw the successive positions of this triangle after the reflections M_1, M_2, M_3 and M_4. Show, by drawing, that the transformation $M_4 M_3 M_2 M_1$ can be replaced by a simple rotation.

10 M stands for a reflection in the line $y = x$ and T stands for a translation of 2 units in the direction of the positive x-axis. Draw diagrams to illustrate the effect of the following transformations on the triangle whose vertices are the

points A (1, 0), B (0, 0) and C (1, 1):

(a) MT;   (b) $T^{-1}MT$;   (c) MTM.

11 In Fig. 8.22, $ABCD$ is a rectangle, $AX = DC$. DY is parallel to XB. Prove that triangles ANX and CPD are congruent.

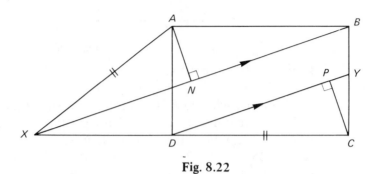

Fig. 8.22

Hence prove that NP is equal and parallel to XD.

12 M_1 is a reflection in the line $y = 3$ and M_2 is a reflection in the line $x + y = 4$. By considering the image of the point A (2, 3) under the transformations (i) $M_1 M_2$, (ii) $M_2 M_1$, show that $M_1 M_2 \neq M_2 M_1$.

Show that $M_1 M_2$ and $M_2 M_1$ can each be replaced by a single rotation with the same centre of rotation. What is this centre of rotation? If these two rotations are denoted by R_1 and R_2 respectively, what is the image of A under the transformation $R_1 R_2$?

13 The following list defines a number of transformations:

R is a rotation of 90° anticlockwise about the origin.

H is a rotation of 180° about the origin.

M_x is a reflection in the x-axis.

M_y is a reflection in the y-axis.

T_x is a translation of 2 units parallel to the x-axis.

T_y is a translation of 2 units parallel to the y-axis.

The ends A and B of a line segment have coordinates (2, 0) and (2, 4) respectively. Show, by clear diagrams, that the effect of the transformation $T_x M_y T_y R$ is to move AB to a position BC. State the coordinates of C.

Show also that $R T_y M_y T_x$ produces a different result, but that $K R T_y M_y T_x$ will transform AB to BC if K is one of the transformations in the list above. Which transformation is K?

14 A, B and C are the points (2, 4), (−3, −6) and (5, −2) respectively.

(a) Write down the components of the translation BC and calculate its magnitude.

(b) The translation which maps B onto C maps A onto D. State the coordinates of D.

(c) Under a dilatation centre the origin B is the image of A. State the scale factor of the dilatation. [SEB]

15 Figure 8.23 shows two unequal squares, $OABC$ and $OPQR$, with centres H and K respectively. Draw a diagram showing the squares and the image of triangle COR when it is rotated through 90° clockwise about H.

Let T be the image of R under the same rotation. Prove that angle TOP = angle CRO.

State the single transformation which maps triangle COR onto triangle TPO.

Let AP meet OT at X. Prove that X is the mid-point of AP. Prove that $2OX = CR$. [OLE]

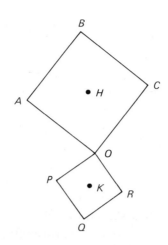

Fig. 8.23

16 A triangle *ABC*, whose vertices are *A* (−1, 2), *B* (−2, 3) and *C* (−4, 2), is subjected to a geometrical transformation *R* followed by another transformation *T*, such that *A*, *B* and *C* are mapped onto *A'* (4, −1), *B'* (5, 0) and *C'* (4, 2) respectively. It is given that *R* is a rotation about *O* (0, 0) and *T* is a translation.

(a) On graph paper, draw the triangles *ABC* and *A'B'C'*. On the same diagram, draw the image of triangle *ABC* under the transformation *R*.

(b) State the angle of rotation of the transformation *R* and find the matrix associated with this transformation.

(c) State the vector of the translation *T*.

(d) Describe geometrically the single transformation which would map triangle *ABC* onto triangle *A'B'C'*. [JMB]

17 Taking the origin *O* near the centre of a sheet of $\frac{1}{2}$ cm square paper, plot the points *A* (2, 0), *B* (0, 4) and *C* (−4, 2).

(a) On your diagram, complete the square *ABCD* and write down the coordinates of the fourth vertex *D*.

(b) Under a half-turn about the point (3, −3), *A* → *P*, *B* → *Q*, *C* → *R* and *D* → *S*. Plot the points *P*, *Q*, *R* and *S* on your diagram and write down their coordinates.

(c) Under the dilatation [*O*, 2], *A* → *K*, *B* → *L*, *C* → *M* and *D* → *N*. Plot the points *K*, *L*, *M* and *N* on your diagram and write down their coordinates.

(d) State the coordinates of the centre and the scale factor of the dilatation under which *K* → *P*, *L* → *Q*, *M* → *R* and *N* → *S*. [SEB]

18 In Fig. 8.24, *PQRS* is a trapezium with *PQ* parallel to *SR*. ∠*PST* = 90°. *PQ* = 6 cm, *PS* = 4 cm, *TR* = 1.5 cm and *QU* = 3 cm.

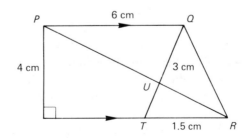

Fig. 8.24

(a) What can be said about triangles *PUQ* and *TUR*?

(b) What can be said about the areas of triangles *TPR* and *TQR*?

(c) Calculate *TU*.

(d) Find in its simplest form the ratio of areas of $\triangle TUR : \triangle PUQ$.

(e) Find, in its simplest form, the ratio of area of $\triangle PUT : \triangle QUP$.

(f) Find the area of the trapezium *PQRT*.

19 *ABC* is a triangle whose sides are all of different lengths; *D* is the mid-point of *BC*, *E* is the mid-point of *CA* and *F* is the mid-point of *AB*. Half-turns with centres *D*, *E* and *F* are denoted by **D**, **E** and **F** respectively. The image of the point *A* under **D** is denoted by **D**(*A*), etc., and the image of the whole triangle is denoted by **D**(△).

Draw a sketch showing in a single diagram the triangle *ABC* and its images under **D**, **E** and **F**. State as fully as you can:

(a) the relationship between the points **D**(*A*), *B* and **F**(*C*);

(b) the relationship between the line segment *CA* and the line joining **D**(*A*) to **F**(*C*);

(c) the transformation mapping **D**(△) onto **F**(△). State the relationship between the line segments *FD* and *AC*. State also the type of transformation mapping the triangle *DEF* onto the triangle formed by the points **D**(*A*), **E**(*B*), **F**(*C*).　　　　　　　　　　　　　　　　[OLE]

20 Triangle *ABC* has *AB* = 4, *BC* = 5, *CA* = 6.

The line *m* bisects angle *A*; *R* is the reflection in *m* and *R* (*B*) = *P*, *R* (*C*) = *Q*.

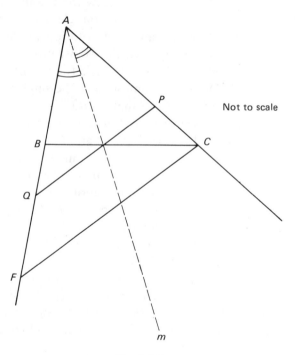

Fig. 8.25

(a) State the lengths of *AP*, *AQ*.

(b) The enlargement *E* has centre *A* and *E* (*AP*) = *AC*. What is the scale factor?

(c) *F* is the point such that *E* (*AQ*) = *AF*.

　(i) Calculate the length of *AF*.

　(ii) Show that *BF* = *BC*.

(d) State the image of angle *ACB* under *R*, and explain why angle *ACB* = angle *AFC*.

(e) Show that angle *ABC* is twice as big as angle *ACB*.　　　　　　　[MEG]

152

9 Matrices

9.1 Array Storage

A great deal of information in everyday life can be represented in a two-dimensional table, called a *matrix*. Table 9.1 shows the milkman's weekly order from one household. The information is compact, and easy to read. This type of *information storage* is commonly used in computers.

Table 9.1

	Mon	Tue	Wed	Thur	Fri	Sat	Sun
Pints of milk	2	2	3	2	1	1	3
Cartons of cream	0	0	1	0	0	0	1
Eggs	6	0	0	0	6	0	0

In this example, the matrix has three *rows* and seven *columns*. We say that the *order* of the matrix is 3×7.

The matrix can be written

$$\begin{pmatrix} 2 & 2 & 3 & 2 & 1 & 1 & 3 \\ 0 & 0 & 1 & 0 & 0 & 0 & 1 \\ 6 & 0 & 0 & 0 & 6 & 0 & 0 \end{pmatrix}$$

if we leave out the headings. The numbers in a matrix are called its *elements*.

9.2 Sum Difference, Multiplication by a Scalar

If $A = \begin{pmatrix} 3 & 4 \\ 1 & 6 \\ 2 & 5 \end{pmatrix}$ and $B = \begin{pmatrix} 4 & -1 \\ 2 & 0 \\ 3 & 1 \end{pmatrix}$

then $A + B = \begin{pmatrix} 3+4 & 4+-1 \\ 1+2 & 6+0 \\ 2+3 & 5+1 \end{pmatrix} = \begin{pmatrix} 7 & 3 \\ 3 & 6 \\ 5 & 6 \end{pmatrix}$.

To add two matrices, simply add the corresponding element.
Two matrices can only be added if they have the same order.

$B + A$ also $= \begin{pmatrix} 7 & 3 \\ 3 & 6 \\ 5 & 6 \end{pmatrix}$,

$\therefore A + B = B + A$.

Addition of matrices is *commutative*, and also clearly *associative*.

153

$$A - B = \begin{pmatrix} -1 & 5 \\ -1 & 6 \\ -1 & 4 \end{pmatrix}. \text{ Simply subtract the corresponding elements.}$$

$$3A = A + A + A = \begin{pmatrix} 9 & 12 \\ 3 & 18 \\ 6 & 15 \end{pmatrix}. \text{ Each element is multiplied by 3.}$$

9.3   Multiplication

To multiply two matrices is a more complicated exercise. The numbers in the following example have been carefully chosen to show the method clearly:

$$\begin{pmatrix} 2 & 5 \\ 6 & 7 \\ 9 & 8 \end{pmatrix} \begin{pmatrix} 10 & 0 & 4 \\ 3 & 16 & 1 \end{pmatrix} = \begin{pmatrix} 2 \times 10 + 5 \times 3 & 2 \times 0 + 5 \times 16 & 2 \times 4 + 5 \times 1 \\ 6 \times 10 + 7 \times 3 & 6 \times 0 + 7 \times 16 & 6 \times 4 + 7 \times 1 \\ 9 \times 10 + 8 \times 3 & 9 \times 0 + 8 \times 16 & 9 \times 4 + 8 \times 1 \end{pmatrix}$$

$$\begin{array}{cc} 3 \times 2 & 2 \times 3 \\ \text{order} & \text{order} \end{array}$$

$$= \begin{pmatrix} 35 & 80 & 13 \\ 81 & 112 & 31 \\ 114 & 128 & 44 \end{pmatrix}$$

$$\begin{array}{c} 3 \times 3 \\ \text{order} \end{array}$$

Two matrices can only be multiplied if the number of columns in the first matrix equals the number of rows in the second. This means that

$$\begin{pmatrix} 10 & 0 & 4 \\ 3 & 16 & 1 \end{pmatrix} \begin{pmatrix} 2 & 5 \\ 6 & 7 \\ 9 & 8 \end{pmatrix} = \begin{pmatrix} 56 & 82 \\ 111 & 135 \end{pmatrix}.$$

$$\begin{array}{ccc} 2 \times 3 & 3 \times 2 & 2 \times 2 \end{array}$$

Clearly, multiplication of matrices is not commutative.

See Worked Example 9.2 for an application of matrix multiplication.

9.4   Algebraic Manipulation 1

If $A = \begin{pmatrix} 4 & 6 \\ 3 & 5 \end{pmatrix}$, then $3A = \begin{pmatrix} 12 & 18 \\ 9 & 15 \end{pmatrix}$; each element is multiplied by 3.

If also $B = \begin{pmatrix} 2 & -1 \\ 3 & 5 \end{pmatrix}$,

then $4A - 3B = \begin{pmatrix} 16 & 24 \\ 12 & 20 \end{pmatrix} - \begin{pmatrix} 6 & -3 \\ 9 & 15 \end{pmatrix} = \begin{pmatrix} 10 & 27 \\ 3 & 5 \end{pmatrix}.$

See Check 27.

9.5 Identity

If $I = \begin{pmatrix} 1 & 0 \\ 0 & 1 \end{pmatrix}$ and $A = \begin{pmatrix} 4 & 1 \\ 2 & -4 \end{pmatrix}$, then $IA = \begin{pmatrix} 1 & 0 \\ 0 & 1 \end{pmatrix}\begin{pmatrix} 4 & 1 \\ 2 & -4 \end{pmatrix}$

$$= \begin{pmatrix} 4 & 1 \\ 2 & -4 \end{pmatrix} = AI.$$

The matrix $\begin{pmatrix} 1 & 0 \\ 0 & 1 \end{pmatrix}$ is called the 2×2 *identity* matrix. It leaves a matrix unchanged if multiplied by it.

$$\text{The matrix} \qquad \begin{pmatrix} 1 & 0 & 0 & \ldots \\ 0 & 1 & 0 & \ldots \\ 0 & 0 & 1 & \ldots \\ \ldots \ldots \ldots \ldots \end{pmatrix}$$

$$n \times n$$

is the $n \times n$ identity matrix; it has 1's on the *leading diagonal*, and zero everywhere else.

9.6 Inverse Matrices

If $A = \begin{pmatrix} 4 & 3 \\ 5 & 6 \end{pmatrix}$ and $B = \begin{pmatrix} \frac{6}{9} & -\frac{3}{9} \\ -\frac{5}{9} & \frac{4}{9} \end{pmatrix}$,

then $AB = \begin{pmatrix} 4 & 3 \\ 5 & 6 \end{pmatrix}\begin{pmatrix} \frac{6}{9} & -\frac{3}{9} \\ -\frac{5}{6} & \frac{4}{9} \end{pmatrix} = \begin{pmatrix} 1 & 0 \\ 0 & 1 \end{pmatrix}$,

and $BA = \begin{pmatrix} \frac{6}{9} & -\frac{3}{9} \\ -\frac{5}{9} & \frac{4}{9} \end{pmatrix}\begin{pmatrix} 4 & 3 \\ 5 & 6 \end{pmatrix} = \begin{pmatrix} 1 & 0 \\ 0 & 1 \end{pmatrix}$.

Since $AB = BA = I$, we say that A is the inverse of B, or B is the inverse of A.

$\therefore A = B^{-1}$ or $B = A^{-1}$.

In general, if $A = \begin{pmatrix} a & b \\ c & d \end{pmatrix}$

then $\qquad A^{-1} = \begin{pmatrix} \dfrac{d}{\Delta} & \dfrac{-b}{\Delta} \\ \dfrac{-c}{\Delta} & \dfrac{a}{\Delta} \end{pmatrix}$ where $\Delta = ad - bc$.

Δ is called the *determinant* of the matrix.

If $\Delta = 0$, then the matrix will have no inverse, and is called a *singular* matrix. A matrix which has an inverse is called *non-singular*.

Check 26

Find the inverse of the following matrices where possible:

1 $\begin{pmatrix} 4 & 2 \\ 5 & 3 \end{pmatrix}$ **2** $\begin{pmatrix} 6 & -7 \\ -5 & 6 \end{pmatrix}$ **3** $\begin{pmatrix} 4 & 2 \\ -8 & -4 \end{pmatrix}$

4 $\begin{pmatrix} 2 & 3 \\ -6 & 9 \end{pmatrix}$ **5** $\begin{pmatrix} 1 & 0 \\ 0 & -1 \end{pmatrix}$ **6** $\begin{pmatrix} 6 & -4 \\ 3 & 11 \end{pmatrix}$

*9.7 Algebraic Manipulation 2

Because multiplication of matrices is not commutative, care has to be taken in manipulating matrix equations.

For example,

$$\text{if } AC = B, \text{ where } A, B \text{ and } C \text{ are matrices,}$$

multiply both sides on the *left* by A^{-1}:

$$\therefore A^{-1}AC = A^{-1}B,$$

$A^{-1}A = I,$ $\qquad \therefore \qquad IC = A^{-1}B,$

$$\therefore \qquad C = A^{-1}B. \quad \text{(Provided } A^{-1}B \text{ is possible.)}$$

9.8 Simultaneous Equations

Consider the equations $\qquad 2x + 4y = 12 \qquad (1)$

$$3x - 7y = 5. \qquad (2)$$

These can be represented using matrices in the following way:

$$\begin{pmatrix} 2 & 4 \\ 3 & -7 \end{pmatrix} \begin{pmatrix} x \\ y \end{pmatrix} = \begin{pmatrix} 12 \\ 5 \end{pmatrix}.$$

If $A = \begin{pmatrix} 2 & 4 \\ 3 & -7 \end{pmatrix}$, $B = \begin{pmatrix} 12 \\ 5 \end{pmatrix}$ and $C = \begin{pmatrix} x \\ y \end{pmatrix}$,

then we have $AC = B$,
as in section 9.6 this means $C = A^{-1}B$.

$$A^{-1} = \begin{pmatrix} \frac{-7}{-26} & \frac{-4}{-26} \\ \frac{-3}{-26} & \frac{2}{-26} \end{pmatrix} = \begin{pmatrix} \frac{7}{26} & \frac{2}{13} \\ \frac{3}{26} & \frac{-1}{13} \end{pmatrix},$$

$$\therefore \begin{pmatrix} x \\ y \end{pmatrix} = \begin{pmatrix} \frac{7}{26} & \frac{2}{13} \\ \frac{3}{26} & \frac{-1}{13} \end{pmatrix} \begin{pmatrix} 12 \\ 5 \end{pmatrix} = \begin{pmatrix} 4 \\ 1 \end{pmatrix};$$

the solution is $x = 4$, $y = 1$.

Examination questions often slightly alter the wording as shown in the following example:

Worked Example 9.1

(a) Find $\begin{pmatrix} 4 & 3 \\ -1 & 9 \end{pmatrix}\begin{pmatrix} 9 & -3 \\ 1 & 4 \end{pmatrix}$.

(b) Use your answer to part (a) to solve the equations

$$4t + 3q = 31, \qquad 9q - t = 41.$$

Solution

(a) $\begin{pmatrix} 4 & 3 \\ -1 & 9 \end{pmatrix}\begin{pmatrix} 9 & -3 \\ 1 & 4 \end{pmatrix} = \begin{pmatrix} 39 & 0 \\ 0 & 39 \end{pmatrix}$

(b) The first part of the question in fact gives us straight away the determinant of the matrix as 39. Notice that the equations have been muddled up, and in fact are

$$4t + 3q = 31,$$

$$-t + 9q = 41.$$

The relevance of the matrices can now be seen.

Find $\begin{pmatrix} 9 & -3 \\ 1 & 4 \end{pmatrix}\begin{pmatrix} 31 \\ 41 \end{pmatrix} = \begin{pmatrix} 156 \\ 195 \end{pmatrix}$.

This answer must be divided by 39.

$\therefore t = 4, q = 5$.

This method is slightly easier in that it does not involve any fractions.

If $X = \begin{pmatrix} a & b \\ c & d \end{pmatrix}$, the matrix $\begin{pmatrix} d & -b \\ -c & a \end{pmatrix}$ is called the *adjoint* of X.

Check 27

1 $A = \begin{pmatrix} 1 & 4 \\ -1 & 3 \end{pmatrix}$, $B = \begin{pmatrix} 2 & -2 \\ 4 & 1 \end{pmatrix}$, $C = \begin{pmatrix} 3 & -1 & -1 \\ 0 & 1 & 2 \end{pmatrix}$,

$D = \begin{pmatrix} 4 & 3 & 0 \\ -2 & -1 & 1 \end{pmatrix}$, $E = \begin{pmatrix} 2 & 1 \\ 4 & -2 \\ 3 & -5 \end{pmatrix}$, $F = \begin{pmatrix} 4 & 3 \\ -1 & 0 \\ 1 & 2 \end{pmatrix}$ and $G = \begin{pmatrix} 1 & -1 & -2 \\ 0 & 1 & 3 \\ 4 & 1 & 6 \end{pmatrix}$.

Evaluate if possible:
(a) $C + 2D$;   (b) $3E - 2F$;   (c) $A - 3B$;   (d) $2D - 3E$;
(e) $4G$;   (f) $A + B + 2C$.

2 Find the matrix M, given that:

$$4M - \begin{pmatrix} 1 & 2 \\ -3 & 5 \end{pmatrix} = \begin{pmatrix} 6 & 1 \\ -1 & 4 \end{pmatrix}.$$

3 Find the matrix A if

$$\begin{pmatrix} 1 & 0 \\ 2 & -1 \end{pmatrix} - 3A = 2A + \begin{pmatrix} -1 & 0 \\ 1 & 2 \end{pmatrix}.$$

4 Evaluate, if possible, the following matrix products:

(a) $(2 \quad 1)\begin{pmatrix} 3 \\ 4 \end{pmatrix}$ (b) $\begin{pmatrix} 3 \\ 1 \end{pmatrix}(2 \quad 1)$ (c) $(1 \quad 3 \quad 4)\begin{pmatrix} 2 \\ -1 \\ -2 \end{pmatrix}$

(d) $(2 \quad 1)\begin{pmatrix} 3 \\ 4 \\ 2 \end{pmatrix}$ (e) $\begin{pmatrix} 3 & 1 & -1 \\ 0 & 1 & 1 \end{pmatrix}\begin{pmatrix} 2 & 1 \\ 4 & 2 \\ 1 & 0 \end{pmatrix}$

(f) $\begin{pmatrix} -1 & 0 \\ 2 & -3 \end{pmatrix}\begin{pmatrix} 4 \\ 1 \end{pmatrix}$ (g) $\begin{pmatrix} 1 & -1 & 0 \\ 2 & 1 & 3 \end{pmatrix}\begin{pmatrix} 2 \\ -1 \\ 0 \end{pmatrix}$

(h) $\begin{pmatrix} 2 & 1 \\ 1 & 2 \end{pmatrix}\begin{pmatrix} 3 & 4 & -1 \\ 0 & 1 & 2 \end{pmatrix}$ (i) $\begin{pmatrix} 2 & 2 & 0 \\ 1 & 3 & 4 \\ -1 & 0 & 6 \end{pmatrix}\begin{pmatrix} 1 & 4 & -2 \\ 0 & 1 & 3 \\ 3 & 1 & 6 \end{pmatrix}$

5 If $X = \begin{pmatrix} 2 & 1 \\ 3 & 0 \end{pmatrix}$, $Y = \begin{pmatrix} -1 & 0 \\ 2 & 4 \end{pmatrix}$ and $Z = \begin{pmatrix} 3 & 1 \\ -1 & 0 \end{pmatrix}$, find XYZ.

6 Solve the following pairs of simultaneous equations by using a matrix method.

(a) $3x + 4y = 1$
$2x - y = 6$

(b) $5x + 3y = 7$
$4x - 5y = 9$

(c) $6x = 5y - 11$
$2y = 8x + 3$

(d) $6x - 9y = 11$
$5x + 17y = 2$

9.9 Networks and Route Matrices

Figure 9.1 shows a network consisting of four *nodes*, A, B, C and D, linked by seven *arcs* in various ways, which divide the plane up into five *regions*. The routes represented by the arcs can be travelled along in either direction.

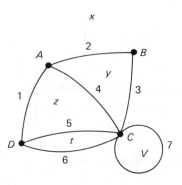

Fig. 9.1

(a) One-stage Route Matrix

A *one-stage* route between any two nodes is not allowed to pass through any of the other nodes. If R is the one-stage route matrix, then

$$
R = \text{from} \begin{array}{c} \\ A \\ B \\ C \\ D \end{array}
\begin{array}{cccc} \overset{\text{to}}{} & & & \\ A & B & C & D \\ \end{array}
\left(
\begin{array}{cccc}
0 & 1 & 1 & 1 \\
1 & 0 & 1 & 0 \\
1 & 1 & 2 & 2 \\
1 & 0 & 2 & 0
\end{array}
\right).
$$

Note that the matrix is *symmetrical* about the leading diagonal.

(b) Two-stage Route Matrix

A *two-stage* route between two nodes passes through one other node on the way. The two-stage routes between A and C are shown in Fig. 9.2. It can be seen that there are five.

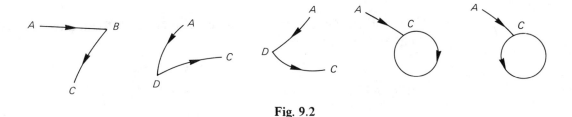

Fig. 9.2

If you now evaluate R^2, you will find that:

$$
R^2 = \begin{array}{c} \\ A \\ B \\ C \\ D \end{array}
\begin{array}{cccc} A & B & C & D \\ \end{array}
\left(
\begin{array}{cccc}
3 & 1 & ⑤ & 2 \\
1 & 2 & 3 & 3 \\
5 & 3 & 10 & 5 \\
2 & 3 & 5 & 5
\end{array}
\right).
$$

— five two-stage routes between A and C

This matrix gives the two-stage routes. You may like to try and justify ten for C to C. Similarly, R^3 gives the three-stage routes for the network.

9.10   Incidence Matrices

Let us look again at Fig. 9.1. Node A lies on (is *incident* on) arcs 1, 2, 4. Node C is incident on 3, 4, 5, 6 and 7 (twice). The matrix N representing the incidence of nodes on arcs is given below:

$$
N = \begin{array}{c} \\ A \\ B \\ C \\ D \end{array}
\begin{array}{ccccccc} 1 & 2 & 3 & 4 & 5 & 6 & 7 \\ \end{array}
\left(
\begin{array}{ccccccc}
1 & 1 & 0 & 1 & 0 & 0 & 0 \\
0 & 1 & 1 & 0 & 0 & 0 & 0 \\
0 & 0 & 1 & 1 & 1 & 1 & 2 \\
1 & 0 & 0 & 0 & 1 & 1 & 0
\end{array}
\right).
$$

If we form the *transpose* N^T of the matrix (interchange rows and columns), we get

$$N^T = \begin{array}{c} \\ 1 \\ 2 \\ 3 \\ 4 \\ 5 \\ 6 \\ 7 \end{array} \begin{array}{cccc} A & B & C & D \\ \begin{pmatrix} 1 & 0 & 0 & 1 \\ 1 & 1 & 0 & 0 \\ 0 & 1 & 1 & 0 \\ 1 & 0 & 1 & 0 \\ 0 & 0 & 1 & 1 \\ 0 & 0 & 1 & 1 \\ 0 & 0 & 2 & 0 \end{pmatrix} \end{array}.$$

This gives the incidence of the arcs on the nodes. The reader should look at NN^T, and compare it with the one-stage route matrix R.

Incidence matrices can also be written down for arcs on regions, and regions on arcs.

9.11 Euler's Theorem

If in any network, R is the number of regions, N the number of nodes and A the number of arcs, then

$$R + N = A + 2.$$

In Fig. 9.1, $\qquad\qquad 5 + 4 = 7 + 2.$

9.12 Traversability

If a network can be drawn without taking the pencil off the paper and without following the same arc twice, it is said to be *traversable*.

A network is traversable if
(a) all its junctions are even or (b) only two of its junctions are odd.

The *order* of a node is the number of arcs leaving the node.
In Fig. 9.3 the order of the nodes is as follows:

$$A(4), B(4), C(4), D(4), E(4).$$

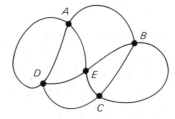

Fig. 9.3

Since these are all even, the network is traversable.

9.13 Transformations

It was stated in section 8.2 that 2×2 matrices can be used to represent transformations in the (x, y) plane. The simplest way to observe the effect of these is to consider the effect that a matrix has on the coordinates of a square with sides of length one, called the *unit square*.

(a) Reflection

The coordinates of a point (Fig. 9.4) are represented as a vector, e.g.

$$B = \begin{pmatrix} 1 \\ 1 \end{pmatrix}.$$

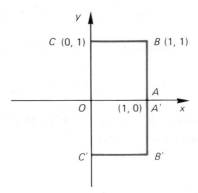

Fig. 9.4

The square can be represented as a 2×4 matrix:

$$\text{Square} = \begin{matrix} O & A & B & C \\ \begin{pmatrix} 0 & 1 & 1 & 0 \\ 0 & 0 & 1 & 1 \end{pmatrix} \end{matrix}.$$

Consider the effect of the matrix $\begin{pmatrix} 1 & 0 \\ 0 & -1 \end{pmatrix}$. The square must be *premultiplied* by the matrix.

$$\therefore \begin{pmatrix} 1 & 0 \\ 0 & -1 \end{pmatrix}\begin{pmatrix} 0 & 1 & 1 & 0 \\ 0 & 0 & 1 & 1 \end{pmatrix} = \begin{matrix} O' & A' & B' & C' \\ \begin{pmatrix} 0 & 1 & 1 & 0 \\ 0 & 0 & -1 & -1 \end{pmatrix} \end{matrix}$$

Note: The first column of the matrix is the image of $\begin{pmatrix} 1 \\ 0 \end{pmatrix}$, the second of $\begin{pmatrix} 0 \\ 1 \end{pmatrix}$.

Transformed points will be denoted by A' etc. It can be seen that the vertices of the square have been reflected in the x-axis. It can also be shown as follows that all points will be reflected in the x-axis.

Consider any point $P(x, y)$, written $\begin{pmatrix} x \\ y \end{pmatrix}$. Transforming this point,

$$\begin{pmatrix} 1 & 0 \\ 0 & -1 \end{pmatrix}\begin{pmatrix} x \\ y \end{pmatrix} = \begin{pmatrix} x \\ -y \end{pmatrix}.$$

Hence $P(x, y) \rightarrow P'(x, -y)$. The x-coordinate has stayed the same, the y-coordinate has changed sign.

Similarly, $\begin{pmatrix} -1 & 0 \\ 0 & 1 \end{pmatrix}$ represents reflection in the y-axis,

$\begin{pmatrix} 0 & 1 \\ 1 & 0 \end{pmatrix}$ represents reflection in the line $y = x$,

$\begin{pmatrix} 0 & -1 \\ -1 & 0 \end{pmatrix}$ represents reflection in the line $y = -x$.

* A very useful formula for finding the matrix which represents the transformation of reflection in the line $y = x \tan \alpha°$ ($\tan \alpha°$ is the gradient of the line which slopes at an angle $\alpha°$ to the x-axis) is given by

$$M = \begin{pmatrix} \cos 2\alpha° & \sin 2\alpha° \\ \sin 2\alpha° & -\cos 2\alpha° \end{pmatrix}.$$

For example, to find reflection in the line $y = x$, means that $\alpha = 45°$.

$$\therefore M = \begin{pmatrix} \cos 90° & \sin 90° \\ \sin 90° & -\cos 90° \end{pmatrix} = \begin{pmatrix} 0 & 1 \\ 1 & 0 \end{pmatrix}.$$

The origin $(0, 0)$ always stays at $(0, 0)$ under a 2×2 matrix transformation, and will be left out from now on. We say that $(0, 0)$ is *invariant*.

(b) Rotation

Consider the matrix $\begin{pmatrix} 0 & 1 \\ -1 & 0 \end{pmatrix}$;

$$\begin{array}{ccc} A & B & C \end{array} \qquad \begin{array}{ccc} A' & B' & C' \end{array}$$
$$\begin{pmatrix} 0 & 1 \\ -1 & 0 \end{pmatrix} \begin{pmatrix} 1 & 1 & 0 \\ 0 & 1 & 1 \end{pmatrix} = \begin{pmatrix} 0 & 1 & 1 \\ -1 & -1 & 0 \end{pmatrix}.$$

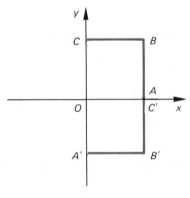

Fig. 9.5

The square appears to be in the same place (Fig. 9.5), but on looking at the labelling of the points, it can be seen that the square has been rotated *clockwise* by 90° about O, i.e. $-90°$. Clockwise angles are designated as being negative. Also, $\begin{pmatrix} 0 & -1 \\ 1 & 0 \end{pmatrix}$ is a rotation of $+90°$ about O, $\begin{pmatrix} -1 & 0 \\ 0 & -1 \end{pmatrix}$ is a half-turn about O.

* In general, the matrix which gives an anticlockwise rotation of $\alpha°$ is given by

$$R = \begin{pmatrix} \cos \alpha° & -\sin \alpha° \\ \sin \alpha° & \cos \alpha° \end{pmatrix}.$$

(c) Shear

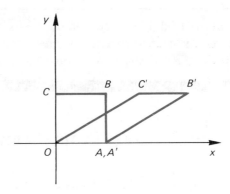

Fig. 9.6

Consider the effect of $\begin{pmatrix} 1 & 3 \\ 0 & 1 \end{pmatrix}$ on the unit square

$$\begin{pmatrix} 1 & 3 \\ 0 & 1 \end{pmatrix}\begin{pmatrix} 1 & 1 & 0 \\ 0 & 1 & 1 \end{pmatrix} = \begin{pmatrix} 1 & 4 & 3 \\ 0 & 1 & 1 \end{pmatrix}.$$

The square has been sheared parallel to the x-axis, the x-axis is the invariant line and $(1, 1) \rightarrow (4, 1)$.

In general, $\begin{pmatrix} 1 & k \\ 0 & 1 \end{pmatrix}$ is a shear of shear factor k parallel to the x-axis,

$\begin{pmatrix} 1 & 0 \\ k & 1 \end{pmatrix}$ is a shear of shear factor k parallel to the y-axis.

See section 8.7.

(d) Enlargement

If the matrix $\begin{pmatrix} k & 0 \\ 0 & k \end{pmatrix}$ is applied to the unit square, it simply enlarges it by a scale factor k, with O as the centre of the enlargement.

See section 8.6.

(e). Stretch

If the matrix $\begin{pmatrix} k & 0 \\ 0 & 1 \end{pmatrix}$ is applied to the unit square, the square is stretched by a factor k in the direction of the x-axis. (See section 8.8.)

Similarly, $\begin{pmatrix} 1 & 0 \\ 0 & k \end{pmatrix}$ is a stretch parallel to the y-axis.

9.14 Combining Transformations

If we want to find the effect of the transformation represented by matrix M_1, followed by the transformation represented by the matrix M_2, simply evaluate the matrix product $M_2 M_1$ (order must be correct).

9.15 Inverse and Identity Transformations

The matrix $\begin{pmatrix} 1 & 0 \\ 0 & 1 \end{pmatrix}$ as a transformation leaves the shape unchanged. For a transformation represented by T, the inverse matrix T^{-1} will represent the transformation that returns the shape to its original position.

Since many transformations are self-inverses, for example all reflections, the inverse of the matrix will be the same as the original matrix.

Worked Example 9.2

The matrix, X, gives information about the number of chocolates of each kind in three different boxes:

$$
X = \begin{array}{c} \text{Box } A \\ \text{Box } B \\ \text{Box } C \end{array}
\begin{array}{ccccc}
\text{Nut} & \begin{array}{c}\text{Soft}\\\text{centre}\end{array} & \begin{array}{c}\text{Hard}\\\text{centre}\end{array} & \text{Toffee} & \text{Plain}
\end{array}
\begin{pmatrix}
3 & 5 & 4 & 2 & 3 \\
4 & 3 & 5 & 3 & 1 \\
6 & 6 & 3 & 0 & 4
\end{pmatrix}.
$$

(a) Multiply matrix X by the matrix $\begin{pmatrix} 1 \\ 1 \\ 1 \\ 1 \\ 1 \end{pmatrix}$ and state what information your answer gives.

(b) Matrix Y gives information about the cost to the manufacturer of each type of chocolate and the number of calories in each type.

	Cost (pence)	Calories
Nut	4	30
Soft centre	3	25
$Y = $ Hard centre	2	30
Toffee	3	40
Plain	1	20

Evaluate the matrix product XY. Hence state the total number of calories in box A. What is the cost to the manufacturer of producing the chocolates in box C?

[OLE]

Solution

(a)

$$\begin{array}{c} A \\ B \\ C \end{array} \begin{pmatrix} 3 & 5 & 4 & 2 & 3 \\ 4 & 3 & 5 & 3 & 1 \\ 6 & 6 & 3 & 0 & 4 \end{pmatrix} \begin{pmatrix} 1 \\ 1 \\ 1 \\ 1 \\ 1 \end{pmatrix} = \begin{array}{c} A \\ B \\ C \end{array} \begin{pmatrix} 17 \\ 16 \\ 19 \end{pmatrix}$$

The answer gives the *total* number of chocolates in box A, box B and box C.

(b)

$$XY = \begin{array}{c} A \\ B \\ C \end{array} \begin{pmatrix} 3 & 5 & 4 & 2 & 3 \\ 4 & 3 & 5 & 3 & 1 \\ 6 & 6 & 3 & 0 & 4 \end{pmatrix} \begin{matrix} \text{Cost} & \text{Cal} \\ \begin{pmatrix} 4 & 30 \\ 3 & 25 \\ 2 & 30 \\ 3 & 40 \\ 1 & 20 \end{pmatrix} \end{matrix} = \begin{array}{c} A \\ B \\ C \end{array} \begin{matrix} \text{Cost} & \text{Cal} \\ \begin{pmatrix} 44 & 475 \\ 45 & 485 \\ 52 & 500 \end{pmatrix} \end{matrix}$$

It should be noted that the headings for the columns in the first matrix are the same as the headings for the rows in the second matrix. The headings for the final matrix are the row headings from the first matrix and the column headings from the second. Providing care is taken, interpreting the answer should not be difficult.

Total number of calories in box A is 475.

Total cost of producing box C is 52p.

Worked Example 9.3

Using a scale of 2 cm to represent 1 unit on each axis, draw on graph paper $\triangle PQR$, where P, Q, R are respectively the points $(3, -1)$ $(3, -2)$ and $(5, -2)$. Find and draw the image of $\triangle PQR$ under the transformation whose matrix is M where $M = \begin{pmatrix} 1 & 0 \\ 0 & -1 \end{pmatrix}$, and describe this transformation.

Find and draw the image of $\triangle PQR$ under the transformation whose matrix is NM, where

$$N = \begin{pmatrix} -\frac{3}{5} & \frac{4}{5} \\ \frac{4}{5} & \frac{3}{5} \end{pmatrix},$$

and describe the transformation whose matrix is N. By finding the coordinates of the point (x, y) under the transformation whose matrix is N, show that the line $y = 2x$ is unchanged under the transformation, and describe the transformation whose matrix is N.   [L]

Solution

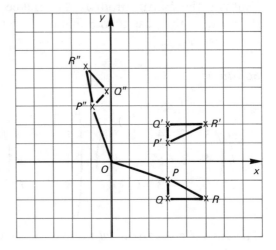

Fig. 9.7

Write the triangle as a 2×3 matrix:

$$\Delta = \begin{matrix} P & Q & R \\ \begin{pmatrix} 3 & 3 & 5 \\ -1 & -2 & -2 \end{pmatrix} \end{matrix}.$$

$$\therefore \begin{pmatrix} 1 & 0 \\ 0 & -1 \end{pmatrix} \begin{pmatrix} 3 & 3 & 5 \\ -1 & -2 & -2 \end{pmatrix} = \begin{matrix} P' & Q' & R' \\ \begin{pmatrix} 3 & 3 & 5 \\ 1 & 2 & 2 \end{pmatrix} \end{matrix}.$$

This is reflection in the x-axis.

$$NM = \begin{pmatrix} -\frac{3}{5} & \frac{4}{5} \\ \frac{4}{5} & \frac{3}{5} \end{pmatrix} \begin{pmatrix} 1 & 0 \\ 0 & -1 \end{pmatrix} = \begin{pmatrix} -\frac{3}{5} & -\frac{4}{5} \\ \frac{4}{5} & -\frac{3}{5} \end{pmatrix},$$

$$\begin{pmatrix} -\frac{3}{5} & -\frac{4}{5} \\ \frac{4}{5} & -\frac{3}{5} \end{pmatrix} \begin{pmatrix} 3 & 3 & 5 \\ -1 & -2 & -2 \end{pmatrix} = \begin{matrix} P'' & Q'' & R'' \\ \begin{pmatrix} -1 & -\frac{1}{5} & -\frac{7}{5} \\ 3 & \frac{18}{5} & \frac{26}{5} \end{pmatrix} \end{matrix}.$$

The triangle has been rotated about O anticlockwise by an angle of $126.9°$.
    Transforming (x, y) by N we have

$$\begin{pmatrix} -\frac{3}{5} & \frac{4}{5} \\ \frac{4}{5} & \frac{3}{5} \end{pmatrix} \begin{pmatrix} x \\ y \end{pmatrix} = \begin{pmatrix} -\frac{3}{5}x + \frac{4}{5}y \\ \frac{4}{5}x + \frac{3}{5}y \end{pmatrix};$$

if $y = 2x$, the matrix on the right becomes

$$\begin{pmatrix} -\frac{3}{5}x + \frac{8}{5}x \\ \frac{4}{5}x \cdot + \frac{6}{5}x \end{pmatrix} = \begin{pmatrix} x \\ 2x \end{pmatrix},$$

hence y is still equal to $2x$.

If a complete line is unaltered, unless some shearing has occurred, which the diagram shows it hasn't, the transformation N is a reflection in the line $y = 2x$.

Exercise 9

1 The inverse of the matrix $\begin{pmatrix} 1 & 4 \\ 2 & 7 \end{pmatrix}$ is:

A $\begin{pmatrix} -7 & 4 \\ 2 & -1 \end{pmatrix}$ B $\begin{pmatrix} 7 & -4 \\ -2 & 1 \end{pmatrix}$ C $\begin{pmatrix} 1 & 2 \\ 4 & 7 \end{pmatrix}$ D $\begin{pmatrix} -1 & -2 \\ -4 & -7 \end{pmatrix}$

[AEB 1981]

2 If $A = \begin{pmatrix} 1 & 1 \\ 1 & 1 \end{pmatrix}$, then A^2 equals:

A $\begin{pmatrix} 1 & 1 \\ 1 & 1 \end{pmatrix}$ B $\begin{pmatrix} 1 & 0 \\ 0 & 1 \end{pmatrix}$ C $\begin{pmatrix} 2 & 2 \\ 2 & 2 \end{pmatrix}$ D $\begin{pmatrix} 0 & 1 \\ 1 & 0 \end{pmatrix}$

3 The matrix $\begin{pmatrix} 1 & 4 \\ -4 & 1 \end{pmatrix}$ represents:

A   a rotation   B   a reflection   C   a shear   D   none of these

4 If $AB = \begin{pmatrix} 3 & 4 \\ 6 & 8 \end{pmatrix}$ and $B = \begin{pmatrix} 3 & 4 \\ 5 & 6 \end{pmatrix}$ then A equals

A $\begin{pmatrix} 6 & -4 \\ -5 & 3 \end{pmatrix}$ B $\begin{pmatrix} 1 & 2 \\ 0 & 0 \end{pmatrix}$ C $\begin{pmatrix} 29 & 36 \\ 58 & 72 \end{pmatrix}$ D $\begin{pmatrix} 1 & 0 \\ 2 & 0 \end{pmatrix}$

5 If $A = \begin{pmatrix} 2 & 3 \\ -4 & -6 \end{pmatrix}$ and $A^2 = kA$ where k is a number, then k equals:

A -4 B 4 C 1 D A

6 If $A = \begin{pmatrix} 4 & 3 \\ 1 & 1 \end{pmatrix}$, $B = \begin{pmatrix} 2 & 0 \\ 2 & 0 \end{pmatrix}$ and $C = (2 \quad 4)$, then $A + BC$ equals:

A $\begin{pmatrix} 8 & 3 \\ 5 & 1 \end{pmatrix}$ B $\begin{pmatrix} 12 & 3 \\ 9 & 1 \end{pmatrix}$ C $\begin{pmatrix} 12 & 12 \\ 6 & 4 \end{pmatrix}$ D   none of these

7 The matrix which represents a reflection in the line $y = -x$, followed by an enlargement, centre O, scale factor 2, is:

A $\begin{pmatrix} -2 & 0 \\ 0 & 2 \end{pmatrix}$ B $\begin{pmatrix} 2 & 0 \\ 0 & -2 \end{pmatrix}$ C $\begin{pmatrix} 0 & 2 \\ 2 & 0 \end{pmatrix}$ D $\begin{pmatrix} 0 & -2 \\ -2 & 0 \end{pmatrix}$

8 The inverse of AB where A and B are 2×2 matrices, whose inverses exist, is always:

A $B^{-1}A^{-1}$ B AB^{-1} C $A^{-1}B$ D $A^{-1}B^{-1}$

9 If $A = \begin{pmatrix} a & b \\ c & d \end{pmatrix}$ and $B = \begin{pmatrix} -c & -d \\ a & b \end{pmatrix}$, then AB equals:

A $\begin{pmatrix} 0 & 0 \\ 0 & 0 \end{pmatrix}$ B $\begin{pmatrix} -ac & -bd \\ ac & bd \end{pmatrix}$ C $\begin{pmatrix} ac + ab & -ad + b^2 \\ c^2 + da & bd - dc \end{pmatrix}$

D none of these

10 The transformation $T = \begin{pmatrix} 1 & 2 \\ 1 & -1 \end{pmatrix}$ maps P onto Q. If P lies on the line $x + 2y = O$, then Q lies on the line:

A $y = \dfrac{3x}{2}$ B $y = 2x$ C $x = 0$ D none of these

11 If x and y are positive, and
$$\begin{pmatrix} x & x \\ y & y \end{pmatrix} \begin{pmatrix} x & y \\ y & x \end{pmatrix} = \begin{pmatrix} 3 & t \\ t & 3 \end{pmatrix},$$
find x, y and t.

12 If $A = (1 \quad 2)$ and $B = \begin{pmatrix} 3 \\ -1 \end{pmatrix}$, evaluate:

(a) AB (b) BA

13 If $A = \begin{pmatrix} x_1 & x_2 \\ x_3 & x_4 \end{pmatrix}$, $B = \begin{pmatrix} y_1 & y_2 \\ y_3 & y_4 \end{pmatrix}$ and $C = \begin{pmatrix} t_1 & t_2 \\ t_3 & t_4 \end{pmatrix}$
show that $A(BC) = (AB)C$.

14 Find x and y given that $\begin{pmatrix} x \\ y \end{pmatrix} = \begin{pmatrix} 4 & -1 \\ 2 & 0 \end{pmatrix} \begin{pmatrix} 3 \\ -2 \end{pmatrix} + \begin{pmatrix} 1 \\ 6 \end{pmatrix}$.

15 The following statements about the 2×2 matrices A, B, C and D are all false. Give examples which demonstrate these statements to be false.

(a) $\begin{pmatrix} 1 & 0 \\ 0 & 0 \end{pmatrix} A = \begin{pmatrix} 0 & 0 \\ 0 & 0 \end{pmatrix} \Rightarrow A = \begin{pmatrix} 0 & 0 \\ 0 & 0 \end{pmatrix}$.

(b) $\begin{pmatrix} 1 & 0 \\ 0 & 0 \end{pmatrix} B = B \begin{pmatrix} 1 & 0 \\ 0 & 0 \end{pmatrix}$ for every 2×2 matrix B.

(c) If $\begin{pmatrix} 1 & 0 \\ 0 & 0 \end{pmatrix} C = \begin{pmatrix} 1 & 0 \\ 0 & 0 \end{pmatrix} D$, then $C = D$.   [OLE]

16 If $A = \begin{pmatrix} 5 & 8 \\ -3 & -5 \end{pmatrix}$, evaluate A^2, and hence solve the equation
$5x + 8y = 2$,
$-3x - 5y = 1$.

17 A triangle is formed by the points $A(2, 0)$, $B(5, 0)$ and $C(4, 2)$. The matrix $\begin{pmatrix} 2 & 4 \\ 1 & 6 \end{pmatrix}$ transforms the triangle into the triangle $A'B'C'$. Find the determinant of the matrix, and hence find the area of triangle $A'B'C'$.

18 On graph paper, plot the square $A(2, 0)$, $B(2, 2)$, $C(0, 2)$ and $D(0, 0)$. Transform this square by means of the matrix $\begin{pmatrix} 0.6 & 0.8 \\ -0.8 & 0.6 \end{pmatrix}$, and hence give a geometrical description of the matrix.

19 Under a certain transformation T, the image (x', y') of the point (x, y) is given by:
$$\begin{pmatrix} x' \\ y' \end{pmatrix} = \begin{pmatrix} 4 & 2 \\ 0 & 3 \end{pmatrix} \begin{pmatrix} x \\ y \end{pmatrix} + \begin{pmatrix} 2 \\ 1 \end{pmatrix}.$$

(a) Find the image under T of $(0, 0)$.

(b) Find the point which under T is mapped onto $(16, 0)$.

(c) Is there a point P such that $T(P) = P$?

20 The following list defines a number of transformations:

R is a rotation of $90°$ anticlockwise about the origin.

H is a rotation of $180°$ about the origin.

M_x is a reflection in the x-axis.

M_y is a reflection in the y-axis.

T_x is a translation of two units parallel to the x-axis.

T_y is a translation of two units parallel to the y-axis.

The ends A and B of a line segment have coordinates $(2, 0)$ and $(2, 4)$ respectively. Show, by clear diagram, that the effect of the transformation $T_x M_y T_y R$ is to move AB to a position BC. State the coordinates of C.

Show also that $RT_y M_y T$ produces a different result but that $kRT_y M_y T_x$ will transform AB to BC if k is one of the transformations in the list above. Which transformation is k? [OLE]

21 (a) For the network shown in Fig. 9.8 write down:

(i) the matrix X giving the number of arcs between any two nodes;

(ii) the 3×7 incidence matrix T for arcs on nodes;

(iii) the corresponding incidence matrix S showing the incidence of nodes on arcs.

(iv) What is the relationship between S and T?

(b) Evaluate (i) TS, (ii) $TS - X$. What does $TS - X$ represent?

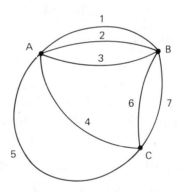

Fig. 9.8

22 (a) $A \begin{pmatrix} 2 & 1 \\ -1 & 3 \end{pmatrix}$, $B = \begin{pmatrix} 4 & 1 \\ -2 & -5 \end{pmatrix}$, and $C = \begin{pmatrix} 3 & -1 \\ 2 & -2 \end{pmatrix}$.

Write, as a single matrix,

(i) $B + C$, (ii) AB.

(b) $T = \begin{pmatrix} 0 & -1 \\ 1 & 0 \end{pmatrix}$. Evaluate the matrix product $T\begin{pmatrix} x \\ y \end{pmatrix}$ and describe clearly the transformation whose matrix is T. Hence, or otherwise, write T^8 as a single matrix. [UCLES]

23 The country of Albion has four local airstrips A, B, C, D, and two international airports G, H. Regular services exist or not between these, as shown by 1 or 0 in the matrix M. Flights from G and H to airports U, V, W in Gaul are given by matrix N.

$$\text{Matrix } M = \begin{matrix} & \begin{matrix} G & H \end{matrix} \\ \begin{matrix} A \\ B \\ C \\ D \end{matrix} & \begin{pmatrix} 1 & 0 \\ 0 & 1 \\ 1 & 1 \\ 1 & 1 \end{pmatrix} \end{matrix} \qquad \text{Matrix } N = \begin{matrix} & \begin{matrix} U & V & W \end{matrix} \\ \begin{matrix} G \\ H \end{matrix} & \begin{pmatrix} 1 & 0 & 1 \\ 1 & 1 & 0 \end{pmatrix} \end{matrix}.$$

Find the product matrix MN and interpret it. Local services in Gaul go from U, V, W to internal airports X, Y, Z as shown by matrix P.

$$\text{Matrix } P = \begin{matrix} & \begin{matrix} X & Y & Z \end{matrix} \\ \begin{matrix} U \\ V \\ W \end{matrix} & \begin{pmatrix} 1 & 0 & 1 \\ 1 & 1 & 0 \\ 0 & 0 & 1 \end{pmatrix} \end{matrix}.$$

A traveller wishes to travel by air between these countries. Find by any method (a) which of the journeys from A or B or C or D to X or Y or Z have no air route; (b) which of them are connected by more than one route. [OLE]

24 (a) Under a certain transformation, the image (x', y') of a point (x, y) is given

by $\begin{pmatrix} x' \\ y' \end{pmatrix} = \begin{pmatrix} 2 & 1 \\ -1 & 1 \end{pmatrix} \begin{pmatrix} x \\ y \end{pmatrix} + \begin{pmatrix} 3 \\ 9 \end{pmatrix}.$

  (i) Find the coordinates of A, the image of the point $(0, 0)$.

  (ii) Find the coordinates of B, the image of the point $(4, 3)$.

  (iii) Given that the image of the point (g, h) is the point $(0, 0)$, write down two equations each involving g and h. Hence, or otherwise, find the values of g and h.

(b) Find the value of x for which the matrix $\begin{pmatrix} x + 3 & 0 \\ 0 & 2 \end{pmatrix}$

  (i) has no inverse;

  (ii) represents an enlargement.

  State the scale factor of this enlargement. [UCLES]

25 Using a scale of 1 cm to 1 unit on both axes, draw on graph paper the flag formed by the points (2 1), (2, 2), (2, 3), (3, 3) and (3, 2). E is the enlargement with centre $(0, 2)$ and scale factor 2. T is the translation $\begin{pmatrix} -1 \\ -5 \end{pmatrix}$ which maps the point (x, y) onto the point $(x - 1, y - 5)$.

R is the anticlockwise rotation of 90° about the point $(3, -2)$.

On your graph, show the image of the flag under each of the following transformations:

(a) E; (b) T; (c) RT.

  Label the images (i), (ii) and (iii) respectively.

The transformation RT is an anticlockwise rotation. State the angle of rotation and find the coordinates of the centre of the rotation. [UCLES]

26 On graph paper, using a scale of 1 cm to represent 1 unit on each axis, draw the square whose vertices are O $(0, 0)$, A $(1, 0)$, B $(1, 1)$ and C $(0, 1)$. Calculate the coordinates of the images O', A', B' and C' of these points under the transformation M whose matrix is M, where

$$M = \begin{pmatrix} 4 & -3 \\ 3 & 4 \end{pmatrix}.$$

Draw the image figure $O'A'B'C'$ on your graph.

Using Pythagoras' theorem or otherwise, calculate $O'A'$ and $O'C'$. Measure $\angle A'O'C'$. Hence calculate the area $O'A'B'C'$, and state a relationship between the ratio $\dfrac{\text{area } O'A'B'C'}{\text{area } OABC}$ and the matrix M.

Find the coordinates of the points P and Q where the line $3y - 4x = 6$ cuts the x-axis and the y-axis respectively. Calculate the images P and Q of these points under the transformation M. Find the tangent of the angle between PQ and $P'Q'$. [L]

27 (a) The vertices of a square A are $(0, 0)$, $(4, 0)$, $(4, 4)$ and $(0, 4)$.

Using x- and y-axes with values from 0 to 8, draw and label A.

(b) Transformation S is defined by

$$S: \begin{pmatrix} x \\ y \end{pmatrix} \rightarrow \begin{pmatrix} 1 & 1 \\ 0 & 1 \end{pmatrix} \begin{pmatrix} x \\ y \end{pmatrix}.$$

(i) Draw the image of A under transformation S. Label it B.

(ii) Describe the transformation S.

(c) Transformation T is 'reflection in the line $y = x$'.

(i) Draw the image of B under transformation T. Label it C.

(ii) Write down the matrix of transformation T.

(d) Transformation U is transformation S followed by transformation T. By evaluating a suitable matrix product, or otherwise, find the matrix of transformation U.

(e) Transformation V is defined by

$$V: \begin{pmatrix} x \\ y \end{pmatrix} \rightarrow \begin{pmatrix} 1 & 0 \\ 1 & 1 \end{pmatrix} \begin{pmatrix} x \\ y \end{pmatrix}.$$

(i) Draw the image of A under transformation V. Label it D.

(ii) Explain why your answer to part (d) is not the same as the matrix for transformation V. [NEA]

28 R is the transformation with matrix $\begin{pmatrix} 0 & -1 \\ 1 & 0 \end{pmatrix}$.

S is the transformation with matrix $\begin{pmatrix} 0 & -1 \\ -1 & 0 \end{pmatrix}$.

A is the point $(1, 0)$, B is the point $(3, 0)$ and C is the point $(1, 1)$.

(a) Find the coordinates of A_1, B_1, C_1, the images of A, B and C under R.

(b) Using scales of 2 cm for 1 unit on both axes, draw a diagram to show ABC and $A_1 B_1 C_1$. Label these points.

(c) (i) Find the coordinates of A_2, B_2 and C_2, the images of A_1, B_1 and C_1 under S.

(ii) Add A_2, B_2 and C_2 to your diagram and label the points.

(d) (i) Calculate $\begin{pmatrix} 0 & -1 \\ -1 & 0 \end{pmatrix} \begin{pmatrix} 0 & -1 \\ 1 & 0 \end{pmatrix}$.

(ii) Describe geometrically the transformation T which this represents.

(iii) What is the relationship between R, S and T? [MEG]

10 Straight Lines and Circles

10.1   Parallel Lines

The basic properties of angles can be seen in Fig. 10.1.

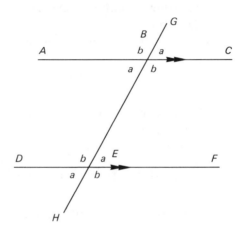

Fig. 10.1

BE can go in any direction; it is only the relative positions that are important.

The pairs ∠*ABG*, ∠*HBC* are called *vertically opposite* angles.
The pairs ∠*GBC*, ∠*BEF* are called *corresponding* angles.
The pairs ∠*ABE*, ∠*BEF* are called *alternate* angles; alternate angles form a characteristic 'Z' shape.
The pairs ∠*ABG*, ∠*GBC* are called *adjacent* angles.
Adjacent angles add up to 180°.
Any two angles that add up to 180° are called *supplementary* angles.

10.2   The Triangle

The angles of a triangle add up to 180°.

The exterior angle of a triangle equals the sum of the two interior and opposite angles.

172

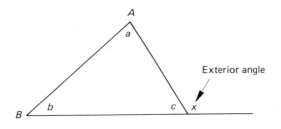

Fig. 10.2

In Fig. 10.2,

$$a + b + c = 180$$
$$a + b = x.$$

10.3   Polygons

The exterior angles of any polygon add up to 360°.

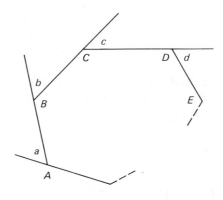

Fig. 10.3

Referring to Fig. 10.3,

$$a + b + c + d + \ldots = 360.$$

To investigate the sum of the interior angles of an *n*-sided polygon, we have:

Sum $= (180 - a)° + (180 - b)° + (180 - c)° + (180 - d)° + \ldots$
$ = (180 + 180 + 180 + 180 \ldots)° - (a + b + c + d + \ldots)°$
$ = 180n - 360 = 90(2n - 4)°$

We have: The sum of the interior angles of an *n*-sided polygon = $(2n - 4)$ right angles.

10.4   Regular Polygons

A *regular* *n*-sided polygon has *n* equal sides and *n* equal angles. Since the sum of the *n* equal exterior angles is 360°, it follows that for a regular polygon, each

exterior angle $= \dfrac{360°}{n}$.

10.5   Symmetry

(a) Line Symmetry

Consider the rectangle in Fig. 10.4. The line *m* divides the rectangle into two equal parts, one half of which can be folded about *m* to fit exactly on the other. We say that *m* is an *axis of symmetry* (or *line of symmetry*).

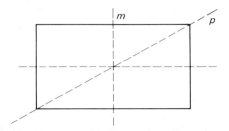

Fig. 10.4

Note that the line *p* divides the rectangle into two equal halves, but one half does not land on top of the other if folded about *p*, which is therefore not an axis of symmetry.

(b) Rotational Symmetry

The hexagon in Fig. 10.5 maps onto itself if rotated about an axis through *O* at right angles to the plane by 60°. If this is repeated 6 times, *A* returns to its original position. We say that the *order* of rotational symmetry is 6.

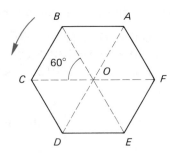

Fig. 10.5

(c) Three Dimensions

In three dimensions, we can have a *plane* of symmetry which divides a solid into two equal halves. For example, a plane through the centre of a sphere.

10.6   Geometric Properties of Simple Plane Figures

(a) Isosceles Triangle

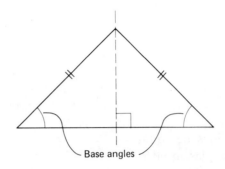

Fig. 10.6

Base angles are equal.
Two sides are equal.
Questions involving isosceles triangles are often made easier if considered as two joined right-angled triangles separated by the line of symmetry.

(b) Equilateral Triangle

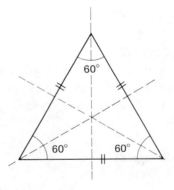

Fig. 10.7

All sides are equal.
All angles equal 60°.
There are 3 axes of symmetry.
Order of rotational symmetry is 3.

(c) Obtuse-angled Triangle

One angle is greater than 90°.

(d) Square

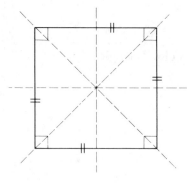

Fig. 10.8

All sides are equal.
All angles equal 90°.
Diagonals are equal in length and bisect each other at right angles.
There are 4 axes of reflective symmetry.
Order of rotational symmetry is 4.

(e) Rectangle

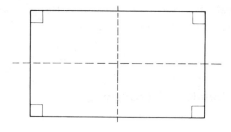

Fig. 10.9

All angles are 90°.
The diagonals are equal in length and bisect each other.
There are 2 axes of reflective symmetry.
Order of rotational symmetry is 2.

(f) Parallelogram

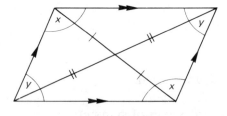

Fig. 10.10

Opposite sides are parallel.
Opposite angles are equal.
The diagonals bisect each other.
There is rotational symmetry of order 2 about the intersection of the diagonals.
There is no line symmetry.

(g) Rhombus

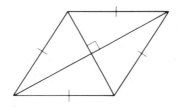

Fig. 10.11

A rhombus is a parallelogram with all sides equal.
The diagonals bisect each other at right angles.
There are two axes of line symmetry.
Order of rotational symmetry is 2.

(h) Kite

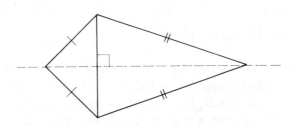

Fig. 10.12

The diagonals are perpendicular.
There is one axis of symmetry.
Two pairs of adjacent sides are equal in length.

(i) Trapezium

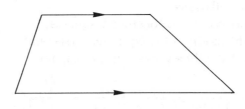

Fig. 10.13

Two opposite sides are parallel. In general, there is no symmetry.

(j) Triangle Mid-point Theorem

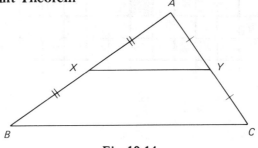

Fig. 10.14

In any triangle *ABC*, if the mid-points *X* and *Y* of *AB* and *AC* respectively are joined, *XY* is parallel to *BC*.

177

10.7　Tessellations

In Fig. 10.15 can be seen a number of repeating patterns, each of which can be extended as far as you like in any direction. Such patterns are called *tessellations*. A shape tessellates if it covers the plane without leaving any gaps.

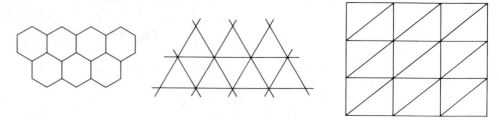

Fig. 10.15

10.8　Regular Tessellations

If the basic shape (referred to as the motif) is a regular polygon, the pattern is called a *regular tessellation*. If you consider any vertex of a regular tessellation, since the angles there must add up to 360°, it follows that the internal angles of a polygon in a regular tessellation must divide exactly into 360°. If you try a few possible angles it can be seen that the only possible regular tessellations are with equilateral triangles, regular hexagons and squares.

10.9　Combined or Modified Polygons

In Fig. 10.16 can be seen a number of tessellations which are based on the regular tessellations.
(a) combines together 5 squares;
(b) modifies the equilateral triangle;
(c) combines together 2 hexagons.

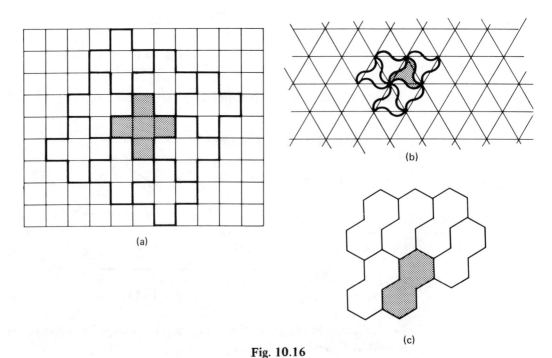

Fig. 10.16

178

10.10   Semi-regular Tessellations

The tessellations shown in Fig. 10.17 are examples of *semi-regular tessellations*, based on two or more different regular polygons.

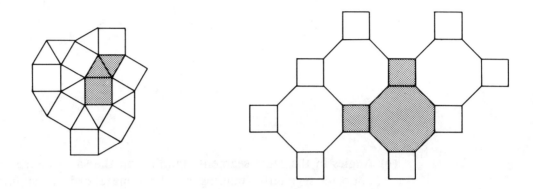

Fig. 10.17

It can be seen, however, that a basic motif, shown shaded, can be found to tessellate the pattern. At each vertex of a semi-regular tessellation there must be the same combination of polygons. For this reason, there are only eight semi-regular tessellations. See if you can find them.

10.11   The Circle (Definitions)

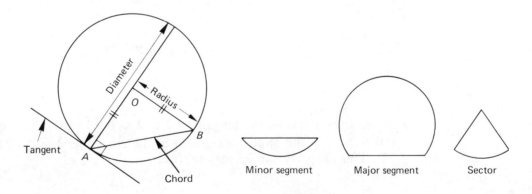

Fig. 10.18

The diameter is twice the radius. OAB is an isosceles triangle.

10.12   The Properties of the Circle

These will be stated here without proof.
(a) The angle between a radius OA and the tangent at A is 90°. See Fig. 10.18.
(b) The angle *subtended* at the centre by two points of the circle A and B is twice the angle subtended by A and B at any point T on the circle. See Fig. 10.19 for various configurations.

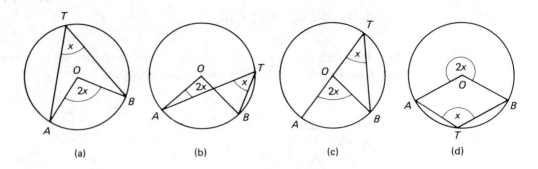

(a)   (b)   (c)   (d)

Fig. 10.19

(c) Angles in the same segment standing on the same chord are equal. Angles in opposite segments standing on the same chord are supplementary. See Fig. 10.20. AT_1BT_2 is called a *cyclic quadrilateral*.

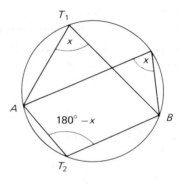

Fig. 10.20

(d) The angle between the tangent at T and a chord through A equals the angle on the chord in the opposite segment of the circle. See Fig. 10.21.
  This property can be very useful.

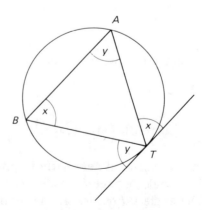

Fig. 10.21

(e) Tangents to a circle from a point are equal in length: In Fig. 10.22, the diagram is symmetrical about OT, hence $AT = BT$.

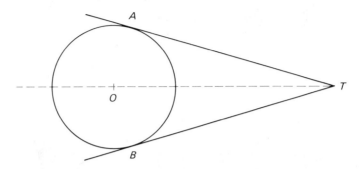

Fig. 10.22

(f) If two chords AB and CD intersect at P, it can be shown that $AP \cdot PB = PC \cdot PD$; see Fig. 10.23.

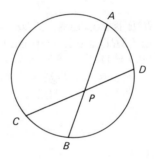

Fig. 10.23

(g) A line drawn from a point P outside a circle which cuts the circle at A and B (this line is called a *secant*) has the property

$$AB \cdot AC = AT^2$$

where T is the point of contact of the tangent from A.

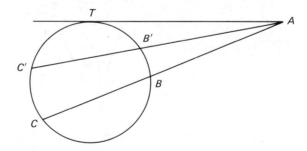

Fig. 10.24

For a second secant, $AB' \cdot AC' = AT^2$ (Fig. 10.21).

Hence, $\qquad\qquad\qquad\qquad AB' \cdot AC' = AB \cdot AC.$

181

Worked Example 10.1

A cyclic quadrilateral *PQRS* has *PQ* = *PS*. The diagonal *QS* = *QR*. If ∠*QSR* = 52°, find ∠*PQR*. See Fig. 10.25.

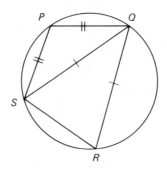

Fig. 10.25

Solution

Since △*SQR* is isosceles, ∠*SQR* = 180° − 104° = 76°.
∠*SPQ* and ∠*SRQ* are in opposite segments,
hence ∠*SPQ* = 180° − 52° = 128°.
△*SPQ* is isosceles, ∴ ∠*PQS* = $\frac{1}{2}$(180° − 128°) = 26°,
∴ ∠*PQR* = 76° + 26° = 102°.

Worked Example 10.2

Find the angles *p* and *q* marked in Fig. 10.26 where *EA* and *ED* are tangents to the circle.

Solution

First attempts at this question might give difficulty in using the recognized circle theorems. However, tangents drawn to a circle from a given point have the same

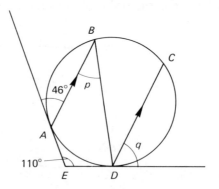

Fig. 10.26

length; see theorem (e) above. Hence, if the line *AD* is joined, since *EA* = *ED*, then *ADE* is an isosceles triangle.

182

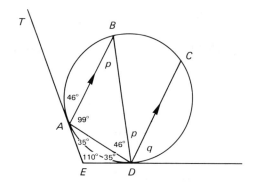

Fig. 10.27

In Fig. 10.27 the angles that can next be found are as follows:
$\angle EAD = \angle EDA = 35°$,
$\angle TAE = 180°$, $\therefore \angle BAD = 99°$.
$\angle BDA = \angle BAT = 46°$ (theorem (d)).
Hence $p = 35°$.
But $\angle BDC = \angle ABD = p$.
$\therefore 35° + 46° + p + q = 180°$,
hence $q = 64°$.

Worked Example 10.3

In Fig. 10.28, PA is 12 mm shorter than PD.

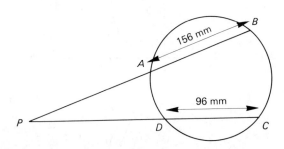

Fig. 10.28

It is also given that $AB = 156$ mm, $CD = 96$ mm and $PA = x$ mm.
(a) Obtain an equation for x.
(b) Calculate x.   [AEB]

Solution

This is not an easy question to do unless the student remembers theorem (g).
(a) It follows that $PA \times PB = PD \times PC$.
$$\therefore x(x + 156) = (x + 12)(x + 12 + 96) = (x + 12)(x + 108).$$
(b) $$\therefore x^2 + 156x = x^2 + 120x + 1296,$$
$$\therefore 36x = 1296,$$
$$\therefore x = 36.$$

Find all the angles marked with a letter in Fig. 10.29. *T* indicates a tangent.

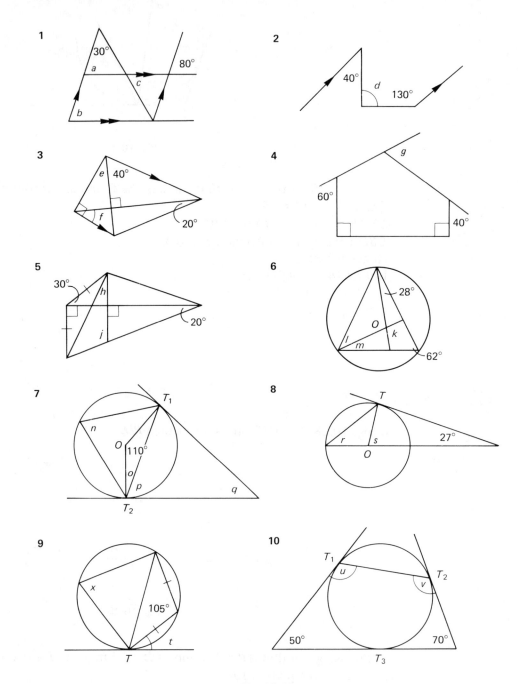

Fig. 10.29

Exercise 10

Multiple choice questions on these topics are usually very straightforward and are therefore not included.

1 In Fig. 10.30, *O* is the centre of a circle of radius 8 cm. $\angle AOB = 80°$. $\angle CBO = 60°$, and *BC* and *AO* produced meet at *D*. Calculate:
(a) $\angle ADB$ (b) *AB*   (c) *OD*   [Trigonometry required.]

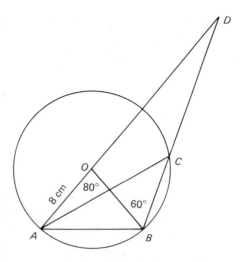

Fig. 10.30

2 *P*, *Q*, *R* and *S* are four points which lie on a circle *PQ* and *SR* produced meet at *T*, and *PS* and *QR* produced meet at *U*. If ∠*PTS* = 30° and ∠*PUQ* = 45°, find the angles of the quadrilateral *PQRS*.

3 *P* is the point inside a circle. A chord of the circle is drawn through *P*. If the shortest chord that can be drawn has length 10 cm, and the greatest distance from *P* to the circumference of the circle is 25 cm, find the radius of the circle.

4 In the diagram, Fig. 10.31, ∠*ADC* = 30° and the lines *DA* and *DC* are tangents to the circle at *A* and *C* respectively. If *AC* = 4 m and *B* is able to move subject

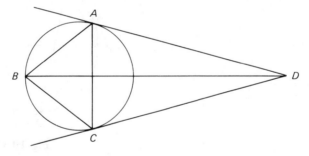

Fig. 10.31

to the condition that 30° ⩽ ∠*ACB* ⩽ 60°, find, by drawing, the angle through which the line *BD* can turn.

5 In Fig. 10.32 *ABC* is a straight line, *O* is the centre of the circle and *AT* is a tangent to the circle. If ∠*BOT* = 100° and ∠*BAT* = 20°, calculate ∠*TOC* (obtuse).

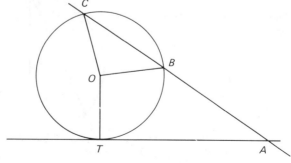

Fig. 10.32

185

6 In Fig. 10.33, *TA* and *TB* are tangents to a circle centre *O*, *TOC* is a straight line and $\angle ATB = 60°$. Calculate:

(a) $\angle ABT$ (b) $\angle AOB$ (reflex)   (c) $\angle BCO$

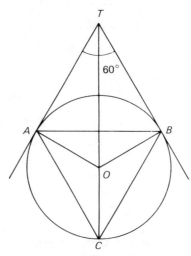

Fig. 10.33

7 In Fig. 10.34, *AC* is a diameter of the circle and the chord *BD* intersects *AC* at *X*. Given that $\angle BCA = 26°$ and $\angle CAD = 47°$, calculate:

(a) $\angle BAC$ (b) $\angle AXD$ [UCLES]

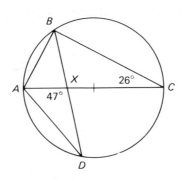

Fig. 10.34

8 *TA* is a tangent to a circle. (*A* is on the circle.) *AB* is a chord of the circle and *O* is the centre of the circle. If $\angle BAT = 50°$, find $\angle BOA$.

9 In Fig. 10.35, *O* is the centre of the circle and *BTC* is a tangent. Given that $\angle BAT = x°$ and $\angle CAT = 2x°$, name three other angles of this figure each equal to $2x°$.

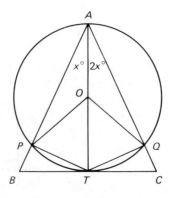

Fig. 10.35

10 A regular polygon has exterior angles of $x°$. Find, in terms of x,
   (a) the interior angle;
   (b) the number of sides;
   (c) the number of lines of symmetry;
   (d) the order of rotational symmetry of the polygon.

11 A pentomino is the name given to an arrangement of five squares such as those shown in Fig. 10.36. The arrangements (a) and (b) are different, but (c) is regarded as the same as (a).

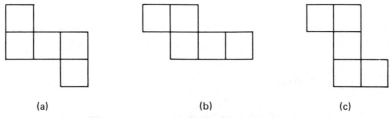

      (a)   (b)   (c)

Fig. 10.36

There are altogether 12 different pentominoes; see if you can find them, and then fit them together to form a rectangle which is 3 squares by 20. How many ways are there of forming this rectangle?

12

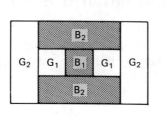
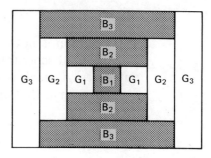

          Cushion 2   Cushion 3

Fig. 10.37

A craft shop sells a range of cushions of different sizes whose fronts are made from strips of blue (B) and green (G) ribbon, each 5 cm wide. Cushions 2 and 3 are shown in the diagram, and the lengths of the strips are given in the table below.

Strip	B_1	B_2	B_3		G_1	G_2	G_3
Length (cm)	10	20	30		5	15	25

The pattern is extended for cushions 4, 5, 6, etc.

(a) (i) State the lengths of strips B_4, B_5 and G_4, G_5.
   (ii) State, in terms of n, the lengths of strips B_n and G_n used in cushion n. Find n if cushion n measures 85 cm by 100 cm.

(b) (i) Find the total length of the green strips used in cushion 3.
   (ii) The total length, R cm, of the green strips in cushion n is given by the formula

$$R = 10n^2.$$

   Show that this is true for cushion 3.

   (iii) 280 cm each of green and blue ribbon are available to make a cushion front. Making no allowance for joins, find the largest possible value of n.   [LEAG]

11 Probability and Statistics

11.1 Sample Space

The set of all possible outcomes in a given situation, or mathematical experiment, is called the sample space, denoted by S or $\mathcal{E}$.

Examples: (a) If a fair die is rolled,

$$S = \{1, 2, 3, 4, 5, 6\}.$$

(b) If three coins are tossed,

$$S = \{HHH, HHT, HTH, HTT, THH, THT, TTH, TTT\}.$$

This notation is not always very satisfactory; for example, if two dice are rolled, and the total score found, although there are only 12 scores, there are 36 possible outcomes. A much better way to illustrate the sample space would be by using a diagram such as that in Fig. 11.1.

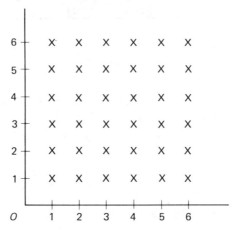

Fig. 11.1

11.2 Definition of Probability

(a) Empirical Definition

If an experiment is carried out n times and results in m successes, then the *empirical* (or experimental) probability is $\dfrac{m}{n}$.

If a die is rolled 18 times, and the score 2 is obtained twice, then the experimental probability is $\frac{2}{18} = \frac{1}{9}$. However, if asked what is the proability when rolling a die of scoring 2, we would probably give the answer of $\frac{1}{6}$. If we increase the number of times that the die is rolled, the probability would get closer to the theoretical value which is defined in the following section.

(b) Theoretical Definition

The theoretical definition is as follows:

$$\text{Probability} = \frac{\text{The number of ways of achieving success}}{\text{The total number of outcomes}}.$$

We have, then, that the theoretical probability of rolling a six with one die is $\frac{1}{6}$.

11.3 Complement, Certain and Impossible Events

The outcomes in a given situation are often referred to as events.

If an event is certain to happen, its probability is 1,
in fact $P(S) = 1$.
If an event is impossible, its probability is zero, i.e. $P(\phi) = 0$.

Returning to the die and rolling a score of 2, we have

$$P(\text{score } 2) = \frac{1}{6}.$$

The probability of not scoring 2 is $\frac{5}{6}$.
The probability of an event not happening is called the *complement* of the event. Using set notation, if the event is denoted by E, its complement is denoted by E';

clearly, $\qquad\qquad\qquad P(E) + P(E') = 1.$

11.4 Set Notation

Questions in probability can often be made easier by the use of set notation. Consider the following example.

Worked Example 11.1

A card is taken from an ordinary pack of playing cards. Find in two different ways the probability of drawing a red picture card, illustrating one of them by a Venn diagram.

Solution

Method (a) The sample space S consists of the 52 cards. If the event of drawing a red picture card is denoted by R, then

$$R = \{J\heartsuit, Q\heartsuit, K\heartsuit, J\diamondsuit, Q\diamondsuit, K\diamondsuit\},$$

$$P(R) = \frac{n(R)}{n(S)} = \tfrac{6}{52} = \tfrac{3}{26}.$$

Method (b) Using the Venn diagram in Fig. 11.2,

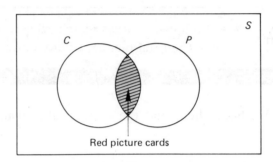

Fig. 11.2

If $C = \{$red cards$\}$ and $P = \{$picture cards$\}$, then the set of red picture cards is denoted by $C \cap P$.

$$P(R) = \frac{n(C \cap P)}{n(S)} = \tfrac{6}{52} = \tfrac{3}{26}.$$

The following check exercise consists of questions on basic probability.

Check 29

1 List all the possible outcomes if a coin is tossed 4 times.
2 A box contains 1 red, 1 white and 1 blue ball. Draw up a sample space for the possible outcomes when two balls are drawn (the first being replaced before the second is drawn).
3 A die is numbered 1, 1, 2, 5, 6, 6. Construct a sample space for rolling the die twice.
4 Determine the probabilities of the following events:
  (a) A king appears in drawing a single card from an ordinary pack of 52 cards.
  (b) A white marble appears in drawing a single marble from an urn containing 4 white, 3 red and 5 blue marbles.
  (c) Choosing a vowel from the word 'probability'.
  (d) A prime number is drawn from a pack of 25 cards numbered 1 to 25.
  (e) Not drawing a red ball from a box containing 6 red, 4 white and 5 blue balls.
5 $\mathcal{E} = \{1, 2, 3, \ldots, 50\}$, $A = \{$multiples of 7$\}$, $B = \{$multiples of 5$\}$, $C = \{$multiples of 3$\}$.
  If any element x is chosen at random from $\mathcal{E}$, find the probability that:
  (a) $x \in A \cup B$; (b) $x \in B \cap C$; (c) $x \in A \cap C'$.

11.5   Combined Events, Tree Diagrams

Consider the following situation. A fair coin is tossed, and a spinner numbered 1, 2, 3, 4 is spun and the results on each are recorded; the possible sample space S is given by

$$S = \{H1, H2, H3, H4, T1, T2, T3, T4\}.$$

We could also use a diagram similar to that in Fig. 11.1.

If E_1 is the event of gaining a head and a score of 2, then since $E_1 = \{H2\}$, we have

$$P(E_1) = \frac{n(E_1)}{n(S)} = \tfrac{1}{8}.$$

If E_2 is the event of gaining a head and an even number or a tail and scoring 1, then

$$E_2 = \{H2, H4, T1\},$$

hence
$$P(E_2) = \frac{n(E_2)}{n(S)} = \tfrac{3}{8}.$$

We will now look at solving a problem of this nature by the use of a *tree diagram*, in which the probability of each event is marked on the appropriate branch of the tree. Since both tossing the coin and using the spinner are carried out at the same time, Fig. 11.3 shows the two possible tree diagrams that can be drawn. This is not the case if the order of the events matters, when only one can be drawn.

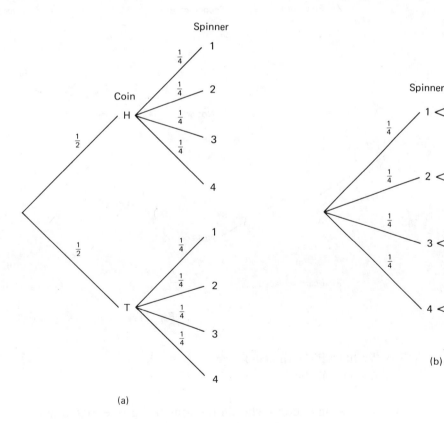

Fig. 11.3

To find $P(E_1)$: find the route on the branches of the tree which corresponds to H2 or 2H, and *multiply* the probabilities together of any branch you travel along:

$$P(E_1) = \tfrac{1}{2} \times \tfrac{1}{4} = \tfrac{1}{8} \text{ diagram (a)}$$

$$= \tfrac{1}{4} \times \tfrac{1}{2} = \tfrac{1}{8} \text{ diagram (b).}$$

The same answer is obtained either way.

To find P(E_2): when there is more than one route that can be taken, you still multiply the probabilities on *each* route and *add* together the different answers.

In this case,

$$P(E_2) = \tfrac{1}{2} \times \tfrac{1}{4} + \tfrac{1}{2} \times \tfrac{1}{4} + \tfrac{1}{2} \times \tfrac{1}{4} = \tfrac{3}{8} \text{ diagram (a)}$$
$$= \tfrac{1}{4} \times \tfrac{1}{2} + \tfrac{1}{4} \times \tfrac{1}{2} + \tfrac{1}{4} \times \tfrac{1}{2} = \tfrac{3}{8} \text{ diagram (b).}$$

The following example considers the problem of the order of events.

Worked Example 11.2

Two cards are drawn one at a time from an ordinary pack of playing cards. Find the probability that they are both aces (a) if the first card is replaced, (b) if the first card is not replaced.

Solution

Although the probability trees are similar, the probabilities on the branches are not the same for the second card (see Fig. 11.4).

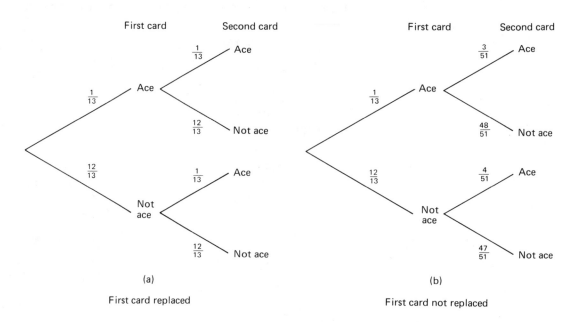

Fig. 11.4

(a) We have P (both aces) = $\tfrac{1}{13} \times \tfrac{1}{13} = \tfrac{1}{169}$.
(b) We have P (both aces) = $\tfrac{1}{13} \times \tfrac{3}{51} = \tfrac{1}{221}$.

The following exercise should be done using tree diagrams.

Check 30

1 Two dice are thrown. What is the probability of a score greater than 7?
2 Six discs, numbered 1 to 6, are placed in a bag. Two discs are drawn out

together. What is the probability that:
(a) the sum of the numbers on the discs is even;
(b) one of the discs has an odd number on it;
(c) at least one of the discs has an even number on it?

3 The probability of an event A happening is $\frac{1}{2}$ and the probability of an event B happening is $\frac{1}{4}$. Given that A and B are independent, calculate the probability that:
(a) neither event happens;
(b) just one of the two events happens.

4 A die numbered 1, 1, 2, 3, 4, 4 is thrown twice. Draw a sample space for the results. What is the probability that the total score on the two throws is (a) odd; (b) greater than 6?

5 A coin is biased in such a way that the probability of a head appearing in one toss of the coin is $\frac{2}{3}$. The coin is tossed three times. What is the probability that there are:
(a) three heads;
(b) at least two heads?

6 Given that the probability of a male birth is 0.52 and that a woman has three children, calculate the probability that:
(a) all three are boys;
(b) at least two are boys.

Worked Example 11.3

(a) Neil and Angela each roll a fair 6-faced die and the number on the top face is noted. What is the probability that:
  (i)   they each roll a 1;
  (ii) Angela scores exactly 4 more than Neil;
  (iii) their numbers differ by 3;
  (iv) neither of them throws an even number;
  (v) Neil's number is larger than Angela's number;
  (vi) the sum of their numbers is 3?
(b) Neil and Angela each roll their die twice. What is the probability that:
  (i)   the total score (of all four numbers) is 5;
  (ii) Neil scores a total of 2 and Angela a total of 3?   [OLE]

Solution

(a) (i) $\frac{1}{6} \times \frac{1}{6} = \frac{1}{36}$.
  (ii) If Angela scores 4 more than Neil, this means Angela scores 5 and Neil 1 or Angela scores 6 and Neil 2, write this A5 and N1 or A6 and N2.
     $\therefore$ Probability $= \frac{1}{6} \times \frac{1}{6} + \frac{1}{6} \times \frac{1}{6} = \frac{1}{18}$.
  (iii) (A6 and N3) or (A5 and N2) or (A4 and N1) or (A3 and N6) or (A2 and N5) or (A1 and N4).
     $\therefore$ Probability $= 6 \times \frac{1}{6} \times \frac{1}{6} = \frac{1}{6}$.
  (iv) If neither throws even, both throw odd (1, 3, 5).
     $\therefore$ Probability $= \frac{1}{2} \times \frac{1}{2} = \frac{1}{4}$.
  (v) If Neil's number is larger than Angela's number, possibilities are:
     (N6, A5), (N6, A4), (N6, A3), (N6, A2), (N6, A1),
     (N5, A4), (N5, A3), (N5, A2), (N5, A1), (N4, A3),
     (N4, A2), (N4, A1), (N3, A2), (N3, A1), (N2, A1),
     i.e. 15 possibilities.
     $\therefore$ Probability $= 15 \times \frac{1}{6} \times \frac{1}{6} = \frac{5}{12}$.

(vi) If the sum is 3, we have
(N1, A2), (N2, A1).
$\therefore$ Probability $= 2 \times \frac{1}{6} \times \frac{1}{6} = \frac{1}{18}$.

(b) (i) The only possible scores on 4 dice to add up to 5 are $1 + 1 + 1 + 2$. The 2 could be on any of the 4 dice.
$\therefore$ Probability $= 4 \times (\frac{1}{6})^4 = \frac{1}{324}$.

(ii) The probability that Neil scores 2 is $\frac{1}{6} \times \frac{1}{6} = \frac{1}{36}$.
The probability that Angela scores 3 is $2 \times \frac{1}{6} = \frac{1}{18}$.
Hence probability required $= \frac{1}{36} \times \frac{1}{18} = \frac{1}{648}$.
This problem could have been solved using either a sample space diagram or a tree diagram. However, the solution here illustrates a method of listing possibilities.

11.6 Statistical Diagrams

It is assumed that the reader has a basic knowledge of how to represent numerical data by means of a diagram. The main types used are bar charts, pie charts, pictograms and histograms. The first three will be considered briefly in this section.

Worked Example 11.4

A survey was carried out of the morning newspapers read by the inhabitants of Steyning. The results were as follows:

Daily Mail	270	*Sun*	340
Guardian	139	*Daily Express*	240
The Times	61	*Daily Mirror*	200
Daily Telegraph	150	*Morning Star*	40

Illustrate this information, using (a) a bar chart, (b) a pie chart, (c) a pictogram.

Solution

In any statistical diagram, clarity is of the utmost importance.
(a) See Fig. 11.5.

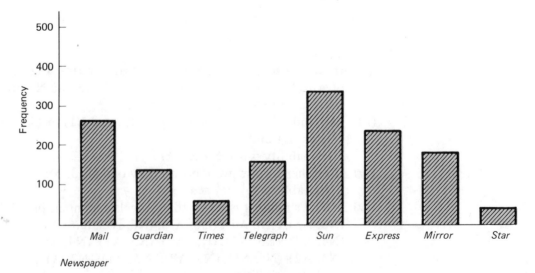

Fig. 11.5

194

(b) When constructing a pie chart, first of all calculate the total number being represented.

$$\text{Total} = 270 + 139 + 61 + 150 + 340 + 240 + 200 + 40$$
$$= 1440.$$

Method 1:

This is being represented by 360°,

hence each degree is $\dfrac{1440}{360}$ = 4 people,

or each person is $\frac{1}{4}°$.

The angles are as follows

$$\textit{Mail} = 270 \times \tfrac{1}{4} = 67.5°,$$

and similarly,

$$\textit{Guardian} = 34.75°, \quad \textit{Times} = 15.25°, \quad \textit{Telegraph} = 37.5°, \quad \textit{Sun} = 85°,$$
$$\textit{Express} = 60°, \quad \textit{Mirror} = 50°, \quad \textit{Star} = 10°.$$

Method 2:

The angles can be found in a more routine method using the following formula:

$$\text{Angle for quantity } Q = \frac{\text{Quantity } Q}{\text{Total}} \times 360.$$

For example, that for the *Mirror* would be

$$\text{Angle for \textit{Mirror}} = \frac{200}{1440} \times 360 = 50°$$

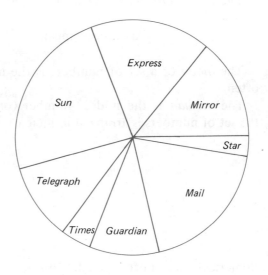

Fig. 11.6

The pie chart can now be drawn (Fig. 11.6). If the numbers are not drawn on the pie chart, this is a very difficult diagram to read.

(c) When drawing a pictogram, first choose a motif to represent a certain unit. In this case, we will use ⚲ to represent 50 people. The pictogram can now be drawn as in Fig. 11.7.

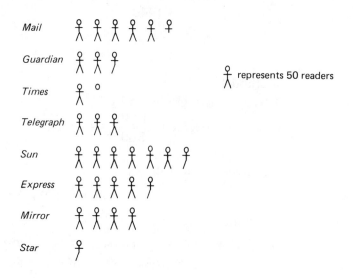

Fig. 11.7

Accuracy again is limited, although it is better than the pie chart to read.

11.7 Averages

Three types of average are commonly used in everyday life (there are others). The *arithmetic mean* (or mean) of n numbers $a_1, a_2, a_3, \ldots, a_n$ is found by

$$\text{Arithmetic mean} = \frac{a_1 + a_2 + a_3 + \ldots + a_n}{n}.$$

The *mode* of a set of numbers is the number (or numbers) which occurs most often.

The *median* is the middle number (or mean of the two middle numbers) if the set of numbers is arranged in increasing order of size.

11.8 Frequency Tables

Numerical data is often much more manageable if it is grouped together in some way. There are two types of situation, as follows:

(a) The marks obtained out of 10 in a single multiple-choice test by 20 students were 8, 6, 5, 0, 1, 4, 3, 4, 6, 7, 6, 5, 5, 6, 3, 4, 7, 6, 9, 10. Calculate (i) the mean score; (ii) the median score; and (iii) the mode, by using a frequency table, as in Table 11.1.

Table 11.1

Score	Tally	Frequency	Score × frequency
0	1	1	0
1	1	1	1
2		0	0
3	11	2	6
4	111	3	12
5	111*	3	15
6	⊮⊬*	5	30
7	11	2	14
8	1	1	8
9	1	1	9
10	1	1	10
	Total	20	105

(i) The mean is found by dividing the sum of score × frequency by the total number of students, not by 10:

$$\text{Mean} = \frac{105}{20} = 5.25.$$

(ii) The median will be the average of the 10th and 11th numbers shown by * in the table:

$$\text{Median} = \frac{5 + 6}{2} = 5.5.$$

(iii) The mode is clearly 6.

(b) The heights of a group of 30 children, measured to the nearest centimetre, are shown in Table 11.2.

Table 11.2

Height (cm)	Frequency	Cumulative frequency	Middle value	Frequency × middle value
90–99	2	2	94.5	189
100–109	5	7	104.5	522.5
110–119	7	14	114.5	801.5
120–129	10	24	124.5	1245.0
130–139	5	29	134.5	672.5
140–149	1	30	144.5	144.5
Total	30			3575

Calculate (i) the mean height; (ii) the modal height.

(i) The middle value column is obtained from the average of the extremes of the group,

i.e. $94.5 = (90 + 99) \div 2$.

$$\text{The average height} = \frac{\text{Sum of frequency} \times \text{middle value}}{\text{Total number of children}}$$

$$= \frac{3575}{30} = 119.2 \text{ cm}.$$

(ii) The modal class is clearly 120–129 cm.

11.9 Cumulative Frequency Curves (Ogives)

Referring again to Table 11.2, the third column gives the cumulative frequencies (or running totals). These could be set out as here:

Height (cm)	< 100	< 110	< 120	< 130	< 140	< 150
Cumulative frequency	2	7	14	24	29	30

When plotting the graph of these figures, since the values are given to the nearest cm, the points are plotted at 99.5 cm, 109.5 cm etc.

The cumulative frequency curve (or Ogive) can then be plotted; see Fig. 11.8. **It always has this characteristic shape.**

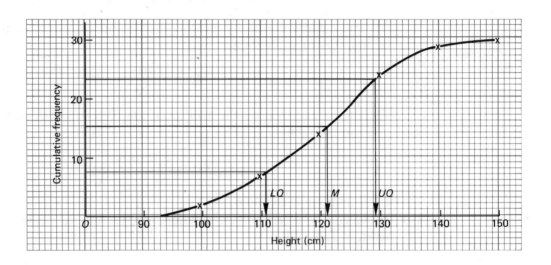

Fig. 11.8

*11.10 Information from the Cumulative Frequency Curve

The main types of information that can be gained from these curves are percentiles, median and interquartile range (or semi-interquartile range). If we divide the total frequency into quarters, the value at the lower quarter is referred to as the lower quartile (LQ), the value at the middle gives the median (M), and the value at the upper quarter is the upper quartile (UQ). The *percentiles* are found by dividing the total cumulative frequency into hundredths.

The semi-interquartile range (SIQR) = $\dfrac{\text{Upper quartile} - \text{Lower quartile}}{2}$.

The values to read off the vertical scale are as follows (N is the total number of items of information):

Median $\qquad \dfrac{(N+1)}{2}$th value.

UQ $\qquad 3\dfrac{(N+1)}{4}$th value.

LQ $\qquad \dfrac{(N+1)}{4}$th value.

Percentiles $\qquad \left(\dfrac{N+1}{100}\right)$ th values.

A quantity sometimes used to measure the range of a set of values is the interquartile range.

Interquartile range = UQ − LQ

Worked Example 11.5

Using the information in Fig. 11.8, find (a) the median height, (b) the semi-interquartile range.

Solution

(a) The total frequency is 30.
   The median is between the 15th and 16th values.
   Reading the frequency of 15.5 gives: median height = 121 cm.
(b) The lower quartile is approximately 7.75.
   The upper quartile is approximately at 23.25.
   ∴ LQ = 110.5
     UQ = 129.

   SIQR = $\dfrac{129 - 110.5}{2}$ = 9.5 cm.

*11.11   Assumed Mean

It is sometimes much easier to work out the mean of a frequency table by assuming the mean, and working from this value.

Worked Example 11.6

Calculate the mean of the frequency table (Table 11.1) by assuming the mean is 5.

Solution

Two extra columns are required, one with score minus assumed mean, i.e. $x - A$, the other with f$(x - A)$. See Table 11.3.

Table 11.3

Score x	x − a	f	f(x − A)
0	−5	1	−5
1	−4	1	−4
2	−3	0	0
3	−2	2	−4
4	−1	3	−3
5	0	3	0
6	1	5	5
7	2	2	4
8	3	1	3
9	4	1	4
10	5	1	5
	Total	20	5

$$\text{Find:} \quad \frac{\text{Total f}(x - A)}{\text{Total f}} = \frac{5}{20} = 0.25.$$

Since we assumed the mean was 5, the correct mean is $A + 0.25 = 5.25$.

11.12 Histograms

A histogram is the display of data in the form of a block graph where the area of each rectangle is proportional to the frequency. When the rectangles are the same width, their heights too are proportional to the frequency and the histogram is synonymous with the bar chart.

An example of a histogram with unequal class intervals follows.

Worked Example 11.7

The following table gives the distribution of the number of employees in the 50 factories in Stenworth:

Number of employees	0–39	40–59	60–79	80–99	100–139
Number of factories	5	15	13	10	7

Construct a histogram to show the distribution.

Solution

The widths of the five class intervals are

$$40 \quad 20 \quad 20 \quad 20 \quad 40$$

Referring to Fig. 11.9, we see that as the widths of the first and last intervals are twice the width of the other three, the heights of the rectangles are reduced in proportion: i.e. if the height of the second rectangle is 15 units, the height of the first rectangle is $\frac{5}{2} = 2\frac{1}{2}$ units and the height of the last rectangle is $\frac{7}{2} = 3\frac{1}{2}$ units.

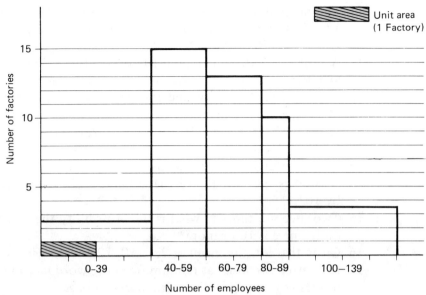

Fig. 11.9

Exercise 11

1 A bag contains 8 red discs and 4 blue discs. If a disc is removed from the bag and not replaced, and then a second disc is removed from the bag, the probability that the two discs are the same colour is:

   A $\frac{2}{3}$ **B** $\frac{17}{33}$ **C** $\frac{1}{2}$ **D** $\frac{5}{9}$

2 The probability of it raining on any day is $\frac{1}{3}$. The probability that it does not rain two days running is:

   A $\frac{2}{3}$ **B** $\frac{5}{6}$ **C** $\frac{4}{9}$ **D** $\frac{1}{2}$

3 The mean of 3 numbers is 14, the mean of 7 other numbers is 20. The mean of the 10 numbers is:

   A 17   **B** 18.2   **C** 18   **D** 16

4 The probability of drawing a picture card from a normal pack of cards is:

   A $\frac{1}{4}$ **B** $\frac{3}{52}$ **C** $\frac{3}{13}$ **D** $\frac{1}{10}$

5 Three coins are tossed together; the probability of obtaining 3 heads is:

   A $\frac{1}{4}$ **B** $\frac{1}{2}$ **C** $\frac{1}{6}$ **D** $\frac{1}{8}$

6 The number which needs to be removed from $\{11, 15, 2, 18, 14, 3, 6\}$ so that the mean of the remainder is 9 is:

   A 14   **B** 15   **C** 6   **D** none of these

7 The average height of 6 boys is 1.8 m and the average height of 9 girls is 1.5 m. The average height of the group is:

   A 1.65 m   **B** 1.62 m   **C** 1.6 m   **D** 1.7 m

8 The mean of 4, 5, a, b is 10. The mean of 7, 8, a, b is:

   A 11.5   **B** 12   **C** 6   **D** indeterminate

9 The probability that a letter drawn at random from the word *statistics* is a consonant is:

   A $\frac{3}{10}$ **B** $\frac{2}{5}$ **C** $\frac{7}{10}$ **D** $\frac{1}{2}$

10 A die is rolled twice, and on each occasion it shows 6. If it is rolled a third time, the probability of obtaining a 6 is:

   A $\dfrac{1}{6^3}$ **B** $\dfrac{1}{6^2}$ **C** $\frac{1}{6}$ **D** 0

11 Raffle tickets numbered 1 to 100 are placed in a drum and one is drawn at random. What is the probability that the number is divisible by (a) 2; (b) 5; (c) 2 and 5?

12 The number which needs to be added to the list of numbers $\{1, 8, 15, 9, 11, 18, 15\}$ to increase their average from 11 to 13 is:

    A 12   **B** 11   **C** 27   **D** 13

13 A target at a rifle range consists of a centre of radius 3 cm which scores 100 and two concentric circles of radius 5 cm and 6 cm, which score 50 and 20 respectively. Assuming that the target is always hit, and that the probability of hitting a particular score is proportional to the area for that score, find the probabilities of scoring 100, 50 and 20 respectively. What is the expected total score for 10 shots?

14 A = {four-digit numbers whose first two digits are greater than or equal to x}.

    What is the probability that a number chosen at random from A is divisible by 10?

15 Two dice are thrown; what is the probability that the product of the numbers on the dice is 10 or more?

16 Given that 9 is the mean of 2, x, 10, 12 and 15, find x.

17 If a letter is chosen at random from the word *method*, what is the probability it does not belong to the word *mathematical*?

18 Six equal balls, numbered 1, 2, 3, 4, 5 and 6 respectively, are placed in a bag. A ball is drawn out of the bag at random and then a second ball is drawn out without replacing the first. Find the probability that:

    (a) the first ball is numbered 4;

    (b) the first ball is not the 6;

    (c) the first ball is numbered 2 and the second 5.

19 A bag contains 40 discs: 8 red, 15 green, the rest black.

    (a) If three are drawn out in succession and not replaced, what is the probability of drawing, in order, 2 reds and 1 green?

    (b) If each disc is replaced after drawing, what would the result be?

20 In a class of 30 children, 2 have the first name John and 5 have the surname Jones. Calculate the probability that a child chosen at random does not have the name John Jones.

    If, further, 2 children have the surname Coates, calculate the probability that a child chosen at random has either the name John Coates or the name John Jones.

21 Four cards numbered 1 to 4 are placed face downwards on a table.

    (a) Two cards are picked up at the same time. Find the number of ways that this can be done. Hence find the probability that if two cards are picked at random from the table, one of them is numbered 2.

    (b) In a second experiment, one card is picked up from the table and marked on the face. The card is replaced, and a second card is picked up and marked. Find the probability that (i) the same card is marked twice; (ii) that the numbers on the two marked cards add up to 5.

22 An engineering firm has 60 employees. The histogram, Fig. 11.10, shows the distribution of their salaries (none of which is a whole number of thousands of pounds). The 14 employees earning less than £4000 p.a. work part-time.

    (a) How many of the part-time workers earn more than £1000 p.a.?

    (b) How many employees earn between £4000 and £5000 p.a.?

    (c) How many employees earn between £6000 and £8000 p.a.?

    (d) The 46 full-time workers have a mean salary of £7000 p.a. and the 14 part-time workers have a mean salary of £1000 p.a. What is the mean salary of the 60 employees?   [NISEC]

23 When John and Henry play darts, the probability that John wins a game is 0.7 and that Henry wins a game is 0.3. They play a match to be decided by the first player to win 3 games (the match is finished as soon as this happens).

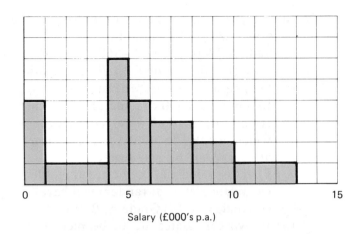

Salary (£000's p.a.)

Fig. 11.10

Calculate the probabilities that:
(a) John wins the first three games;
(b) John loses the first game but wins the next three;
(c) John wins by three games to one;
(d) John wins the match in not more than four games. [OLE]

24 The lifetimes in hours of 100 electric light bulbs are decided by the following table:

Lifetimes x	$300 < x \leqslant 400$	$400 < x \leqslant 450$	$450 < x \leqslant 500$	$500 < x \leqslant 550$
Frequency	3	2	6	35

Lifetimes x	$550 < x \leqslant 600$	$600 < x \leqslant 650$	$650 < x \leqslant 700$	$700 < x \leqslant 750$
Frequency	17	10	3	11

Lifetimes x	$750 < x \leqslant 850$	$850 < x \leqslant 1000$
Frequency	10	3

Draw a histogram to illustrate this information.

Estimate the probability that an electric light bulb drawn at random from this sample has a lifetime of over 700 hours.

Calculate an estimate of the mean lifetime of these electric light bulbs.
  [OLE]

25 Anne and Jane play a game against each other which starts with Anne aiming to throw a bean bag into a circle marked on the ground.
(a) The probability that the bean bag lands entirely inside the circle is $\frac{1}{2}$, and the probability that it lands on the rim of the circle is $\frac{1}{3}$. Show that the probability that the bag lands entirely outside the circle is $\frac{1}{6}$. What are the probabilities that two successive throws land:
  (i) both outside the circle;
  (ii) the first on the rim of the circle and the second inside the circle?
(b) Jane then shoots at a target on which she can score 10, 5 or 0. With any one shot, the probability that she scores 10 is $\frac{2}{5}$, the probability that she scores 5 is $\frac{1}{10}$, and the probability that she scores 0 is $\frac{1}{2}$. With exactly two shots, what are the probabilities that she scores
(i) 20;   (ii) 10?
(c) When the bean bag thrown by Anne lands outside the circle, Jane is allowed two shots at her target. If, however, the bean bag lands on the rim of the circle, Jane has one shot, and if it lands inside the circle Jane is not allowed any shots. Find the probability that Jane scores 10 as a result of any one throw from Anne. [O & C]

26 In last year's mathematics examination, there were 20 000 candidates who were awarded grades as follows:

Grade A 2780, Grade B 4360, Grade C 6320,

Grade D 1600, Grade E 1380, Unclassified 3560.

(a) On graph paper, draw a bar chart to represent this information. Use 2 cm to represent 1000 candidates, and 1 cm to represent each grade.

(b) If the information were represented on a pie chart, calculate the angle which would be used for the sector representing Grade C, giving your answer to the nearest degree.

(c) Find, as a decimal correct to three decimal places, the probability that a candidate picked at random will have

(i) Grade C   (ii) Grade A, B or C.

(d) If two candidates are to be picked at random, write down, but do not simplify, an expression for the probability that they will both have Grade C. [L]

27 The matrix shown, denoted by M, is one whose entries are all probabilities relating to chances in the weather:

$$\text{Today} \begin{array}{c} \\ \text{Fine} \\ \text{Wet} \end{array} \overset{\begin{array}{cc} \text{Tomorrow} & \\ \text{Fine} & \text{Wet} \end{array}}{\begin{pmatrix} \frac{2}{3} & \frac{1}{3} \\ \frac{1}{2} & \frac{1}{2} \end{pmatrix}}$$

For example, the entry in the top left-hand corner indicates that if today's weather is fine, then the probability of tomorrow's being fine is $\frac{2}{3}$.

(a) Write down the probability that if today is fine, tomorrow will be wet.

(b) Assume that today is Sunday and that it is fine. Calculate the probabilities that:

(i) Monday and Tuesday will both be fine;

(ii) Monday will be wet and Tuesday will be fine.

(c) Calculate M^2. Interpret the entry in the bottom right-hand corner of this matrix as a probability.

(d) It is desired to find numbers x and y such that $x + y = 1$ and such that:

$$(x \quad y)\begin{pmatrix} \frac{2}{3} & \frac{1}{3} \\ \frac{1}{2} & \frac{1}{2} \end{pmatrix} = (x \quad y).$$

Verify that $x = \frac{3}{5}$ and $y = \frac{2}{5}$. [OLE]

28 As a test of general knowledge, 200 pupils from a city school had to mark the names of as many streets as they could on a map of the area. The results are given in the following table. For example, 12 pupils named 46 streets correctly, and so on.

Number of streets correct (x)	46	47	48	49	50	51	52	53
Number of pupils (f)	12	25	46	44	30	17	16	10

(a) Draw the frequency polygon of this distribution, using the following scales. On the horizontal axis take values of x from 46 to 53 and a scale of 2 cm to represent 1 street. On the vertical axis take values of f from 0 to 50 and a scale of 2 cm to represent 10 pupils.

(b) For this distribution, find (i) the mode, (ii) the median.

(c) Copy and complete Table 11.4, which uses an assumed mean of 50.

Table 11.4

No. of streets correct x	No. of pupils f	$x - 50$	$f(x - 50)$
46	12	-4	-48
47	25		
48	46		
49	44		
50	30		
51	17		
52	16		
53	10		
	Total = 200		Total =

(d) Hence, or otherwise, calculate the mean of the distribution.   [UCLES]

29 Government statistics giving motoring and criminal offences in England and Wales for 1979 were as shown in the table.

	Offences (thousands)
Motoring Offences	
Drunken driving	56
Other motoring offences	1045
Criminal offences	
(including 53 000 violent offences)	509

(a) Calculate the percentage, correct to two decimal places, of motoring offences which were drunken driving.

(b) (i) Explain the entry 456 in the table below.

    (ii) Copy and complete the table showing the angles required to make a pie chart.

	Offences (thousands)	*Angle (to the nearest degree)*
Drunken driving	56	13°
Other motoring offences	1045	
Violent offences	53	12°
Other criminal offences	456	

    (iii) Draw this pie chart, using a circle of radius 6 cm.   [MEG]

30 A student asked 30 people arriving at a football ground how long, to the nearest minute, it had taken them to reach the ground. The times they gave (in minutes) are listed below:

35   41   22   15   31   19   12   12   23   30

30   38   36   24   14   20   20   16   15   22

34   28   25   13   19   9   27   17   21   25

(a) (i) Copy and complete the frequency table here.

Time taken in minutes (to nearest minute)	8–12	13–17	18–22	23–27	28–32	33–37	38–42
Number of people	3	6	7	5	4		

205

(ii) Draw a histogram to represent the information in the frequency table.

(b) Of the 30 people questioned,

    6 paid £2 each to see the football match,
    8 paid £3 each,
    4 paid £4 each,
  10 paid £5 each and
    2 paid £6 each.

(i) Calculate the total amount paid by these 30 people.
(ii) Calculate the mean amount paid by these 30 people.   [MEG]

31 In a survey 100 motorists were asked to record the petrol consumption of their cars in miles per gallon. Each figure was rounded to the nearest mile per gallon and the frequency distribution shown in the table was obtained.

Miles per gallon	26–30	31–35	36–40	41–45	46–50	51–55	56–60
Frequency	4	6	18	34	20	12	6

(a) (i) State the limits of the modal class of this distribution.

    (ii) Complete the 'less than' cumulative frequency table here.

Miles per gallon (less than)	30.5	35.5	40.5	45.5	50.5	55.5	60.5
Number of motorists	4	10					

    (iii) On graph paper draw the cumulative frequency curve (ogive) from your completed cumulative frequency table.

(b) Use your cumulative frequency curve to estimate:
    (i) the median of the distribution,
    (ii) the interquartile range.

 A 'good' petrol consumption is one which lies between 38 and 52 miles per gallon.

(c) Estimate the number of motorists whose petrol consumption was 'good'.

                                                                         [NISEC]

32 A set of 15 dominoes is shown below. The face of each domino is a rectangle divided into two squares and each square is marked with 0, 1, 2, 3 or 4 spots to give the 15 different faces illustrated in Fig. 11.11.

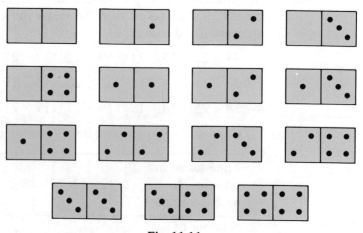

Fig. 11.11

This set of dominoes is placed face down on a table and shuffled. If one domino is chosen at random, find the probability of obtaining

(a) a double (a domino with the same number of spots on each half);

(b) a domino whose total number of spots is odd;

(c) a domino which either is a double or whose total of spots is odd.

If two dominoes are chosen at random (without replacement) from the complete set, find the probability of obtaining

(d) two doubles,

(e) only one double,

(f) two dominoes which together have a total of 3 spots.

If three dominoes are chosen at random (without replacement) from the complete set, find the probability of obtaining at least one double.　　[NISEC]

33　The pie chart represents the number of homes in a village that are heated by either coal, gas, or electricity.

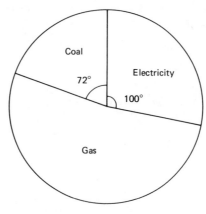

Fig. 11.12

(a) 2000 homes are heated by electricity. Calculate the number of homes that are heated by

   (i) coal,

   (ii) gas.

(b) What percentage of homes are heated by coal?　　[WJEC]

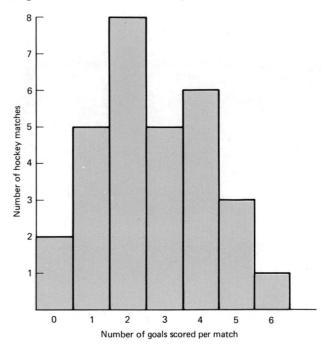

Fig. 11.13

34 The chart in Fig. 11.13 shows the goals scored per match in league hockey matches on a certain Saturday.

(a) Write down the number of matches in which 2 goals were scored.

Calculate

(b) the number of matches played,

(c) the number of goals scored altogether,

(d) the mean number of goals scored per match. [WJEC]

12 Trigonometry

12.1 Trigonometrical Ratios (Sine, Cosine, Tangent)

There are a number of ways of defining the trigonometrical ratios. The method of coordinates is used here, which also allows extension to any angle.

In Fig. 12.1 *OP* is a line of length r, which can rotate in an anticlockwise direction (positive angle).

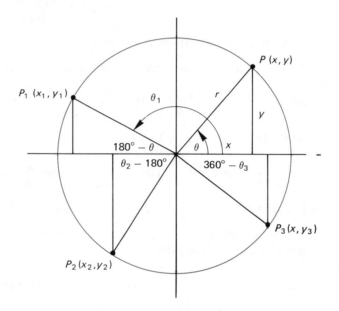

Fig. 12.1

The quadrants of the circle are defined as follows:

$0° \leqslant \theta \leqslant 90°$ is called the *first quadrant*.
$90° < \theta \leqslant 180°$ is called the *second quadrant*.
$180° < \theta \leqslant 270°$ is called the *third quadrant*.
$270° < \theta \leqslant 360°$ is called the *fourth quadrant*.

We have the following definitions:

$$\sin \theta = \frac{y}{r}, \tag{1}$$

$$\cos \theta = \frac{x}{r}, \tag{2}$$

$$\tan \theta = \frac{y}{x}. \tag{3}$$

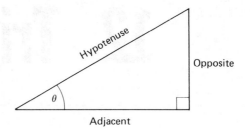

Fig. 12.2

If we restrict ourselves to the first quadrant, we find as in Fig. 12.2:

$$\sin \theta = \frac{\text{opposite}}{\text{hypotenuse}}, \tag{1A}$$

$$\cos \theta = \frac{\text{adjacent}}{\text{hypotenuse}}, \tag{2A}$$

$$\tan \theta = \frac{\text{opposite}}{\text{adjacent}}. \tag{3A}$$

Formulae (1)–(3) can be rewritten:

$$y = r \sin \theta, \quad (4) \qquad x = r \cos \theta, \quad (5) \qquad y = x \tan \theta. \quad (6)$$

or
$$r = \frac{y}{\sin \theta}, \quad (7) \qquad r = \frac{x}{\cos \theta}, \quad (8) \qquad x = \frac{y}{\tan \theta}, \quad (9).$$

* *Note:* In more advanced work:

$$\frac{1}{\sin \theta} = \operatorname{cosec} \theta, \quad (10) \qquad \frac{1}{\cos \theta} = \sec \theta, \quad (11) \qquad \frac{1}{\tan \theta} = \cot \theta. \quad (12)$$

hence $\quad r = y \operatorname{cosec} \theta, \quad (13) \qquad r = x \sec \theta, \quad (14) \qquad x = y \cot \theta, \quad (15).$

In the second quadrant, when P reaches P_1 after rotating an angle θ_1 then y_1 is positive but x_1 is negative.

$$\sin \theta_1 = \frac{y_1}{r} \quad \text{is still positive,}$$

$$\cos \theta_1 = \frac{x_1}{r} \quad \text{is negative,}$$

* and
$$\tan \theta_1 = \frac{y_1}{x_1} \quad \text{is negative.}$$

But $\dfrac{y_1}{r} = \sin (180 - \theta_1), \quad \therefore \sin \theta_1 = \sin (180 - \theta_1),$ \hfill (16)

$\dfrac{-x}{r} = \cos (180 - \theta_1), \qquad \therefore \cos \theta_1 = -\cos (180 - \theta_1),$ \hfill (17)

* $\dfrac{-y}{x} = \tan \theta_1, \qquad \therefore \tan \theta_1 = -\tan (180 - \theta_1).$ \hfill (18)

In the third quadrant, when P reaches P_2 after rotating an angle θ_2, then y_2 is negative and x_2 is negative.

We find
$$\cos \theta_2 = -\cos (\theta_2 - 180), \tag{19}$$
$$\sin \theta_2 = -\sin (\theta_2 - 180), \tag{20}$$
$$\ast \tan \theta_2 = \tan (\theta_2 - 180). \tag{21}$$

In the fourth quadrant, when P reaches P_3 after rotating an angle θ_3, then y_3 is negative and x_3 is positive.

We find that

$$\cos \theta_3 = \cos (360 - \theta_3), \qquad (22)$$
$$\sin \theta_3 = -\sin (360 - \theta_3), \qquad (23)$$
$$*\tan \theta_3 = -\tan (360 - \theta_3). \qquad (24)$$

We illustrate the use of these formulae by the following examples:

(a) $\cos 127° = -\cos (180° - 127°) = -\cos 53° = -0.6018$ (see equation 17).

(b) $\sin 290° = -\sin (360° - 290°) = -\sin 70° = -0.9397$ (see equation 23).

* (c) $\tan 210° = \tan (210° - 180°) = \tan 30° = 0.5774$ (see equation 21).

The final answers can be obtained directly by using the calculator.

The reverse process is slightly more involved.
Find x if:

(a) $\cos x = -0.5,$ (b) $\sin x = 0.8,$ (c) $\tan x = 2.3.$

(a) Since $\cos x$ is negative, x could be in the second or third quadrant. On the calculator, first find the inverse cosine of 0.5; this gives 60°.

Hence: $x = 180° - 60° = 120°,$

or $x = 180° + 60° = 240°.$

(b) Since $\sin x$ is positive, x could be in the first or second quadrant. On the calculator, first find the inverse sine of 0.8; this gives 53.1°.

hence: $x = 53.1°,$

or $x = 180° - 53.1° = 126.9°.$

* (c) Since $\tan x$ is negative, x could be in the second or fourth quadrant. First find the inverse tangent of 2.3; this gives 66.5°.

hence: $x = 180° - 66.5° = 113.5°$

or $x = 360° - 66.5° = 293.5°.$

The graphs of $\sin x$, $\cos x$ and *$\tan x$ are shown in Fig. 12.3 for $0 \leqslant x \leqslant 360°$. The functions can be extended in either direction.

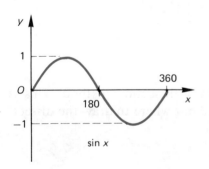
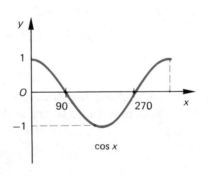
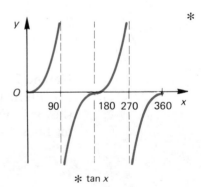

Fig. 12.3

12.2   Pythagoras' Theorem

In any right-angled triangle ABC ($\angle ABC = 90°$), Pythagoras' theorem states that:

$$AC^2 = AB^2 + BC^2. \qquad (25)$$

The first proof relies on ideas developed in Chapter 9. ABC is a right-angled triangle (Fig. 12.4). Consider squares drawn on the sides AB, BC and CA.

Method 1:
Draw XX' at right angles to AC. The area of $ABB'A'$ = area $ABXR$ (shear parallel to AB).

211

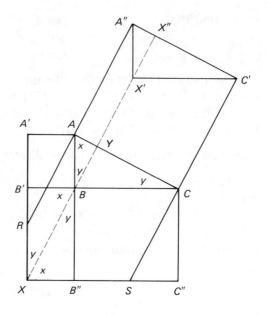

Fig. 12.4

The area of $BCC''B''$ = area $BCSX$ (shear parallel to CB).
$ABC \rightarrow BB'X$ (by a rotation of 90°),

$$\therefore XB = CC'.$$

$ABC \rightarrow A''X'C'$ (by a translation $\vec{CC'}$),

$$\therefore \text{area } BCSX = \text{area } BCC'X' = \text{area } YCC'X'' \text{ (shear parallel to } CC').$$

Similarly,

$$\text{area } ABX'A'' = \text{area } ABXR = \text{area } AYX''A'' \text{ (shear parallel to } AA'),$$
$$\therefore \text{area } BCC''B'' + \text{area } ABB'A' = \text{area } AA''C'C.$$

$$\therefore AC^2 = AB^2 + BC^2.$$

Method 2:

An alternative way of proving the theorem is by a dissection method. This is shown in Fig. 12.5. You might like to try and find out where to draw the dissecting lines.

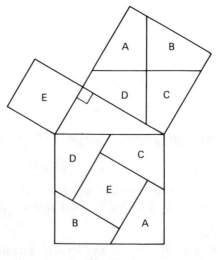

Fig. 12.5

12.3 Relationship Between sin x, cos x and tan x

Pythagoras' theorem applied to the triangle in Fig. 12.6 gives:

$$c^2 = a^2 + b^2. \tag{26}$$

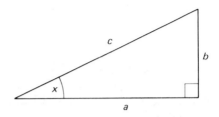

Fig. 12.6

Divide equation (26) by c^2:

$$1 = \frac{a^2}{c^2} + \frac{b^2}{c^2}.$$

But $\qquad \frac{a}{c} = \cos x, \therefore \frac{a^2}{c^2} = (\cos x)^2$, written $\cos^2 x$,

$$\frac{b}{c} = \sin x \therefore \frac{b^2}{c^2} = (\sin x)^2, \text{ written } \sin^2 x,$$

hence $\qquad\qquad 1 = \cos^2 x + \sin^2 x. \tag{27}$

This is in fact true for x in any quadrant.

Consider $\dfrac{\sin x}{\cos x} = \dfrac{b/c}{a/c} = \dfrac{b}{\cancel{c}} \times \dfrac{\cancel{c}}{a} = \dfrac{b}{a} = \tan x$;

$$\therefore \tan x = \frac{\sin x}{\cos x}. \tag{28}$$

This is also true for x in any quadrant.

*Worked Example 12.1

If $\cos x = \dfrac{1}{\sqrt{5}}$, and $x \geqslant 180°$, find

(a) $\sin x$;   (b) $\tan x$.

In any question of this type, make sure that you determine the quadrants that any angle must be in.

Solution

(a) Since $\cos x$ is positive and $x \geqslant 180°$, x must be in the *fourth* quadrant, hence $\sin x$ is negative.

$$1 = \cos^2 x + \sin^2 x = \left(\frac{1}{\sqrt{5}}\right)^2 + \sin^2 x,$$

$$\therefore 1 - \frac{1}{5} = \sin^2 x,$$

213

$$\therefore \ \sin^2 x = \frac{4}{5},$$

$$\therefore \ \sin x = \frac{-2}{\sqrt{5}}.$$

(b) $\tan x = \dfrac{\sin x}{\cos x} = \dfrac{-2/\sqrt{5}}{1/\sqrt{5}} = -2.$

12.4   Solution of Right-angled Triangles

The ideas of sections 12.1 and 12.2 are now used in the solution of problems as indicated below.

Worked Example 12.2

The diagram in Fig. 12.7 shows part of a girder. Find:
(a) $\angle RPQ$,   (b) RQ,   (c) SQ.

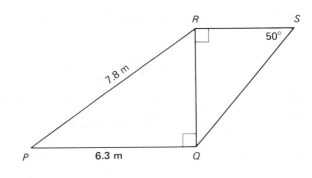

Fig. 12.7

Solution

Since two sides are given in triangle *PRQ*, either the sine, the cosine or the tangent ratio can be used. Relative to $\angle RPQ$, 7.8 is the hypotenuse and 6.3 is the *adjacent*, hence the cosine ratio is needed.

(a) Using formula (2A), $\cos R\hat{P}Q = \dfrac{PQ}{PR} = \dfrac{6.3}{7.8} = 0.8077.$

Pressing the inverse cosine button on the calculator, we get:

$\angle RPQ = 36.1°.$

(b) The easiest way to find RQ is using Pythagoras' theorem:

$$PR^2 = RQ^2 + PQ^2,$$

$$\therefore \ 7.8^2 = RQ^2 + 6.3^2,$$

$$\therefore \ 60.84 = RQ^2 + 39.69$$

$$\therefore \ 60.84 - 39.69 = 21.15 = RQ^2.$$

Remember, Pythagoras' theorem gives the square of the side. The square root must now be found:

$$RQ = \sqrt{21.15} = 4.599 \text{ m}$$

(c) In triangle *RQS*, we now have one side and one angle, hence we can use formulae (4)–(9). *RQ* is *opposite*, and *SQ* is the hypotenuse. Since the hypotenuse is unknown, we require formula (7).

$$\therefore QS = \frac{QR}{\sin RSQ} = \frac{4.599}{\sin 50°} = \frac{4.599}{0.766},$$

$$\therefore QS = 6.004 \text{ cm}.$$

*12.5 Special Triangles

There are certain triangles which occur frequently in examination questions where the sides or angles are related in a particularly simple way. The triangles are often disguised (see Worked Example 12.3). Figure 12.8 shows a number of these triangles.

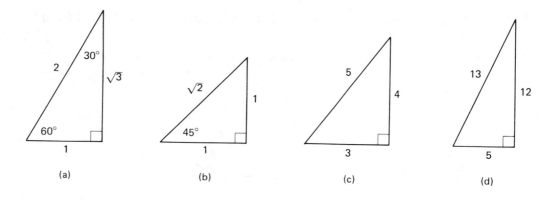

Fig. 12.8

Worked Example 12.3

In Fig. 12.9, *ABCD* is a square of side 24 cm. $\angle EAC = 90°$. Calculate *EC*.

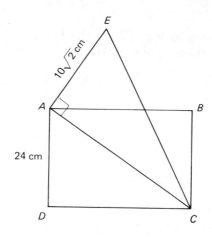

Fig. 12.9

Solution

The fact that $\sqrt{2}$ appears in the diagram immediately suggests one of the special triangles.

In triangle *EAC* only one side is known. Hence, before *EC* can be found, we must find *AC*. △*ADC* is an enlargement, scale factor 24, of triangle (b) in Fig. 12.8.

$$\therefore AC = 24\sqrt{2} \text{ cm.}$$

Careful observation of △*AEC* shows that it is an enlargement of triangle (d) in Fig. 12.8 with scale factor $2\sqrt{2}$.

Hence $$EC = 26\sqrt{2} \text{ cm.}$$

12.6 Angles of Elevation and Depression

Figure 12.10 illustrates the meaning of the two terms

angle of elevation (measured upward from the horizontal),

and   *angle of depression* (measured downward from the horizontal).

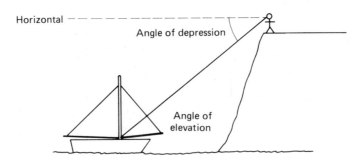

Fig. 12.10

It can be seen that:

the angle of depression of the boat from the man $=$ the angle of elevation of the man from the boat.

12.7 Bearings

Referring to Fig. 12.11, the bearing of *B* **from** *A* (always measured clockwise) is 025° (three figures are always given). To find the bearing of *A* **from** *B*, we need to find *y*.

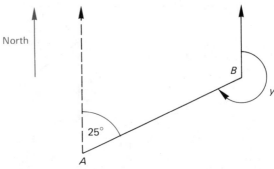

Fig. 12.11

Clearly, $y = 180° + 25° = 205°$.

Note: Bearings are still sometimes given using the compass points. However, they are not used in this book.

Worked Example 12.4

The points B, P and Q lie in the same horizontal plane, and AB is a vertical monument of height 75 m. From the point A at the top of the monument, the angles of depression of the points P and Q are $17°$ and $20°$ respectively. Calculate, to the nearest metre, the distances BP and BQ.

The bearings of P and Q from B are $026°$ and $116°$ respectively. Calculate the distance PQ to the nearest metre, and the bearing of Q from P to the nearest degree.

[London]

Solution

In Fig. 12.12, we have $\dfrac{75}{PB} = \tan 17° = 0.3058$.

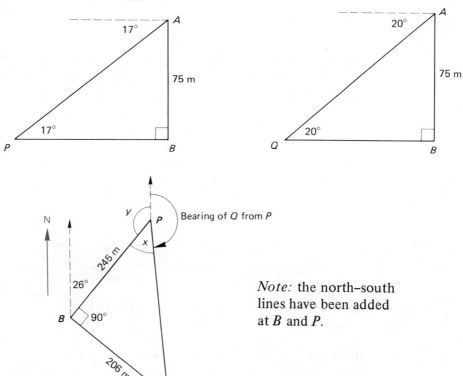

Note: the north–south lines have been added at B and P.

Fig. 12.12

$$\therefore PB = \frac{75}{0.3058} = 245 \text{ m}.$$

Also, $\dfrac{75}{QB} = \tan 20° = 0.3640$,

$$\therefore QB = \frac{75}{0.3640} = 206 \text{ m}.$$

217

Note: $\angle PBQ = 90°$ because the bearing of Q from B is $116°$ and $26° + 90° = 116°$.
Using Pythagoras,

$$PQ^2 = 245^2 + 206^2 = 102\,461,$$

$$\therefore \quad PQ = \sqrt{102\,461} = 320 \text{ m.}$$

To find the bearing of Q from P, we must first find x.

$$\tan x = \frac{206}{245} = 0.8408,$$

$$\therefore \quad x = 40° \text{ (nearest degree).}$$

We know $y + 26 = 180$, $\therefore y = 154$,
hence the bearing of Q from P is $360° - (154° + 40°) = 166°$.

12.8   Reduction to Right-angled Triangles

There are many situations where triangles which at first sight are not right-angled triangles can be reduced to right-angled triangles. The following examples should illustrate this.

Worked Example 12.5

The diagram in Fig. 12.13 shows the cross-section of a cylindrical oil-storage tank of radius 2.6 m. Find the depth of the oil above the bottom of the tank when $\angle AOB = 109°$.

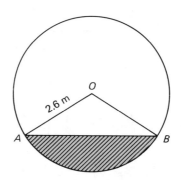

Fig. 12.13

Solution

First recognize that triangle AOB is an isosceles triangle. If divided in half, it becomes two right-angled triangles, as in Fig. 12.14.

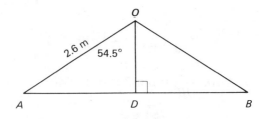

Fig. 12.14

$$\cos 54.5° = \frac{OD}{2.6}, \therefore OD = 2.6 \times 0.5807$$

$$= 1.509.$$

To get the depth of the oil, we must subtract OD from the radius:

$$\text{depth of oil} = 2.6 - 1.509 = 1.091 \text{ m.}$$

The next example is slightly more complicated.

* Worked Example 12.6

In order to measure the height of a vertical tower OT which is in an inaccessible position, the angles of elevation of the top of the tower are taken from two points A and B distance 100 m apart as shown in Fig. 12.15.
Find the height of the tower.

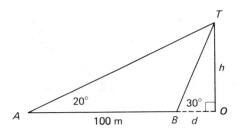

Fig. 12.15

Solution

This question can be solved using the sine rule (see section 12.10). The following method involves simultaneous equations.

In triangle BTO,
$$\frac{h}{d} = \tan 30° = 0.5774,$$

$$\therefore \frac{h}{0.5774} = d. \tag{1}$$

In triangle TAO,
$$\frac{h}{(d + 100)} = \tan 20° = 0.3640,$$

$$\therefore \frac{h}{0.364} = d + 100. \tag{2}$$

Subtract (1) from (2):

$$\frac{h}{0.364} - \frac{h}{0.5774} = 100.$$

By using the $1/x$ button on the calculator or reciprocal tables, this can more easily be written:

$$2.747h - 1.732h = 100, \qquad \left[\frac{1}{0.364} = 2.747 \text{ etc.}\right]$$

$$\therefore 1.015h = 100,$$

$$\therefore h = \frac{100}{1.015} = 98.52 \text{ m.}$$

12.9　Perpendicular Height of a Triangle

The following method is a useful way of finding the perpendicular height of a triangle, given the three sides of the triangle. It will be illustrated by a worked example.

Worked Example 12.7

In triangle ABC, Fig. 12.16, $AB = 8.3$ cm, $CB = 4.9$ cm and $AC = 6.7$ cm. Find the perpendicular distance of C from AB.

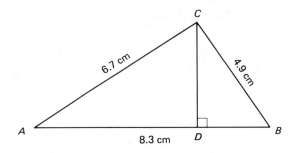

Fig. 12.16

Solution

Referring to the diagram, we are trying to find CD.
　We begin by finding the area of the triangle using the formula

$$\text{Area} = \sqrt{s(s-a)(s-b)(s-c)} \text{ (see Chapter 4)},$$

$$s = \tfrac{1}{2}(6.7 + 8.3 + 4.9) = 9.95.$$

$$\text{Area} = \sqrt{9.95 \times 5.05 \times 3.25 \times 1.65} = 16.42 \text{ cm}^2.$$

Using $\tfrac{1}{2}$ base $\times$ height = area, we get $\tfrac{1}{2} \times 8.3 \times CD = 16.42$.

$$\therefore 4.15CD = 16.42, \therefore CD = \frac{16.42}{4.15} = 3.96 \text{ cm}.$$

*12.10　The Sine Rule

The first of the rules which can be used in solving non-right-angled triangles is the sine rule.
　The rule states:

$$\frac{a}{\sin A} = \frac{b}{\sin B} = \frac{c}{\sin C} = 2R \qquad (29)$$

where R is the radius of the circumscribing circle through A, B and C; see Fig. 12.17.

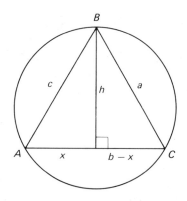

Fig. 12.17

Part of the formula can be proved as follows:

$$\frac{h}{c} = \sin A, \qquad \therefore h = c \sin A;$$

$$\frac{h}{a} = \sin C, \qquad \therefore h = a \sin C;$$

$$\therefore \ c \sin A = a \sin C, \text{ i.e. } \frac{a}{\sin A} = \frac{c}{\sin C}.$$

The sine rule should be used if two angles and one side are given, or two sides and one angle which is opposite either of the two given sides.

*12.11   Sine Rule (Ambiguous Case)

When using the sine rule to find angles, it is important to have an approximate idea of the answer, as in some cases more than one solution is possible.

Worked Example 12.8

In triangle XYZ, $\angle XYZ = 30°$, $XY = 8$ cm, and $XZ = 5$ cm. Find the two possible values of XYZ and illustrate with a diagram.

Solution

If you try to draw triangle XYZ, then the two possible triangles can be seen in Fig. 12.18: XYZ_1 and XYZ_2.

$$\frac{XY}{\sin Z} = \frac{XZ}{\sin Y}, \qquad \therefore \frac{XY}{XZ} \sin Y = \sin Z;$$

$$\sin Z = \frac{8 \sin 30°}{5} = 0.8.$$

Since $\sin Z$ is positive, Z could be in the first or second quadrant.
    Hence, $Z_1 = 53.1°$,
        $Z_2 = 126.9°$.

See Fig. 12.18.

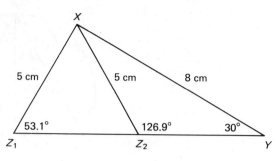

Fig. 12.18

*12.12 The Cosine Rule

The cosine formula is used if either three sides of a triangle are given, or two sides and the angle between the two sides.

With the notation of section 12.10:

$$a^2 = b^2 + c^2 - 2bc \cos A \qquad b^2 = a^2 + c^2 - 2ac \cos B \qquad c^2 = a^2 + b^2 - 2ab \cos c$$

or $\qquad \cos A = \dfrac{b^2 + c^2 - a^2}{2bc}.$ $\qquad \cos B = \dfrac{a^2 + c^2 - b^2}{2ac}$ $\qquad \cos C = \dfrac{a^2 + b^2 - c^2}{2ab}$

Proof:

$$c^2 = h^2 + x^2 \qquad \text{and} \qquad a^2 = h^2 + (b - x)^2 \, ;$$

$$c^2 - x^2 = a^2 - (b - x)^2 = a^2 - (b^2 + x^2 - 2bx)$$

$$c^2 = a^2 - b^2 + 2bx \qquad \text{but} \qquad x = c \cos A,$$

hence $\qquad a^2 = b^2 + c^2 - 2bc \cos A.$

Remember, for an obtuse angle cos A will be negative.

*Worked Example 12.9

In triangle PQR, $PQ = 5$ cm, $QR = 6$ cm and $RP = 7$ cm. Find the smallest angle of the triangle.

Solution

The order of size of the angles of a triangle is always the largest angle opposite the largest side and the smallest angle opposite the smallest side.

We need to find the angle opposite PQ, which is R.

$$\cos R = \frac{6^2 + 7^2 - 5^2}{2 \times 6 \times 7} = \frac{60}{84} = 0.7143,$$

$$\therefore \angle R = 44.4°.$$

*Worked Example 12.10

In Fig. 12.19, the circle centre A has radius 3 cm, and the circle centre B has radius 5 cm. If $AB = 6$ cm, find the shaded area common to both circles.

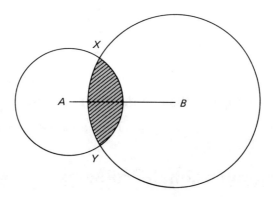

Fig. 12.19

Solution

This problem is more involved than it might seem at first sight. We begin by joining XY and looking at half of the diagram as shown in Fig. 12.20.

The shaded area = Area of sector AXY − Area of triangle AXY.

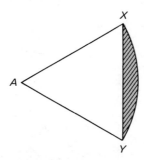

Fig. 12.20

The next problem to overcome is that we need angle XAY, and this cannot be found from triangle AXY as XY is not known. We now go to triangle AXB; see Fig. 12.21.

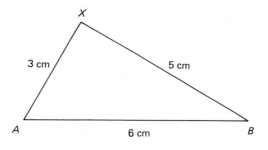

Fig. 12.21

Using the cosine rule for angle A, we have:

$$\cos A = \frac{6^2 + 3^2 - 5^2}{2 \times 6 \times 3} = \frac{20}{36} = 0.5556,$$

hence $A = 56.2°$.

$\angle XAY = 2 \times 56.2° = 112.4°$.

The shaded area in Fig. 12.20 $= \pi \times 3^2 \times \dfrac{112.4}{360} - \dfrac{1}{2} \times 3^2 \times \sin 112.4°$

$$= 4.67 \text{ cm}^2.$$

A similar method on the other half gives

Total area $= 4.67 + 2.24 = 6.91 \text{ cm}^2$.

12.13   Three-dimensional Problems

In order to tackle most three-dimensional problems at this level, it is necessary to have a clear understanding of how to find the angle between a line and a plane, and also the angle between two planes.

Figure 12.22 shows a line L passing through a plane P, cutting the plane at O. N is a point in the plane, and Q a point on the line, and $\angle QNO = 90°$. QN is *perpendicular to the plane*. For this position, angle QON is the angle between the line and the plane.

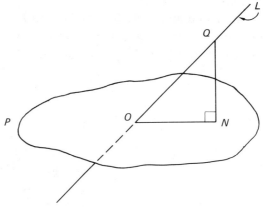

Fig. 12.22

Figure 12.23 shows two planes P_1 and P_2 which have a common line m. q is a line in P_1 at right angles to m, and n is a line in P_2 at right angles to m. The angle between n and q is the angle between the planes.

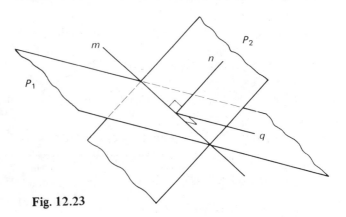

Fig. 12.23

Worked Example 12.11

In Fig. 12.24 $ABCDA'B'C'D'$ is a cube of side 6 cm. M is the midpoint of CC'. Find
(i) the angle between AM and the plane $BB'C'C$,
(ii) the angle between the planes ABM and $ABCD$.

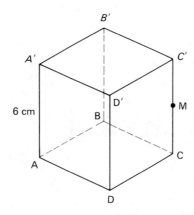

Fig. 12.24

Solution

The simplest way of tackling a question similar to part (i) is to draw the equivalent triangle to QON which appears in Fig. 12.25.

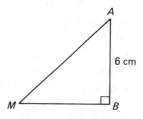

Fig. 12.25

(a) AM represents L in Fig. 12.22 and $BB'C'C$ represents P, hence B is the point N.
BM^2 must be found first:
$BM^2 = 6^2 + 3^2 = 45$.
$BM^2 = 6^2 + 3^2 = 45$. (Using triangle BCM.)
$BM = 6.71$.
The required angle is AMB,
$\therefore \tan A\hat{M}B = \dfrac{6}{6.71} = 0.8942$,
$\therefore \angle AMB = 41.8°$.

(b) In Fig. 12.23 the lines n and q will be BM and BC, because AB is the line m.
The angle between the planes is MBC.
$\therefore \tan M\hat{B}C = \dfrac{3}{6} = 0.5$,
$\therefore \angle MBC = 26.6°$.

*12.14 Latitude and Longitude

(This topic could be ideal for a project.)

Another problem in three-dimensional work is linked to the earth, considered as a perfect sphere of approximate radius 6370 km. See Fig. 12.26 for definitions.

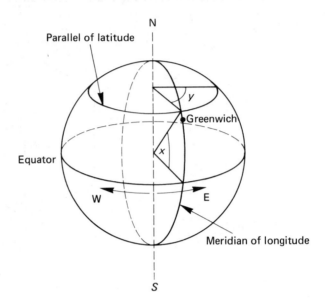

x is the angle of latitude (N or S)
y is the angle of longitude (W or E)

Fig. 12.26

Great circle: Any circle on the surface of the earth whose centre is the centre of the earth, including circles of longitude, and the equator, is called a *great circle*.

Nautical mile: The length of arc on a great circle which subtends an angle of 1′ at the centre is called a *nautical mile* (n mile).

Radius of circle of latitude: In Fig. 12.27, if A is in latitude x° N, r is the radius of the circle of latitude, and R is the radius of the earth, then

$$\frac{r}{R} = \cos x°, \quad \therefore \ r = R \cos x°.$$

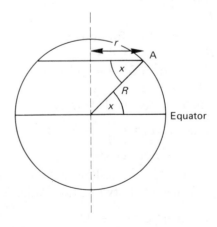

Fig. 12.27

*Worked Example 12.12

A is the point (18° E, 60° N), B is the point (12° W, 60° N) and C is the point (12° W, 18° S). Find

(a) the distance between A and B along a circle of latitude, measured in nautical miles,

(b) the distance between B and C along a circle of longitude measured in km.

Solution

All problems in latitude and longitude are best solved by drawing either the relevant circle of latitude (remember its radius may have to be found), or the circle of longitude.

(a) r is not required if we are working in nautical miles. Angle between A and B is

$$12° + 18° = 30° = 30° \times 60 = 1800'.$$

Add angles because
A is east and B is west.

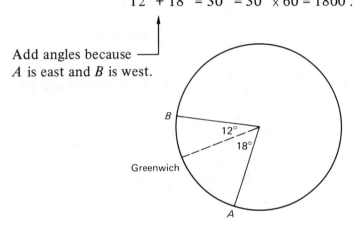

Fig. 12.28

Since we are not on a great circle,

the distance in nautical miles = 1800 cos 60° = 900 n miles.

(b) Angle between B and C is 60° + 18° = 78°;

$$\text{distance } BC = 2 \times \pi \times 6370 \times \frac{78}{360} = 8672 \text{ km.}$$

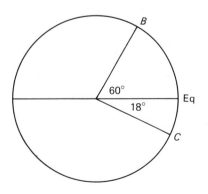

Fig. 12.29

Exercise 12

1 *ABCD* is a square of side 2 cm. *P*, *Q*, *R* and *S* are the mid-points of *AB*, *BC*, *CD* and *DA* respectively.
AP + *AQ* + *AR* + *AS* equals:
   A 6 cm   **B** $2 + 2\sqrt{5}$ cm   **C** $2 + \sqrt{5}$ cm   **D** $2(1 + 2\sqrt{5})$ cm

2 Given that *PR* = 4 cm, Fig. 12.30, an expression in cm for the length of *QS* is:

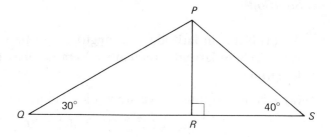

Fig. 12.30

  A $\dfrac{4}{\tan 30°} + \dfrac{4}{\tan 40°}$ **B** $4 \tan 30° + 4 \tan 40°$

  C $\dfrac{4}{\sin 30°} + \dfrac{4}{\sin 40°}$ **D** $\dfrac{4}{\cos 30°} + \dfrac{4}{\cos 40°}$ [AEB 1980]

3 In Fig. 12.31, sin *x* equals:
  A $-b/c$ **B** $-a/b$ **C** b/c **D** $-b/a$

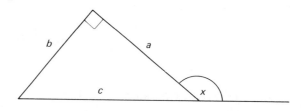

Fig. 12.31

4 The length of the diagonal *AB* of the rectangular box shown in Fig. 12.32 is:
  A 7 cm   **B** 5 cm   **C** $\sqrt{29}$ cm   **D** 9 cm

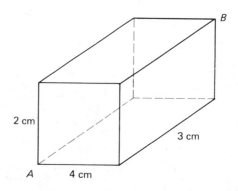

Fig. 12.32

5 In Fig. 12.33, PQ is parallel to SR; $PQ = 10$ cm, $QR = 12$ cm, $PR = 15$ cm. Given that $\angle SPR = \angle PQR$, the length, in cm, of PS is:

A 8.0 **B** 12.5 **C** 13.5 **D** 18.0 [AEB 1980]

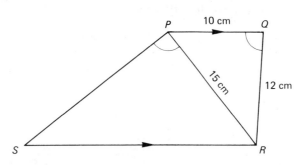

Fig. 12.33

6 Fig. 12.34 shows the position of 3 yachts in a race, A, B, C. The bearing of B from A is 040°, and the bearing of B from C is 310°. It follows that the bearing of A from C must be:

A 350° **B** 260° **C** 270° **D** none of these

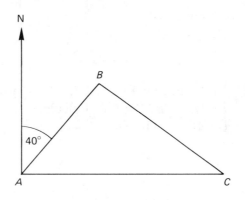

Fig. 12.34

7 In triangle ABC, it was found that $AB^2 < AC^2 + BC^2$. It follows that

A $\angle C$ is obtuse **B** $\sin C < \frac{1}{2}$ **C** $\cos C > 0$ **D** $\angle ABC = 90°$

∗8 A is the point (10° E, 60° N) and B is the point (14° W, 60° N). The shortest distance measured in nautical miles between A and B along a circle of latitude is:

A 240 **B** 1440 **C** 120 **D** 720

∗9 In Fig. 12.35, ABD is a straight line, and angle x is an acute angle such that $\sin x = \frac{3}{5}$. It follows that AC equals:

A 5 cm **B** $\sqrt{5.8}$ cm **C** $\sqrt{44.2}$ cm **D** 6 cm

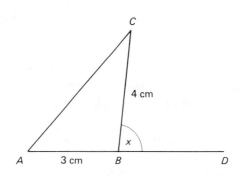

Fig. 12.35

10 In Fig. 12.36, calculate:
  (a) the length of *PS*
  (b) the size of ∠*SRP*
  (c) the length of *RQ*

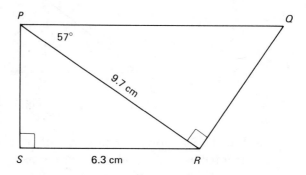

Fig. 12.36

11 In the diagram Fig. 12.37, *ABC* is a straight line, *BE* = 20 cm, and *BD* = 10 cm. ∠*EAB* = ∠*BCD* = 90°. Calculate:
  (a) *AC*   (b) *DC*   (c) tan *x*   (d) *x*   [AEB 1980]

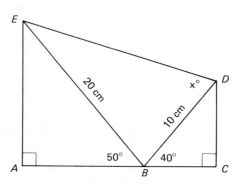

Fig. 12.37

12 In the kite *ABCD*, where *AB* = *AD*, the diagonals *BD* and *AC* meet at *E*; *P* is the mid-point of *AE* and *Q* is the mid-point of *CE*. Given that *BD* = 12 cm, *AC* = 13 cm and *AE* = 4 cm:
  (a) calculate *AB* and *CB* in cm;
  (b) prove ∠*ABC* = 90°;
  (c) calculate ∠*EBC*;
  (d) calculate ∠*PBQ*.   [L]

13 In Fig. 12.38 *ABCD* represents part of the cross-section of a circus tent with *BC* and *AD* being vertical poles. *FECD* is level ground and *AF* and *BE* are guy-ropes to support the tent.

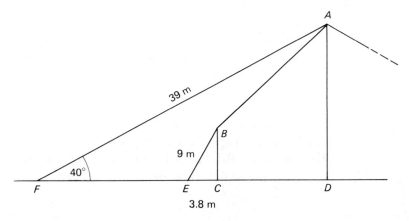

Fig. 12.38

AF = 39 m, *BE* = 9 m, *EC* = 3.8 m and ∠*AFE* = 40°. Calculate:
(a) the height of the tent *AD*;
(b) the size of ∠*BEC*. [WJEC]

14 Two ships *X* and *Y* leave a port *P* at 12.00 hours. Ship *X* sails at 18 knots on a bearing 040°, and ship *Y* sails at 20 knots on a constant bearing so that *Y* is always due south of *X*. Calculate:
(a) the bearing on which ship *Y* is sailing;
(b) the distance between the ships at 14.00 hours.
(c) At 14.00 hours, *X* and *Y* are 70 nautical miles and 50 nautical miles respectively from a lighthouse *L* which is east of the line *XY*. Calculate the bearing of *L* from the ship *Y*. [L]

15 *A*, *B* and *C* are three points in a straight line on horizontal ground and *CD* is a vertical rock face, as shown in Fig. 12.39.

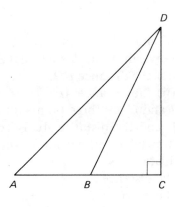

Fig. 12.39

Bruce and Stephanie each wish to estimate the height of the rock face. Their methods are as follows:
(a) Bruce estimates that, at *A*, the angle of elevation of *D* is 20°, the distance *AB* is 200 m and the distance *BC* is 500 m. Using Bruce's estimates, calculate:
  (i) the height of the rock face;
  (ii) the angle *CBD*.
(b) Stephanie estimates that, at *A*, the angle of elevation of *D* is 20°, the

distance *AB* is 200 m and angle *CBD* is 25°. Let *BC* = *d* metres and *CD* = *h* metres. Using Stephanie's estimates, write down two equations involving *d* and *h*. Hence calculate the values of *d* and *h*.   [OLE]

*16 *A*, *B* and *C* are three points on a map. *AB* = 6.8 cm, *AC* = 5.3 cm and ∠*BAC* = 44.6°.

(a) Calculate the length of *BC*.

(b) Given that the actual distance represented by *AB* is 13.6 km, calculate the scale of the map in the form 1 : *n*, and the actual distance represented by *BC* in kilometres.

(c) Given that *B* is due east of *A* and that *C* is north of the line *AB*, calculate the bearing of *C* from *A*.

*17 (a) Find two angles whose sine is 0.55.

(b) Figure 12.40, which is not drawn to scale, shows two points *A* and *B* on a coastline which runs from west to east where *AB* = 5 miles. A boat leaves

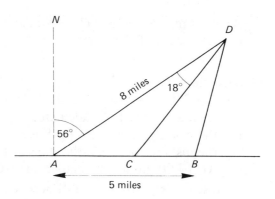

Fig. 12.40

A and sails 8 miles to *D* on a course 056° (N 56° E). The point *C* is between *A* and *B* such that ∠*ADC* = 18°. Calculate:

(i) the distance *BD*;

(ii) the distance *AC*.   [WJEC]

18 *A*, *B* and *C* are three points on level ground. *B* is due east of *A*, *C* is due north of *A*, and the distance *AC* is 160 m. The angles of elevation from *A* and *B* to the top of a vertical mast whose base is at *C* are respectively 30° and 28°. Calculate:

(a) the distance *BC*;

(b) the bearing of *C* from *B*.

19 The points *O*, *P*, *Q* and *T* lie in a horizontal plane, but, because of an obstruction, the point *T* is not visible from the point *O*. The bearings of the points *P* and *Q* from *O* are 029° and 062° respectively; *OP* = 0.8 km and *OQ* = 1.2 km. The bearing of *T* from *P* is 126° and the bearing of *T* from *Q* is 160°.

Using a scale of 10 cm to 1 km, draw a diagram showing the points *O*, *P*, *Q* and *T*. From your diagram, obtain the bearing and distance of *T* from *O*.

[O & C]

20 Figure 12.41 shows a storage shed on a building site.

(a) Calculate the angle of inclination of the roof to the horizontal.

(b) Calculate the length of the longest rod that can be stored in the shed.

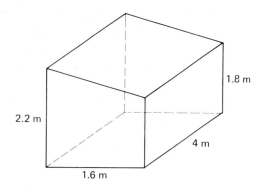

1.8 m

2.2 m

4 m

1.6 m

Fig. 12.41

21 The diagram in Fig. 12.42 shows a pyramid whose horizontal base is a square *ABCD*. The vertex *V* is vertically above *N*, the centre of the base.

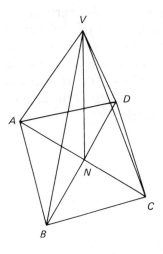

Fig. 12.42

(a) Given that the base has an area of 50 cm², find the length of a diagonal of the square *ABCD*.
(b) Given also that each slant edge of the pyramid is 13 cm, find the volume of the pyramid. [EAUCJ]

22 A square pyramid has base *A'B'C'D'* of side 50 cm. The top is cut off to give a square top *ABCD* of side 20 cm, height 1.5 m. Each of the four sloping sides is a trapezium of the same dimensions as *ABB'A'*. Find:
(a) the inclination of face *ABB'A'* to the base;
(b) the length of *AA'*;
(c) inclination of *AA'* to the horizontal.

23 In Fig. 12.23 *G* and *D* represent the positions of guns, *T* the position of a target and *O* that of an observation post.
Given that *OG* = 3500 m, *OT* = 2000 m, *OD* = 4000 m, angle *AOG* = 63°, angle *TAG* = 90° and *DOG* and *AOT* are straight lines, calculate the distances
(a) *AG*, (b) *AT*, (c) *TD*. [EAUCJ]

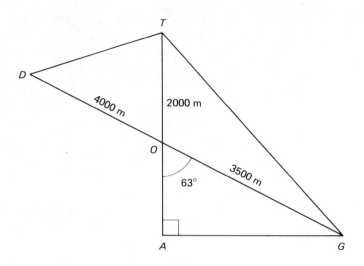

Fig. 12.43

24 The sails of a yacht form a triangle ABC with BC horizontal and A the top of the mast. The bottom of the mast D is the foot of the perpendicular from A to BC. $AD = 6.5$ m, $DC = 2$ m, $BD = 3$ m. When the mast is inclined at an angle $10°$ to the vertical, calculate the height of A above the water level (assumed to be the level of BC). When the mast is vertical the sun shines from the direction perpendicular to BC and at an elevation of $60°$, calculate the area of the shadow cast by the sails on the water.

* 25 In Fig. 12.44 ABC is a straight line, $CD = 6.4$ cm and $AB = 7.3$ cm. Calculate (a) BD; (b) AD; (c) the area of triangle ABD; (d) the perpendicular distance of B from AD.

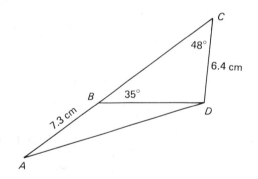

Fig. 12.44

* 26 From a lighthouse L a boat is seen at a point A which is due north of L, and 1.2 km away from it. The boat travels in a straight line, and 10 minutes later it is at a point B on a bearing of $105°$ from L and 1.8 km away from L. Calculate:
(a) the speed of the boat in km/h;
(b) the direction in which the boat is travelling;
(c) the shortest distance between the boat and the lighthouse.

* 27 On a certain golf course, the distance from the tee T to the hole H is 350 m. A player drives his ball from T to a point S where $TS = 160$ m and $\angle STH = 3°$.
Calculate, correct to 0.1 m, the distance SH.
A second player drives his ball from T to a point O, such that $\angle HTO = 6°$ and $\angle TOH = 160°$. Calculate, correct to 1 m, the distance TO. A third player drives his ball a distance of 180 m from T to a point P which is 180 m from H. Calculate the angle PTH.

28 ABC is a triangle in which $AB = 4$ cm, $BC = 6.7$ cm and $\angle ABC = 105°$. Calculate AC.

AB is produced to D so that $\angle BDC = 60°$. Calculate BD. Calculate also the area of the triangle ACD.

29 The points A and B lie on the circumference of a circle, of centre O and radius 49 cm, such that $\angle AOB = 80°$. Taking $\pi = \frac{22}{7}$, find the difference in length between the minor arc AB and the chord AB.

30 O is the centre of a circle of diameter 12 cm. P and Q lie on the circle and $\angle POQ = 80°$. Calculate:
(a) the length of the minor arc PQ;
(b) the area of the minor sector POQ;
(c) the area of the triangle POQ;
(d) the length of the chord PQ.

31 Figure 12.45 shows the vertical cross-section of an oil drum, being fastened to the ground by a wire $PQRS$. The radius of the drum is 0.6 m. Calculate:
(a) RS;
(b) PS;
(c) angle ROQ (where O is the centre of the circle);
(d) the total length of the wire $PQRS$.

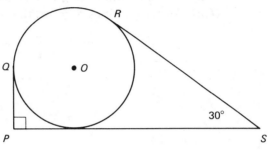

Fig. 12.45

* **32** State the latitude and longitude of the point A on the surface of the earth, if AB passes through the centre of the earth and B is (56° N, 37° W).

* **33** On a globe whose diameter is 21 cm, two points on the same parallel of latitude differ in longitude by 120°. The distance between the two points measured along the line of latitude is 5.5 cm. Calculate the latitude of the two points ($\pi = \frac{22}{7}$).

* **34** P and Q are two points on the same parallel of latitude 64° 25′ S, whose longitudes differ by 180°. Assuming the earth to be a sphere with centre O and radius 6370 km, calculate in kilometres:
(a) the radius of the parallel of latitude;
(b) the distance of P from Q measured along the parallel of latitude.
Calculate the shortest distance in nautical miles between P and Q measured on the surface of the earth.

* **35** A (28° N, 162° W) and B (28° N, 18° E) are two places on the earth's surface. Calculate in nautical miles, the distance between A and B:
(a) travelling by the shortest route;
(b) travelling along a parallel of latitude.
Two jet aircraft leave A simultaneously, flying at the same speed, one along each of the two different routes. Calculate the latitude and longitude of the other when the first aircraft arrives at B. The second plane is flying eastwards.

36 Figure 12.46(a) represents a strip of sticky tape of uniform width laid across a sheet of card near to one corner of the sheet which is right-angled. The strip is

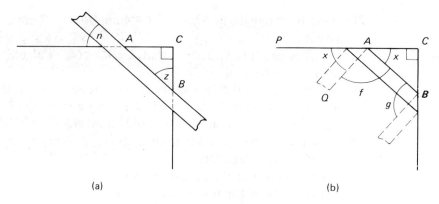

(a)   (b)

Fig. 12.46

then neatly folded under the sheet and pressed to the sheet, such that angle
PAQ = angle BAC, as shown in (b). Similarly, the tape is folded at B so that
equal angles are formed with the edge of the card.

(a) If $x = 37°$, calculate the sizes of the angles:

    (i) n; (ii) z; (iii) f; (iv) g.

(b) (i) Find a formula for f in terms of x;

    (ii) find a formula for g in terms of x;

    (iii) for what values of x are the folded parts of the tape parallel?

[UCLES]

13 Drawing and Construction

13.1 Constructions Using Ruler and Compass

In the following diagrams, points numbered ①, ② etc. show where and the order in which the compass point is placed and the corresponding arcs have the same numbers. Notes about restrictions on the radii are given at the side.

(a) Bisecting a Line *PQ* at Right Angles

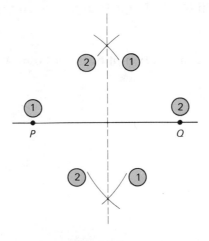

Fig. 13.1

Radius ① = radius ②, and must be greater than half of *PQ*.

(b) Bisecting an Angle *ABC*

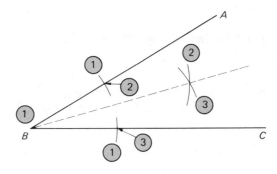

Fig. 13.2

① Any radius;
radius ② = radius ③, large enough for two arcs to meet.

(c) Perpendicular from a Point P to a Line AB

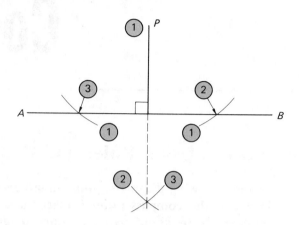

Fig. 13.3

Radii ①, ②, ③ equal, large enough for ① to meet line *AB*.

(d) Construction of 60° at a Point X on XY

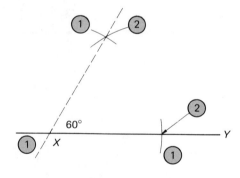

Fig. 13.4

Radius ① = radius ②, any length.

(e) Construction of 30°, 45°, 75° etc.

30° can be obtained by bisecting 60°.
45° can be obtained by bisecting 90°.
75° can be obtained by constructing 45°, and then 30° on this.

Many other angles could be constructed using these basic angles,

e.g. $52\frac{1}{2}° = 15° + 37\frac{1}{2}° = $ half of 30° + half of 75°,
or $\qquad = $ half of 105° = half of (90° + 15°).

(f) Drawing a Line Through _P_ Parallel to _AB_

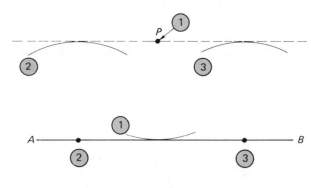

Fig. 13.5

Radii ①, ②, ③ equal, the arc ① just touches _AB_.

(g) To Construct an Angle of 90° at _A_ on _AB_

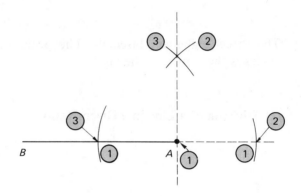

Fig. 13.6

_BA_ must be produced at _A_ ;
radii ①, ②, ③ equal.

(h) To Construct the Circumscribing Circle of a Triangle _ABC_

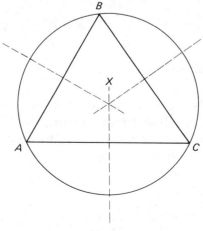

Fig. 13.7

239

To find the centre of the circle, bisect each side in turn. The intersection of the bisectors is the centre of the circle.

(i) To Construct the Inscribing Circle of Triangle *PQR*

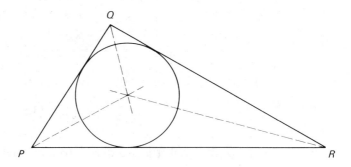

Fig. 13.8

The three angles are bisected. The point of intersection of the bisectors of the angles is the centre of the circle.

(j) Division of a Line in a Given Ratio

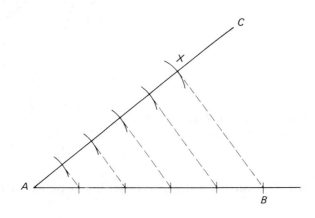

Fig. 13.9

Strictly speaking, this is not a ruler and compass construction.

Divide a line *AB* into 5 equal parts.

Draw line *AC* (any reasonable angle). Use a compass to mark off 5 equal lengths on *AC*. Join the end point *X* to *B*.

Then using two set squares, draw 4 lines parallel to *BX*. *AB* is then divided into 5 equal parts.

In all construction work, the construction lines must be faint, and not detract from the main details of the diagram.

Worked Example 13.1

Three towns O, A and B are such that O is the point $(0, 0)$, $\overrightarrow{OA} = \begin{pmatrix} 8 \\ -2 \end{pmatrix}$ and $\overrightarrow{OB} = \begin{pmatrix} 24 \\ 6 \end{pmatrix}$, where the units are kilometres.

(a) Using a scale of 1 cm to 2 km, illustrate O, A and B on squared paper.

(b) A motorway is constructed so that it is equidistant from A and B. An interchange on this motorway is to be located so that it is not more than 10 km from A. Assuming that the motorway can be represented by a straight line, accurately construct and label on your diagram the line segment p which represents possible locations for the interchange.

(c) Circle and label the point X on p which is closest to A. Calculate, in kilometres, the distance AX, giving your answer correct to two significant figures.

(d) A new town C is to be situated so that it is equidistant from the motorway and the line AB. Mark clearly on your diagram all the possible locations for C if $CX = 8$ km.

[AEB 1980]

Solution

(a), (b) The diagram in Fig. 13.10 shows accurately the position P_1 and P_2 at the end of the line segment p. These are found by drawing a circle, centre A, radius

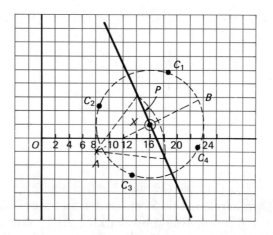

Fig. 13.10

10 km (5 cm), and finding the intersection of it with the perpendicular bisector of AB. (So that the motorway is equidistant from A and B.)

(c) The closest point X is the mid-point of AB, hence X is $(16, 2)$.
   AX can be found by Pythagoras' theorem.
   The horizontal distance from A to X is 8.
   The vertical distance from A to X is 4.
   $\therefore AX = \sqrt{8^2 + 4^2} = 8.9$ km

(d) Draw a circle centre X radius 8 km (4 cm). The new town must lie on the bisectors of angle $P_1 XB$ and $P_2 XB$. (These have been left out for clarity.) We thus obtain four points, C_1, C_2, C_3, C_4 as shown.

Worked Example 13.2

Using ruler and compasses throughout, construct a rectangle *PQRS* in which *PQ* = 10 cm and the diagonal *QS* = 11 cm. Measure and state the length of PS.

Construct a triangle *TPQ* having *PQ* as base, the point *T* on *SR* and the angle *TQP* = 45°. Measure and state the length of *PT*. Find, by construction, a point *X* on *SR* between *S* and *T* and such that the angle *PXQ* = 90°. Complete the parallelogram *PXYQ*.

Without any further measurement, calculate:
(a) the area of the triangle *TQP*;
(b) the area of the parallelogram *PXYQ*;
(c) the product of *PX* and *QX*.   [AEB 1980]

Solution

Draw *PQ* and mark off 10 cm. Construct 90° at *P*. Mark off *QS* = 11 cm. Repeat to find *R*.

By measurement, *PS* = 4.6 cm.

Bisect ∠*RQP* to get 45°; locate *T*, join *TP*.

By measurement, *PT* = 7.9 cm.

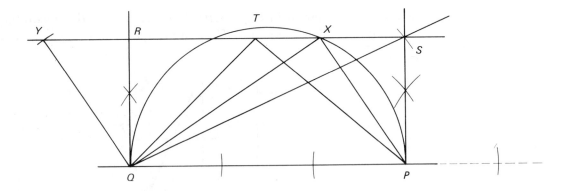

Fig. 13.11

To find *X*, *QP* will be the diameter of a circle if *QXP* = 90°. Hence, draw a semicircle radius 5 cm, centre mid-point of *QP*, to cut *RS* at *X*.

Y can be found by marking off 10 cm.
(a) Area of △*TQP* = $\frac{1}{2}$ × 10 × 4.6 = 23 cm².
(b) Area of parallelogram = 10 × 4.6 = 46 cm².
(c) Since *PXQ* is a right-angled triangle, *PX* multiplied by *QX* is twice the area of the triangle. But △*PXQ* and △*PTQ* have the same area.

∴ *PX* · *QX* = 46.

Worked Example 13.3

A circle is inscribed inside a square *ABCD*. Any point *P* of the circle is joined to any point *Q* of the square and *PQ* is produced to *R*, so that *PR* = 2*PQ*. Describe and illustrate:
(a) the locus of *R* as *Q* moves round the square for any fixed point *P* not a point of contact;

(b) the locus of R as P moves round the circle for any fixed point Q not a point of contact;

(c) the locus of R for one of the points of contact of the circle with the square.

[L]

Solution

This is quite a difficult question, and an explanation is not easy to give. The approach will be to look at several positions of R for each case and see how this leads to a solution.

(a) Figure 13.12 shows five different positions of Q and the corresponding positions of R. Since Q is the mid-point on each occasion, the locus is a square with sides parallel to the original square and sides of twice the length. The centre of enlargement will be P.

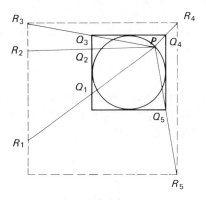

Fig. 13.12

(b) This time three positions of P are given. The resulting locus is an enlargement, scale factor -1, centre of enlargement Q. It is another circle.

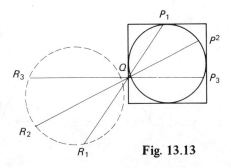

Fig. 13.13

(c) Two positions of Q are shown; it can easily be seen that the locus is another circle which is an enlargement, scale factor 2, centre of enlargement P.

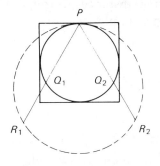

Fig. 13.14

243

13.2 Plans and Elevations

The solid shown in Fig. 13.15 is similar to the shape of a house. Hidden edges are dotted. Three different views of it are shown alongside.

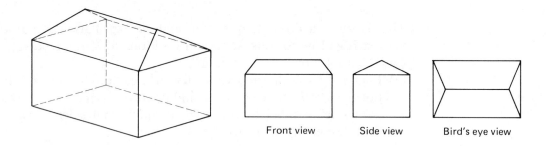

Front view   Side view   Bird's eye view

Fig. 13.15

The front and side views are referred to as *elevations*, and the bird's eye view is called the *plan*. These can be combined together in a more technical fashion as shown in Fig. 13.16.

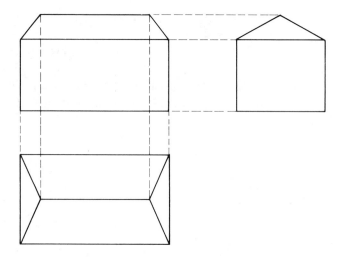

Fig. 13.16

Diagrams of this nature are commonly used in engineering. They are very useful for finding distances through three-dimensional objects, as illustrated by the following example.

Worked Example 13.4

Figure 13.17 shows a framework made from 12 rods of length 8 cm, forming a cube. $A'X = 3$ cm. Draw a plan and elevation from the direction of the arrow, and hence find the length of DX.

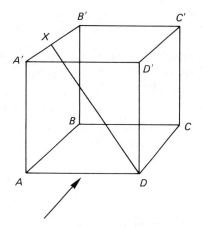

Fig. 13.17

Solution

The plan and elevation are shown in Fig. 13.18. In order to find the real distance *DX*, read the *horizontal* distance from the plan, and the *vertical* distance from the elevation.

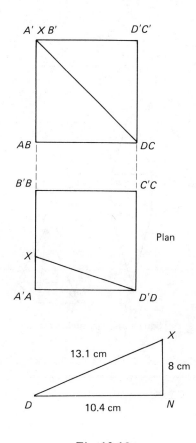

Fig. 13.18

The triangle *XDN* can then be drawn, where *N* is the point vertically beneath *X*.

The actual distance *XD* = 13.1 cm.

13.3 Nets

Many problems in three dimensions can be simplified if the situation can be reduced to a two-dimensional one — for example in finding surface areas.

In Fig. 13.19, a number of nets are shown together with the three-dimensional shapes that they fold up into (flaps for joining have been left out). Each net is not necessarily unique for a given shape. You should investigate different nets, and also look at other shapes.

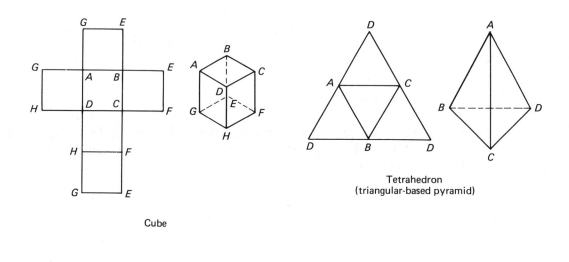

Cube

Tetrahedron
(triangular-based pyramid)

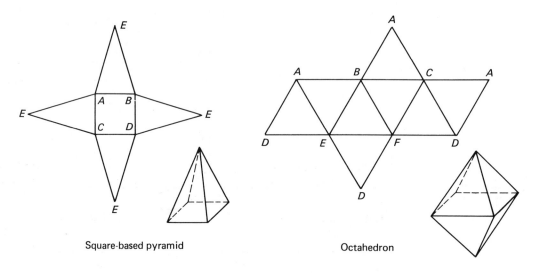

Square-based pyramid

Octahedron

Fig. 13.19

Worked Example 13.5

A fly is at one corner X of a wooden cube of side 8 cm. If it walks along the surface of the cube to the corner Y that is furthest from X, what is the shortest distance it would have to walk?

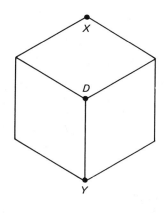

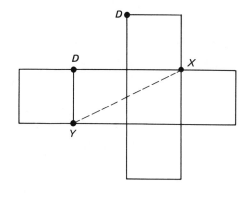

| Fig. 13.20 | Fig. 13.21 |

Solution

Look at Fig. 13.20. You may be tempted to say that the shortest distance is *XDY*. This turns out to be 19.3 cm. However, if you look at the net of the cube in Fig. 13.21, the shortest distance is the straight line *XY* on the net.
　The distance is 17.9 cm.

13.4　Locus

The definition used in section 6.6 can be used here.

Worked Example 13.6

AB is a fixed line of length 6 cm. Construct the locus of a variable point *P* such that $\angle APB = 45°$, and *P* is on one side of *AB* only.

Solution

If $\angle APB$ is always 45°, then *P* moves along the arc of a circle as shown in Fig. 13.22. To find the centre of the circle, one position of *P* must be found. The easiest case is if $\hat{A} = 45°$ and $\hat{B} = 90°$.
(a) Construct $\hat{B} = 90°$.
(b) Bisect 90° at *A*.
(c) Bisect the sides to find the centre of the circle.
(d) Draw the arc. See Fig. 13.23.

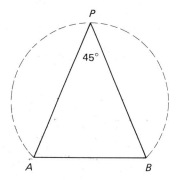

Fig.　13.22

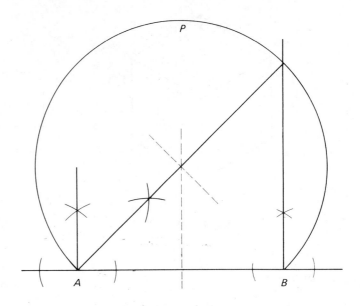

Fig. 13.23

Exercise 13

This exercise does not contain multiple-choice questions as they are not relevant.

1 State the locus in two dimensions of the centre of a variable circle:
(a) which touches a given line at a given point;
(b) which touches both of two fixed parallel lines.
On graph paper, draw the rectangle $ABYX$ in which $AB = 10$ cm, $BY = 8$ cm.
Draw also the line LM where L is the mid-point of AX and M is the mid-point
of BY.

Determine, by construction, the point P lying inside the rectangle $ABYX$,
such that it is equidistant from AB and LM, and $AP = 5$ cm.

Construct a circle which passes through P touching AB and XY.

Construct a further circle which touches the circle you have drawn and also
the lines LM and XY. Label its centre R and measure and write down the
length of PR.   [L]

2 In Fig. 13.24 construct, using ruler and compasses only, and leaving all your
construction lines clearly visible:

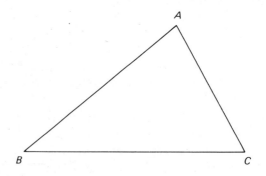

Fig. 13.24

248

(a) the perpendicular bisector of BC;

(b) the bisector of angle ABC. D is the point at which the two bisectors meet.

(c) Measure the length of DC.

(d) Shade, with horizontal lines, the set of points P, inside triangle ABC, for which $PB \leqslant PC$.

(e) Shade, with vertical lines, the set of points Q, inside triangle ABC, for which angle $QBC \leqslant \frac{1}{2}$ angle ABC. [OLE]

3 Using ruler and compasses only, construct in a single diagram:

(a) the triangle ABC such that $AB = 7$ cm, $AC = 10$ cm and $BC = 6$ cm;

(b) the circle centre P which touches AC and also touches CB produced and is such that $CP = 8$ cm;

(c) the triangle QAB, equal in area to the triangle ABC, where QA is perpendicular to AB and Q is on the opposite side of AC to B.

State the length of CQ. [AEB 1982]

4 Using ruler and compasses only, construct the triangle ABC in which $AB = 8$ cm, $BC = 9.2$ cm, and $\angle ABC = 120°$. Construct also (a) the perpendicular from B to AC; (b) the bisector of angle BAC.

5 Three equal spheres stand on a plane so that they touch each other. An identical sphere is placed on top. Draw the plan of this configuration.

6 Draw a line XY of length 7 cm. Construct a line PQ parallel to XY, and distant 4 cm from XY. Construct the circle which passes through X and Y, touching PQ. Measure the radius.

7 Draw any acute-angled triangle BAC. Produce BC to D where $CD = CA$. Produce CB to E where $BE = BA$. Construct the bisectors of angles ABE and ACD. Label the point of intersection of these two bisectors O. By drawing a circle through A with centre O, deduce that OB is the line of symmetry of the quadrilateral $OABE$. Construct also the bisector of angle BAC. What do you notice?

8 Describe the locus, in a plane, of

(a) the vertex A of $\triangle ABC$ when BC is fixed in length and position and $\angle BAC$ is of constant size;

(b) the vertex P of $\triangle PRQ$ when QR is fixed in length and position and $\triangle PQR$ is of constant area.

Using ruler and compasses only and drawing any necessary area of such length and clarity to permit assessment, construct a $\triangle XYZ$ in which $YZ = 8$ cm, $\angle YXZ = 60°$ and the area of $\triangle XYZ = 24$ cm^2. In the case when XY is longer than YZ, measure and write down

(c) the length of XY to the nearest mm;

(d) the $\angle XYZ$ to the nearest degree. [L]

9 The $\triangle PQR$ lies in a fixed plane, has a fixed base QR and a constant area. State the locus of the vertex P.

Using ruler and compasses only in the remainder of this question, and drawing any necessary arcs of such length and clarity to permit assessment, construct:

(a) a $\triangle ABC$ in which $AB = 8$ cm, $BC = 6$ cm and $AC = 7$ cm;

(b) the circumcircle of $\triangle ABC$;

(c) the cyclic quadrilateral $BCAX$, where X is such that area $\triangle BCX$ = area $\triangle BCA$;

(d) $\triangle XBY$, with Y on BC produced, which is such that the area of $\triangle XBY$ is equal to the area of quadrilateral $BCAX$. Measure, and write down, the length of XY. [L]

10 Figure 13.25 illustrates a model of a building, made from two solid blocks of wood fixed together, standing on a horizontal table. One block is rectangular; its height is 6 cm and its cross-section is a square of side 3 cm. The other

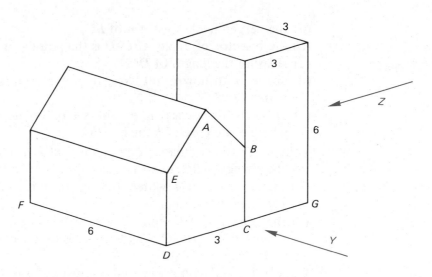

Fig. 13.25

block is a prism of length 6 cm with cross-section $ABCDE$. The vertical height of A above DC is 5 cm, $ED = BC = DC = 3$ cm, $EA = AB$ and $\angle EDC = \angle DCB = 90°$.

Draw full size:

(a) the plan of the model;

(b) the elevation, as viewed from Y, on a vertical plane parallel to the straight line DCG;

(c) the elevation, as viewed from Z, on a vertical plane parallel to DF.

Find the volume of wood used to make the model. [UCLES]

11 Two points P and Q are 6 cm apart.

(a) Construct the locus of points R such that $AR = 2.5$ cm.

(b) Construct the locus of points R such that $\angle ARB = 90°$.

(c) Construct the locus of points R such that $\angle ARB = 60°$.

12 A plot of land on a proposed housing estate is in the shape of a triangle ABC with $AB = 12.5$ m, $AC = 9$ m and the angle $BAC = 60°$. There is a preservation order on a tree T on the plot and T is equidistant from CA and CB and is also 8 m from B.

Using ruler and compasses only, draw a scaled diagram of this plot of land and by construction show the position of T.

Measure and state the distance AT.

An architect's plan of this housing estate is drawn to a scale of 1 : 250. Calculate the length on the architect's plan, in cm, of the side AB.

The area of a garden is represented by 44 cm² on the plan. Calculate, in m², the actual area of the garden. [AEB 1980]

13 Construct the triangle XYZ in which $XY = 5$ cm, $\angle X = 60°$ and $\angle Y = 90°$. Measure and write down the length of YZ. On the same diagram,

(a) Construct the circumcircle of $\triangle XYZ$.

(b) Construct, on the same side of XY as Z, the locus of the point P such that the area of $\triangle XYP$ equals half the area of $\triangle XYZ$.

(c) Mark, and label clearly, a point Q such that $\angle XQY = 30°$ and the area of $\triangle XYQ$ is half the area of $\triangle XYZ$.

Given that M is a point such that $\angle XMY = 30°$, find the largest possible area of $\triangle XMY$. [UCLES]

14 Figure 13.26, diagram I, shows a bowl in which rests a stiff rectangular card $ABCD$. The bowl is a thin hollow hemisphere of radius 62 mm with part of it cut off by a plane parallel to the plane of the rim to form the base. The bowl is 49 mm deep. Diagram II is an elevation, in which the card is seen edge-on.

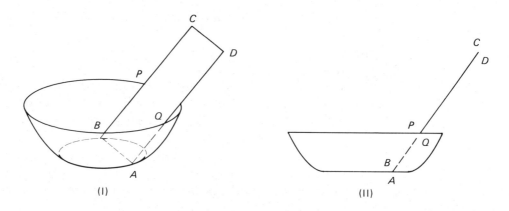

(I)   (II)

Fig. 13.26

(a) Draw, full-size, the elevation of the bowl without the card. Measure the diameter of the base and draw, full-size, the plan of the bowl.

(b) The area of the outer curved surface can be found by multiplying the depth by the circumference of the rim. Calculate the area of the whole of the outer surface, including the base.

(c) The corners A and B of the card are on the circumference of the base and the edges BC and AD rest on the rim at P and Q. The length AB is 58 mm. Show $ABPQ$ first in your plan and then in your elevation. Measure the inclination of the card to the base.   [O & C]

15 Use a ruler and protractor to answer this question, but do not use graph paper.

The front view of a large house is a rectangle with a trapezium-shaped roof on top.

The width of the house is 20 metres and its height, to the start of the roof, is 16.8 metres.

The sloping sides of the symmetrical roof are 9 metres long, at an angle of 35° to the horizontal (inwards).

Using the scale of 1 cm = 2 m, draw a diagram which represents the front view of the house.

Use your drawing to find:

(a) the actual length of the horizontal part of the top of the roof;

(b) the overall height of the house.

16 Figure 13.27 shows the net of a solid in which ABH is an equilateral triangle, $HBDF$ is a rectangle, $HB \neq BD$ and $BC \neq CD$.

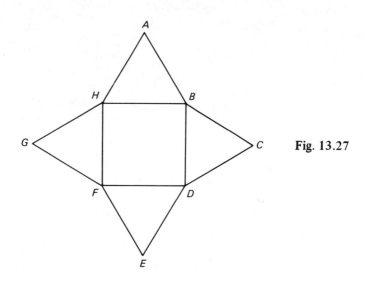

Fig. 13.27

(a) Which points will coincide with *A* when the net is folded up to make the solid?

(b) Describe the symmetry of
(i) the net,   (ii) the solid.

(c) How many faces, edges and vertices has the solid?

(d) A new solid is to be formed from a modification of this net. *HGF*, *BCD* and *HBDF* are unaltered but *ABH* is replaced by a square. Describe the shape which must replace *FED*.   [O&C]

17 (a) Figure 13.28 represents a view of a cubical die. The number of dots on opposite faces add up to seven. Write down the number of dots on the back face and on the bottom face, as indicated in the diagram.

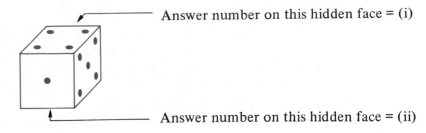

Answer number on this hidden face = (i)

Answer number on this hidden face = (ii)

Fig. 13.28

(b) Figure 13.29 represents the net of another die. As before, the number of dots on opposite faces add up to seven. Write down the number of dots that would appear on each of the faces marked as A, B and C respectively.
                    [MEG]

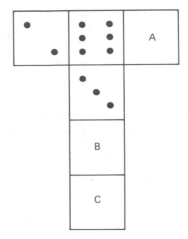

Fig. 13.29

14 Aural Examinations

The GCSE examination aims to encourage students to talk about the mathematics they are doing, describe the strategies they have used in problem solving, and indicate how they might extend the work they have done. It is also possible that you may be asked to take some form of mental arithmetic test (aural examination) as part of the coursework. The author has included four such test papers in this chapter for you to try. You will need a friend or relation to read the questions to you. Try to write down the answers without any working. Tests 3 and 4 have an information sheet which you will need to remove from the book first. Before attempting the papers, look at the following questions which contain a few hints.

Worked Example 14.1

How many 17p stamps can you buy for £2?

Solution

17 does not go exactly into £2 (200p). If you gave 200 ÷ 17 = 11.8 as the answer, it would be marked wrong.
   The correct answer is 11.

Worked Example 14.2

Work out the area of a rectangle whose sides measure 3.5 m by 8 m.

Solution

3.5 × 8 in your head is much easier if you do 3 × 8 = 24 and add 0.5 × 8 = 4.
   ∴ the area is 28 m².

Worked Example 14.3

The diameter of a circle is 12 cm; estimate the circumference.

Solution

The formula for the circumference of a circle is $2\pi r$ or πd. If you approximate $\pi = 3$, then the circumference = 3 × 12 = 36 cm.

Worked Example 14.4

A square has side of length 7 cm. What is the approximate length of the diagonal?

Solution

Using Pythagoras' theorem to find the length D of the diagonal, we have

$$D^2 = 7^2 + 7^2 = 98.$$

Hence $D^2 \approx 100$ ($\approx$ means approximately equals.)

$\therefore D$ is approximately 10 cm.

You are now in a position to try one of the following tests. Try to find somewhere quiet, and the person reading the questions to you should read each question *twice*, give you enough time to write down each answer, and then move on to the next question. Try to complete the test in the allocated time.

Mental Arithmetic Test 1 (time 20 minutes)

1. How many seventeen pence stamps can you buy for one pound?
2. What is the approximate value of forty-one multiplied by thirty-nine?
3. How many posts spaced half a metre apart would be needed in fencing a length of six metres?
4. A train service runs every twenty minutes. If one train leaves at nine forty-seven, what time will the next train leave?
5. What is the smallest number that six and eight divide into exactly?
6. What is the cost of four reels of cotton at twenty-nine pence each?
7. If today Monday is the twenty-eighth of January, what is the date on Tuesday next week?
8. What time p.m. is sixteen thirty-eight on the twenty-four hour clock?
9. How many tiles fifty centimetres by fifty centimetres are needed to cover an area of floor which measures two metres by one metre?
10. Jane normally earns one pound eighty an hour. On Saturdays, she is paid time-and-a-half. How much an hour does she earn on Saturday?
11. Write down in figures one hundred and twenty thousand eight hundred and five.
12. Two angles of a triangle are fifty-four degrees and thirty-seven degrees. What is the third angle?
13. Jason is playing darts. With his three darts he scores eight, double five and treble twenty. What is his total for that throw?
14. The train fare to London is seven pounds. If fares are increased by four per cent, what is the new fare?
15. It costs twenty-five pounds a day to hire a Ford Sierra. You get a twenty per cent reduction if you hire the car for a week. How much does it cost to hire the car for one week?
16. The average weight of three parcels is twelve kilograms. If the average weight of two of the parcels is fourteen kilograms, how much does the third parcel weigh?
17. A car travels at an average speed of thirty-five miles per hour. How far does it travel in two and a half hours?
18. A committee is made up from four men and two women. A chairperson is selected from the six. What is the probability that it is a woman?
19. The mortgate rate is increased by one and three quarters per cent from ten and a half per cent. What is the new interest rate?
20. David was sent to the shops to buy ninety bolts. Unfortunately, they were only sold in bubble packs of twelve, which cost twenty pence. How much did he have to pay to get the bolts he required?

Mental Arithmetic Test 2 (time 20 minutes)

1 Tickets to see Dire Straits cost £10.50 each. How much did Jill and her three friends pay altogether to see the concert?

2 Eight glasses of wine can be poured from one bottle of wine. How many glasses can be poured from six bottles?

3 A tin of emulsion covers ten square metres. How many tins are needed to paint a wall which measures nine metres by eight metres?

4 The sides of a rectangle measure six metres and three metres. Estimate the length of the diagonal.

5 A batsman scored eight, twenty-three and fifty in three innings. What was his average score?

6 Ann and Bill went picking peas. Ann picked twice as many peas as Bill, and altogether they picked seven and a half pounds. How many peas did Ann pick?

7 Write down the cube root of 125.

8 How many vertices has a cuboid?

9 The radius of a circle is 8 cm. Estimate the area of the circle.

10 David bought half a pound of tea at forty-five pence a quarter and two cut loaves which cost thirty-five pence each. How much did he spend?

11 Rashid just missed the 1415 train. If the service is every fifty minutes, what is the earliest train he can catch next?

12 Simplify as far as possible four x multiplied by two x.

13 A car averages seventy miles an hour on a motorway. How long does it take to travel one hundred and seventy-five miles?

14 A piece of glass has an area of twelve hundred square millimetres. Express this area in square centimetres.

15 Write down any fraction that lies between two-thirds and five-sixths.

16 Two angles of a triangle are eighty degrees and thirty-five degrees. What is the third angle?

17 Peter's radio-controlled car can travel at twenty miles an hour. How many minutes would it take to drive around a quarter-mile course?

18 The number of customers attending the first day of a sale was twenty-eight thousand, seven hundred and nine. Write this correct to two significant figures.

19 The surface area of a box is four square centimetres. The surface area of a similar box is sixteen square centimetres. If the volume of the smaller box is one point five cubic centimetres, what is the volume of the larger box?

20 What time p.m. is twenty-one twenty-one on the twenty-four hour clock?

Mental Arithmetic Test 3 (time 15 minutes)

1 A rectangle measures three point five centimetres by eight centimetres. What is its area?

2 What is the largest prime number less than forty?

3 All goods in a shop are reduced by ten per cent in a sale. If the sale price of a washing machine is one hundred and eighty pounds, how much was it before the sale?

4 I buy four pens costing sixty-five pence each. How much change should I get from a five-pound note?

5 Write down in full, the number one hundred and five thousand and eight.

6 The Battle of Hastings was fought in ten sixty-six. How long ago was this?

7 The temperature overnight fell from twelve degrees Celsius to minus nine degrees Celsius. How much did the temperature fall by?

8 What is the perimeter of a square which has an area of sixty-four square centimetres?

For the rest of the questions, you will need to remove the information sheet which comes after Test 4.

9 How far is it from Cambridge to Norwich?
10 The parallelogram is drawn to scale. The length of the longest side is six centimetres. What is the approximate area of the parallelogram?
11 How many kilometres an hour is thirty-four miles an hour?
12 Estimate the size of angle x.
13 How long does the return journey from Honiton to Worthing take on a Saturday?
14 How much would it cost to have two films, each with twenty-four pictures, developed in a matt finish including postage?
15 How much would it cost to send a letter weighing thirty grams to India?

Mental Arithmetic Test 4 (time 15 minutes)

1 How many seconds are there in one hour?
2 What is the cost of twenty-two pens at twelve pence each?
3 What is the volume of a box whose dimensions are eight centimetres by five centimetres by six centimetres?
4 The height of a horse is measured in hands. One hand is four inches. How high is a horse measuring fifteen hands?
5 A photograph has an area of twenty-four square centimetres. If it is enlarged by a scale factor of two, what is the area of the new picture?
6 Write down the fraction that lies half-way between one-eighth and one-quarter.
7 A large tube of gum contains two hundred millilitres. What area in square centimetres would it cover if spread to a depth of two millimetres?
8 A night storage heater normally costing one hundred and twenty pounds is offered at a twenty per cent discount. What is the reduced price?

For the rest of the questions, you will need to remove the information sheet which comes after this test.

9 How far is it from York to Cambridge?
10 The parallelogram is drawn to scale, and the largest side is six centimetres. Estimate the length of the longest diagonal.
11 What is ninety kilometres per hour in miles per hour approximately?
12 Estimate the size of angle y.
13 I wish to travel from Axminster to Plymouth on Saturday, September the twentieth. What time does my train depart?
14 How much, including postage, would it cost to have a fifteen-exposure disc developed, including a duplicate set of prints?
15 A letter to Japan costs sixty-four pence to post. What is the heaviest that the letter could weigh?

9

	Aberdeen								
Brighton	540								
Cambridge	445	105							
Dover	560	76	118						
Exeter	555	166	218	241					
Glasgow	142	442	352	460	440				
Leeds	310	241	145	255	268	210			
Norwich	474	167	61	161	276	376	172		
York	302	250	151	262	290	206	24	172	

Distance in miles (vertical axis)

Distance in miles

10

11 Miles per hour (A) to kilometres per hour (B)

A	B	A	B	A	B
1	1.6	7	11.3	25	40.2
2	3.2	8	12.9	30	48.3
3	4.8	9	14.5	50	80.5
4	6.4	10	16.1	75	120.7
5	8.0	15	24.1	90	144.8
6	9.7	20	32.2	100	160.9

12

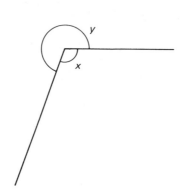

257

13

TO PLYMOUTH and PENZANCE & BACK

		FRIDAYS		SATURDAYS		
		OUTWARD		OUTWARD		RETURN
BRIGHTON	dep	11 11	dep	09 13	arr	18 13
WORTHING	dep	11 26	dep	09 27	arr	17 58
BARNHAM	dep	11 42	dep	09 44	arr	17 42
CHICHESTER	dep	11 52	dep	09 54	arr	17 33
HAVANT	dep	12 06	dep	10 06	arr	17 21
COSHAM	dep	12 19	dep	10 19	dep	—
FAREHAM	dep	12 29	dep	10 29	dep	17 05
SOUTHAMPTON	dep	12 52	dep	10 53	dep	16 42
SALISBURY	dep	13 23	dep	11 25	dep	16 09
YEOVIL JUNCTION	dep	14 07	dep	12 07	dep	15 21
AXMINSTER	dep	14 31	dep	12 36*	dep	14 56
HONITON	dep	14 50	dep	12 51*	dep	14 44
EXETER CENTRAL	arr	15 08	arr	13 10*	dep	14 21
EXETER (ST DAVIDS)	arr	15 13	arr	13 15*	dep	14 17
NEWTON ABBOT	arr	15 43	arr	13 53	dep	13 39
PLYMOUTH	arr	16 26	arr	14 40	dep	13 00

CALLS CERTAIN STATIONS BETWEEN PLYMOUTH and PENZANCE

TRURO	arr	18 03	arr	16 02	dep	11 34
PENZANCE	arr	18 50	arr	16 48	dep	10 50

Notes: *—Until 28 June and from 13 September departs Axminster 12 30, Honiton 12 45, and arrives Exeter Central 13 07 and Exeter St. Davids 13 13.

14

SUPERB GLOSSY OR MATT PRINTS

TICK A BOX TO MAKE YOUR CHOICE				

GLOSSY . . . A shiny finish for extra sharpness. Ideal for albums. ☐   **MATT** . . . A lustrous finish, attractive but durable, resistant to marking. ☐

24 EXPOSURES FOR ONLY **£2.09** + P&P

NUMBER OF EXPOSURES	OUR PRICE	NO. OF FILMS SENT	WRITE AMOUNT HERE
12 OR 15 (DISC)	£1.89		£ .
24	£2.09		£ .
36	£2.69		£ .
Add 35p per film for postage and packing			£ . Add P&P
A duplicate set of prints only £1.40 more per film			£ .
TOTAL			£ .

15

Inland Letters
United Kingdom, Channel Islands,
Isle of Man and Irish Republic.

	60g	100g	150g	200g
1st clas	17p	24p	31p	38p
2nd class	12p	18p	22p	28p

The rates shown here are effective from November 1985.

Please use the postcode

Overseas Air

Letters	10g	Each extra 10g
Zone A	29p	11p
Zone B	31p	14p
Zone C	34p	15p

Postcards 26p
Aerogramme 26p
Europe Surface rates apply

Overseas Surface
Letters and Postcards

	20g	60g	100g
All countries	22p	37p	53p

Zone A
N Africa
Middle East

Zone B
Americas
Africa
India
SE Asia

Zone C
Australasia
Japan
China

15 Coursework

Until 1991, the coursework element of the GCSE will not be compulsory. Some candidates, however, will be required to offer coursework, and it is important that you acquaint yourself fully with what is required. You will be asked to carry out a certain number of tasks (depending on which examination board you are taking); some will be quite short, others will be extended over a few weeks. Your work will then be marked according to a fixed scheme, again depending on the examination board you are taking. The sort of areas for which marks will be awarded are summarised in the table.

1	2	3	4	5
Overall strategy	Mathematical content	Accuracy	Presentation	Summary

It is important that the work submitted is your own work. Your teacher will probably have to indicate to the examination board any extra help you had to ask for. This will be reflected in the mark awarded. The following three examples of investigation should give some idea as to the approach that will be required.

Investigation 1

Look at the squares shown in Fig. 15.1. Investigate how many squares you can find in each diagram.

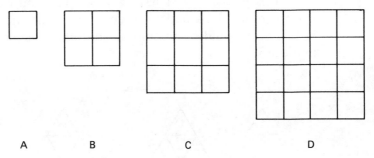

A   B   C   D

Fig. 15.1

Solution

At first sight, this does not seem a particularly difficult question. Let us look, however, at how we can turn this into an investigation that might be used as a piece of coursework.

In A, the number of squares is clearly 1.

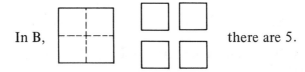

In B,   there are 5.

261

In C 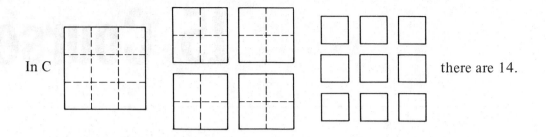 there are 14.

Similarly, in D you can find 30.

This counting method is not very systematic, however, and would gain a low score under strategy.

Look again at the totals:

A   1   = 1
B   1 + 4   = 5
C   1 + 4 + 9   = 14
D   1 + 4 + 9 + 16 = 30

We return to the ideas of number patterns discussed in section 2.2. By now, you should recognise the square numbers, and so you can predict a 5 x 5 square which would give $1^2 + 2^2 + 3^2 + 4^2 + 5^2 = 55$ squares. At this stage, you should begin to think about how many squares you could find if the square measured $n \times n$. In other words, how can we find

$$1^2 + 2^2 + 3^2 + 4^2 + \ldots + n^2?$$

The problem suddenly becomes very difficult. You may be clever enough to work this out, or you may have to ask somebody for a hint. Remember that your teacher has to write on your project report any outside help that you may need.

The answer is $\dfrac{n(n + 1)(2n + 1)}{6}$;   check for $n = 5$.

At this point, if you have got this far, you may be tempted to give up. The examiners will look and see if you can extend the problem. An obvious extension in this case would be to consider different shapes. Take, for example triangles, as in Fig. 15.2.

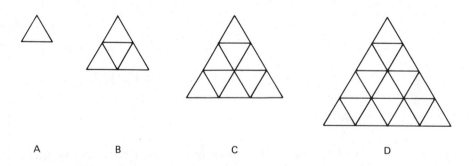

A   B   C   D

Fig. 15.2

Can you now find number patterns associated with these? Can you extend to further shapes?

Investigation 2

Figure 15.3 shows a four-figure security code which is fitted to an electrical device. Each digit can be any number from 1 to 6. How many codes are there? How is your answer altered if each digit can only occur once? Investigate other such number codes.

Fig. 15.3

Solution

You might first of all try to list the possible codes:

1111	1112	1113	1114	1115	1116
1121	1131	. . .	. . .	. . .	. . .
1131	. . .	. . .	. . .	. . .	. . .
. . .	. . .	. . .	. . .	. . .	. . .

It soon becomes clear that the list is rather long. Can this listing be shortened? How many choices are there for the first digit? If you look at the partly drawn tree diagram in Fig. 15.4, you should be able to see that the total number of routes on this diagram is 6 x 6 x 6 x 6 = 1296.

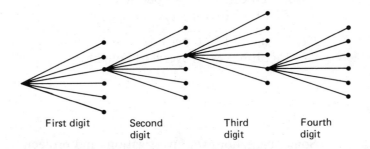

Fig. 15.4

If we are restricted to no repetition of digits, the tree becomes much smaller. Again, it is shown partly drawn in Fig. 15.5.

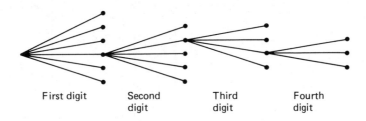

Fig. 15.5

If completed, the total number of routes would be

6 x 5 x 4 x 3 = 360.

This investigation can be extended in many ways, by changing the number of digits used, introducing letters, or increasing the length of the code.
You could investigate car number plates and many other areas.

The third example is from the LEAG. It is stated without a solution for obvious reasons, but it indicates that the investigations should not always be thought of as based around number patterns.

Investigation 3

You have taken over the running of the school tuckshop. The sales come mainly from crisps, which at present are bought from three different suppliers. Each of the three suppliers has different ways of pricing their crisps, making it awkward for you to decide who really is the cheapest.
The tuckshop cannot hold more than 25 boxes of crisps.
Using the information given, decide from whom you are going to buy your crisps.
The three suppliers and their prices are as follows:
AB Supplies: £3.50 per box
5 per cent discount on 8+ boxes.
12.5 per cent discount on 15+ boxes.
15 per cent discount on 30+ boxes.

Associated Crisps: £3.48 per box
1 FREE box with every 8 bought.

Gold Crunch: £3.40 per box
1 FREE box with every 12 bought.

Exercise 15

Some suggestions for investigations and projects:
1 A rectangle measures 4 cm by 5 cm as shown in Fig. 15.6. A diagonal is drawn across the rectangle. How many squares does it cut? Now vary the length of the sides. What happens? What happens if the figure is a square and not a rectangle?

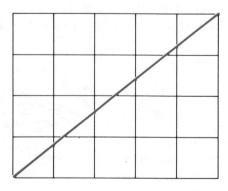

Fig. 15.6

2 Figure 15.7 shows a configuration formed from 6 lines. How many triangles are there in the diagram? What happens if 2 of the lines are parallel? What happens if you change the number of lines? Do you always get the same number of triangles for a given number of lines?

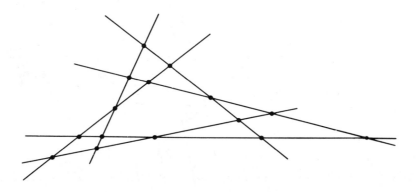

Fig. 15.7

3 Figure 15.8 shows a magic square, where the numbers in each row, column or diagonal add up to 15. Is this the only square with this property?
   Investigate other magic squares.

4	9	2
3	5	7
8	1	6

Fig. 15.8

4 Write a flowchart for one of the following:
   (i) buying a house;   (ii) buying a motorbike;
   (iii) decorating a room;   (iv) a problem of your choice.
5 Using your knowledge of tessellations, design 8 different tiles that would be suitable for a kitchen floor. Design a catalogue that a manufacturer might produce, indicating colours, prices and measurements.
6 A sheet of cardboard measuring 80 cm by 50 cm is to be made into a small gift box. Investigate suitable nets for the box if the box is to hold the largest volume (remember flaps will be needed to stick the box together). You are not restricted to any particular shape. A 'hit and miss' method will not be acceptable.
7 What do we mean by 'best buy'?
8 Figure 15.9 shows a road junction with four sets of traffic lights. The possible directions in which traffic can travel are shown by the arrows. You have been asked to design a traffic light system so that traffic should flow as freely as

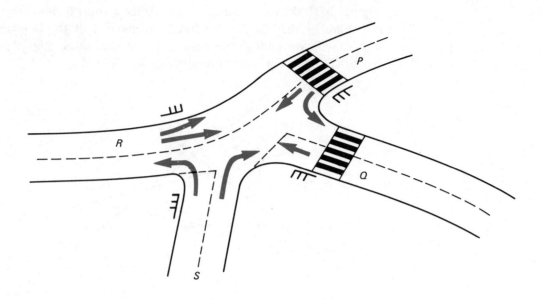

Fig. 15.9

possible. Traffic travelling from *S*, and from *P* to *Q*, is much less than the other directions. You may add filter lights if required and remember the two pedestrian crossings.

9 How would you measure the height of a tree which was standing on the opposite bank of a river from you, and you had no means of crossing the river?

10 How fast do cyclists accelerate or brake? Can you answer this with just a stop watch?

Answers

Check 1

1 (a) {11, 13, 17, 19, 23, 29} (b) {$1\frac{1}{2}$} (c) ϕ
(d) {(0, 8), (1, 7), . . ., (8, 0)} (e) {30, 150}

2 (a) {4, 5} (b) {3, 5, 7, 8} (c) {1, 4, 6}
(d) {2, 3, 4, 5, 6, 8} (e) {1, 2, 4, 6, 7} (f) { 3, 5, 8}
(g) {1, 4, 5, 6, 7}

4 13, 8

5 19

6 (a) {3, 4, 5, 6, 7, 8} (b) {4, 5, 6} (c) {$-\infty$, . . ., 0, 1, 2}

Check 2

1 25, 36   **2** 63, 127   **3** 4, 16   **4** 125, 216   **5** 2.5, 1.25
6 9, −11   **7** 17, 19   **8** $\frac{1}{16}$, $\frac{1}{32}$ **9** 42, 89   **10** 29, 41

Check 3

1 8.69, 26.13, 0.09, 0.10, 2.02, 2.19, 10.00
2 86.4, 187, 0.0900, 2.00, 170, 3.00, 8690, 10 000

Check 4

(a) 94   (b) 140   (c) 1128   (d) 11   (e) 61   (f) 35   (g) 420
(h) 587   (i) 2133   (j) 2343

Check 5

1 110000, 1010110, 10001, 10111011000, 10111, 11001111, 111110, 1011100
2 13, 27, 333, 125

Check 6

1 10100   **2** 100001   **3** 1111   **4** 1443   **5** 10100   **6** 35552
7 417   **8** 31   **9** 33   **10** −111   **11** 11110   **12** 14
13 1202   **14** 2225   **15** 1215

Check 7

1 $1\frac{7}{20}$	2 $\frac{8}{15}$	3 $1\frac{1}{12}$	4 $\frac{3}{20}$	5 $\frac{1}{10}$	6 $\frac{5}{24}$
7 $\frac{1}{4}$	8 $1\frac{1}{8}$	9 $1\frac{1}{2}$	10 $\frac{3}{5}$	11 $6\frac{5}{6}$	12 $1\frac{9}{16}$
13 $\frac{1}{5}$	14 $2\frac{4}{7}$	15 $\frac{31}{240}$	16 3	17 $29\frac{1}{2}$	18 $1\frac{11}{25}$
19 $8\frac{8}{9}$	20 $\frac{1}{3}$				

Check 8

1 0.6	2 0.12	3 0.625	4 0.714	5 $0.1\dot{8}$	6 0.52
7 $0.2\dot{7}$	8 0.368	9 0.4375	10 0.354		

Check 9

1 40, 279, $16\frac{2}{3}$, 3.75, 0.5, 55, 150, 9.8

2 $\frac{1}{3}$, $\frac{18}{25}$, $\frac{1}{8}$, $\frac{3}{500}$, $\frac{3}{25}$, $\frac{73}{200}$

Check 10

1 4.86×10^2, 6.93×10^3, 8.57×10^5, 10^{-2}, 9.6×10^{-2}, 8.31×10^{-3}, 9.09×10^{-2}

2 45 000, 3840, 8 010 000, 0.085, 0.000 695, 0.000 008 801

Check 11

0.9, 0.007, 40, 0.1, 1, 100, 400 000, 0.006

Check 12

1 $6\sqrt{2}$, $7\sqrt{6}$, $\sqrt{2}$, $5\sqrt{10}$, 0, $\sqrt{7}$, $-\sqrt{11}$, $6\sqrt{7}$, $10\sqrt{2} - 2\sqrt{3}$, $5\sqrt{5}$

2 $\frac{\sqrt{2}}{2}$, $\frac{\sqrt{5}}{25}$, $\frac{\sqrt{2}}{2}$, $\frac{\sqrt{2}}{2}$, $\frac{\sqrt{10}}{2}$, $\frac{\sqrt{5}}{5}$, $\frac{\sqrt{7}+\sqrt{2}}{5}$

Check 13

1 -6	2 -16	3 12	4 $-1\frac{1}{8}$	5 $-\frac{2}{3}$	6 -7	7 $-\frac{3}{20}$
8 $-\frac{1}{32}$	9 $-1\frac{57}{160}$	10 $1\frac{3}{32}$	11 -10	12 $7\frac{14}{15}$	13 $\frac{9}{40}$	14 0
15 $35\frac{47}{80}$						

Check 14

1 100	2 9	3 0.3	4 $\frac{1}{25}$	5 $\frac{1}{3}$	6 4	7 1
8 7	9 4	10 $\frac{1}{25}$	11 $2x^3$	12 $5p^{-8}/4$		13 $12x^{-6}$
14 $-27m^3$		15 $3x^2$	16 $5y^8$	17 $4q^{4/3}$		18 u
19 $9v^4$		20 $\frac{8}{27}$				

Check 15

1 $y(a + 4y)$ 2 $t(3t^2 + 2t + 5)$ 3 $p^2q^2(q - p)$ 4 $4(p - 2)$
5 $(p + q)(y - z)$ 6 $(r - p)(q + s)$ 7 $(t - 3)(t - p)$
8 $(x - y)(a + b + c)$ 9 $(x - 3)(x - 8)$ 10 $(x + 3)(x - 1)$
11 $(x + 13)(x - 2)$ 12 impossible   13 $(2x + 3)(x + 5)$
14 $(2x + 1)(2x + 3)$ 15 $(3x - 1)(2x - 1)$ 16 $(9x + 2)(x - 1)$
17 $(4x^2 + 1)(x - 1)(x + 1)$ 18 $(2x - 5)(2x + 5)$ 19 $(1 - x)(1 + x)$
20 $\pi(R - r)(R + r)$ 21 $x(x - 6)$ 22 $(11xy - 2)(11xy + 2)$
23 $(2x - 3y)^2$ 24 $(5x - y)^2$ 25 $(5 - b)^2$

Check 16

1 (a) $\dfrac{x + 1}{x^2}$ (b) $\dfrac{2b + 3}{ab}$ (c) $\dfrac{8t - 3}{2t^2}$ (d) $\dfrac{13x}{12}$ (e) $\dfrac{25}{3y}$

(f) $\dfrac{28x^2 - 15y^2}{21xy}$ (g) $\dfrac{4x^2 + 1}{x}$ (h) $\dfrac{7a + 12b}{8}$ (i) $\dfrac{2x - 1}{6}$

(j) $\dfrac{7x + 5}{(x - 1)(x + 2)}$ (k) $\dfrac{-1}{x(x - 1)}$ (l) $\dfrac{x^2 - 2x + 1}{(x - 3)(x - 2)}$ (m) $\dfrac{4x}{x^2 - 1}$

2 (a) $\dfrac{2}{y}$ (b) $\dfrac{4tq}{3}$ (c) $\dfrac{3q}{5t}$ (d) $\dfrac{8x}{15y}$ (e) $\dfrac{8}{15}$

(f) $\dfrac{2q}{3}$ (g) $\dfrac{c}{a + b}$ (h) $\dfrac{25}{18t}$ (i) $4tp$ (j) $\dfrac{a + b}{a - b}$

Check 17

1 $\dfrac{2x - 5}{3}$ 2 $kq + \dfrac{py}{2000}$ 3 $\dfrac{xy}{10}$ 4 $150 + x + y$

5 $yt + v(50 - y)$ 6 $\dfrac{10p}{11}$ 7 $4f + 6s + 9$ 8 1.2%

9 $\dfrac{(E - D)I}{100}$ 10 $85W + M$

Check 18

1 (a) 2   (b) 4   (c) $-\frac{4}{3}$ (d) $-\frac{10}{3}$ (e) $\frac{19}{5}$ (f) $\frac{8}{5}$
(g) $1\frac{1}{2}$ (h) $-\frac{8}{5}$ (i) $\frac{15}{26}$ (j) $\frac{1}{2}$ (k) $\frac{34}{23}$ (l) -9
(m) $\frac{7}{9}$ (n) 8   (o) $-\frac{13}{5}$
2 (a) $3, -1$ (b) $2, 8$ (c) $\frac{1}{2}, -1$ (d) $\frac{1}{3}, 3$ (e) 1   (f) $0, 9$
(g) $1.85, -4.85$ (h) $-1 \pm \sqrt{2}$ (i) $-4 \pm \sqrt{19}$ (j) $-0.11, 2.36$
(k) $1.82, 0.18$ (l) $-6 \pm \sqrt{19}$ (m) no solution
(n) $\pm\dfrac{2}{\sqrt{3}}$ (o) 1
3 (a) $5, 2$ (b) $-2, -5$ (c) $2, 1$ (d) $2, 4$ (e) $\frac{11}{10}, \frac{3}{10}$ (f) $3, 2$
(g) $1\frac{1}{2}, -3$ (h) $6, -\frac{1}{2}$ (i) $5, 1$ (j) $-3, -\frac{11}{3}$

Check 19

1 $\frac{9}{8}$ 2 $\frac{4}{9}$ 3 $121\frac{1}{2}$

4 (a) $(x-1)(x^2+x+1)$ (b) $(x+2)(x-1)(x+1)$
  (c) $(x-2)(x^2+9x+15)$ (d) $(x-1)(x-2)(x-3)$
  (e) $(x-1)(x+1)(2x-1)$ (f) $(3x-1)(x+1)(x+2)$
  (g) $(x+2)(x-3)(x-5)$

5 $-\frac{3}{2}, \frac{1}{2}$

Check 20

1 430, 68.4, 40 000, 5, 0.25, 8.63×10^7, 4000, 125.5
2 6.25×10^{-3}, 0.08, 9.4×10^{-3}, 0.895, 8.69×10^{-4}
3 8000, 40, 0.685, 65 000, 1.8×10^{-3}, 9×10^5
4 9.6×10^4, 28.75, 4.8×10^8
5 0.6, 2.8×10^4, 2×10^{12}
6 72, 6.94, 8

Check 21

1 10.3, 13.44, 11.72, 15.32, 32.0, 53.92, 92.52, 28.56
2 2.176×10^7
3 93.5 cm²
4 3.5
5 616, 484, 14, $201\frac{1}{7}$, 2.2, 10.68, 1232, 2, 38 808, 5544, $50\frac{2}{7}$, 2, 91 989, 28,
  11.5, 24.64, 91.99, 2.8, $205\frac{1}{3}$, 177.4, 331.4, 8.06, $314\frac{2}{7}$, 204.3, 282.9, 5, 167.2,
  321.2, 7, 7.6, 1797, 905.1, 26.8, 28, 2932, 880, 14.28, 20.

Check 22

1 3.34
2 7.3
3 8.55 cm, 14 453 km, 0.448 m, 2513 km
4 14.32 cm, 32.17 cm, 630.2 km, 203.7 km
5 86, 57, 5, 1

Check 23

1 $-7 \leqslant y \leqslant 5$, {0, 1, 4, 9}, {$x \in R, x \neq 0$}, $-1 \leqslant y \leqslant 1$
2 $2x^2 + 1$, $(2x-3)^2$, $4x - 9$, $8x^2 - 24x + 19$
3 1, 0, $\frac{3}{4}$
4 (a) 3, 11   (b) $3 < x < 11$
5 30, 55
8 -4
9 $3y = 2x + 12$, $y = 3x - 2$, $2y = 3x - 6$, $y + 3x = 10$
10 $(1\frac{1}{2}, 5)$, $(\frac{1}{2}, -\frac{1}{2})$, $(1, -1\frac{1}{2})$, $(2\frac{1}{2}, 2\frac{1}{2})$

Check 24

1 $x < \frac{11}{3}$

2 $x < 1$

3 $\{1, 2, \ldots, 10\}$

4 -1

5 $-2 < x < 12$

6 $7, 8$

7 $-3 < x < 4$

8 $-4.6 < x < -2.2$

9 $\{2, 3, \ldots, 7\}$

10 $-1 < x < 4$

11 $2 < x < 3$

12 $-\sqrt{15} < x < \sqrt{15}$

13 $-3 < x < 2$

14 $0 < x < 2\frac{1}{2}$

15 $x > 2$ or $x < -2$

Check 25

1 $\begin{pmatrix} 1 \\ 2 \end{pmatrix}, \begin{pmatrix} -6 \\ 3 \end{pmatrix}, \begin{pmatrix} 8 \\ 1 \end{pmatrix}, \begin{pmatrix} 5 \\ 0 \end{pmatrix}, \begin{pmatrix} 7 \\ 4 \end{pmatrix}, \sqrt{10}, \sqrt{5}, \sqrt{10} + \sqrt{5}$

2 $\mathbf{b} + \mathbf{c}, \mathbf{a} + \mathbf{b} + \mathbf{c}, \mathbf{a} + \mathbf{b}$

3 $\mathbf{b} - \mathbf{a}, -\mathbf{b} - \mathbf{a}, 2\mathbf{b}$

4 $\begin{pmatrix} -6 \\ -2 \end{pmatrix}, \begin{pmatrix} 7 \\ -2 \end{pmatrix}, \begin{pmatrix} 1 \\ -4 \end{pmatrix}$

5 $(5, -3), \begin{pmatrix} 2 \\ -4 \end{pmatrix}$

6 $(6, 4), (18, 8), \sqrt{265}$

Check 26

1 $\frac{1}{2} \begin{pmatrix} 3 & -2 \\ -5 & 4 \end{pmatrix}$

2 $\begin{pmatrix} 6 & 7 \\ 5 & 6 \end{pmatrix}$

3 impossible

4 $\frac{1}{36} \begin{pmatrix} 9 & -3 \\ 6 & 2 \end{pmatrix}$

5 $\begin{pmatrix} 1 & 0 \\ 0 & -1 \end{pmatrix}$

6 $\frac{1}{78} \begin{pmatrix} 11 & 4 \\ -3 & 6 \end{pmatrix}$

Check 27

1 (a) $\begin{pmatrix} 11 & 5 & -1 \\ -4 & -1 & 4 \end{pmatrix}$ (b) $\begin{pmatrix} -2 & -3 \\ 14 & -6 \\ 7 & -19 \end{pmatrix}$ (c) $\begin{pmatrix} -5 & 10 \\ -13 & 0 \end{pmatrix}$

(d) impossible (e) $\begin{pmatrix} 4 & -4 & -8 \\ 0 & 4 & 12 \\ 16 & 4 & 24 \end{pmatrix}$ (f) impossible

2 $\begin{pmatrix} \frac{7}{4} & \frac{3}{4} \\ -1 & \frac{9}{4} \end{pmatrix}$

3 $\begin{pmatrix} \frac{2}{5} & 0 \\ \frac{1}{5} & -\frac{3}{5} \end{pmatrix}$

4 (a) (10) (b) $\begin{pmatrix} 6 & 3 \\ 2 & 1 \end{pmatrix}$ (c) (-9) (d) impossible

(e) $\begin{pmatrix} 9 & 5 \\ 5 & 2 \end{pmatrix}$ (f) $\begin{pmatrix} -4 \\ 5 \end{pmatrix}$ (g) $\begin{pmatrix} 3 \\ 3 \end{pmatrix}$

(h) $\begin{pmatrix} 6 & 9 & 0 \\ 3 & 6 & 3 \end{pmatrix}$ (i) $\begin{pmatrix} 2 & 10 & 2 \\ 13 & 11 & 31 \\ 17 & 2 & 38 \end{pmatrix}$

5 $\begin{pmatrix} -4 & 0 \\ -9 & -3 \end{pmatrix}$

6 (a) $\frac{25}{11}, \frac{-16}{11}$ (b) $\frac{62}{37}, \frac{-17}{37}$ (c) $\frac{1}{4}, 2\frac{1}{2}$ (d) $\frac{205}{147}, \frac{-43}{147}$

Check 28

1 80, 80, 70 **2** 90 **3** 50, 50 **4** 80 **5** 30, 110
6 124, 28, 34 **7** 55, 35, 55, 70 **8** 63, $31\frac{1}{2}$
9 $37\frac{1}{2}$, 75 **10** 120, 120

Check 29

4 (a) $\frac{1}{13}$ (b) $\frac{1}{3}$ (c) $\frac{4}{11}$ (d) $\frac{9}{25}$ (e) $\frac{3}{5}$
5 (a) $\frac{8}{25}$ (b) $\frac{3}{50}$ (c) $\frac{1}{10}$

Check 30

1 $\frac{5}{12}$ **2** $\frac{2}{5}, \frac{3}{5}, \frac{4}{5}$ **3** $\frac{3}{8}, \frac{1}{2}$
4 $\frac{1}{2}, \frac{2}{9}$ **5** $\frac{8}{27}, \frac{20}{27}$ **6** 0.14, 0.53

Exercise 1

1 D **2** C **3** D **4** B **5** C **6** A **7** A **8** A **9** C **10** D
11 (a) $\{3, 7\}$ (b) $\{13, 15\}$
12 (a) $\{36\}$ (b) $\{6, 12, 18, 24, 30, 42, 48, 54, 60\}$.
(c) $\{4, 8, 16, 26, 44\}$
13 62 **14** 16

15 (a) $(A \cap B \cap C') \cup (A \cap B' \cap C) \cup (A' \cap B \cap C)$
   (b) $(A \cup C) \cap B'$ (c) $((A \cup C)' \cap B) \cup ((A \cup B)' \cap C) \cup ((B \cup C)' \cap A)$
   (d) $((A \cup B)' \cap C) \cup (A \cap B \cap C')$
16 (a) ϕ (b) cyclic
17 (a) (i) S (ii) ϕ (b) (i) 6 (ii) 47
18 (a) There are no fast red cars   (b) Some red cars are fast
   (c) Some red cars are not fast
19 $\{5, 10, 15, 20, 25\}, \{3, 6, \ldots, 27\}, \{5, 10, 20, 25\}\ldots$
20 (b) $\{3\}$ (c) $\{1, 4, 6, 9, 12, 15, 18, 21, 24, 27, 30, 33, 36, 39\}$.
21 (d) $\{2, 3, 13, 17, 19\}$ (e) $\{1, 14, 15, 16, 18, 20\}$
   (f) $\{1, 6, 8, 9, 12, 14, 15, 16, 18\}$
22 (a) 19   (b) 32
23 (a) 32   (b) 44   (c) 3   (d) 20   (e) 4
24 (a) {multiples of 70} (b) 83
25 14   26 (a) 10   (b) 3   (c) 15   (d) 59
28 (a) (i) $\{3\}$ (ii) $\{1, 2, 3\}$ (iii) $\{1, 2, 3, 4, 5\}$
   (b) (i) $\{4, 16, 36\}$ (ii) $\{25, 36, 49\}$ (iv) $\{36\}$
29 (a) 34% (b) (ii) 24 (iii) 3   30 (b) 100, n (bad steering only) = 0

Exercise 2

1 C 2 B 3 A 4 D 5 B 6 A 7 B 8 D 9 C 10 B 11 D
12 C   13 C   14 £30.17 15 £288 000, £300, 82p
16 (a) 9, 6 (b) $3n + 4$ 17 0.02   18 £87.72 19 (a) 101010 (b) 110
(c) 111000011   (d) 100011 21 (a) 6 (b) 4 (c) 8
22 7.44×10^5, -2.08×10^5 23 (a) 0.0025 (b) (i) 0.05263   24 2
25 (a) 2.4393 (b) 0.141 (c) 22.41 or 22.28   26 9%
26 (a) 300 (b) 10p (c) 11p (d) 31.4% (e) £141.45   27 £120 33.10, 9%
28 (a) £75 000 (b) (i) 3.2p (ii) £17.28 (c) (i) £230 (ii) 2.7%
29 (a) (i) £159 (ii) £223 (iii) £205 (b) £624 (c) £245.30
30 (a) £104.13 (b) £178.50 (c) 6.25% (d) £233.50
31 (a) 2361.6 (b) 85 000 (c) 125 (d) 1676
32 (a) 2660   (b) 9.5, £434, 2.2, £84
33 (a) 31 (b) 17 (c) 0 (d) R, U   34 (a) 300 (b) £25 320 (c) £410.64

Exercise 3

1 D 2 C 3 D 4 B 5 C 6 B 7 C 8 A 9 C 10 B 11 D 12 A
13 ± 6 14 $by^2/(x - 1)$ 15 $(x - 3)(2x + 1)(x - 1)$
16 $(2a + 4b + 5c)(2a + 4b - 5c)$ 17 $(v^2 - u^2)/2s$ 18 (a) $\sqrt{29}$ (b) $\frac{1}{3}$
19 -1

20 (a) 200.016 (b) 1.96 (c) $\sqrt{\dfrac{k}{T - 100n}}$

21 (a) $(x + 1)(4x + 1)$ (b) $4(3a + b)(2b - a)$ (c) $x(x + 3)(x - 2)$
22 (a) ϕ, (b) $\frac{1}{3}$, (c) $\sqrt{2}$ (d) $\sqrt{2}, \frac{1}{3}$ 23 (a) $2p^2$ (b) $8x$ (c) $18x^4$

24 (a) $x - 1$ (b) x, $\dfrac{1}{(x - 1)}$ (c) 1.62

25 (a) $\sqrt{\dfrac{qy^2 - 3t}{4t}}$ (b) $\dfrac{-(ky + m)}{h}$ (c) $\dfrac{yt}{4 + k}$

26 (a) (i) $17\frac{1}{2}$ (ii) 2   (b) 1.77

27 (a) $\frac{7}{8}$ (b) $-2, 1\frac{1}{2}$ (c) $0, -3$ (d) $2\frac{1}{7}$ (e) 1 (f) ± 5 (g) $-\frac{1}{4}$ (h) -1

(i) ±3 (j) 2

28 (a) $q - 4y$ (b) $(4 - 2T^2)/T^2$ (c) $t/(y - 4)$ (d) $\sqrt{r^2 - y^2}$ (e) $\sqrt{4 + y^2}$

(f) $\sqrt{\dfrac{A^2 t^2 - 16y^2}{16}}$ (g) $-(by + c)/a$ (h) $\sqrt{\dfrac{2E}{m}}$ (i) $\dfrac{f}{Ff - 1}$

29 (a) $2t(q - 3)(q + 3)$ (b) $4t(q + 2t)$ (c) $(2t - 3)(x + y)$

(d) $(8x + 11)(4x - 9)$ (e) $(x - 1)(x^2 + 2x + 2)$

30 (a) 4   (b) 13   (c) 9   (d) −38

31 (a) 2, −1   (b) $vf/(v - f)$ (c) $(x + 4)^2 + 9$

32 $(wy + (52 - w)r)/52$ **33** 6.52

34 (a) 1600   (b) 8 **35** 366

36 (a) (ii) $(A + b^2)/2b$ (b) $4l$ **37** (a) 137   (b) 51, 52, 53, 61, 70

38 (b) correct to 2 d.p. **39** (a) (ii) $x^3 = 12$

41 1.74 × 1.74 × 4.74 **42** 240, 2 h 5 min

43 (a) 0, 1, 3, 6, 10   (b) 1, 2, 3, 4   (c) n (e) 99

44 (a) (i) 4   (ii) 49   (iii) 484

46 (b) 58   (c) 48   (d) $W = 2R + 4$ (e) 44   (f) $5\frac{1}{3}$ (g) not possible

Exercise 4

1 B   **2** A   **3** D   **4** A   **5** C   **6** B   **7** A   **8** D   **9** B   **10** D   **11** D

12 64 cm² **13** (a) 8.8×10^5 (b) 2.72×10^{-2} **14** (a) 90   (b) 90

15 £982 600, 520 km

16 (a) £6000, £3600, £2400   (b) 370, £4500, 75%

17 (a) 2240 m³   (b) 1640 cm³   (c) $\frac{70}{33}$

18 (a) 5960 mm   (b) £178.80   (c) £208.60   (d) £47.25   (e) £434.65

(f) £43.46$\frac{1}{2}$ (g) £23.91

19 (c) 52 **20** 48 m³, 5 min, 384 m³, 37.5 cm

21 (c) (i) 64 m/s   (ii) 8 m/s²   (iii) 672 m **22** (a) 60   (b) 11.3   (c) $3\frac{3}{4}$ m/s²

23 $3\frac{1}{3}$ min, 67 min

25 (b) 160°   (c) 7.8 km   (d) 0.7 km   (e) 50 min   (f) 9.4 km/h

26 (b) 11.25 **27** (a) 0.5 h   (b) 1 h 30 min   (c) 180 km   (d) 2 h

(e) 90 km/h   (f) 13.15

28 (a) 1054   (b) 1 h 54 min   (c) 14 min   (d) 47 km   (e) 47 km/h   (f) 18 km

Exercise 5

1 D   **2** B   **3** B   **4** A   **5** C   **6** D   **7** B   **8** C   **9** D   **10** D   **11** C

14 (a) 2   (b) $(-1\frac{1}{2}, 3)$ (c) $(3, -6)$

15 (a) (ii) $\frac{11}{5}$ (b) $y + 2x + 3 = 0$ **16** $x^3 + 1.6x^2 + x + 1 = 0$

17 (a) $x = 2.24$ (b) 3.3 or 1.5 **18** (c) (i) 0.81   (ii) −4.1   (iii) 11.3

(d) −2.4   (e) 1, $-2\frac{1}{3}$

19 (a) 6   (b) $6\sqrt{3}, 2\sqrt{3}$

20 (a) (10, 0) (0, 5)   (b) −0.5   (c) $y = 2x$ (d) (2, 4)   (e) (4, 8)   (f) $(5, 2\frac{1}{2})$

(g) $5\sqrt{5}/2$ **23** (a) $-\frac{1}{60}$ (b) 0, (−4, −5)   (c) 1.93

21 (a) (i) $x \mapsto 2$ (ii) $x \mapsto 4$ (b) gh   (c) $x \mapsto 3(x - 1)$

22 (a) 2   (b) 0, 1, 2   (c) 0

23 (a) $(3 - x)/2$ (b) $2/3x$ (c) $3\sqrt{x}$ (d) $3\sqrt{x - 2}$ (e) $(1 - x)/2x$

(f) $(b - dx)/(cx - a)$ **25** 4 solutions, 2.65

26 (a) −22   (b) −2   (c) −22   (d) −4, 9   (e) 9.92, −1.92

27 (a) 18.8   (b) ±5.29   (c) $-\frac{7}{4}$ (d) $y \geqslant 6$

28 (a) 2.5   (b) 3.6   (c) $2.5 < x < 4.1$

29 (b) 100   (c) $A = 170 - 10t$ (d) between 6.30 and 8.30 Sunday

30 (b) (ii) 2   (c) 2.73, −0.73 **31** (a) 175, 315   (d) 46 mile/h   (e) 30 mile/h

32 (a) $(x - 3)(x - 2)$ (b) $x = 3, 2$ (c) (0, 6) (2, 0) (3, 0)   (d) −4, −5

274

Exercise 6

1 D   2 C   3 A   4 D   5 A   6 D   7 C   8 B   9 D   10 C   11 8, 9, 10
12 (a) 24   (b) (i) $2\frac{1}{4}$ (ii) 0
13 £4.80   14 $x + y \leqslant 1000$, $y \geqslant 2x$, $x \geqslant 100$, $y \leqslant 800$, 333, 667
15 (a) $h \geqslant 15$ (b) $p > 25$ (c) $45 \leqslant h + p < 60$; 25. 30

Exercise 7

1 D   2 B   3 C   4 B   5 C   6 C   7 C   8 B   9 A   10 D   11 (a) 34   (b) 26
12 7, 4   13 $5\overrightarrow{PT}$ 14 6, 0
15 (a) (i) $2\mathbf{v}$ (ii) $3\mathbf{v} + 2\mathbf{u}$ (iii) $-2\mathbf{v} - 2\mathbf{u}$ (b) $\overrightarrow{QN}$
16 (a) $\mathbf{q} - \mathbf{p}$, $\frac{1}{2}(\mathbf{q} - \mathbf{p})$, $\frac{1}{2}(\mathbf{p} + \mathbf{q})$ (b) $\frac{1}{3}(\mathbf{p} + \mathbf{q})$, $\frac{1}{3}\mathbf{q} - \frac{2}{3}\mathbf{p}$ (c) $\frac{1}{2}\mathbf{q} - \mathbf{p}$ (d) $\frac{2}{3}$
17 (d) 5.1 km   (e) 12.14   18 $h = k = \frac{1}{3}$, 1 : 3   19 (b) $\frac{1}{3}$ (c) $\frac{21}{16}$ (d) $\frac{4}{9}$
20 (c) $(\mathbf{a} + \mathbf{b} + \mathbf{c} + \mathbf{d})/4$
21 (a) $10\mathbf{a} - 2\mathbf{b}$ (b) $2\mathbf{b} + k(10\mathbf{a} - 2\mathbf{b})$ (c) $10m\mathbf{a} + (2\mathbf{b} - 10\mathbf{a})$
22 (a) (i) $-\mathbf{x}$ (ii) $2\mathbf{x}$ (iii) $\mathbf{y} - \mathbf{x}$ (iv) $\mathbf{x} + \mathbf{y}$ (v) $2\mathbf{x} - \mathbf{y}$ (b) (i) $3\mathbf{x}$ (ii) $4\mathbf{x} - 2\mathbf{y}$
   (c) (i) 2   (ii) 6   24 (a) (i) $2\mathbf{n} + 2\mathbf{e}$ (ii) $2\sqrt{2}$ (b) $k = \frac{5}{2}$
25 (a) (i) $\begin{pmatrix} -6 \\ -2\frac{1}{2} \end{pmatrix}$ (ii) 13   (b) $3\mathbf{a} + 3\mathbf{b}$, $-\mathbf{a} + 3\mathbf{b}$, $m = 4$, $n = 3$
26 (a) $\frac{2}{5}\mathbf{b}$, $\frac{3}{5}\mathbf{b}$, $-\mathbf{b} + \mathbf{a}$ (b) $\frac{3}{5}(\mathbf{a} - \mathbf{b})$, $\frac{3}{5}\mathbf{a}$ (c) trapezium   (d) $\frac{25}{9}$ (e) 27 cm²
27 (a) equal   (b) $\begin{pmatrix} 6 \\ -4 \end{pmatrix}$ $\begin{pmatrix} -9 \\ -6 \end{pmatrix}$ (d) $\begin{pmatrix} 6 \\ -4 \end{pmatrix}$ (e) returns to A

Exercise 8

1 B   2 D   3 C   4 A   5 D   6 D   7 B   8 1 : 8   12 (1, 3), (2, 3)
13 (6, 4), H 14 (a) $\begin{pmatrix} 8 \\ 4 \end{pmatrix}$, $4\sqrt{5}$ (b) (10, 8)   (c) $-1\frac{1}{2}$

15 90° anticlockwise about k 16 (b) $-90°$ $\begin{pmatrix} 0 & 1 \\ -1 & 0 \end{pmatrix}$ (c) $\begin{pmatrix} 2 \\ -2 \end{pmatrix}$
                    (d) $-90°$ about (0, -2)
17 (a) D (-2, -2)   (d) (4, -4), $-\frac{1}{2}$
18 (a) similar   (b) equal   (c) $\frac{3}{4}$ (d) 1 : 16   (e) 1: 4   (f) 15 cm²
19 (a) straight line   (b) parallel line × 2 (c) translation, parallel 1 : 2,
enlargement × 4   20 (a) 4, 6   (b) $1\frac{1}{2}$ (c) (i) 9   (d) AQB

Exercise 9

1 A   2 C   3 D   4 D   5 A   6 D   7 D   8 A   9 D   10 C   11 $\sqrt{\frac{3}{2}}$, $\sqrt{\frac{3}{2}}$, 3
12 (1) $\begin{pmatrix} 3 & 6 \\ -1 & -2 \end{pmatrix}$ 14 $\begin{pmatrix} 15 \\ 12 \end{pmatrix}$ 16 18, -11

17 8, 24   18 rotation 53° clockwise
19 (2, 1), $(3\frac{2}{3}, -\frac{1}{3})$, $(-\frac{1}{3}, -\frac{1}{2})$ 20 (6, 4), H

21 (a) (iv) $S = T^{\mathrm{T}}$ (b) (ii) $\begin{pmatrix} 5 & 0 & 0 \\ 0 & 5 & 0 \\ 0 & 0 & 4 \end{pmatrix}$ 22 (a) (i) $\begin{pmatrix} 7 & 0 \\ 0 & -7 \end{pmatrix}$ (ii) $\begin{pmatrix} 6 & -3 \\ -10 & -16 \end{pmatrix}$
                    (b) rotation 90° about 0, $\begin{pmatrix} 1 & 0 \\ 0 & 1 \end{pmatrix}$

24 (a) (i) (3, 9)   (ii) (14, 8)   (iii) (2, -7)   (b) (i) -3 (ii) -1, 2   25 90° (6, 0)

26 5, 5, 90°, 25, $\frac{3}{4}$ **27** (b) (ii) shear   (c) (ii) $\begin{pmatrix} 0 & 1 \\ 1 & 0 \end{pmatrix}$ (d) $\begin{pmatrix} 0 & 1 \\ 1 & 1 \end{pmatrix}$

28 (c) (i) $(-1, 0)$, $(-3, 0)$, $(-1, 1)$ (d) (ii) reflection in Oy (iii) $T = SR$

Exercise 10

1 (a) 20°   (b) 10.3 cm   (c) 20.3 cm   **2** $52\frac{1}{2}°$, $82\frac{1}{2}°$, $127\frac{1}{2}°$, $97\frac{1}{2}°$

3 13 cm   **5** 140°   **6** (a) 60°   (b) 240°   (c) 30°

7 (a) 64°   (b) 107°   **8** 100°

9 POT, AQO, QTC **10** (a) $180 - x$ (b) $360/x$ (c) $360/x$ (d) $360/x$

11 2   **12** (a) (i) 40, 50, 35, 45   (ii) $10n$, $10n - 5$, 9   (b) (i) 90 cm   (iii) 5

Exercise 11

1 B   **2** C   **3** B   **4** C   **5** D   **6** B   **7** B   **8** A   **9** C   **10** C   **11** $\frac{1}{2}$, $\frac{1}{5}$, $\frac{1}{10}$

12 C   **13** $533\frac{1}{3}$ **14** $1\frac{1}{10}$ **15** $\frac{19}{36}$ **16** 6   **17** $\frac{1}{3}$ **18** $\frac{1}{6}$, $\frac{5}{6}$, $\frac{1}{30}$ **19** $\frac{7}{494}$, $\frac{3}{200}$

20 $\frac{89}{90}$, $\frac{7}{450}$ **21** (a) $\frac{1}{2}$ (b) (i) $\frac{1}{4}$ (ii) $\frac{1}{4}$

22 (a) 6   (b) 12   (c) 12   (d) £5600

23 (a) 0.343   (b) 0.1029   (c) 0.3087   (d) 0.6517

24 0.24, 600   **25** (a) (i) $\frac{1}{36}$ (ii) $\frac{1}{6}$ (b) (i) $\frac{4}{25}$ (ii) $\frac{41}{100}$ (c) 0.202

26 (b) 114°   (c) (i) 0.316,   (ii) 0.673   (d) $\frac{6320}{20\,000} \times \frac{6319}{19\,999}$

27 (a) $\frac{1}{3}$ (b) (i) $\frac{4}{9}$ (ii) $\frac{1}{6}$ **28** (b) 48, 49   (d) 49.1

29 (a) 5.09%   (b) (ii) 233°, 102°   **30** (a) 3, 2   (b) (i) £114   (ii) £3.80

31 (a) (i) $40.5 - 45.5$ (b) (i) 43.5   (ii) 8   (c) 70

32 (a) $\frac{1}{3}$ (b) $\frac{2}{5}$ (c) $\frac{11}{15}$ (d) $\frac{2}{21}$ (e) $\frac{10}{21}$ (f) $\frac{4}{105}$, $\frac{67}{91}$

33 (a) (i) 1440   (ii) 3760   (b) 20 per cent

34 (a) 8   (b) 30   (c) 81   (d) 2.7

Exercise 12

1 B   **2** A   **3** C   **4** C   **5** D   **6** D   **7** C   **8** D   **9** C

10 7.38 cm, 49.5°, 14.9 cm   **11** 20.5 cm, 6.43 cm, 2, 63.4°

12 (a) 7.2, 10.8   (c) 56.3°   (d) 55.3°   **13** 25.1 m, 65°

14 144.7°, 60.2 n miles, 78.3°   **15** (a) (i) 254.8 m (ii) 27°   (b) 711.3 m, 331.7 m

16 (a) 4.8 cm   (b) 9.6 km   (c) 45.4°

17 (a) 33.4°, 146.6°   (b) (i) 4.76 miles   (ii) 3.14 miles

18 (a) 173.8 m   (b) 337°   **20** (a) 14°   (b) 4.84 m

21 (a) 10 cm   (b) 200 cm³   **22** (a) 84.3°   (b) 151.4 cm   (c) 82°

23 (a) 3119 m   (b) 3589 m   (c) 3569 m   **24** 6.4 m, 9.38 m²

25 (a) 8.29 cm   (b) 14.9 cm   (c) 17.4 cm²   (d) 2.34 cm

26 (a) 14.4   (b) 133.8°   (c) 0.87 km   **27** 190.4 m, 248 m, 13.5°

28 8.65 cm, 5.47 cm, 30.6 cm²

29 5.45 cm   **30** (a) 8.38   (b) 25.13   (c) 17.73   (d) 7.71

31 (a) 2.24 m   (b) 2.84 m   (c) 120°   (d) 4.1 m

32 (56° S, 143° E)   **33** 75.5°

34 (a) 2751 km   (b) 8642 km, 3070 n miles

35 (a) 7440 n miles   (b) 9536 n miles, (28° N, 21.6° W)

36 (a) (i) 37°   (ii) 53°   (iii) 106°   (iv) 74   (b) (i) $f = 180 - 2x$, (ii) $g = 2x$
(iii) all values

Exercise 13

1 (a) perpendicular line (b) parallel line, 4.5 cm
3 CQ = 8.1 cm 6 3.5 cm 9 10 cm 10 126 cm³ 12 275 m² 13 8.7 cm, 23.3 cm²
15 (a) 5.2 m (b) 22 m 16 (a) GCE (c) 5, 8, 5 (d) rectangle
17 (a) (i) 6 (ii) 3 (b) 5, 1, 4

Test 1

1 5 2 1600 3 13 4 10.07 5 24 6 £1.16
7 5 February 8 4.38 p.m. 9 8 10 £2.70 11 120 805
12 89 13 78 14 £7.28 15 £140 16 8 kg 17 87.5 miles
18 $\frac{1}{3}$ 19 $12\frac{1}{4}\%$ 20 £1.60

Test 2

1 £42 2 48 3 8 4 6.5 − 7 m 5 27 6 5 lb 7 5
8 8 9 192 cm² 10 £1.60 11 1505 12 $8x^2$ 13 $2\frac{1}{2}$ h
14 12 cm² 15 $\frac{3}{4}$ 16 65 17 45 s 18 29 000 19 12 cm³
20 9.21 p.m.

Test 3

1 28 cm² 2 37 3 £200 4 £2.40 5 105 008
7 21°C 8 32 cm 9 61 10 18 cm² 11 54.7 12 110°
13 0314 14 £4.88 15 59p

Test 4

1 3600 2 £2.64 3 240 cm³ 4 5 ft 5 96 cm² 6 $\frac{3}{16}$
7 1000 cm² 8 £96 9 151 miles 10 8 cm 11 56 mile/h
12 250° 13 1230 14 3.99 15 30 g

Index